Praise for

New York Diaries

"*New York Diaries*…is the most convivial and unorthodox history of New York City one is likely to come across. This book's editor, Teresa Carpenter, a longtime *Village Voice* writer, has had the ingenious idea to comb through hundreds of diaries, written by the famous, the infamous and the unknown in New York, and to liberate these chronicles of their crunchiest and most humane bits."

—Dwight Garner, *The New York Times*

"The voices from the past we hear in these entries reassure us that we're all part of a great cosmic parade, [and] that restlessness and self-doubt have always been a constant of the human condition…. Given the limitations of recorded history…Carpenter has unearthed an impressive range of New York diary entries…. [Her] smart move was to arrange this collection not chronologically, but day by day throughout the calendar year…. The effect, oftentimes, is of a chorus of voices, separated by decades, even centuries, unconsciously echoing the same sentiments and complaints."

—Maureen Corrigan, NPR

"*New York Diaries* is an absolute masterpiece blending a curator's discernment, an archivist's obsessive rigor, a writer's love of writing, and a New Yorker's love of New York—the ultimate celebration of the city's tender complexity and beautiful chaos."

—Maria Popova, *The Atlantic*

"As hilarious as it is heartbreaking, *New York Diaries* is a must read for anyone who has fallen in love with the Big Apple. It is, in essence, a celebration of the complexity, beauty and chaos of New

York City by means of capturing the voices of those who have repeatedly trodden its sidewalks. It will prove to be one of the most essential books when discussing the history of the living, breathing metropolis."

—DARREN RICHARD CARLAW, *New York Journal of Books*

"Required reading...as comprehensive as it is revealing, making the city come alive."

—SUSANNAH CAHALAN, *New York Post*

"Fascinating...too compelling to put down."

—WHITNEY MATHESON, *USA Today*

"These journal entries [allow] New York natives and visitors, writers and artists, thinkers and bloggers, to reach across time and share vivid and compelling snapshots of life in the Capital of the World."

—The Rising Hollywood

"Whether you're a resident, a tourist, or a far-off admirer, pick up a copy and enjoy the stories of those who helped create a world of hope, glamour, pride, grit and greatness."

—New York Fantasy World

"What makes *New York Diaries* so compelling is that, as you read the 400 years' worth of reflections, it feels like the layers of myth enshrouding the city slowly come off, only to reveal, still, a metropolis that fully deserves its nickname: the Capital of the World."

—NATHALIE ROTHSCHILD, *Spiked*

New York Diaries

NEW YORK DIARIES

DIARIES

1609 TO 2009

EDITED BY

TERESA CARPENTER

MODERN LIBRARY

NEW YORK

2012 Modern Library Paperback Edition

Published in the United States by Modern Library,
an imprint of The Random House Publishing Group,
a division of Random House, Inc., New York.

MODERN LIBRARY and the TORCHBEARER Design are registered
trademarks of Random House, Inc.

Originally published in hardcover in the United States by Modern Library,
an imprint of The Random House Publishing Group,
a division of Random House, Inc., in 2012.

Permissions acknowledgments can be found on page 483.

LIBRARY OF CONGRESS CATALOGING-IN-PUBLICATION DATA
New York diaries, 1609 to 2009/edited by Teresa Carpenter.
p. cm.
ISBN 978-0-8129-7425-6
1. New York (N.Y.)—History—Diaries. 2. New York (N.Y.)—
Social life and customs—Diaries. I. Carpenter, Teresa.
F128.36.N49 2012
974.7'1—dc23 2011023580

Printed in the United States of America

www.modernlibrary.com

4 6 8 9 7 5 3

FOR ANDREW

Contents

PREFACE

First, the anthology apology. I have not read *every* diary written by New Yorkers or those written about New York. There are thousands, possibly hundreds of thousands, and most have never been published or made available to archives. Some, no doubt, are locked in attics or safes. Some were lost at sea; others burned. Some were destroyed by their creators for fear of discovery. I can only assure the reader that I've made a rigorous survey of the discoverable. What you will find here is an unorthodox history covering roughly four centuries of the New York experience from September 11, 1609— the first incursion of Europeans into the Upper Bay—through the destruction of the World Trade Center, a short distance upriver, on September 11, 2001, through the healing thereafter.

This compilation is *not* a literary anthology, though common sense dictates that a disproportionately large number of published writers will find their way into the mix. It is not a chronicle of military exploits, although diaries of officers and enlisted men from the Revolutionary and Civil wars are particularly numerous.

These journals are not limited to the famous. George Washington, Thomas Edison, Jack Kerouac, Charles Dickens, Mark Twain, and other luminaries do make appearances, but in the company of more obscure columnists, naturalists, coffin makers, clergymen, and precocious Victorian adolescents.

The criterion for selection was simple. I chose these entries because I liked them. They moved me, fascinated me, made me angry, made me laugh, invited tears, or simply satisfied my curiosity. They also serve a more vital purpose, and that is to transform the New York of postcards, the gray, still abstraction of granite, the denatured Gotham of science fiction, the out-of-time videoscape of crumbling towers, into a living city. And so in this spirit, they provide the kind of detail of daily life that so delights the armchair anthropologist.

A baked apple from Schrafft's. The contents of Tiffany's *knicknackatory*. Mario Cuomo's turtle story. Oysters the size of "cheeseplates." "Jewells" in the ears of colonial Dutch women. Heinrich Schliemann's divorce. Thomas Edison's sexual fantasies. The eerie pallor of the Rosenbergs in their caskets. The diarists you are about to read are skillful observers who offer an intimate memoir of lives and deaths set against a dynamic interplay of elements—"A violent orgy of lights," writes Albert Camus of one New York night. More "mercury to magenta to slate," suggests composer Ned Rorem of the daylight in Central Park. Sunrise in New York, the poet James Schuyler insists, is "peach" and "Nile green," reminiscent of lingerie. Wild winds whip through the canyons, sending people flying. Insistent tides confound mariners at Hell Gate on the Sound or slosh hypnotically under the piers, encircling Manhattan and linking her to the boroughs, binding Greater New York to its destiny. But the city is never gray and never still.

Why the calendar and not a more linear, traditional format? It is an homage to one of my own favorite anthologies, *The Faber Book of*

Diaries, edited by the English mystery writer Simon Brett. Strongly recommended reading. Even if you imagine that you cannot learn more formal British history, I promise you will find out a great deal more about the Brits.

The cyclical form, Brett points out, gives a collection such as this a beginning and an end—the advantage of which is incalculable. I would add that the calendar is an excellent convention for raising certain patterns to high relief. The seasons, to a large extent, shape our experience. September to early June historically finds café society in the city attending the balls described to condescending perfection by George Templeton Strong. By July the wealthy have migrated to posh watering holes while, from July through August, the poor who remain in the city are visited by plague—cholera, yellow fever, and influenza—brought in through the port, also a dubious gift of the tides. (The manifestations of yellow fever are described here in the fascinating case histories of an anonymous physician thought to be a Dr. James L. Phelps.) Wars are typically waged in the midsummer through early winter. As a consequence, the period of late July through the first couple of weeks of December is a particularly treacherous passage. Into this unsettled and unsettling period fall the events of September 11, 2001.

Did the 9/11 hijackers intend to hit New York at a vulnerable point in our calendar? Did they sense somehow that September is the mean season? We'll probably never know. The challenge facing this collection was, on one hand, to do justice to the horrors of that day and the heroism that followed in its wake and, on the other, to put the attack into some perspective. The Internet bloggers of 9/11, several of whom were composing accounts on laptops even as the towers fell, contribute some of the most compelling entries of this anthology. Their observations are so powerful, in fact, that they threaten to overshadow the preceding four centuries. Here again, the cyclical construction is helpful. What one can see in history

overlain, year upon year, is that the city has been wracked more
or less continuously by cataclysms—plagues, riots, financial panics,
battle carnage, and countless fires. Every century produces a diarist who laments, "This is the worst catastrophe ever to befall New
York!" Surely it seems that way at the moment. The city takes the
blow, catches its breath, then moves along to the insistent rhythm
of the tides. New York, as it emerges from these pages, is by turns
a wicked city, a compassionate city, a muscular city, a vulnerable
city, an artistic wonder, an aesthetic disaster, but forever a resilient
city—and one loved fiercely by its inhabitants.

I would like to express my gratitude to archives that have made
their holdings available to me: The New York Public Library,
Astor, Lenox, and Tilden Foundations, notably the Henry W. and
Albert A. Berg Collection of English and American Literature,
the Manuscripts, Archives and Rare Book Division, and the Paul
and Irma Milstein Division of United States History, Local History and Genealogy; the Patricia D. Klingenstein Library of the
New-York Historical Society; the Elmer Holmes Bobst Library,
New York University; the Museum of the City of New York; the
Whitney Museum of American Art; the New York State Library;
the Morgan Library and Museum; The Metropolitan Museum
of Art's Thomas J. Watson Library; the Kurt Weill Foundation
for Music; and the Cooper Union Library in New York City;
the Rosenbach Museum and Library and the American Philosophical Library & Museum in Philadelphia; the Lilly Library,
Indiana University–Bloomington; the Ellis Library, University
of Missouri–Columbia; the Earl Gregg Swem Library, College
of William and Mary, Williamsburg, Virginia; the Archives of
American Art and the National Museum of American History
[Smithsonian Institution] in New York and Washington, D.C.;
the Collection of American Literature, Beinecke Rare Book and

Manuscript Library, Yale University, New Haven, Connecticut; the Schlesinger Library of Radcliffe Institute for Advanced Study and the Houghton Library, Harvard College in Cambridge, Massachusetts.

As usual, the errors are exclusively my own.

TERESA CARPENTER
New York City
May 2011

A Word About Style

Many of the diarists you will encounter here wrote in irregular, imperfect English. Spellings and grammar were not standardized until the twentieth century. I have tried to stay as true as possible to the original expression, and in the interest of clarity, altered punctuation or graphic format—but only slightly. If a word or phrase is unintelligible, I identify it as such. If material has been omitted from the interior text of an entry, I indicate this with ellipses. It was my intent that each entry should stand on its own. In some instances a reference requires explanation and I have made those in brackets, either within the text or beneath the signature.

All of the writers included here are identified in "About the Diarists" (page 429). These bios identify the sources from which the present entries are drawn. In several instances I have cited other documents or publications containing the same entries in slightly different form. In short, any reader wishing to look into the work of any diarist or diarists found here has been given a rich set of sources upon which to draw.

Lovers of diaries, please enjoy.

New York Diaries

January 1

1844

Yet another year has overtaken me and how much advance can I reckon for myself.... My taste in writing is chastened some. My social position is not only elevated but widened though my visiting circle is very much limited. I called today only upon about 25 families. Professionally I do not feel that I have advanced at all.

JOHN BIGELOW

1851

On duty at the office all day between 12 & 1 o'clock helping give out new year's cake at the Hall. In the evening went up to the 18th ward Station House saw there the young man who was thrown out of the sleigh & killed at the corner of Madison Avenue & 29th St. I called on Alderman Atwood [*sic*] had a good time of it—went home.

INSPECTOR WILLIAM H. BELL

1906

Played golf today with [Robert] Henri and [Edward Wyatt] Davis. We welcome the New Year at James B. Moore's "Secret Lair Beyond the Moat"—450 West 23rd Street. A very small party.... I'm going to try to do a bit less smoking this year.

JOHN SLOAN

[The "Secret Lair" in question was the home of one café proprietor, James B. Moore, a flamboyant bohemian and host of bawdy parties.]

1953

A blissful moment alone with Julian [Beck] in the apartment, drinking to the year with wordless laughter.

Then four friends arrived: Jerry Newman and John Clellon Holmes, Allen Ginsberg and Jack Kerouac, and we drank port and got high on gage.

Holmes is the author of *Go,* a novel now popular among the vipers [potheads], and he it was who wrote that *New York Times Magazine* oddity, "The Beat Generation."...

Jack Kerouac, who he credits with inventing the phrase,... is a novelist who was a contemporary of Julian's at Horace Mann. He was the football champ who surprised everyone by winning scholastic honors.

Kerouac is a hero, a free-flowing spirit. He can't do anything except display his talent. Sardonic and handsome to a fault, he became raucous, drunk and incoherent as the night wore on to morning. But a hero on the binge is still a hero.

JUDITH MALINA

JANUARY 2

1850

Yesterday was New Year's Day, and I had lovely presents. We had 139 callers, and I have an ivory tablet and I write all their names down on it.... Some of the gentlemen come together and don't stay more than a minute; but some go into the back room and take some oysters and coffee and cake.... My cousin is always the first to come, and sometimes he comes before we are ready, and we find him sitting behind the door, on the end of the sofa, because he's bashful. The gentlemen keep dropping in all day and until long after I have gone to bed; and the horses look tired, and the livery men make a lot of money.

CATHERINE ELIZABETH HAVENS

1880

After breakfast took Alice out to drive in the Park.

THEODORE ROOSEVELT

JANUARY 3

1837

Mr. Lawrence, the Mayor, kept open house yesterday, according to custom from time immemorable [*sic*], but the manners as well as the times have sadly changed. Formerly gentlemen visited the mayor, saluted him by an honest shake of the hand, paid him the compliment of the day, and took their leave; one out of twenty perhaps taking a single glass of wine or cherry bounce and a morsel of pound cake or New Year's cookie[s]. But that respectable functionary is now considered the mayor of a party, and the rabble considering him "hail fellow well met," use his house as a Five Points tavern.

PHILIP HONE

1924

Grey [*sic*], rainy days, how I hate you! I am almost twenty-two, and still unloved. You remind me that beauty is a brief thing. You remind me that death hovers over me on dark wings. You even make me want to think of death....

I don't for a moment suppose it's the weather that ails me. Too much New York cheer, no doubt! I am exhausted, mentally and physically, unable to see things as they are. Straight normalities have a dark and crooked look when I am low and fagged. I cannot write any more—it requires the living death of loneliness and solitude to make me write—and no writing ever done is worth it.

WINIFRED WILLIS

1925

To dinner, in Rye, and I ordered a great steak for myself, but so many wanted it I went from the table as hungry as when I sate down. So at cards till late, and I had fair success, but [*New Yorker* publisher] Raoul Fleischmann had a royal flush, and there was talk of calling him Royal Flushman, but nought [*sic*] more momentous than that was said the whole night, and so to bed a moment or two before dawn.

FRANKLIN P. ADAMS

JANUARY 4

1780

The Snow continued very deep in the Streets. Some people froze to Death.

HUGH GAINE

1798

Jan[y] 4th 1798. Our Theatrical business is still bad except Monday [the] first of Jan a house of 494 Ds:. With much difficulty we prevailed in having the finishing of [the] New Theatre postponed and a temporary close made of [the] business so that we play in it, in 2 or 3 weeks.

WILLIAM DUNLAP

JANUARY 5

1844

Used D. Wilke's eyewash last night and think it has a good effect, also this morning. Office. Dinner. Read some of Burton's anatomy of melancholy which Henry Goodhue lent me. It is a rather curious book for its learning and superstition. But it is a compilation rather than a production.... I went up stairs and the full moon was shining in my window. I tried to feel sentimental but failed. I got out my telescope and looked and I think the magnifying power had some effect on the sentimentals [*sic*] but not much. I drew a picture of the appearance.... It looks very beautiful through a telescope.... Do they say that the bright part is the sea, and the dark land, or which way. It seems altogether absurd to suppose that they are mountains & valleys as they are great surfaces of often a regular brilliancy.

GEORGE CAYLEY

1864

Snowed all day. Commenced to take out our Guns.

WILLIAM B. GOULD

1924

Opening bill at [Provincetown Playhouse] under directorship of Kenneth, Bobby & me. Strindberg's "Spook Sonata" (using masks— my suggestion).

EUGENE O'NEILL

JANUARY 6

1795

Attended Chemical Lecture,—to obviate costiveness, with which I am much troubled, I had recourse to a very agreeable remedy—eat 11b½ of Raisins,—... About 4, came home and engrav'd—return'd and took out medicines,—came home again, at 7—Before 1—I finished the wooden cut.

DR. ALEXANDER ANDERSON

1842

I was indefatigable this morning and tonight I stayed quietly at home, smoked volcanically, and read Burns, of whose writings I ought to know more than I do.

GEORGE TEMPLETON STRONG

1864

Brooklyn Navy Yard. Verry cold. Giveen charge of the Wine Mess Ward Room.

WILLIAM B. GOULD

1912

Great cold and like to continue. To the playhouse to see Mr. Lew Fields do "The Hen-Pecks," which I liked not at all save when Mr. Fields is doing his anticks. For him I can laugh at greatly and he did nothing more than to mouth the alphabet, his manner being the drollest ever I saw, yet with a sad note therein, as ever in the best drolleries. To a publick where I have a beaker of ale and so to bed.

FRANKLIN P. ADAMS

JANUARY 7

1793

Beautifully, beautifully pleasant for the season.... Stopped at the shoe maker's to get measured for a pair of shoes. Learned coming from the hospital after lecture [that] Ludlow was taken by the undersheriff.... Was informed by the constable who stood at the door, [that] he was now in jail. The reason was because he had committed a rape, upon the daughter of a Parson H[ettelafs] at Long Island. Most horrid idea. I cannot conceive the truth of it. It made me feel cold when I was informed of it. He has been a dissipated character, but of late has very much attoned [*sic*] so as to become quite Studious and attentive to his business. If it is true, poor unfortunate lad[,] it will leave an eternal blott upon his character ... also an excommunication by our club. Had it not been poor L. this would not have ... happened.

JOTHAM POST

1798

Teach my children: read in Gibbon & NY Mag: for Dec.ʳ Write additional songs for *Sterne's Maria.*

WILLIAM DUNLAP

1878

Studies now fairly under way again. I think I shall do well in all except French 4, and very well in the Natural History courses.

I am boxing with my "Tutor" five times a week; I am going to try hard for the light weight cups in boxing and wrestling.

THEODORE ROOSEVELT

JANUARY 8

1790

According to appointment, at 11 Oclock I set out for the City Hall in my Coach—preceded by Colonel Humphreys and Majr. Jackson in Uniform (on my two White Horses) & followed by Mesr. Lear & Nelson in my chariot. ... In their rear was the Chief Justice of the United States & Secretaries of the Treasury and War Departments in their respective Carriages and in the order they are named. At the outer door of the Hall I was met by the Doorkeepers of the Senate and House, and conducted to the Door of the Senate Chamber; and passing from thence to the Chair through the Senate on the right, & House of Representatives on the left, I took my Seat. The Gentlemen who attended me followed & took their stand behind the Senators; the whole rising as I entered. After being seated, at which time the members of both Houses also sat, I rose (as they also did) and made my Speech; delivering one Copy to the President of the Senate, & another to the Speaker of the House of Representatives—after which, and being a few moments seated, I retired, bowing on each side to the Assembly (who stood) as I passed, and descending to the lower Hall attended as before, I returned with them to my House.

In the Evening, a *great* number of Ladies, and many Gentlemen visited Mrs. Washington.

On this occasion I was dressed in a suit of Clothes made at the Woolen Manufactury at Hartford, as the Buttons also were.

PRESIDENT GEORGE WASHINGTON

1793

Some of us then went to the jail to See Ludlow to know for what he was confined in reality. As I had been informed that it was not a rape which he had committed, but that he had only got her with child, the act having been committed, by her own consent, and willingness... at 6 went to Taylor's for our Examinations... the gentlemen got in a notion of drinking wine, and therefore we had to give up scientific pursuits, for the vain, and idle whim of a too prevailing sensation... all I would say or do proved ineffectual for fun as they called it, he would have it.... What a most horrid thing is it that we must be continually talking of people's faults instead of their virtues.—

JOTHAM POST

1851

On duty—left the office at 11 O'clock [and] went up to the Tombs to appear before the Grand Jury as witness against Hall & Miller[.] remained there until I was informed by Officer Lamont to report myself forthwith to the Chief. [H]aving done so I was ordered by the Chief to go in my office and await further orders. (The decision of Judge Judson in the case of the negro Henry Long, a fugitive slave from Virginia, was this morning given[;] it was that Henry Long be delivered to Dr. [Parker] the authorized agent of Dr. Smith, the owner of Long, to be taken back to Virginia.) After the decision was given, a large number of Persons both black & White collected around the Building and in the Park expressing various opinions concerning the decision as one of the witnesses (a Southern Gentleman) was leaving the Park he was followed by a number of Negroes [and] *white kined* Abolitionists who gathered to beat him. he Called upon a Policeman for protection who at once with the assistance of other Policemen Kept the mob back until he went in at the (Lossing?) House. when they arrested 3 of the ringleaders—at 4 O'clock I was ordered by the Chief to the U.S. Marshall's office along with the other officer. Henry Long in custody of Deputy U.S. Marshalls Brown, DeAngelis & Talmage. Then started for the 8 O'clock Train for Philadelphia protected by about 200 Policemen. The Chief & the U.S. Marshalls walking ahead of the nigger. We crossed the Ferry at the foot of Courtlandt St. and arrived in Jersey City. he was placed in the car and started for Philadelphia. I returned to the office and then went Home.

INSPECTOR WILLIAM H. BELL

JANUARY 9

1778

Visitors came on board in whose honor the guns were made to thunder and we were treated to fresh meat.... Here I sold an old white Prussian cloth vest with silver buttons for $6. (Congress money) to a sailor.

LT. JOHN CHARLES PHILIP VON KRAFFT

1863

Mrs. [William F.] Ritchie is a pretty woman who aids nature a little by art. Her hair was dressed in the modern Phrygian style in two great hills on either side of her head, the center being occupied on full-dress occasions with a bunch of hair full of feathers, birds, or flowers. One lady, a Mrs. Ronaldi, who is now the toast of the town, wears a bird's nest with eggs, making her head a hatchery. I doubt if there is enough brain there to hatch anything.

MARIA LYDIG DALY

1912

A daily practice on the typewriter now. On the piazza all morning after various chores.... Much excitement over the burning of the Equitable Life Building... [accounts] have not said whether the vaults are safe.

MARJORIE RICHARDS REYNOLDS

1935

Lately—due to not working and due, too, to observing how much more prestige and authority other people with less ability carry—It seems to me, now that I definitely want rewards during my lifetime, that given a good talent, its recognition and elevation to great are utterly dependent on exploitation and outside funny-business, the personal approach. If someone doesn't do this for you, you must do it yourself.

Walter Duranty at Carol [Hill Brandt]'s the other day described to me Bolitho's attitude toward this—sweep into a room no matter what your height. Above all, be a great genius to your friends.... Since I have always been disparaging about my work to my friends, I read a lesson in this. Observing elsewhere, I see how certain friends make good by sheer social contact—a flair for knowing who's who, for using these people without aggression. Success is a gift—like any knack for weaving something out of a few strings which to the rest of us are nothing but a few strings.

DAWN POWELL

1981

Tonight I watched several girls who were my peers and many younger race ahead to stardom on the big stage. As the curtain rose, all my friends became goddesses, and I felt alone and mortal. I forced myself to face the fact that I refuse to face every day; I am going nowhere. I can stay and stagnate, or I must change my life. I really find it grossly unfair to have to feel such impending doom at my age.

I had a nightmare last night about Balanchine. He told me I danced like a Biafran—no substance. I awoke with a great fear and knew I must go and dance before him. My faith in dancing is gone, but my faith in life cannot be, or else I would not be here writing this page.

TONI BENTLEY

1982

Dined at Maggie Paley's. She's at work, like everyone else, on a novel.

NED ROREM

JANUARY 10

1793

At 7 we all went to college to See M...he had invited us several days ago....Ludlow attended with us this afternoon. Poor fellow, he seems when sitting still to be much agitated by contending emotions. Is it just that a woman should be allowed such liberty as to swear away the life of a man...[be] that he committed a rape or not. I am fully persuaded that he did not commit one and yet she comes forward and Swears that he did. No man is absolutely safe if Women are disposed to injure them.

JOTHAM POST

1950

Dinner with Goddard Liebersons [producers] at Algonquin.... "The Member of the Wedding" beautifully written and acted for 2 acts. 3rd act very ordinary and disappointing.

KURT WEILL

JANUARY 11

1880

If these rehearsals of the *Middy* don't drive us all into asylums it will be a wonder....

Now we are learning the music for the third and last act of the *Middy;* it is as pretty as all the rest.... There is a charming love duet between...the Queen and Miss Lewis, disguised as a young man. The coquettish young Queen has been flirting mildly with what she supposes to be a young midshipman of noble birth; and Fanchette, the gipsy, is obliged to pretend that she is smitten with the Queen in order to hide her own identity as a girl until she can get away safely from Portugal.

The "royal game of chess" is going smoother; the fencing will be one of the showy bits of the piece, and the grand entrance of the royal midshipmen at the end of the first act will be tremendously effective, both in posing and music. We begin work now at nine in the morning and keep it up till five o'clock, with only an hour for luncheon.

A sensation was sprung on us...this week, in the second act. When we were in the midst of the fencing business Mr. Moore came forward with a package of cigarettes and informed us that we were to light up and smoke in that scene in every performance! We all protested and said we couldn't, didn't want to do it.... We looked so disturbed that Mr. Daly laughed at us; then he asked whether we ever had smoked cubeb cigarettes, and had we any objection to them? Two or three had used them for colds or sore throats, and the rest of us said we didn't mind trying them; so a package of cubebs was sent for, and we all began to practice on them. Nasty things they are, too; in a few minutes we were coughing, choking, and gasping, but I would rather smoke them than real tobacco.

DORA RANOUS

1922

Met Mrs. Dorothy Parker, and to dinner with her, but all she would take was some chicken salad. So to the Central, and saw a cinema play called "Foolish Wives." ... Von Stroheim. Lord, how these films do concern themselves with matter extraneous to the story for the sake of pictorial effect! Weary with the picture by midnight, we made charades, and one scene showing a dog and the next a piece of bread, D. said it was Barcarole, which made us very merry, and the play not ended until quarter past midnight, and when we came to Broadway we were astonished to find all the same, no new buildings up. Took D. home, and so home by subway, the weariest ever I was, and to bed.

FRANKLIN P. ADAMS

1981

Called Vincent and woke him up. He said a lot of my paintings at the office cracked from the cold.

I watched *Giant* on TV from 1:00 to 5:30. It's so long. I even went to church in between and when I came back it was still on. James Dean's acting when he gets old is the worst thing. But they did a good thing—when he's drunk and talking into the microphone it's like a rock star, he's right on top of the microphone and it's just noises coming out and so it's abstract.

I had some wine and a couple of aspirin to try to get rid of the pain in my back. I'm also trying to take two aspirin a day so I don't becòme senile because I just read that it stops the hardening of the arteries. But I don't know, my mother took millions of aspirin and it didn't do any good.

Bob [Colacello] said the inauguration is on Saturday. I didn't realize it was so soon. Bob doesn't care about discoing now, he's just so happy with all his Republicans—with Doria and Jerry Zipkin calling him.

ANDY WARHOL

JANUARY 12

1834

At night a fire broke out in Mr. Long's Bookstore which was totally consumed. The houses next adjoining were nearly destroyed. Mr. Long's was 161 Broadway.

Among persons engaged in extensive business there exists at the present time a great pressure for money; caused in part by the hostility of the Bank of the United States, which hostility arose from the acts of the Government towards it. A fearfull [*sic*] struggle is now going on between the Bank of the N.Y and the Government, which [it] is to give us, time will soon show. So for myself I have no great fears as to the result. The old General [Andrew Jackson] who is now at the head of Government, has passed through many a dark struggle without flinching, and it is not to be supposed that he will flinch now when our very liberty is at stake.

JAMES CRUIKSHANK

1920

[Robert] Benchley tells me he hath resigned his position with "Vanity Fair" because they had discharged Mistress Dorothy Parker; which I am sorry for.... To the opera house and hear "Martha," a tuneful score, and E. Caruso and Miss Mabel Garrison sang well, but the story of the opera is a second-rate affair.

FRANKLIN P. ADAMS

JANUARY 13

1777

A very pleasant, though cold, Morning, induced me to take the Exercise of walking upon the Banks of the North River [Hudson], which now begins to shine with immense Floats of Ice, brought by the ebbing Tide from the upper Parts. The *Eagle*, upon this Account, was hauled nearer Shore in the East River.

AMBROSE SERLE

1790

After duly considering on the place for receiving the address of the House of Representatives, I concluded that it would be best to do it at my own House—first, because it seems most consistent with usage & custom—2d. because there is no 3d. place in the Fedl. Hall ... to which I could call them, & to go into either of the Chambers appropriated to the Senate or Representatives, did not appear proper; and 3d. because I had appropriated my own House for the Senate to deliver theirs in and, accordingly appointed my own House to receive it.

PRESIDENT GEORGE WASHINGTON

1859

Poor Hanslein has had a dreadful struggle with subtraction. The educational hour before dinner today was tragic and tearful. He grasps new notions slowly and hardly, and the instant he gets wrong, loses his self-possession and becomes hopelessly muddled. But he is decidedly a brick and his future promises none the worse for his developing slowly.

GEORGE TEMPLETON STRONG

JANUARY 14

1798

Hodgkinson suggested an Idea of naming the Boxes from the principal dramatic Authors & Actors of Great Britain, I changed it to [the] dramatic Authors of Europe to the exclusion of [the] Actors & adopted it.

WILLIAM DUNLAP

1850

My mother said she could not afford to give me another pair of kid gloves now, but my sister took me down to Seaman and Muir's, next door to the hospital on Broadway, and bought me a pair. I like salmon color, but she said they would not be useful....

I like best to go to Arnold and Constable's on Canal Street, they keep elegant silks and satins and velvets, and my mother always goes there to get her best things....

My Staten Island sister gave me a nice silk dress, only it is a soft kind that does not rustle. I have a green silk that I hate, and the other day I walked too near the edge of the sidewalk, and one of the stages splashed mud on it, and I am so glad, for it can't be cleaned.

CATHERINE ELIZABETH HAVENS

1951

Yesterday I went to eat with Len Perskie, my boss at Graphic Studios where I now work as a messenger boy and all-around-hand.

We talked about Charles. Charles is our chemist.... He is almost blind, makes mistakes, Charlie. Each time he weighs the chemicals, he calls me to check the scales. All he does, and does really well, is stir them....

[Charlie] always buys the *Journal American,* and everybody's waiting for it. When we are all back, Al and Phil will ask Charlie: What's nude? And we take up the search for the nude picture, there is always one planted somewhere in the *Journal American,* we just know, it never fails. But not Charlie, who is crazy about dog and cat pictures. That's what he's looking for, in the *Journal American,* and if he finds one, he walks around showing it off to us, telling us how sweet pets are. His hands, when they touch you, they are like dough, so uncomfortably flabby. Whenever he runs out of things to do, he stands by Lizzie's table—she is thirty, unmarried, petite—and giggles.

Henry is no more than 25 but he is already old. He serves as an "elder" in his church, in Chinatown, eventually he wants to study theology, to work as a missionary in Africa. His camera and working table are cluttered with Sunday School pamphlets. He speaks softly, piously. Walks most of the time on the tips of his toes, like a stork looking for frogs. He also spends a lot of time at Lizzie's table. He stands right behind her, runs his hand down her back, scratches her neck, giggles. He constantly reproaches me for not having a savings account and why I am not collecting receipts for things I buy. When I drop them into a waste basket, he retrieves them, saves them, and brings them to me a few weeks later, asking me to keep them. He says I'll end up badly, one of these days, because of my lack of practicality.

JONAS MEKAS

JANUARY 15

1879

Arrived at New York. Went to a rehearsal of the wedding. One of my old flames, pretty Helen White, is a bridesmaid.

THEODORE ROOSEVELT

1939

I cannot really love the art of Van Gogh; I am too American, that is, a believer in good fortune and good temper and good looks; a lover of the calm and definite kind of form set apart somehow in brilliant uncluttered space; a lover of the deliberate pose, the steady brush, the third (not the fourth) dimension. That, roughly speaking, always has been the style of our American painting when it has been very good: the farm pictures of Homer, before he began splashing watercolor about like Sargent; the scenes of shooting and sculling by Eakins which have the background of dewy field or geometrically rippled water. You can always tell that we are a people very empiric and sportive, not over-educated and not really religious, not maniacal, not even logical; and that our continent is not narrow, our atmosphere not opalescent or shadowy. Even our "primitives" and odds and ends are not consciously artistic, have it: a certain insolent or childish simplicity, very neat, very spacious, almost vacuous; a little look of constant sensuality without much moral trend one way or the other. Even the aquatints of old Audubon, intended to be merely informative of the native birdlife, seem now emblematic of what kind of native art we are apt to have, if any.

GLENWAY WESCOTT

1988

Feeling in an oysters and clams mood, I decided yesterday afternoon that if I went to Grand Central for an early supper (we're talking 3:30), I could be in and out and back before rush hour. Of course it didn't work out that way. After the oysters—Belons, and rather nasty, tasting of iodine and disagreeably chewy—and the fried clams, I lingered in that book store too long and was totally, utterly chilled trying to cop a cab. It was only when I was safely tucked up in bed, in a flannel nightshirt, that it got through to me that, rush hour or no rush hour, the shuttle across town and the Seventh Avenue to 23rd would have spared me much pain. The thermia was never more hyper.

But I did find Elmore Leonard's *Bandits* finally in paperback. Also Ed McBain's *Shotgun*, almost the only 87th Precinct novel I haven't read. And a George V. Higgins and a Simenon. Not bad.

JAMES SCHUYLER

JANUARY 16

1778

...I was now determined to make my escape, though hardly able to undertake it. Just at dusk, having made the Sentinel intoxicated, I with others, went out into the backyard to endeavor to escape over the fence. The others being backward about going first, I climbed upon a tombstone and gave a spring, and went over safe, and then gave orders for the others to do so also. A little Irish lad undertook to leap over, and caught his clothes in the spikes on the wall, and made...a noise. The sentinel being aroused called out "Rouse!" which is the same as to command the guards to turn out. They were soon out and surrounded the prison. In the mean time I had made my way to St. Paul's Church, which was the wrong way to get out of town.

The guards, expecting that I had gone towards North River, went in that direction....I wished much to cross the river, but could not find any boat suitable. While going along up the side of the river,... I was challenged by a sentinel with the usual word (Burdon), upon which I answered nothing.... He bade me advance and give the countersign, upon which I fancied [pretended] I was drunk, and advanced in a staggering manner.... I still entreated him to let me go. Soon he consented and directed my course [toward what was presumed to be his home].... Soon the moon arose and made it very light, and there being snow on the ground, crusted over, and no wind, therefore a person walking could be heard a great distance.

At this time the tumor in my lungs broke, and being afraid to cough for fear of being heard, prevented me from relieving myself of the pus that was lodged there.

I had now to cross lots that were cleared and covered with snow,... and for fear of being heard I lay myself flat on my stomach and crept along on the frozen snow. When I come to the fence I climbed over, and walked down the road, near a house where there was music and dancing.... One of the guards came out. I immediately fell down upon my face. Soon the man went into the house. I rose again and crossed the fence into the field, and proceeded towards the river....

I found a Sentinel every fifteen or twenty rods until I came within two miles of Hell Gate. Here I stayed until my feet began to freeze, and having nothing to eat I went a mile further up the river. It now being late I crept into the bushes and lay down to think what to do next. I concluded to remain where I was during the night, and early in the morning to go down to New York and endeavor to find some house to conceal myself in.

In the morning as soon as the Revelry Beating commenced I went on my way to New York.... I passed the sentinels unmolested down the middle of the road, and arrived there before many were up. I met many British and Hessian soldiers whom I knew very well, but they did not know me.

I went to a house, and found them friends of America, and was kindly received of them, and [they] promised to keep me a few days.

... The good lady of the house gave me some medicine of my

own prescribing, which soon gave me relief. Soon after, a rumor spread about town among the friends of America of my confinement, and . . . they took measures to have me conveyed to Long Island, which was accordingly done.

DR. ELIAS CORNELIUS

1940

Very cold. Got up late. Worked on the book [*Other Men's Houses*]. Took a walk up to the park and to see the skaters in Rockefeller Center. Then in the evening went off to a dinner of the Euthanasia Society. Mostly doctors. Made a short speech. They thought I was Maxwell Anderson so I let it go at that.

SHERWOOD ANDERSON

JANUARY 17

1899

Passing out into the sunlight we walked along the driveway overlooking the park as far as 125th street where we took the car going three quarters of an hours . . . down to Brooklyn Bridge on the east side. What a change in the scene. . . . Here was life in the Bowery, old men, young men, women and children all jostling, crowding and yelling at each other in their bowery slang. Looking so queer in their odd dress. We caught a glimpse of the celebrated Chinese quarters with its dark and dinginess. Presently we came to the Brooklyn bridge. Here again was great hurrying and bustling. Down below . . . there was the dark deep water of the East river . . . with the vessels and steamboats and large ferries running to and fro. We just went to the center of the bridge . . . then turned around and started back. . . . It was just dusk and it looked as if the buildings were a great dark mountain and the lights looked like gems among them.

NAOMI R. KING

1934

Saw jacket of *Story of a Country Boy* which is set for March 22. Then went to that Gypsy Tea Room for lunch at Fifth Avenue and 38th. Booths with not the usual tearoom chatter of women's voices since most of the lunchers are alone. They sit with their teacups already overturned waiting for a gypsy to sit down at their table and reveal....

In a corner booth a sign says "Palmistry, Rajah, the White Hindu" and here a big Irish policeman (Rajah) sits with fez on, reading palms. A cat roams about and a kettle hangs on three sticks. The gypsies are named Ramona, Juanita, etc. Ramona sat down by me, said I was to go on a sea journey; sleep soon in a strange bed; sign a contract with the letter P; that I was a dancer; said something about my foot; said I would make more money than any man but must concentrate on it as I had a highly spiritualized mind to which practicality was foreign;... September people attracted to me but make me unhappy. In four weeks an old friend comes back and trip is discussed; also, follow first impressions always of everything.

Dawn Powell

1980

The children keep the [Nixon] house under steady surveillance. There have been signs of activity: Lights dimly on, workmen plodding through, Christmas wreaths hung (adorned incongruously with doves of peace); still no curtains. But the second coming impends. Today Alexandra was meeting in the living room with a group working on the Kennedy campaign. Suddenly one of them said, "You won't believe what I see through the window." They all looked. There was the unforgettable profile briefly framed in the window across the fence. He was there for an instant, oblivious, then he turned away. A daughter was with him. Apparently he was inspecting the property.

Arthur M. Schlesinger, Jr.

JANUARY 18

1790

Still indisposed with an Aching tooth, and swelled and inflamed Gum.

PRESIDENT GEORGE WASHINGTON

1943

Monday Night (about 3 A.M.)

What [Paul] Bigelow calls my "occupational disease"—crab lice—is back on me. Only one discovered but I shall have to procure a bottle of "The Personal Insecticide" tomorrow. Who shall I blame? Who is the father of these bastards I am reluctantly bearing. Qui sait?

(Elizabethan humor!)

Tomorrow I see [producer] Carly Wharton and a verdict will presumably be handed down on "You Touched Me"—an occasion important enough to alter the whole future course of my strange term on earth.

And so we come to the end of another journal. We are not afraid. We are prepared to go on. So En Avant!

TENNESSEE WILLIAMS

1979

It was the first time I ever saw people actually flying around the streets, it was so windy. Cabbed to Union Square ($3) and that's where I really saw people in the air. If you were on the sunny side of the street it was nice, beautiful, but then when you'd hit a corner you'd get blown away. People were holding on to things. Went to the office. Stephen Mueller and Ronnie were finishing stretching Shadow paintings for my show next week.

ANDY WARHOL

JANUARY 19

1922

Early up, and hastily to the dentist's, and stopt [*sic*] at a haberdasher's to buy A[lexander]. Woollcott a birthday gift, and bought two tyes for him. Shall you wear one? asked the clerk. Nay, quoth I, these do go to Sergeant Woollcott. But, said the clerk, you must not go forth thus tyeless. And he shewed me I had no tye on at all, I having been in so great a hurry and not having looked at myself in the mirror, which I seldom do unless necessary. So I bought a fine green tye, and so to the office.

FRANKLIN P. ADAMS

JANUARY 20

1850

We have a Dutch oven in our kitchen beside the range, and in the winter my mother has mince pies made, and several baked at once, and they are put away and heated up when we want one. My mother makes elegant cake, and when she makes rich plum cake, like wedding cake, she sends it down to Shaddle's on Bleecker Street to be baked.

CATHERINE ELIZABETH HAVENS

1899

Mama wanted to see A. T. Stuart's [*sic*] large store.... On the [second] floor in a large rotunda is what was called "Cotton Picking"...there was the log cabin and the old darkies which looked just like reality...to represent the cotton fluff were long strings of little crystal balls hung from the top of the building...the whole dome looked like a great large cotton ball. This store is lighted by electricity plants which give wonderful brilliancy to the whole store and these electric plants are said to be worth $150,000.

NAOMI R. KING

1943

La Wharton has turned thumbs down on the re-write and my castles have tumbled again. I will probably return to Clayton and live on the folks for a while. Worse things are possible, since I have been away so long I'm really longing for home a bit. Excepting, of course, the old man. Perhaps he is too old a dragon to be still very fearsome. We shall see. *Mon devoir* is to Grand [mother] and Grandfather—and Mother.

It was a blow at Wharton's. She is way up on the 29th story and from her window we could see the Statue of Liberty. I had an admirable composure for <u>me</u> and I took the medicine which she gave me straight in a manner becoming a "veteran of discouragement" which I told her I was. We parted on good terms. I shall make no outraged comments on producers. They are fools—like everyone else—only a <u>little</u> more so. Unfortunately they have the power to wring a poet's heart, if not his neck, when he comes into the theatre—or tries to.—See [agent] Audrey [Wood] tomorrow. Then probably—
    En avant!

TENNESSEE WILLIAMS

1958

Today I presented my Letters of Credence to Dag Hammarskjöld. He twinkled at me and turned on the charm. What is he like? Modest conceit, subtlety, vanity, intimacy switched on and off. . . . In the long bar at the U.N. I met John Hood, the Australian Representative. We had three or four jumbo-sized Manhattans each. I don't know if this is the order of the day. . . . In the afternoon walked in Central Park—icy wind, cloudless blue sky, the wild animals shrunken in their cages, bored jaguars, comatose pumas, a wild-animal smell that hung about one for an hour afterwards. To a cocktail party in the evening. I had forgotten how much the Americans love talking on social occasions about international affairs and how earnestly distressed they are about the conduct of everyone everywhere.

CHARLES RITCHIE

JANUARY 21

1844

Breakfast. Wrote a long valentine to Miss Depeyster. Trashy but amusing from the nature of the circumstances.

GEORGE CAYLEY

1855

The unemployed workmen, chiefly Germans, are assembling daily in the Park and listening to inflammatory speeches by demagogues (who should be "clapt up" for preaching sedition) and marching in procession through the streets. The large majority of the distressed multitude is decently clad and looks well fed and comfortable. People anticipate riot and disturbance; there have been two or three rumors of [it] in various quarters. Friday night it was rumored that a Socialist mob was sacking the Schiff mansion in the Fifth Avenue, where was a great ball and a mass meeting of aristocracy. Certainly the destitute . . . are a thankless set and deserve little sympathy in their complaints. The effort to provide them employment and relief, the activity of individuals and of benevolent organizations, the readiness with which money is contributed do credit to the city. More could be done and ought to be done, of course, but what is done is beyond precedent here, and more than our "unemployed" friends have a right to count on.

GEORGE TEMPLETON STRONG

1952

Merce Cunningham's dance is the healthiest and the most pleasant modern dance. Instead of the sorrows, he dances the joyous discoveries.

A lady named Ann Lovett invites us to a small party. . . .

I enjoy a long talk with the unsettlingly handsome [mythologist]

Joseph Campbell. He speaks with uncanny exuberance when he describes the beauty of Sanskrit, in which each word is an actual expression of the concept.

Campbell believes in the power of magic and encourages me to experiment in the darker arts.

I say I would be morally obliged to practice only white magic.

"There can be no real power unless it is used for evil first."

He lies.

He tells me stories of magic and bewitchment.

I should not mind bewitching him in a much simpler sense. But no, the resplendent Jean Erdman is wearing a red dress. And I am quite powerless, even in my black satin. No, especially in black satin.

JUDITH MALINA

JANUARY 22

1846

Our dear little Mary [Hone's two-year-old granddaughter] gave a *déjeuner à la fourchette* at Grandfather Hone's. About twenty-odd little Responsibilities, whose joint ages did not amount to the sum of mine, after a royal romp, sat down to a grand banquet of cold chickens, sandwiches, jellies, confectionery, etc. And the table, after the feast was ended, gave evidence that nature's first [?] and the pap days of the children were past. The lady hostess did the honors at the head of the table, with her usual grace and propriety, and at 3 o'clock the dining room had become a banquet hall deserted.

PHILIP HONE

1924

I have had the chance of a publicity job at a salary of about 75 dollars a week or more! But have not even tried to put it over since it is not writing, and write I must.... I have written an essay on "Oscar Wilde and Modern Review"—a gem. It is the same with everything I write; I do nothing with them but put them by, because I shrink from seeing editors, and it is no use to send MSS in. But I am living perhaps some thousand paces ahead of the "successful ones" now, so it doesn't matter—except that I am so poor!

I sit, with a glass of exquisite sherry wine, soul of leisure. When I read Wilde I feel that I must be drinking wine slowly or smoking an expensive cigaret [*sic*].

WINIFRED WILLIS

1954

These are the best rehearsals. In our living room where the furniture is disarranged to approximate a stage, the actors move easily and securely, and the static poem becomes a moving play, the means clear. I am in love with what I am doing; therefore the actors work well.

Every night after rehearsals we plunder the ruins for floorboards, dodging the ubiquitous policemen.

JUDITH MALINA

JANUARY 23

1891

I always love to attend one of Mrs. William Astor's balls... they are perfect in every respect. I danced with Mrs. Stevenson, *née* Brady, Mrs. Paget, Mrs. King... and Mrs. Whitney. The supper was served at small tables. Mrs. [Cornelia] Bradley-Martin, Mrs.... Whitney, Mr. Elliott Shefford... and a... German count were at the table with me.

EDWARD NEUFVILLE TAILER

1907

Well, New York looks good and big and prosperous but the prosperity don't seem to come my way.

JOHN SLOAN

1924

I love the great twilit canyon of lower Broadway—I can dream it is some fairy place of shifting lights and shadows if I shut my eyes and ears to the noisy little men who hustle, two [by] two, everywhere, gesticulating, mouthing, and exclaiming. How different, tho, is my world, from the world that is out there. How secret and clean and sweet is the world of thoughts, books, writings and dreams, and how far removed from the bare ugliness of office-rooms, and the mad rush for money! How can people live, when it is only for the sake of dying!

WINIFRED WILLIS

1997

Paris Review parties have always had a satyric quality to them—jowly novelists well into their third marriages and fifth drinks, the latest batch of overripe lit chicks off the bus from Oberlin, George Plimpton, glissading through the throng, urging everyone on to great gin-and-tonic consumption. One half expects a Brueghel painting to break out.... When I had just arrived on the New York literary / media scene—which, as are all such scenes, is made up of about 1 [*sic*] percent literati and 99 percent pseudos—I began going to these parties with some regularity and learned the essential art of talking to novelists whose books one hadn't read. I also met my wife there, and so will always have fond feelings toward the place.

I went back tonight and found virtually the entire late-'80s crowd gone. No Jay. No Bret. No Tama. And as if to confirm that times had really changed, the young novelist being honored bounded up to me and said, "Hey, you're the only person left here I haven't met." Plimpton was still there, of course, and he continues to be an object of wonder. No younger person could ever pull off his brand of élan, his ability to greet someone whose name he can't remember, or possibly never knew, with a magisterial, "Ah, there you are." People just don't live life grand cru anymore, though there are a surprising number in the younger generation who play at being baby Plimptons. It doesn't quite work. For one, Plimpton actually wrote a lot of books and continues to produce on a regular basis. The new literati have more or less ditched the achievement part—a few bylines for branding purposes—and focused entirely on the lifestyle part....

I'm sad to say that our generation's main gift to the culture may turn out to be self-promotion. We have precious little to promote, but we do it with ferocious ingenuity.

MICHAEL HIRSCHORN

JANUARY 24

1795

Morning—finish'd the drawings for Cressin—I Inoculated two patients in Capt. Smith's family—spent 6d for Figs.... Got my bottle of shoe-blacking, which has been a second time in the care of Capt. Hardy for alteration—he pretends that it is made by another person.—Call'd at my Father's before dinner, where I found James Sacket, drew a couple of Cyphers for a set of China which he is going to send for.—After-noon, finish'd a wooden cut. Evening—Read 'till 8.—began another wooden cut.

DR. ALEXANDER ANDERSON

1980

Victor Bockris came over with William Burroughs. I introduced Bianca to William Burroughs. Bianca's hair is really short now, like a crewcut, it looks terrible. Jade was painting in the back with me and she sat on her first painting. I gave her some diamond dust to throw on the canvas.

ANDY WARHOL

JANUARY 25

1850

My oldest aunt went to Miss Pierce's school, and got acquainted with a young gentleman...who became a clergyman, and Queen Victoria ordered him to come to Edinburgh to try to get an estate [file a lawsuit].... He took my aunt and their children and went away in a ship, and it took them ninety days to cross the Atlantic Ocean, and when they get the estate they will live in the castle, and my mother and I will go and visit them....

A young lady in Edinburgh told one of my Scotch cousins that she supposed all the Americans were copper colored, and he said, "Well, you know my father is a Scotchman, so that is why I am white."

CATHERINE ELIZABETH HAVENS

1880

At last everything is settled; but it seems impossible to realize it.... I am so happy that I dare not trust in my own happiness. I drove over to the Lees determined to make an end of things at last; it was nearly eight months since I had first proposed to her, and I had been nearly crazy during the past year; and after much pleading my own sweet, pretty darling consented to be my wife. Oh, how bewitchingly pretty she looked! If loving her with my whole heart and soul can make her happy, she shall be happy; a year ago last Thanksgiving I made a vow that win her I would if it were possible; and now that I have done so, the aim of my whole life shall be to make her happy, and to shield her and guard her from every trial;

and, oh, how I shall cherish my sweet queen! How she, so pure and sweet and beautiful can think of marrying me I can not understand, but I praise and thank God it is so.

THEODORE ROOSEVELT

1940

Pretty bum—no sleep but did work. Walked about, tired and distraught in the early p.m. Then John Dos Passos and a man named Henry Miller—just home after 10 years in Europe—came. We drank and talked together. Had late dinner alone with E. [wife, Eleanor]. Took sleeping powder and had big sleep.

SHERWOOD ANDERSON

1951

Newsweek, eleventh floor. The same tiny receptionist girl, typing. Boy, they keep them busy here, even the receptionist has to type.... busy with the next edition. Typewriters clacking in every corner. It's a pleasure to walk past them all, carelessly. Messengers have their own privileges.

I walk straight to the editor's desk:

"Anything for me?"

The man points at a small package on the corner of the desk.

I take the package and walk back, retracing my steps through the maze of typewriters, past the typing receptionist, and out into the street.

Now, during the holiday season, the streets are full of beautiful girls. There are more of them than ever. Last night there was some snow, so now they all had pulled out their water boots—it's a rare occasion to show them off to the world.... Yes, the boots do fit them nicely.... I remember Mikšys, he said: "Maybe I don't know what New York really has, it may have nothing. But one thing I know, it does have beautiful girls."

JONAS MEKAS

JANUARY 26

1838

My wife, daughter Margaret, Jones and I dined with Mr. & Mrs. Olmstead.... The dinner was quite *à la française*. The table, covered with confectionery and gew-gaws, looked like one of the shops down Broadway in the Christmas holidays, but not an eatable thing. The dishes were all handed around, in my opinion, in a most unsatisfactory mode of proceeding in relation to this important part of the business of man's life. One does not know how to choose, because you are ignorant of what is coming next, or whether anything more is coming. Your conversation is interrupted every minute by greasy dishes thrust between your head and that of your next neighbor, and it is more expensive than the old mode of shewing a handsome dinner to your guests and leaving them free to choose. It will not do. This French influence must be resisted. Give us the nice French dishes, *fricandeau de veau, perdrix au choux,* and *côtelettes à la province* but let us see what we are to have.

PHILIP HONE

1870

Splendid day. In the morning all the tools were removed to Shed opposite, At 10 A.M. the Bellymen with 18 Carts, music band and a number of men, outsiders, after loading the tools, march around the factory, down Lexington Ave. & past our store on 14th str. some of the outsiders, hooting & whistling. Otherwise all orderly. At home in eveg. writing letters to germany [*sic*].

WILLIAM STEINWAY

["Bellymen," as the term suggests, were skilled workmen who climbed inside pianos to repair them.]

1947

I drink orange juice at the edge of a counter, sitting in a polished booth on one of three armchairs raised on a little dais; little by little,... the city grows familiar. The surfaces become facades; the solids turn into houses. On the pavement the wind stirs up dust and old papers. Beyond Washington Square, the grid begins to bend. The right angles break down; the streets are no longer numbered but have names; the lines curve and tangle together. I'm wandering through a European city. The houses have only three or four storeys and come in opaque colors somewhere between red, ochre, and black. Sheets dry on the fire escapes that zigzag against the facades. These sheets that promise sunshine, the shoeshine boys posted on the street corners, the rooftop terraces—they vaguely evoke a southern city, yet the worn red of the houses makes one think of the London fog. The fact is, this neighborhood is like nothing I've ever seen. But I know I will love it.

The landscape changes. The word "landscape" suits this city that's been deserted by men and invaded by the sky. Rising above the skyscrapers, the sky surges through the straight streets; it's too vast for the city to tame, and it overflows—it's a mountain sky. I walk between the steep cliffs at the bottom of a canyon where no sun penetrates: it's filled with a salt smell. Human history is not inscribed on these carefully calibrated buildings; they are more like prehistoric caves than the houses of Paris or Rome. In Paris, in Rome, history has permeated the bowels of the ground itself; Paris reaches down into the center of the earth. In New York, even the Battery doesn't have such deep roots. Beneath the subways, sewers, and heating pipes, the rock is virgin and inhuman. Between this rock and the open sky, Wall Street and Broadway bathe in the shadows of their giant buildings; this morning they belong to nature. The little black church with its cemetery of flat paving stones is as unexpected and touching in the middle of Broadway as a crucifix on a wild ocean beach.

The sun is so beautiful, the waters of the Hudson so green that I take the boat that brings midwestern tourists to the Statue of Liberty. But I don't get out at the little island that looks like a small fort. I just want to see a view of [*sic*] Battery as I've so often seen it in the movies. I do see it. In the distance, its towers seem fragile. They rest so precisely on their vertical lines that the slightest shudder would knock them down like a house of cards. When the boat draws closer, their foundations seem firmer, but the fall line remains indelibly traced. What a field day a bomber would have!

SIMONE DE BEAUVOIR

JANUARY 27

1844

Delightful book is Mr. D[ickens's]. [*A Christmas Carol*.] He's not dead yet, though *Martin Chuzzlewit* is flat and the [*American*] *Notes* a libel on this model republic of enlightened freemen.

GEORGE TEMPLETON STRONG

1947

I have a rendezvous at six o'clock at the Plaza Hotel on Fifty-ninth Street. I climb the stairs of the elevated railway. This railway is touching, like a memory; it's scarcely bigger than a provincial miniature railway. The walls are wooden; it seems like a country station. The gate is also made of wood, but it turns automatically—no employee. To go through, all you need is a nickel, the magic coin that also activates telephones and opens the doors of toilets, which are modestly called "restrooms." We roll along above the Bowery at second-story level. The stations whiz by: we're already at Fourteenth Street, then Thirty-fifth, Forty-second. I'm waiting for Fifty-ninth, but we rush past—Seventieth, Eightieth—we're not stopping anymore. Below us, all the streetlamps are lit. Here is the nocturnal celebration I glimpsed from up in the sky: movie houses, drugstores, wooden horses. I'm transported through a wondrous amusement park, and this little elevated train is itself a fairground attraction. Will it ever stop? New York is so big.

SIMONE DE BEAUVOIR

JANUARY 28

1939

I bought a newspaper to read on top of the Fifth Avenue bus, and therein came upon the news of the death of Yeats, and to my astonishment experienced an auditory illusion: two or three claps of thunder, not loud, at a distance, but awe-inspiring on that bright winter day.

GLENWAY WESCOTT

1947

It's not customary here to do work in places where people drink: this is the land of specialization. In places where drinks are served, you drink. As soon as my glass is empty, the waiter comes over to inquire; if I don't empty it fast enough, he prowls around me, looking at me reproachfully. This morning the taste of whiskey doesn't seem so bad. But it seems wiser to leave before the fourth glass.

I give my lecture to a French audience. I go to a cocktail party at the home of a Frenchwoman. All the guests are French, except for two French-speaking Americans.... I'm quite excited by the time I arrive at the house of A.M. . . . who has invited me for dinner; at long last I'm getting inside an American home. But apart from Richard Wright, whom I knew in Paris and whom I'm delighted to see again, everyone is French....

All these French people I meet are pleased to explain America to me—according to their experience, of course. Nearly all of them

have a strong bias: either they hate it and can think only of leaving
or they shower it with excessive praise....

I'm utterly taken with New York. It's true that both camps tell
me, "New York is not America." V. irritates me when he declares,
"If you like New York, it's because it's a European city that's strayed
to the edge of this continent." It is all too clear that New York is not
Europe. But I'm even more distrustful of P., another pro-American
Pétain supporter, when he contrasts New York—a city of foreigners and Jews—to the idyllic villages of New England, where the inhabitants are 100 percent American and endowed with patriarchal
virtues. We have often heard "the real France" praised this way in
contrast to the corruption of Paris.

SIMONE DE BEAUVOIR

1997

McD. calls with good news. He's the music director of *The Rosie
O'Donnell Show,* where I used to work. "I'm putting up the theme
song for a Daytime Emmy." McD. composed the music; I wrote the
lyrics. Unlike most TV themes, ours is actually sung; the words are
heard. Most opening themes are arranged as instrumental music,
but nearly all have lyrics. Even if the words are never heard, the
lyricist receives a royalty each time the theme is played.... In television, writing lyrics that will never be sung is regarded as a fabu-
lous opportunity.

McD. isn't optimistic about our chances: "Patti LaBelle wrote
that new *Oprah* thing." But a nomination would mean seats at the
awards luncheon, which is sure to be attended by many soap stars.
I'd go in a second. I'm disconcerted but not displeased that Patti
and Oprah may have a genuine effect, if not on my happiness, at
least on my lunch plans.

RANDY COHEN

JANUARY 29

1847

Our good City of New York has already arrived at the state of society to be found in the large cities of Europe; overburdened with population, and where the two extremes of costly luxury in living, expensive establishments, and improvident waste are presented in daily and hourly contrast with squalid misery and hopeless destitution. This state of things has been hastened in our case by the constant stream of European paupers upon the shores of this land of promise. Alas! How often does it prove to the deluded emigrant a land of broken promise and blasted hope. If we had none but our own poor to take care of, we should get along tolerably well; we could find employment for them, and individual charity, aiding the public institutions, might save us from the sights of woe with which we are assailed in the streets.... Nineteen out of twenty of these mendicants are... indigent, helpless, having expended the last shilling in paying their passage-money, deceived by the misrepresentations of unscrupulous agents, and left to starve amongst strangers, who, finding it impossible to extend relief to all, are deterred from assisting any.

PHILIP HONE

1917

Early up, and I took a short walk, but find I am so grown away from the habit of violent exercise that I grudge the time spent in any, exercise, which is silly; for in the summer I do grudge the time wasted in doing aught else but outdoor strenuosities.

FRANKLIN P. ADAMS

1997

Looking out my bedroom on this bright January morning, I see that the parking garage across the street has again deposited several cars on the sidewalk, using it as a kind of annex. Folks heading for work have to squeeze past the Toyotas. This is illegal, of course, as are many routine transactions of New York life, from running red lights to selling insurance to transit cops. B. told me that all the deliverymen from all of the Chinese restaurants bring you your food on stolen bicycles. Thieves sell bikes to restaurants at a price so low, their felonious origins are undeniable.

When I lived on 13th Street, there was a numbers parlor around the corner, halfheartedly disguised as a stationery store, with two packs of yellowing, loose-leaf paper and a dozen Flair pens fanned out in the window. On summer days, the door was propped open; any passerby could see the counter shielded with heavy glass and the sign above it listing that day's winning numbers. I knew about it....Surely the police knew about it, but of course did nothing. Corruption or incompetence? Indifference, perhaps....

New York is not Mexico City, but twice a year, we parents at the 96th Street school-bus stop collect money for Mr. R., the driver. "You have to give, or he'll drop your kid in Times Square alone," someone jokes. And it is a joke. New York is not Lagos, Mr. R. is a responsible man, and the money is a gift.

RANDY COHEN

JANUARY 30

1790

Exercised with Mrs. Washington and the children in the coach, in the forenoon. Walked round the Battery in the Afternoon.

PRESIDENT GEORGE WASHINGTON

1908

Out to the bank and bought $49 worth of stamps, took them up to Macbeth's for mailing catalogues. Here is a crying shame. The beastly daubs of Paul Dougherty, N.A. (with whom I have no acquaintance personally) are selling—five of them have been bought. If posterity ever reads these lines, I know that the heirs of these buyers, when they look at the shrunken values on these pot boilers, will know that I knew them for what they are—vile—low—and, come to think of it, not worth this much comment.

John Sloan

1925

AT THE CHINESE RESTAURANT: A fly—although it was not summer, but January, but winter, but snow outside halfslush [*sic*] and the air dull wet cold—a fly, pointed microscopic, absurd, intelligent jigged about a small area which was visibly no different [*sic*] from the rest of the tablecloth and which was in fact created merely by his motion...

I...picked my table well...I did well to sit at this second table-for-two and not at the one in front of it, when (on the further side of the chin-high partition at the table-for-two which corresponded to my own) the girl with the small head, the oval face, the icy-black bobbed hair, the minute hat, began discussing their lives with her man who wore tortoiseshell spectacles and tried to see, if not through, at least a slight way into, her green, smooth hardest eyes as her small perfectly white teeth with their pale smile lied to him.

Wonderful [last in red]—again I'm intouch [*sic*] with life—the prostitute is fooling her man, as Elaine fooled me. I'm participating in living, again.

I must call up Alice Hall & get her to sleep with me.

E. E. Cummings

JANUARY 31

1847

Going to be sick, I think, so specially wretched have I been today with every sort of horrid dyspeptic sensation. My little black friend Teufelchen [Little Devil] ... —I mean my black squirrel, is an invalid too, and has been sitting grunting on my lap all afternoon in great affliction....

Robert Weeks's big party Friday; went thither through the great waters of a most rainy evening. Pleasant affair, rather. Wonder why people always look so solemn when they dance a quadrille. Perhaps it originated in the Homeric funeral games.

GEORGE TEMPLETON STRONG

FEBRUARY 1

1857

Epidemic of crime this winter. "Garroting" stories abound, some true, some no doubt fictitious, devised to explain the absence of one's watch and pocketbook after a secret visit to some disreputable place, or put a good face on some tipsy street fracas. . . . Most of my friends are investing in revolvers and carry them about at night. . . . I think I should make the like provision; though it's a very bad practice carrying concealed weapons.

GEORGE TEMPLETON STRONG

1908

The pictures left for Macbeth's in the morning. Now the time that we have all waited and worked for months past is here. . . . After the hanging, Lawson, Luks, Henri, Glack, Shinn and I went to the "Tavern," a café which is fitted up in an old fashioned way, and there held forth over ale till we saw by such hints as turning out lights, putting out chairs, barkeep putting on street togs, etc., that our departure would be appreciated. Shinn had left before—and we were then, by Glackens, treated to oysters across 42nd St., after which we sought a dimly lit side entrance on 41st, and having by now dwindled to three—Luks, Glack and myself—had a "night cap" and parted. This last saloon was interesting and was evidently an undercover sort of place. Saw two officers of the Police, their blue coats and brass buttons and red typical faces, strong against a gray wall paper with color prints of fish, as they sat behind a screen.

JOHN SLOAN

1969

I am still after Jesus to comb his hair. He is Puerto Rican and therefore different from the other children in color and hair texture. He says he is white and all he has to do is put water on his hair.

I have explained to him that he is Puerto Rican and that some Puerto Ricans are white and others are black, but Puerto Ricans on the whole are a mixture of black and white, and at any rate, everyone should comb his hair, no matter what color he is.

JIM HASKINS

FEBRUARY 2

1798

This Day Capt. Dennis cut his Throat in his own House in Partition Street. Cause not known; but I heard he lost his Place as Commander of the Custom House Cutter.

HUGH GAINE

1867

The only trouble about this town is, that it is too large. You cannot accomplish anything in the way of business, you cannot even pay a friendly call, without devoting a whole day to it—that is, what people call a whole day who do not get up early. Many business men only give audience from eleven to one; therefore, if you miss those hours your affair must go over till next day. Now if you make time at one place, even though you stay only ten or fifteen minutes, you can hardly get to your next point, because so many things and people will attract your attention and your conversation and curiosity, that the other three-quarters of that hour will be frittered away. You have but one hour left, and my experience is that a man cannot go *any*where in New York in an hour. The distances are too

great—you must have another day to it. If you have got six things
to do, you have got to take six days to do them in.

Mark Twain

1921

What a funny life! I do not know myself, nor what I have become,
and yet when I look in the glass I am the same. . . .

From morning till night newspaper reporters ask me questions,
I am told I have to submit—if I were impatient or cross they would
write something nasty. So I am amiable. I go on talking the same
stuff about Lenin and Trotsky! How they would laugh if they could
hear me!

I go out to lunch with a reporter in a taxi—and what luncheons:
hen luncheons in Fifth Avenue! Lovely women with bare white
chests, pearls, and tulle sleeves.

Today I lunched with Rose Post, who is a great kind dear. I had a
very pleasant woman on my right, but on my left was a Mrs. Butler,
whose husband is president of Columbia University. She wouldn't
speak to me—she couldn't bear even to look at me. I expect she
thought I was a Bolshevik. I went from there to see Mrs. Otto Kahn.
She received me among Botticellis and tapestries. It was a beautiful room, and one had a feeling of repose. Money can buy beautiful things, but it cannot buy atmosphere, and that was of her own
creating.

She dropped me at the *Vanity Fair* office, and I went up to the fif-
teenth floor and saw Mr. Crowninshield and Mr. Condé Nast, editors respectively of *Vanity Fair* and *Vogue*. I knew them in London. . . .

"Crownie" was an angel; he and Mr. Nast decided to give a dinner for me. A "fun" dinner, all of the people who "do" things, what
he called "tight-rope dancers" and "high divers"—not social swells!
He offers me a peace[ful] room to write in—a lawyer to protect
me, and advances of money! Truly I have good friends!

Clare Sheridan

1955

I've spent the last few hours rereading the Journal and find it less exciting than I thought, and quite unpublishable in its present form.... But there is a lot in it. I have to develop it.

I can probably generalize on the effects of Lipton's [marijuana] and Seconal. Lipton's releases vast amounts of exciting material and trivial material with very little selection. It enables me to work at a tremendous rate, but everything is equally exciting to me. Which is mystically, philosophically valid, but is almost impossible for a novelist to deal with—at least in my present stage. That is, I could not write novels on it, although it might be good to turn to it when I got writing blocks. The Seconal is what is bad for it is beginning to give me bad letdowns and deep depressions. Except I know how to handle those too, now. If I can't sleep. I must just sit up and read instead of trying to fight myself into sleep. Enough for today. I think I'll lay off the Journal for a few days.

NORMAN MAILER

FEBRUARY 3

1844

I have done nothing this week scarcely but go to parties.... During my absence from the city Mrs. Osgood the poetess has come to tabernacle with us. I think I shall like her. She tells me that she has been invited to contribute to the *Home Critic* a new paper (weekly) on the plan of the London Athenaeum as far as possible to be edited by H. Farrar assisted by Duykinck ... & others of that ilk. Their purpose they profess to be the rendering of Justice to American writers, which means the securing of a reputable organ to tickle themselves or some of them. Duykinck is a modest man [and] Mrs. Osgood a modest woman.

JOHN BIGELOW

1908

Exhibition at Macbeth's opens. Davies called, said that he thought the show looked quite well but a little crowded in some places—which is true enough, but don't seem to me to matter in a group arrangement—hang "taste" anyway! Mrs. Kirby, Kirby and Dolly went to see the exhibition in the afternoon. I felt that my clothes were not of the prosperous aspect necessary in this city. The appearance of poverty is the worst possible advertising these days.

JOHN SLOAN

1947

I'm happy to be escorted this evening to the Savoy by Richard Wright; I'll feel less suspect. He comes to fetch me at the hotel, and I observe that in the lobby he attracts untoward notice. If he asked for a room here, he would surely be refused. We go eat in a Chinese restaurant because it's very likely that they wouldn't serve us in the uptown restaurants. Wright lives in Greenwich Village with his wife, a white woman from Brooklyn, and she tells me that every day when she walks in the neighborhood with her little girl, she hears the most unpleasant comments....

The Savoy is a large American dance hall, nothing exotic. On one side, the dance floor is bounded by a wall where the orchestra sits. On the other side, there are boxes with chairs and tables, and beyond, there is a kind of great hall that looks like a hotel lobby. The floor is covered with a carpet, and people are sitting in the armchairs looking bored. These are customers who don't drink anything; they pay only the entrance price, and during the dances the woman [*sic*] do needlepoint, as at a town ball. We sit in one of the boxes, and Wright puts a bottle of whiskey on the table. They don't sell whiskey here, but the customer has the right to bring his own. We order sodas; we drink and look around. Not a white face.... Most of the women are young. They wear simple skirts and little pullovers, but their high-heeled shoes are sometimes bizarre.

The light or dark tint of their skin dresses their bare legs better than nylon stockings. Many are pretty, but they all seem especially lively. What a difference from the strained coldness of white American women. And when you see these men dance, their sensual life unrestrained by an armor of Puritan virtue, you understand how much sexual jealousy can enter into the white Americans' hatred of these quick bodies.... Many of these young women belong to respectable families and probably go to church on Sunday mornings. They have worked all day and have come to enjoy themselves quietly with their boyfriends. They dance simply and quite naturally; you need perfect inner relaxation to allow yourself to be so utterly possessed by the music and rhythms of jazz. It's this relaxation that also allows dreaming, feeling, loafing, and laughing of the sort that's unfamiliar to most white Americans.

I listen to the jazz, watch the dancing, and drink whiskey; I am beginning to like whiskey. I feel good. The Savoy is the biggest dance hall in New York, the biggest in the world: something in this statement is soothing to the spirit. And this jazz is perhaps the best in the world; in any case, there's no other place where it can more fully express its truth.

SIMONE DE BEAUVOIR

FEBRUARY 4

1780

This week sleighs have crossed over the ice from Staten Island to this city, which has hardly been known before.

BROTHER EWALD GUSTAV SCHAUKIRK

1861

[The] Rev. [Dr.] Seabury has put forth a book maintaining the right to hold slaves on religious and ethical principles. It looks sound and sensible. The complaint of Christendom and of all humanity against the South is not founded on their exercise of that right (though most people take for granted that it is a wrong), but on the diabolical peculiarities of the Southern system—separation of families and the like—which I suppose to be mere accidents of slaveholding, not of its essence.

GEORGE TEMPLETON STRONG

1917

Meyer called up in morning to tell me he was waiting on B'way for me. I hurried down expecting to see a Ford, when lo and behold it was a marvelous Buick—latest model. He took me to dressmakers along Riverside Drive, introduced me to his sister, dad, and family and then home. I was the first one to be invited out in his car. Honored. Ahem!

SARA HOEXTER BLUMENTHAL

1947

During the night, New York was covered with snow. Central Park is transformed. The children have cast aside their roller skates and taken up skis; they rush boldly down the tiny hillocks. Men remain bareheaded, but many of the young people stick fur puffs over their ears fixed to a half-circle of plastic that sits on their hair like a ribbon—it's hideous.

At five o'clock I have an appointment at the Plaza bar with the editor of a big magazine to discuss a projected article. The discussion is difficult because he's more than half-drunk. I take him to a party J.C. [Jean Condit] is giving for me; she's a beautiful young American woman who works for *Vogue* and is friends with a Frenchwoman I know. For my benefit, she's brought together the editors of different magazines and other people likely to help me make my way in New York. Such kindness confounds me; I'm nothing to her, she expects nothing from me. I'm even ashamed—we're not so outgoing in France.

It's a very American party—lots of people, lots of alcohol....
Everyone continues to stand, except my hostess, who is soon reclin-
ing on a sofa. The conversational tone rises. I argue bitterly with
a magazine publisher, whose air of superiority irritates me. Then
I find myself violently at odds with an insistently insolent young
man: Have you read the Hindu philosophers? Do you know Con-
fucius? And Jakob Böhme? And if not, how can you dare to have
philosophical opinions? Taking a good look at him, I see he's not so
young: he's thirty, perhaps thirty-five. I try to explain to him that
he's confusing thought and erudition, but he takes advantage of his
knowledge of English to talk faster than I can. He points out one of
his friends, saying, "There's the most intelligent man in America."
I find myself surrounded by the staff of a journal [*Partisan Review*]
that calls itself "left-wing" and "avant-garde," and their aggressive-
ness surprises me. In even sharper tones, they renew the reproaches
I heard from [one] who was part of the same group for a long time,
then separated from them. To like the American literature we like
in France is an insult to the country's intelligentsia. They, too, make
an exception for Faulkner, but they tear into Hemingway, Dos Passos, Caldwell, and especially Steinbeck, who seems to be their bête
noir. I'm a little bewildered; I'm not familiar with their journal,
I don't know what they're implying or what their values are, and
through the virulence of their attacks, I can't make out what points
we have in common or what underlying disagreements separate us.
The martinis, the whiskeys, and my difficulties in understanding
English increase my confusion. Around nine o'clock in the evening I find myself in the company of "the most intelligent man in
America" in a restaurant below street level, where they serve us
magnificent steaks. But the feverish discussion dampens my appetite. Now they're after me about politics in relation to an article by
Merleau-Ponty, "The Yogi and the Proletarian." They hate Stalin-
ism with a passion that makes me realize they are old Stalinists. I
think alcohol is making us choose our words unwisely; it seems

my statements are worthy of a Soviet agent. But these free spirits might easily be taken for American imperialists. The tall, insolent young man declares in the middle of the conversation, "Anyway, it isn't the Russians who send you food; America created UNRRA [the United Nations Relief and Rehabilitation Administration]." If even so-called left-wing intellectuals are so proud of the boxes of condensed milk their government dispenses to us, how can we be surprised by the arrogance of the capitalist press, by that tone of condescension that I've observed almost everywhere when France is mentioned and that is beginning to exasperate me? I'm indignant, and we argue in earnest. The very excess of our anger gradually calms us. It's hot. G.F. is streaming with sweat. We're embarrassed at not really knowing, any of us, whom we're dealing with. Doubtless a more thoughtful exchange of ideas would have been more profitable: they spoke with such fire that they weren't listening to me, and I didn't understand them very well. We leave the restaurant. It's snowing outside, and under the pure sky the cold is penetrating.... My mouth is dry, and I still feel a few pangs of anger in my chest. It's past midnight; we'll meet another day.

SIMONE DE BEAUVOIR

FEBRUARY 5

1846

Grace Church. The new church at the head of Broadway is nearly finished and ready for consecration. The pews were sold last week and brought extravagant prices, some $1200 to $1400, with a pew rent on the estimated value of eight per cent; so that the word of god, as it came down to us from fishermen and mechanics, will cost the Quality who worship in this splendid temple about three dollars every Sunday. This may have a good effect; for many of them, tho[ugh] rich, know how to calculate, and if they do not go regularly to church they will not get the worth of their money.

This is to be the fashionable church and already its aisles are filled especially on Sundays after the morning services in other churches with gay parties of ladies in feathers and *mousseline-de-laine* dresses, and dandies with mustaches and high-heeled boots; and the lofty arches resound with astute criticisms upon Gothic architecture from fair ladies who have had the advantage of foreign travel, and scientific remarks upon acoustics from elderly millionaires who do not hear quite so well as formerly. The church is built of white marble, in the extreme of the florid Gothic, in the form of a cross. The exterior is beautiful, and its position at the commencement of the bend of Broadway, which brings it directly in view from below, striking and prominent.

PHILIP HONE

2003

A Peregrine falcon just flew past my window.

JOHNNY/QUIPU BLOGSPOT

FEBRUARY 6

1790

Walked to my newly engaged lodgings to fix on a spot for a New Stable which I was about to build. Agreed ... to erect one 30 feet sqr., 16 feet pitch, to contain 12 single stalls; a hay loft, Racks, mangers &ca.—Planked floor and underpinned with Stone with Windows between each stall for 65 £.

PRESIDENT GEORGE WASHINGTON

1923

Emotional specialists—Edna St. Vincent Millay—She may be sincere—I'm such a [case] where if I had a big loss ... I'd feel it a long time, while they seem to have a great sorrow in the morning & a great joy at noon.

Marianne Moore

1950

Meeting with [G.] Wilson at Steinway Hall. Slightly disappointed with drawings [for] "Moby Dick," but agreed to read libretto.

Kurt Weill

February 7

1840

Glorious warm weather, but we're all under a positive *ne exeat* [a public order to remain where one is], though decidedly better than yesterday....

Dr. N[eilson] says there was arsenic in the cheese. I don't believe it. I don't believe the primitive Pillsburies on Cow Island know what arsenic means, nor is it likely they have ever have [*sic*] occasion to use any mineral poison whatever. There can't be any rats on the island. If this has been caused by anything other than some unhealthiness in the pork, or some vegetable put in by mistake, I'm inclined to think a badly tinned copper boiler has been the discomforter of our stomachs. I couldn't get my old chemical gimcracks together to test the stuff in a scientific way, so I applied a spirit blowpipe, without producing any of the fumes of arsenic.... I'm anxious to hear from Boston whether they've been poisoned or not, and if not, what poor E[loise] will say when she hears of this unlucky result from her present.

George Templeton Strong

1906

In the afternoon I went a part of the rounds of the publishers. No work for me.

JOHN SLOAN

1950

Read libretto [of] "Moby Dick"—very bad.

KURT WEILL

1955

After lunch, and how I hated giving up time for lunch. So many ideas I had while I bolted my food, and so many of them must be lost.

NORMAN MAILER

FEBRUARY 8

1921

Paul Manship [American sculptor] called for me and took me to his studio which is near Washington Square in a side alley that used to contain stables. The moment one turned into that side alley one had left New York! He has a beautiful studio and house, and his work is modern and archaic and has a great sense of design. It interested me to discover how he gets his surfaces and the feeling of the thing being carved; this is done by working on the plaster. He is going to have an exhibition in London at the Leicester Galleries in the spring. I shall be very interested to know the result. I am sorry for the artist who goes from here to London, instead of from London here.

CLARE SHERIDAN

1932

Lunch with John Farrar who disturbed me by saying no hurry on novel—not coming out till August. Since I was getting along fine by being in a hurry, what to do?

DAWN POWELL

FEBRUARY 9

1910

A note of appreciation for my work as appearing in the Sunday Call from Hayden Carruth of the Editors of *Woman's Home Companion*. One of those loving streaks of lightning out of a clear sky, which are very encouraging or should be.

Started on a puzzle drawing. Went up to [Albert] Ullmans' for dinner, spaghetti. After dinner we played cards till after 12, then in some way we got into a talk of death and the sensations of entering the shadow. From this we naturally turned to the universe, The Beginning! If ever such a thing could be conceived, or an End! I feel that it is against our instinctive understanding of the rhythm of the universe to say that we, who have no consciousness of a former state or states of the ego—will go on with this same ego to a future state. Anything is possible in the way of passing of the Spirit or the Life Force but hardly the "I." In other words why should I as I know *myself* ignorant of a past existence expect to be *conscious* of a future one?

JOHN SLOAN

1921

Mr. Liveright, my publisher, fetched me and took me to the Ritz where we dined with Mr. Pulitzer, Mr. and Mrs. Swope and Mr. B. M. Baruch. Mr. Pulitzer looks much too young to be the owner of *The World* and has the face of a well-bred Englishman. Mr. Baruch (whose name I mistook for Brooke) has white hair, fine features and stands 6 ft. 4. I gathered from the general conversation that I was talking to someone whom I should have heard of, and as I could think of no distinguished Brooke but Rupert Brooke the poet, I asked if he was related. And then Mr. Baruch rather reprovingly spelt his name for me. Instantly by a faint glimmer of memory "Wall Street" came to my mind and I seemed to have heard in London that he was a friend of Winston [Churchill]. He was interesting and unprejudiced. Most of these brilliant men are unprejudiced about Russia when one talks to them individually. It is the same in England.

CLARE SHERIDAN

FEBRUARY 10

1779

A servant of Mrs. Morris's called for an Order to prevent Waste of Wood on her part of Morrisania. I backed her request.... He [Royal Governor William Tryon] slighted it with, "The King's Troops must be supplied and I gave the General's Orders to cut on all Morrisania."... How wanton is military power! On my asking "Is it right to destroy the Property of the King's friends," he answered, "They will be paid for it." "Will they?" said I. "May be so," says he, "after the war is over," with a Smile. Tryon sacrifices his Civil Character to gain a reputation in the Army, and [British Major General John] Vaughan, with whom he is intimate, does him Harm. This Man is hot, rash, vain, and ignorant.

WILLIAM SMITH

FEBRUARY 11

1776

This was a gloomy day. The carts went all the day with the goods of the people that are moving; moreover, in the forenoon the Soldiers began to take away all the guns from the Battery and the Fort, and continued till late. This caused an hourly expectation, especially in the afternoon, that the men of war would fire; however they did not.

BROTHER EWALD GUSTAV SCHAUKIRK

1844

A week has elapsed since I wrote up my Journal which reminds me that I have not been much of a Student for if [I] had been I should have not neglected this. I have spent too much time at chess for which I have conceived a perfect passion.... I have attended a meeting or rather I was invited by Duyckinck to meet some of the contributors of the *Home Critic* last evg. at his house.... They have nearly a hundred subscribers but I fear they will not make it go.

JOHN BIGELOW

2005

Nothing announced Fashion Week in New York more meretriciously than a surfeit of model sightings around town, especially in the subway.

I had one yesterday, most likely a second or third tier girl in a non primetime showcase of an up and coming Parson Design grad or she would have been chauffeured already to the big tent at Bryant Park. This as I jostled for a seat in the D train on my way to my tax preparer.

Of course, her build was improbably tenuous and her legs just sprouted from under her boobs and jetted all the way down to this mortal earth.

Although she wasn't made up yet, her tresses still wrapped up shabbily in a silk logo scarf, the rest of the jaded morning commuters in my car couldn't keep their eyes off of her, to say the least. Models are New Yorkers' Hollywood stars.

Maybe this is what they teach ravishing girls in the pulchritude academy. Whenever you expect to be stuck in people places, be sure to lug along a weighty book. A Shakespeare is best.

As the rest of us mortals were ogling her, our divinity was deep into a Folger paperback edition of Hamlet. Something indeed smells rotten in the state of New York when the most beautiful creatures in the world assembled for this week-long Saturnalia are also the most literary.

My model, as expected, got off at 42nd [Street] Bryant Park, as she gathered all her other stuff, an unopened one liter Pellegrino bottle, a crisp Burberry plaid trench, her head scarf unlaced and her luminous face revealed to us, the Puerto Rican guy in front of her wearing a tatty Sean John hoodie could not help himself but exclaimed "dang…"

It was only when the train pushed on that [we] realized our model [had] left her Hamlet behind. No one dared to scoop the book out of the still glowing chair.

STAYING PINOY IN NEW YORK

FEBRUARY 12

1790

Sat from 9 Oclock until 11 for Mr. John Trumbull for the purpose of Drawing my picture.

A good deal of Company (Gentlemen & Ladies) to visit Mrs. Washington this afternoon.

PRESIDENT GEORGE WASHINGTON

1878

He [Theodore Roosevelt, Sr.] has just been buried. I shall never forget these terrible three days: the hideous suspense of the ride on [home]; the dull, inert sorrow, during which I felt as if I had been stunned, or as if part of my life had been taken away; and the two moments of sharp, bitter agony, when I kissed the dear dead face and realized that he would never again on this earth speak to me or greet me with his loving smile, and then when I heard the sound of the first clod dropping on the coffin holding the one I loved dearest on earth. He looked so calm and sweet. I feel that if it were not for the certainty that, as he himself has so often said, "he is not dead but gone before," I should almost perish.

THEODORE ROOSEVELT

1934

I want this new novel to be delicate and cutting—nothing will cut New York but a diamond. Probably should do a night job on it as on *Tenth Moon*—it should not be a daylight book but intense and brilliant and fine like night thoughts. No wandering but each detail should point to the one far-off star and be keyed by Lila's own waiting excitement and preserved youth. It should be crystal in quality, sharp as the skyline and relentlessly true. No external details beyond the swift eager glance over the shoulder.

DAWN POWELL

FEBRUARY 13

1790

Walked in the forenoon to the House to which I am about to remove. Gave directions for the arrangement of the furniture &ca. and had some of it put up.

PRESIDENT GEORGE WASHINGTON

1921

I lunched with "The Kingfisher" as we call Mrs. Cornelius Vanderbilt in London! I was rather disappointed with her Fifth Avenue
Palazzo, it does not compare with the Otto Kahns' and has not the
atmosphere. There was a beautiful Turner in one of the drawing rooms and a gallery full of Corots and Millets, but they were
not very interesting or decorative, or else there were too many of
them....

After lunch when the women left the dining room someone haz-
arded a remark to the effect that the big rooms were pleasant with
nobody in them. Our hostess said that was not an idea with which
she was in sympathy, that she thought a big house should be full of
people and as many enjoy it as possible, "Whatever I have I want
to share," she said and then turning to me, "Please tell that to the
Bolsheviks—"... Then, suddenly, conversation drifted onto me and
my plans.

I was asked if when I returned I was going to live in Ireland,
hadn't my father got a place there? I answered that I lived where
there was work, and, therefore, I might remain where I was, or go to
Russia. Mrs. Vanderbilt looked rather surprised, and asked whether
Russia paid better than any other country. That I did not know, but
certain it is that any country pays more than England!

Altogether, it was rather unpleasant, and I left as soon as I could,
and wondering, as I walked home, why she had asked me to her house.

CLARE SHERIDAN

FEBRUARY 14

1884

The light has gone out of my life.

THEODORE ROOSEVELT

[Upon the occasion of the deaths, the same day, of his wife and mother.]

1952

Valentine's Day....

   A formal party at Maria Piscator's. It is beautiful, of course, to drink champagne in the company of all this elegance, but I keep thinking of the equally fraudulent but comfortable degradation of the *maudit* San Remo [hang-out for actors and poets] and the spirit of Valentine, patron of lovers. I leave in depression.

JUDITH MALINA

FEBRUARY 15

1842

The agony is over; the Boz ball, the greatest affair in modern times, the tallest compliment ever paid a little man, the fullest libation ever poured upon the altar of the muses, came off last evening in fine style. Everything answered the public expectation.... [A] curtain was raised in the intervals between the cotillions and waltzes to disclose a stage on which were exhibited a series of *tableaux vivants*, forming groups of the characters in the most striking incidents of "Pickwick," "Nicholas Nickleby," "Oliver Twist," "The Old Curiosity Shop," Barnaby Rudge, etc.... On the arrival of the "observed of all observers," a lane was opened through the crowd, through which he and his lady were marched to the upper end, where ... I, as chairman of the committee, received him, made a short speech, after which they joined in the dancing.... The author of the "Pickwick Papers" is a small, bright-eyed, intelligent-looking fellow, thirty years of age, somewhat of a dandy in his dress, with "rings and things and fine array," brisk in his manner and of a lively conversation. If he does not get his little head turned by all this, I shall wonder at it. Mrs. Dickens is a little, fat, English-looking woman, of an agreeable countenance, and, I should think, a "nice person."

PHILIP HONE

1924

I have been so happy today! For a story came to me beautifully complete. I wrote the end of it early in the day, and shall do the first half...tomorrow. It's the only way one should write stories. I never can rest until I get the climax off my mind.... I am so happy in my little room, but sometimes I wonder if I am losing [my] Mother. I suppose no one could ever understand how I love her....José is a fine sweet boy, a great singer, an ardent lover—but will he make Mother happy[?] I call him a boy for he seems one and looks one, but they say he is thirty-five years old. Mother seems about thirty, so *that's alright.* So long as she's happy, I am content, but I know no passion can fill her love of me, her need of me. I must cling to her silently until she finds she needs me again. God bless my mother.

WINIFRED WILLIS

1954

Ruth Draper [the monologuist] is the most fascinating phenomenon in the theater this season. I can find no explanation for her prodigious impact. She is a lady, essentially a lady of old New York family (the Danas on one side) and so Jewish [-seeming] (the Drapers on the other—were they Jewish?). She has a rigid middle, as such gently-reared ladies always had. She is almost nondescript in coloring, pale, aristocratic, would be unnoticed in a crowd, and yet she peoples her stage with myriads. She is by turns, almost in the same moment, a girl of sixteen, an old woman of ninety, and no makeup, no excessive costuming, the basic straight up and down long brown dress, shawls, a jacket, some period hats, accessories, a twentyish evening coat, and her indefinable genius. It is impossible to pin down the genius of her magic. Only the greatest have this: Toscanini, Raquel Meller, [the dancer] Argentina, Margot Fonteyn, Yvette Guilbert—but not an actor in my experience—yes, Duse. These transcend the art in which they are supreme, transporting all beholders beyond this art and its mechanics, transporting them out of themselves. Stark [Young] and Wales [Bowman, architect] say that Miss Draper does not read, wears good quiet clothes, lives quite elegantly. But when she went on a journey to Istanbul (I think they said Istanbul), a friend reported that always Miss Draper seemed to be the well-known Miss Draper's maid. She met [poet] Lauro de Bosis and fell instantly in love with him. He seems to have been typical *jeunesse dorée*. Later, he flew his plane out over the ocean and fell to his death, having opposed Mussolini. Miss D was inconsolable. Meeting Stark, she reproached him with not having written her a condolence. But all of her friends believe her to be a virgin. And they said of her long ago: Ruth is a genius, but watch her love scenes.

LEO LERMAN

1961

Dinner with Bunny [Edmund Wilson] at the Princeton Club and then to Edward Albee's "American Dream"—extraordinarily fresh. Bunny and I, determined to be less than our sleepy age, afterward knew we wanted a drink but were hardly able to sit up and stay awake. Our feet with one accord strolled into Liquor Store where we each selected pints of rye, strolled out into cab and tore to our separate beds where we could drop our clothes, put nipple on bottle and slurp the whole thing down with ease.

DAWN POWELL

FEBRUARY 16

(16TH AND 17TH)
1884

Alice Hathaway Lee. Born at Chestnut Hill [Massachusetts], July 29, 1861. I saw her first on October [18th,] 1878; I wooed her for over a year before I won her; we were betrothed on January 25th 1880, and it was announced on Feb. 16th; on Oct. 27th of the same year we were married; we spent three years of happiness greater and more unalloyed than I have ever known fall to the lot of others; on February 12th 1884 her baby was born and on Feb. 14th she died in my arms, as my mother had died in the same house, on the same day, but a few hours previously. On Feb. 16th they were buried together in Greenwood....

On Feb. 17 I christened the baby Alice Lee Roosevelt.

For joy or for sorrow, my life has now been lived out.

THEODORE ROOSEVELT

1911

Such long stops between illustrations that I get out of the swing of the thing. It makes me feel poorly in my mind—and that worries Dolly. She said tonight that she wished I was a bricklayer. I said so too. Then I could etch, paint and draw when I was out of bricklaying work (and not looking for a Job)!!

JOHN SLOAN

1959

Dinner at Sardi's East with Gerald and Sara [Murphy] and Mr. Cornish, their estate manager. He is a smooth, rather secret-looking young man;... single; lives at the Harvard Club, reflective and genuinely literary in angles.

About the Harvard Club—the men who live there. The younger ones drinking moodily at bar, marriages on the rocks. Somewhat older, the more serious drinkers, glad of a refuge from overwhelming family, glance occasionally at the old ones, the admitted defeated ones—deserted, deserting and defeating, frankly and wholeheartedly and systematically Scotching themselves into the grave.

DAWN POWELL

FEBRUARY 17

1777

Sr. Wm. Howe dined with us to-day, and many officers of the Army & Navy.

Important Intelligence was brought by Lieut. Jones of the Navy from Philadelphia, where he was lately a prisoner, that a Part of Maryland has taken up Arms, declared for the Crown, and disarmed many of the Rebels in that Province.... The *Randolph* Frigate, built by the [Continental] Congress, together with several other Ships, laden chiefly with Tobacco, & bound to France, had got out of the Delaware [River]; and that a Vessel, with a large Cargo of Salt, had got in. He also says, that the Congress have [*sic*] remitted all the Produce they could collect to France during the Summer, and ... that they are to purchase 11 new Frigates for the Use of the Continent.

AMBROSE SERLE

1777

This Evening another Alarm of Fire. This was no more than a Chimney.

HUGH GAINE

FEBRUARY 18

1853

I maintain the cause of the French Empress sturdily in these times, with no very tangible reason except that she has auburn hair and Eugenie is a very pretty name. I rather like the notion of Napoleon 3rd, who, 10 or 12 years ago, was a disreputable, dirty, drinking, penniless, foreign prince prowling about these streets and ordered out of the bar room of the old Washington Hall ... because he was too great a loafer to be allowed to hang about even those disreputable premises, who had so long been wriggling in the gutters and cloaca of the social system, being now on terms of equality with kings and czars, and making something his friends call a *mésalliance* with the beautiful representative of one of the first among the haughtiest nobility in Europe. There's a romance about it that's altogether refreshing.

GEORGE TEMPLETON STRONG

1867

The police of Broadway seem to have been selected with special reference to size. They are nearly all large, fine-looking men, and their blue uniforms, well studded with brass buttons, their jack boots and their batons worn like a dagger, give them an imposing military aspect. They are gentlemanly in appearance and conduct. . . . I hear them praised on every hand for their efficiency, integrity and watchful attention to business. It seems like an extravagant compliment to pay a policeman, don't it? I am charmed with the novelty of it.

MARK TWAIN

FEBRUARY 19

1864

Heard that war has brokeen out in Europe on the Holsteine question. The Prushen and Austrien nine thousand strong, defeated by Danes two thousand strong.

WILLIAM B. GOULD

1927

Edna [St. Vincent Millay] in New York. Our formal dinner across a too-wide table drinking Boissevain's whiskey and sauterne [*sic*]. He tactfully withdrew with a book called *Wine, Women and War* and came back at 10:15 sharp. She inquired about *New Republic*— I resented this piece of politeness—I saw her wince and the collapse for a moment of her manner: nervous, trembling, worried and dismayed—the new slang, too (which she didn't know)—like her never having heard of Hart Crane, "The Master of Us All."— "I'm not a pathetic figure—I'm not!" "Whoever said you were?"— I had previously talked her into an enthusiasm for the country, then talked her out of it—I now talked her into it again. . . .

She was all burning and lit up when I came in, quite different from her paleness and brittleness when I had seen her in bed the winter before, and she put her arms around me and kissed me, leaving Boissevain behind in the bedroom, and it was I who was too stiff and unresponsive.

EDMUND WILSON

February 20

1908

Mrs. Luks called me on the phone and told me that George was started on a tear again since yesterday.... A pathetic request from her to tell Macbeth not to pay G.B.L. the money for the picture sold in the exhibition, but to send the check to the house by mail. I did so and Macbeth says that he will. All the sales (7) in the exhibition were to three buyers. Mrs. Harry Payne Whitney, the rich sculptress—at least she has a fine studio for the purpose—bought four. Henri's "Laughing Child" bought by her, he told me.

JOHN SLOAN

1931

To see Eva Le Galienne in "Camille." The audience wept; hundreds of old ladies dabbed handkerchiefs under their glasses, gentlemen coughed and blew their noses, and Joe [Gousha, her husband], always delighted with old traditions, was very happy. I was bored and unconvinced until the last act. The thing is romantic and needs to be overplayed. Modern sophisticated acting and naturalistic reading of lines only emphasizes the highly artificial plot. It is theatrical and should be played theatrically.

DAWN POWELL

2005

As temperature dropped to the teens again, around 30 nudists came for their monthly "clothing optional" buffet dinner in a mid-manhattan bistro just before weekend.
their coats, their shirts, and their undergarments all wound up folded in plastic bags by the bar while they dined nude but, I believe, never under accessorized.

STAYING PINOY IN NEW YORK

FEBRUARY 21

1780

The Ice between the Governor's and Bidelow's Island being cut, several vessels came up that had been below for some time.

HUGH GAINE

1924

(Sensational stuff in papers all over country for past week about "*All God's Chillun*")

EUGENE O'NEILL

[*All God's Chillun Got Wings*, about marriage between a black man and white woman, was widely reviled as miscegenation.]

1960

I spent the morning with Hammarskjöld, who was in marvellous form, giving me vignettes of the political leaders with whom he has been dealing—Salazar, de Gaulle, and Franco. He is certainly the most charming, witty, intelligent companion and a delight to be with, glinting with malice and playing with political schemes, ideas, devices, and stratagems.

CHARLES RITCHIE

FEBRUARY 22

1848

Mother died of Typhus Fever. After two weeks of sickness.

MARIA LOUISA MAVERICK

1955

A black day to begin a blue journal—
"Cat on a Hot Tin Roof" in rehearsal. The leading actress [Barbara

Bel Geddes] inadequate, the play not coming to life enough. I'm tired and a bit drunk and I have a beastly cold—I am already making plans for a far away flight (perhaps as far as Ceylon) the night the play opens in New York!

TENNESSEE WILLIAMS

[*Cat* opened on Broadway, March 24, to critical acclaim.]

1962

Mad Magazine very funny this issue. I decided that the sheer ugliness of this magazine is very wise. A beautiful layout means art director is going to rule copy for beauty, not for wit. Any choice between a comic line and a harmonious picture goes to the picture. The other preservation of comedy is in the low salaries of staff which keeps them bitter and irreverent.

DAWN POWELL

FEBRUARY 23

1848

J. Quincy Adams died. Louis Phillipe Dethroned.

MARIA LOUISA MAVERICK

1867

I only got over a calamitous cold in the head yesterday, and to-day I felt like the breaking up of a hard winter.... my thoughts persistently ran on funerals and suicide. I was in a fit frame of mind for any desperate enterprise, and with a recklessness that even stirred a sort of dull admiration within me, I resolved to go and take a bath.

In five minutes I was breasting the frosty wind and ploughing through the soft new snow, and in fifteen I stumbled upon the place where they keep the monster they call the Russian Bath.... I went up stairs, in the stylish building, and along a carpeted hall, and entered a large and sumptuously furnished and decorated drawing-room....

A very polite man entered my name in a book, taxed me a dollar and a quarter, took charge of my watch and portmonnaie [wallet], gave me a ticket and turned me over to an attendant who conducted me into another part of the house and gave me a neat stateroom wherein to undress. When I came out of there, a fine healthy young descendant of Adam (I think he was a descendant of Adam because he hadn't anything on but a fig-leaf made of a rag), took me into a large apartment that was as hot as sin, and gave me a basin of cold water to wash my face in, and a cup of ice water to drink, and then left me. The place had a latticed floor, and a great plunge bath in the middle of it…. The room began to fill with steam, and I began to sweat. I oozed drops of water from every pore as large as marbles—marbles of the small kind…. The fog grew thicker and thicker, till the gas lights were only faint blurs in the mist. I could not breathe through my nose any more, because the steam was so thick; I had to inhale it through my mouth—and if I hadn't had a mouth like a ship's hatchway, I must have suffocated anyhow….

At this critical period Adam appeared…. Then this inhuman Russian posted me in a corner and discharged a volley of boiling hot and ice cold streams of water against every part of my body…. Then I was told to jump into the plunge bath. I said with some irony, that if I was to go into a furnace next, and afterwards into an ice-chest and then suffer an earthquake and be struck by lightning, I would prefer to tackle those outrages first and get them off my mind, if it would be all the same to the Russian Bath Company. But the foreigner said no, and looked perplexed—delicate sarcasm always perplexes a foreigner.

MARK TWAIN

1878

I came back to Cambridge to day.

I am left about $8,000 a year; comfortable although not rich.

THEODORE ROOSEVELT

1924

Threatening letter from K.K.K.

EUGENE O'NEILL

1952

Eliot's *Sweeney Agonistes* has become increasingly funereal.

I try to make it funny at first. Soon we were trying to laugh inside the gloom. The laughter became weaker and weaker. The actors could not even laugh themselves, much less evoke laughter. Then we gave up and gave in to the gloom....

Saw Dylan Thomas last night at the Remo, boorishly banging at the locked door after closing time. Tomorrow night he reads at our theater.

JUDITH MALINA

1980

Standing in the waterfront bar, having stopped in for a beer in midafternoon, smoky sunlight fading in through the large plate-glass windows and a thumping roll of music beating invisibly in the air.... Over by one window and side wall a group of guys hanging out playing pool, one of them this Chicano boy, muscular and smooth with a thin cotton shirt of olive green black cowboy hat pushed down over his head, taut neck rising out of the cut of his shirt, strong collarbones pressing out, a graceful curve of muscles in his back and a solid chest, his stomach pressed like a slightly curved washboard.... Standing there drinking from my bottle I could see myself taking the nape of his neck in my cold white teeth, a shudder of eroticism as he turned and stared out the window for a moment at the traffic.

DAVID WOJNAROWICZ

FEBRUARY 24

1907

Walked down Fifth Avenue in the snowstorm from 40th Street to South Washington Square. Miss Pope and Miss Niles have a fine dinner.... After eating to excess almost, we sit about and try to amuse each other... all seem dry. Dolly gets in an argument (quite senseless) with Henri. A horrid evening on the whole, and they are all invited to dine with us on Tuesday next.

JOHN SLOAN

1997

There are two marine creatures that I have always identified with. One of them is the juvenile sea squirt. This is a little thing that wanders through the sea looking for a nice rock or hunk of coral to make its home for life. When it finds the right spot and takes root, it no longer has any use for its brain. So it eats it. In much the same way, I have been wandering through Manhattan these 20 years in search of a suitable hunk of coral to attach myself to. A month ago I found it. It is a magazine called the *New Leader*. Finally, I can eat my brain....

I am by way of being work-shy, not exactly a man of ginger and push. Since college I have had only two real jobs, for a total of 37 months' employment. Being unoccupied is fine if you are under the age of 40. Until you pass that milestone, you are "young and brilliant."... At 40 you are suddenly "veteran," a status you retain until 60, whereupon you become "distinguished." In my young-and-brilliant phase I had one good idea.... I figured out why there is Something rather than Nothing.... (I'll save the explanation for later..., as a hedge against uneventfulness.) That gratified whatever intellectual ambition I had.... After all, when Epimenides thought up the Liar's Paradox...he called it a day's work and proceeded to sleep soundly for 57 years, right through his "veteran" and "distinguished" phases. He would have been even better off declining into the editorship of a small political bi-weekly....

By the way, the other marine creature...is the hagfish. It is a jawless thing that, when attacked, secretes enough slime to cover itself and repel the predator.

JIM HOLT

FEBRUARY 25

1921

Dick took me out to lunch. He insisted I should go alone with him. He knew exactly where to take me. We crossed Fifth Avenue and went along West 55th Street and down some steps to a restaurant called the "Mayflower," where he seemed to be known there. Dick ordered the food, talked familiarly to the waitress and produced two dollars to pay the bill. He then took me to a toy shop in Fifth Avenue; he knew the way there, too, and I had to pay five dollars for a submarine——!

I dined with Mr. and Mrs. Barmby, who took me to Carnegie Hall to hear Sir Philip Gibbs' lecture on the Irish question. It was a subject that seemed to demand great courage to tackle, and, of course, it asked for trouble. Outside on the side walk, women went back and forth with placards full of insults about England. It roused all my fighting instincts. I said to one of them aggressively, "I'm proud I'm English!" and she put her tongue out at me. Why was I proud to be English? I never feel very English ordinarily, but these people affected me that way.

CLARE SHERIDAN

FEBRUARY 26

1643

I remained that night at the Governor's, sitting up. I went and sat by the kitchen fire, when about midnight I heard a great shrieking, and I ran to the ramparts of the fort, and looked over to Pavonia. Saw nothing but firing, and hear the shrieks of savages murdered in their sleep. I returned again to the house by the fire. Having sat there awhile, there came an Indian with his squaw, whom I knew well, and who lived about an hour's walk from my house, and told me that they two had fled in a small skiff, which they had taken from the shore at Pavonia; that the Indians from Fort Orange had surprised them; and that they had come to conceal themselves in the fort. I told them that they must go away immediately; that this was no time for them to come to the fort to conceal themselves; that they who had killed their people at Pavonia were not Indians, but the Swannekens [Dutch].... They then asked me how they should get out of the fort. I took them to the door, and there was no sentry there and so they betook themselves to the woods. When it was day the soldiers returned to the fort, having massacred or murdered eighty Indians, and considering they had done a deed of Roman valor, in murdering so many in their sleep; where infants were torn from their mother's breasts, and hacked to pieces in the presence of the parents, and the pieces thrown into the fire and in the water, and other sucklings, being bound to small boards, were cut, stuck, and pierced, and miserably massacred in a manner to move a heart of stone.

DAVID PIETERSZ. DE VRIES

1985

I don't understand why Jackie O. thinks she's so grand that she doesn't owe it to the public to have another great marriage to somebody big. You'd think she'd want to scheme and connive to get into history again.

ANDY WARHOL

FEBRUARY 27

1847

News from Mexico—guerrilla parties and yellow fever. Polk said to be going off to the seat of war in person. Nobody believes it. Hope he'll go, and like Don Sebastian of Portugal, never come back again.

GEORGE TEMPLETON STRONG

FEBRUARY 28

1917

Home to dinner, very late,... but I was in no jovial frame of mind, what with depression over the Germans, who, I hear, have plotted to make Mexico and Japan join them against us; and those who still think Germany is friendly toward us I have no patience with.

FRANKLIN P. ADAMS

2009

My sourdough bread mother is well over a year old now, my job has taken its' [*sic*] tole on it. I finally had a chance to make a nice loaf of bread today. It came out pretty good. I don't have a recipe. I do it by feel.

THE DEADICATED GROUP

FEBRUARY 29

1836

I have taken up my pen again after an interval of two months, caused partly by my ardor for laziness and partly by my ardor for science, exemplified in blowing up my hand. *Mem*[*orandum*]. Never to pound chlorate of potass[ium] and sulphur together again without thick gloves and never to pound them at all when I can help it.

GEORGE TEMPLETON STRONG

MARCH 1

1783

The soldiers have been lately employed in filling up and raising the grade in Trinity Church yard, it having grown too shallow for the graves, whence injurious effects were apprehended. Various reports of peace, and now a separate peace between England and America prevailed.

BROTHER EWALD GUSTAV SCHAUKIRK

1822

There are a great many of the African race in the city and they are generally in a most woeful condition. It's slavery no doubt to which this is to be traced but it is not slavery which does it now. They are almost all free. By an act of the legislature the state of New York every male negroe that arrives at the age of twenty-eight and every female at twenty five within its jurisdiction are to be free and none are allowed now to bring slaves in from other states. The consequences are the blacks are let loose without restraint and without information or knowledge to guide themselves so that not one in ten has behaved with propriety but have become drunken lascivious and thievish. I cannot conceive from their lazy lounging conduct how the half of them find sustenance. If one walks through the back streets in which they [gather] he sees the Negro shops crammed to the door with them.

SCOT [ANONYMOUS]

1930

Out to cable Picasso to ask if he will illustrate *Nigger Heaven*.

CARL VAN VECHTEN

[While the title drew criticism, the book itself was a celebration of Harlem.]

MARCH 2

1842

Once more in Broadway! Here are the same ladies in bright colours walking to and fro, in pairs and singly; yonder in the very same light blue parasol which passed and repassed the hotel-window twenty times while we were sitting there. We are going to cross here. Take care of the pigs. Two portly sows are trotting up behind this carriage, and a select part of half-a-dozen gentlemen-hogs have just now turned the corner....

The street and shops are lighted now; and as the eye travels down the long thoroughfare, dotted with bright jets of gas, it is reminded of Oxford Street or Piccadilly. Here and there a flight of broad stone cellar-steps appears, and a painted lamp directs you to the Bowling Saloon, or Ten-Pin alley: Ten-Pins being a game of mingled chance and skill, invented when the legislature passed an act forbidding Nine-Pins. At other downward flights of steps, are other lamps, marking the whereabouts of oyster-cellars— pleasant retreats, say I: not only by reason of their wonderful cookery of oysters, pretty nigh as large as cheese-plates..., but because of all kinds of eaters of fish, or flesh, or fowl, in these latitudes, the swallowers of oysters alone are not gregarious; but subduing themselves, as it were, to the nature of what they work in, and copying the coyness of the thing they eat, do sit apart in curtained boxes, and consort by twos, not by two hundreds.

But how quiet the streets are! Are there no itinerant bands; no wind or stringed instruments? No, not one. By day, are there no Punches, Fantoccinis, Dancing-dogs, Jugglers, Conjurers, Orchestrinas, or even Barrel-organs? No, not one. Yes, I remember one. One barrel-organ and a dancing-monkey—sportive by nature, but fast fading into a dull, lumpish monkey, of the Utilitarian school.

Beyond that, nothing lively; no, not so much as a white mouse in a twirling cage.

CHARLES DICKENS

[Dating inferred from content.]

1844

Writing. Breakfast. Chinese. I intend to read a psalm every morning after breakfast in Chinese to keep up a sort of nodding acquaintance with the language which without this I run some chance of forgetting outright. New test. Revelation[s]. Is hard to understand.... Almost incline[d] to think St. John was not in his right mind when he wrote it.

GEORGE CAYLEY

1854

Schermerhorn fancy ball; costume of *Louis Quinze*.... It was quite successful. No fancy ball can approximate to common sense that does not adopt some single period. The chaos of nuns and devils, Ivanhoe and Harlequin, Loyola, Paul Pry, the cavalier and the Swiss peasant, presented by a ball on any other principle, or rather without principle of any sort, is so incoherent and insane that a thoughtful spectator would certainly be qualified for the Bloomingdale Asylum after some assignable period of inspection.

GEORGE TEMPLETON STRONG

1969

Last night, to Paula [Laurence] and Chucky [Bowden], to dine with the Lunts. What a wonderful evening, to be with Lynn ("Lynnie," as she is called) and Alfred after years of adoring (I don't exaggerate) her. She is very old, but still has her beautiful, highly individual figure—the chin held high, the broad lids artificially lashed, the nacreous skin (so like Sargent's *Madame X*). She came in tottering a bit, but she has made this into a sort of wandering calculated glide, a sort of swing through a room (rather like Ellen Terry's walk). When she saw the Sargent drawing of Ruth Draper, she said that Sargent was a great portrait painter but this drawing was the worst Sargent portrait she'd ever seen. "Ruth wasn't a pretty girl. This is a pretty girl...." She slides her voice, which is quite high—like a high-pitched pale color, a rich lavender—and then falls an octave or more. Her lower register was always ugly—really unattractive—but she managed.... She tells wonderful stories and suddenly forgets what she's been telling. One has to help get her on the central track, but it is all done with incredible charm and staging. Lunt is a great, genuine gentleman full of Scandinavian chuckles. He was delighted with the success of his modestly blue-and-white striped shirt, a departure for him, this coming to dine in a colored shirt. Lynnie rang Paula up to ask whether the last time they lunched Lynnie was wearing a dress with white sleeves. Paula said no. Lynnie didn't want to repeat the dress, which she had sewed, every stitch of it, herself, and a beautiful dress it is. The choice of Lynn's words is so fantastic. She is so right about the visual things.

LEO LERMAN

MARCH 3

1754

[For] Robert Levingston [*sic*] Dr. [Made] ... a Large Cofin for his negro.

JOSHUA DELAPLAINE

1844

Got up and took more than usual pains in toggery.... After church went to the [Goodhues].... Talked a good deal of nonsense and touched it off with writing out from memory my valentine to

Tiny which I did not dare send, but being able to make a prelude, I dare[d] do in person. They were civil enough to say it was good... T... attribute[d], or pretended to attribute my long Valentine to somebody else which I am not sorry for since it was rather absurd, however she laid it at the door of a person who writes well enough... her conduct might always be interpreted 50 ways and I don't know exactly how deep she is. Whether from drowsiness or for effect she grew sleepy and laid herself on the sofa; I sat watching her as she lay with her head thrown back over a very diminutive pillow, which by the way is a very natural position for it in her. Thought I would write a poetics about it but thought better of it.

GEORGE CAYLEY

MARCH 4

1790

Dined with the President of the United States [George Washington]. It was a dinner of dignity. All the Senators were present, and the Vice-President. I looked often around the company to find the happiest faces. Wisdom, forgive me if I wrong thee, but I thought folly and happiness most nearly allied. The President seemed to bear in his countenance a settled aspect of melancholy. No cheering ray of convivial sunshine broke through the cloudy gloom of settled seriousness. At every interval of eating or drinking he played on the table with a fork or knife, like a drumstick. Next to him, on his right, sat Bonny Johnny Adams, ever and anon mantling his visage with the most unmeaning simper that ever dimpled the face of folly.

WILLIAM MACLAY

1980

On February 14, Nixon came at last to 65th Street. I returned late on March 2. The next morning, Sunday, Peter called, "Look out the window." I did and saw the unmistakable figure on the terrace picking up some logs. He returned to the house; then inexplicably came out in a few minutes, still carrying the logs. He deposited them, picked up some other logs (perhaps shorter?) and disappeared.

Logs seemed to be the dominating theme of the presence so far. Peter reports an earlier appearance, in which he filled his arms with logs and, as he approached the door, dropped them. Mr. Pashkoff, who installed some energy-saving storm windows during our absence, later told me that he too saw Nixon in search of logs. This time the door closed behind him. When he approached it, he discovered that he was locked out. He began banging on the door and, after a few minutes, someone opened up, and he was rescued. One recalls the White House accounts of his passion for log fires, often accompanied by intensified air conditioning in order to make the room cold enough to justify a fire. Actually the weakness for open fireplaces must count as one of his more disarming characteristics.

ARTHUR M. SCHLESINGER, JR.

MARCH 5

1841

The prospect of war with England seems to be in everybody's sight and the general opinion is that we shall be most lamentably used up for the first three years perhaps; after that, the public opinion is very strong that the British Empire would be wiped out from the face of the earth. If tall talking can do it, John Bull is a used-up man.

GEORGE TEMPLETON STRONG

1864

A verry fine day.... [I] took A stroll up Broadway. Departure of the 20th Regmt of U.S. (colard) Volunteers, the first colard Regement

raised in New York pronounce[d] by all to be A splendid Regement.

WILLIAM B. GOULD

1917

Up, and walked to the office, in the slush and snow, and my shoes,
albeit waterproof, were not impervious; so I removed them and set
them to dry, and worked all afternoon in my bare feet, which was
a strange experience. Home and finished reading Mr. Maugham's
"Of Human Bondage," which I think is a great book.

FRANKLIN P. ADAMS

MARCH 6

1849

Wrote a few lines to my beloved Catherine, an occupation that
takes me out of this *odious country*—let me speak the truth!—where
taste, and high feeling, and the spirit of a gentleman are understood
and appreciated only by the *very, very few*—the helpless minority.
Let me die in a *ditch* in England, rather than in the Fifth Avenue of
New York here.

WILLIAM MACREADY

1907

Up early and down to Tombs Court. Met Judge C. S. Whitman and
he was most courteous. He sent his probation officer Al Thomas
to show me through the building. The Tombs prison and last but
not least important—The [Harry K.] Thaw Trial.... This was a
great experience and opportunity.... I ... heard some testimony of
Mrs. W. Thaw, the defendant's mother. A fine old lady. Jerome, the
prosecutor, is decidedly a player to the Press representatives. I was
disgusted with him and put him down as a sham. Thaw himself

impressed me as not mentally regular though it's hard to look at a man in this sort of fix dispassionately.

JOHN SLOAN

MARCH 7

1878

Looking back on [my father's] life, it seems as if mine must be such a weak useless one in comparison.

I should like to be a scientist: oh, how I shall miss his sweet, sympathetic advice!

THEODORE ROOSEVELT

1924

My Tommy seems too good to be true—I didn't know God made men like him.... He is like a woman for tenderness—he is utterly selfless where I am concerned...and yet he is so vitally a man!... Tommy took me to the subway and somehow for the first time I found it actual[ly] hurt to leave him—you hate to leave a man at dusk, just when lovers are going out to dine somewhere together.... I don't know why. It's one of the queer things New York does to you. Love in N.Y. is lights and dancing and restaurants and cocktails and the continual excitement of changing faces and new places. Queer! I wonder if I could love on a farm?

WINIFRED WILLIS

MARCH 8

1777

The Weather moderates, but produces nothing worthy Remark, but that Mutton has this Day been sold in Market for 2/3 and Veal at 2/9 per lb. tho' Provisions are plenty. It seems an attack was made on the Light House at Sandy-Hook yesterday morning by about 250 Rebels, both Horse and Foot, but they were repulsed by the Garrison, consisting of no more than about 30 Men.

Hugh Gaine

1921

Walking down Fifth Avenue in the afternoon, a woman caught me up and asked if I was Mrs. Sheridan. She said she was the Communist woman who came up and spoke to me after my lecture at the Aeolian Hall. I remembered her emotional Russian face. Her name, she said, was Rose Pastor Stokes. She had liked my sincerity and impartiality about the Soviet leaders. She apologized for not being able to ask me to a meal in her house (why should she apologize or ask me?) Her explanation was that she had married a millionaire, and he had "reverted to type" with the result that their meals were rather silent! I asked her to come and see me, but she said that she was under police surveillance and she did not wish to compromise me.

We walked some way together.

Clare Sheridan

1959

I sit here trying to write. [Housekeeper] Matilda, her hair in curlpapers, comes tidying things under my nose. Then she begins to shake two bathroom mats out of the window on to the terrace. Then she changes the cigarette in my ashtray beside my notebook so that all the smoke goes into my eyes. She has a passion for [pet pup] Popski. She takes him away for weekends with her to stay with her German sister—puts him in a box with an air-hole in it. He seems to accept this with resignation, although he has bitten her three times.

I am reading a book about the American Revolution. As I was brought up in a nest of United Empire Loyalists, I always instinctively sympathize with them, but I am swinging to the side of the Revolution. How insufferable it must have been for the Americans to be patronized by petty British officials and third-rate line officers.

CHARLES RITCHIE

MARCH 9

1907

Took a stroll on Ninth Avenue through the muck covered streets with dirty heaps of melting snow. Children swarming in the pools of dirt, sledding down three- or five-foot slushy heaps—having lots of fun. The curb vegetable market, meat wagons and blue looking chickens—in the mud and the sun that gets by the elevated railway structure. A small boy sees a huge wagon loaded with empty unused crates. "My, I wish I had that wood!"

JOHN SLOAN

1927

Today on the front page of the *World* we come upon "One hundred dollars a day for Poet of King's Henchman" and a [*sic*] article telling how my book has already sold ten thousand copies. Sometimes I get a kick out of things like this—often I don't. But this time I did. I was thrilled to death. That the amounts of royalties I get for a book of poems should be of front page interest to the great new york [*sic*] public—well, I just sat for ten minutes with my eyes sticking out, drinking it in.—Oh, what a thrilling winter this has been. Ugin and I—what fun we've had!—how happy we are.

EDNA ST. VINCENT MILLAY

MARCH 10

1957

Parting at shipboard standing high on the ship rail top gallant deck delight in the rain waving farewell to receding smaller-ing pier with black dressed girls…and T.S. Eliot-like-umbrella'd Lafacadio [Orlovsky] taller disappearing into space smallness with apron of water before their stage, & curtains of rain descending, and the back bank box black house wharf pier they sat on waving growing smaller under foot and ascending the harbor over the sea rising like an airplane past the docks of Brooklyn and black dirty ships' asses stuck out in void green water floating with mercury and condom doom and alas alast [*sic*] the towers of Manhattan spiring & rocking on the Island behind us symmetrical the four stanchions of miniature buildings displayed on the side glued together in the wind, green statue standing & turning in the world as we passed, Isles of Staten & houses ahill, Brooklyn apartments on the banks of Channel Park, Sandy Fort, Coney Island Ferris Wheel and miniature hotel and the grey rainy sea ahead for life.

ALLEN GINSBERG

MARCH 11

1840

My daughter Margaret received as a present from London a piece of the Queen's wedding cake, enclosed in a letter from Mrs. Stevenson, lady of the American minister, and brought in the Great Western by Mr. Cracroft, who was introduced by the same letter. This is all very well, but nothing to the present which I am told was received by the same conveyance by Miss Rush, daughter of the former Minister from the United States. Hers came from the queen itself—a piece of the cake, with a letter enclosed in a beautiful satinwood box, on which the letter V is emblazoned in diamond. This young lady was probably a companion of Victoria's in their youthful days, when perhaps her childish dreams did not soar to the heights of her present greatness, and the "Sea of Glory" on which she now swims had no place on the map of her imagination.

PHILIP HONE

1897

L—— is more or less spoiled by being too much with boys, and so is P——. But M—— is as good as gold, and I hope she will not affect the craze too. All the girls now run after the ones that are going to help them, and worth seems to go for nothing, unless it is in the introducing line. They hug and kiss to the face but behind the back they are deceited [*sic*] and I don't like it. I am not in any of the "sets", having friends in all but belonging to none and being an outsider to all. At dancing class one night I went in and said how-de-do and only M—— answered, and she seeing that my face got red (the room was very hot) whispered to A—— to speak to me. M—— did it but with the best intention but it hurt just the same; I don't believe anyone noticed it, though....

Men may come and men may go but I go on forever in the same old rut, doing no good or harm, but always hoping at some time to be some good in the world, always wanting to walk on something but finding only air.

SUSAN BLISS

1978

I had a lot of dates but decided to stay home and dye my eyebrows.

ANDY WARHOL

MARCH 12

1790

Attended this day at the Hall.... The committee on the Naturalization bill reported, but far short of the points which I wished established in it. There really seems a spirit of malevolence against Pennsylvania in this business. We have been very liberal on the subject of admitting strangers to citizenship. We have benefited by it and still do benefit. Some characters seem disposed to deprive us of it. I moved postponement of a day that we might consider of this amendment. It was easily carried; but [South Carolina's Senator Ralph] Izard snapped, ill-natured as a cur, and said "No" alone.

WILLIAM MACLAY

1847

My wife and I went this morning to see the celebrated Tom Thumb at the American Museum. He appears to have increased in *littleness* during his European visit. He is said to have realized by showing himself £150,000 sterling and been kissed by a million pairs of the sweetest lips in Europe, from Queen Victoria down; and now he is making here a thousand dollars a day. He performs four or five times each day to a thousand or twelve hundred persons; dances, sings, appears in a variety of characters with appropriate costumes, is cheerful, gay, and lively, and does not appear to be fatigued or displeased by his incessant labors.

PHILIP HONE

1861

Nothing definite about Fort Sumter, but the impression grows stronger that its surrender is unavoidable and that [the] government has not the means to hold it. Lincoln's administration cannot fairly be held responsible for this national disgrace.... Traitors

[Strong refers here to "Cobb," likely John B. Cobb, a speaker of the House of Representatives who defected to the Confederates] have been diligently paralyzing our national strength for months, if not for years. Their successors in office cannot undo the spell at once.

But, whoever may be responsible for the calamity, this is a time of sad humiliation for the country. Every citizen of what has heretofore been called the Great Republic of America, every man, woman, and child, from Maine to Texas, from Massachusetts to California, stands lower among the inhabitants of this earth tonight than in March, 1860. We are a weak, divided, disgraced people, unable to maintain our national existence.... I'm tempted to emigrate, to become a naturalized British subject and spend the rest of my days in some pleasant sea-side village in the southern counties of old Mother England. It's a pity we ever renounced our allegiance to the British Crown.

GEORGE TEMPLETON STRONG

MARCH 13

1917

I sure am in love! Can't wait until the evening when Meyer comes to love me and make a fuss about me. He keeps repeating God, I love you so much, so much! I know he does too!

He sure is splendid to darling Ma & Pa who are crazy about him. School-teachers all jealous wish they were me! Great excitement.

SARA HOEXTER BLUMENTHAL

MARCH 14

1777

Reports current that George Washington was dead, and his Army passing the Delaware, however not credited with any Body [*sic*].

HUGH GAINE

1953

An extraordinary stranger—dark-maned, ponderous—enters the Remo; I point him out and asked around "Who's that?" He has a snarling look....

Someone says, "James Agee." And the animal cry of "A Mother's Tale," and the transcendent poetry of *Let Us Now Praise Famous Men*—is what I remark in this handsome face.

I begged Julian to introduce me, for he had once met him, but that was years ago, and he was shy to approach him.

Agee had several drinks. Julian was still talking to Frank O'Hara/ stray child of the Muses/when Agee left....

Feeling thwarted and seething, I went off to Washington Square, to thoughts of the past, present, and future.

Of the past: how I dived for pennies tossed from the Fifth Avenue buses to the half-naked children in the fountain.

Of the present: I smoke a reefer and contemplate the motto on the monument, thrown into relief by the moonlight, "The event is in the hand of God."

Of the future: I want Jim Agee to be my lover.

JUDITH MALINA

1976

I write to Mr. Shawn, enclosing a list of twelve people from whom to choose the six I shall write about for *The New Yorker*. They are: Pinter, Stoppard, Shirley MacLaine, Irving Lazar, Bob Kaufman, Peter Sellers, John Curry, Mel Brooks, George Burns, Johnny Carson (No. 1 on my list), Robert de Niro, and Ralph Richardson. (When I asked Mr. Shawn why the magazine no longer published critical profiles, he said (a) that although it had published "playful" or satirical profiles, they had never been really hostile, and (b) that he simply shrank from the idea of destroying people in print and would rather leave that to other magazines. For him, merely to be ignored by *The New Yorker* is punishment enough.

KENNETH TYNAN

MARCH 15

1888

The first oriole had already been spied hanging its nest from a cedar in Central Park; the bare poplars were putting forth their plush of spring; and the leaves of the chestnut were burgeoning, like chattering women poking their heads out of their hoods after a storm.... The first straw hats had made their appearance, and the streets of New York were gay with Easter attire, when, on opening its eyes after the hurricane had spent its force, the city found itself silent, deserted, shrouded, buried under the snow....

At no time in this century has New York experienced a storm like that of March 13. It had rained the preceding Sunday, and the writer working into the dawn, the newspaper vendor at the railroad station, the milkman on his round of the sleeping houses, could hear the whiplash of the wind that had descended on the city against the chimneys, against walls and roofs, as it vented its fury on slate and mortar, shattered windows, demolished porches, clutched and uprooted trees, and howled, as though ambushed, as it fled down the narrow streets. Electric wires, snapping under its impact, sputtered and died. Telegraph lines, which had withstood so many storms, were wrenched from their posts....

A shopkeeper, a man in the prime of life, was found buried today, with only a hand sticking from the snow to show where he lay. A messenger boy, as blue as his uniform, was dug out of a white, cool tomb, a fit resting place for his innocent soul, and lifted up in the compassionate arms of his comrades. Another, buried to the neck, sleeps with two red patches on his cheeks, his eyes a filmy blue....

Without milk, without coal, without mail, without newspapers, without streetcars, without telephone, without telegraph, the city arose today. What eagerness on the part of those living uptown to read the newspapers, which thanks to the intrepidity of the poor newsboys, finally came up from the downtown presses! There were four theatres open last night, but all the stores and offices are closed, and the elevated struggles in vain to carry the unwitting crowds that gather at its station to their places of work.

José Martí

1952

Last night at San Remote [San Remo bar], I talk with Kimon Friar, who didn't approve of my interpretation of *Sweeney Agonistes*. He introduces me to Christopher Isherwood.

I had met Isherwood briefly during *The Dog Beneath the Skin*. Very much inside himself, he reaches outward tentatively. He says, "I am looking for complete directness and honesty...."

We talk a long time. He warns me fervently against the practice of black magic, which Joseph Cambell has encouraged.

"It is because it does work that we must avoid it."

Judith Malina

1961

Ides of March in the evening. The Buffalo stint is over. Back in New York.

If I never write here anymore it's because I write nothing no-where. Haven't put down a note of music in six months—the longest ever. Been six weeks back from Buffalo, a city that never existed, harboring some unknown Ned Rorem who for a year and a half did his job in a trance brilliantly, then vanished ... Waiting, waiting immobile again for something (what?) while others scurry ambitiously for money and love. It's ambition here that breaks the spirit, sterilizing all endeavor: can no longer work for pleasure.... Who am I trying to fool? In less than three years I'll be forty. And next month I finally return to France seeking the insane, the grey-haired, the dead and dying, those caught in their own problems, and my not-forgotten yet vanished boyhood.... (I wrote Virgil [Thomson] in Paris: "Have you seen my lost youth around?" He answered: "There's plenty of lost youth around but I don't know if any of it's yours.")

NED ROREM

MARCH 16

1790

Exercised on horseback between 10 & 12 Oclock. Previous to this, I was visited (having given permisn.) by a Mr. Warner Miflin, one of the People called Quakers; active in pursuit of the Measures laid before Congress for emancipating the Slaves. After much general conversation, and an endeavor to remove the prejudices which he said had been entertained of the motives by which the attending deputation from their Society were actuated, he used Arguments to shew the immorality—injustice and impolicy of keeping these people in a state of Slavery; with declarations, however, that he did not wish for more than a gradual abolition, or to see any infraction of the Constitution to effect it. To these I replied, that as it was a matter which might come before me for official decision I was not inclined to express any sentimts. on the merits of the question before this should happen.

PRESIDENT GEORGE WASHINGTON

1998

It was a fun weekend for my show....

The musical takes the form of one of Hedwig's pathetic gigs. The rock band Cheater backs me up, and we perform in the ballroom of an ancient flophouse where the surviving crew of the *Titanic* once stayed. Nowadays, a bunch of welfare cases and a few German backpackers loiter around the coffee machine in the lobby (the condoms are in the candy machine). Our dressing room is in the Rapunzel-like tower at the top of the hotel....

Last week, somebody over-dosed, and the body was carried out through the incoming audience. Last night, the audience was annoyingly quiet. A few too many uptown, button-down folks. The show was tough-going at first—my voice was strained by our Saturday doubleheader—but the audience warmed up to us by the end....

On our way back up to the dressing room, a very cute Israeli cornered me. He had just seen the show and tried to pull me into his hotel room. I considered this a rave.... On my way out, two very self-possessed 13-year-old twin girls told me they had heard about us on the Internet and come all the way from Toronto to see the show... and to shop at Saks.

JOHN CAMERON MITCHELL

MARCH 17

1924

Rehearsal my adaption [*sic*] "*The Ancient Mariner*" at [Provincetown Playhouse] ... N.Y. Opening of "Welded"—A Flop!

EUGENE O'NEILL

1941

Drama critics of New York have lived together so long that (like married couples) they think and look alike. There should be little uniforms for them to wear. The fault is not that they know little about drama, it's that they know so little else. "Life-like" is a word they use for a form of life they have seen sufficiently on the stage for it to seem normal to them. They never disagree—they have an adolescent fear in differing one iota from their associates. They permit one playwright a year to enter, and one actress. Century Club technique of membership.

DAWN POWELL

1998

- A nice note from a *Hedwig* idol, Madeline Kahn, thanking me for inviting her to opening night. Wrote her a thank you note. Will she write back to thank me for it?
- A Screen Actors Guild check for 14 cents compensating me for the fourth Serbian re-run of a *MacGyver* episode....
- A letter from someone wanting me to contribute to a book titled *How to Be Successful in America*. Other contributors include Bart Conner [Olympic gymnast] and Norm Crosby [Borscht Belt comedian].

On the lobby floor of my apartment building is a monthly flyer from the New York Hemlock Society addressed to a Mr. and Mrs. Clive Small. Handwritten next to the address: "No longer at this address."

JOHN CAMERON MITCHELL

MARCH 18

1864

All day I have been receiving company. I had an amusing talk about the degeneracy of modern manners with old Mrs. Webster and Mrs. LeRoy. Mrs. Webster is shocked at the song figure introduced by Pierre Marié into the German cotillon. It consists of a gentleman driving round with reins and whip, married ladies supping with gentlemen at Delmonico's without their husbands, and the rompishness of the younger ladies....

There is a clique of fast young married women in New York who are very much loosening the reins of good and decorous manners. In one family, there has been a great scandal—that of Mr. Austin Stevens, one of the most respectable men of the city. His daughter, Mrs. Peter Strong, has behaved most shamelessly with her brother-in-law, and her outraged husband is seeking a divorce.

Society seems to have gone mad, giving itself up to every kind of extravagance and dissipation.

MARIA LYDIG DALY

1914

College. Danced hesitation and tango at chapel hour.

SARA HOEXTER BLUMENTHAL

1939

Two months since we left England. Here we are—still at the George Washington. What has happened?

This time in New York has been a bad, sterile period for me. I've done practically nothing. Every day, I think: now I must get busy, now I must start work. But at what? My money—including the advance I got from [Bennett] Cerf—is rapidly running out. Wystan [Auden] still has several hundred dollars, and the prospect of a teaching job, later on. I have no prospects. I don't even know what kind of job I want. My whole instinct is against teaching, or lecturing, or exploiting my reputation in any way. I would like some sort of regular, humble occupation. I got to know Berlin because I was doing something functional—the natural occupation for a poor foreigner—teaching his own language. If I can't do something of the same kind here, I shall never get to know America. I shall never become a part of this city....

Wystan himself is going through a curious phase. He's as energetic as I'm idle. He takes Benzedrine regularly, in small doses, followed by Seconal at night. He says that "the chemical life" solves all his problems. He writes a great deal—poems and articles and reviews—makes speeches, goes to tea parties, and dinners, is quite brilliantly talkative. It's a little as if he and I had changed places....

There is much that is majestic but nothing that is gracious in this city—this huge, raw, functional skeleton, this fortress of capital, this jungle of absolutely free competition. Every street is partly a slum. Where the banks and the brownstone houses end, the slum tenements begin, with their rusty fire escapes and crowds of baseball-playing Dead End Kids. Beyond, on the mainland, is a wilderness of scrapyards and shacks. This country is insanely untidy.

CHRISTOPHER ISHERWOOD

MARCH 19

1906

A very heavy snowstorm swept over the city and between noon and 6 o'clock had dropped three inches of snow....I delivered my drawings at *Collier's*—no verdict....Walked around through West 4th Street neighborhood in the storm and afterward about Madison Square. Rain followed the snow and Dolly and I had a slushy trip around the corner to Fox's studio. He cooked an elegant dinner—steaks on charcoal fire and some delicious salad after dinner.

JOHN SLOAN

1943

I took a taxi to some place on 48th & B'way where they have pre-view studios. Mr. [Herbert] Morgan [in charge of short subjects for Metro Goldwyn Mayer] met us. We saw the movie [*Fala, the President's Dog*] twice through & liked it very much. The only trouble is that it hasn't enough of the President—But we have to be thankful they could get the one scene where he gives Fala his supper! Mr. Morgan explained some "secret" details: a squirrel was brought in a cage & let out at the proper moment so that Fala could chase him to a tree on the W.H. lawn; a piece of bacon was put under the bottom of a scrapbook which Diana [Hopkins] & Fala are looking at with such interest; a piece of bacon was buried with the bone Fala dug up in the lawn; a substitute for Fala had to be put in for the kitchen scene, as the photographers were not allowed to take the kitchen in the W.H. This was also true of the telephone girl scene. The substitute dog had shorter hair than for Fala, so they glued extra hair on him. The P.'s room & the breakfast tray were all faked, but very well, for I asked Mr. Morgan if the bed wasn't really the President's....

On the whole it is a very amusing little "short" & should be popular in the newsreel.

MARGARET "DAISY" SUCKLEY

MARCH 20

1780

On watch as guard at *Sik Rebls Prison*.

LT. JOHN CHARLES PHILIP VON KRAFFT

1854

Bill Guess, died aged 22.

A thoughtless, strong, generous animal nature, fond of direct pleasures, eating, drinking, women, fun &c.—Taken sick with the small-pox, had the bad disorder and was furious with the delirium tremens.—Was with me in the Crystal Palace,—a large broad fellow, weighed over 200.—Was a thoughtless good fellow.

WALT WHITMAN

MARCH 21

1920

A fair day, which put me in a joyous mood, and I rode about in my petrol-waggon, and took Hilda [Gaige] for a ride, she looking very pretty, and I lent her some books to read.... A. Samuels to my house today, playing on the piano, and contending that the musick of Victor Herbert hath more melody in it than that of Sir Arthur Sullivan, a silly contention.

FRANKLIN P. ADAMS

1955

Auden and his birthday party: I have got to like him and usually see him when I come to New York. . . .

(Elena likes him but finds a little hard to take on account of his boorishness. Once, in a previous winter, when I had gone out to buy liquor and left her alone with Auden, she said the conversation stopped completely till I had come back. After his coming to dinner the other night, she said that he made her feel as if she were not there.)

Nonetheless, I have the impression now more than ever that, whether he knows it or not, he deliberately goes in for uncomfortable, sordid, and grotesque lodgings. A few years ago he was living on lower Sixth (?) Avenue. He had told me while we were dining in a restaurant that he was happy about his new apartment, which had an extra room in which he could put up Spender or Isherwood. . . . The place was completely without heat when we entered . . . and Wystan started up some queer kind of little stove, but we sat in our overcoats and our breath went up in vapor. . . . The guest room was a thing like a doghouse built completely *inside* the loft (which was hardly or not at all divided by partitions into rooms). . . . Yet, as I looked out on the night of Sixth Avenue, I had something like a moment of wistfulness as I thought of my own independence in the poverty and responsibility of my one-room apartment on West 13th St. Many writers and artists have a phase of this, and it makes them feel their independence and helps them, in a sort of asceticism, to assert their virtue and power. It is a way of putting oneself to a test, makes a base for more prosperous days and guarantees one against compromises. But Wystan has condemned himself to this, so far as I can see, for all the rest of his life—as he has to homosexuality—and, in a puritanical way, seems to feel he is acquiring merit by living—with a touch of fantasy—in the most unattractive way possible.

EDMUND WILSON

MARCH 22

1790

Sat for Mr. Trumbull for my Picture in his Historical pieces—after which conversed for more than an hour with Mr. Jefferson on business relative to the duties of his office.

PRESIDENT GEORGE WASHINGTON

1950

In the cafeteria, after I had finished eating, I stayed a little while, watching the people. I felt good, life was looking brighter. Without knowing it, I began to hum a tune.

I was awakened from my daydream by the voice of a man sitting at the table next to me. "Singing?" he said.

"Yes," I said. "My belly is full, I am happy, why not sing?"

"But your song doesn't sound like you're happy," the man said.

I suddenly realized that I was, in fact, humming one of the saddest folk songs I know… "Oh, the misery, the misery of my life, when will it end…"

Those Lithuanian songs, they are always so sad…. Lithuanians have always been in the path of bigger neighbors, always trampled by them….

Yesterday we visited Professor P. He said, he had received a request to investigate the brothers: they must, most certainly, be communists. We told him that it made no difference to us any longer who says what.

JONAS MEKAS

MARCH 23

1859

I go to City & returned at 7—Find Uncle has had a quiet day—without cough & very little shortness of breath—an improvement over his condition for a week or more to be attributed to the return to the [illeg.] in stronger doses than before— 3 table spoonsfull per day—... Went to church to morning prayers [Lent] No fire in church—caught cold—wouldn't catch him again at "their confounded morning prayers."

PIERRE MUNRO IRVING

1921

I spent the afternoon at [the art dealer] Knoedler, who has very generously taken on my exhibition from the Numismatic Society for two weeks. My things look well in their big room, and it is comic to see the Soviet leaders daring to show their faces in Fifth Avenue! No one looks at Winston [Churchill] or Asquith, they go straight to the Russians, as though fascinated with horror!

CLARE SHERIDAN

MARCH 24

1790

Prevented from Riding by the unfavourableness of the weather.

PRESIDENT GEORGE WASHINGTON

1888

Why this laughing sun, these thronged streets, this thunder of artillery and blare of bugles, this coming and going of aides on horseback? Carriages surround the armory of the Twelfth Infantry Regiment. It is a cold morning, but the turnout is large. Who is arriving now that everybody makes way and friendly greetings rise on every side? He carries a black-plumed tricorne in his hand; how can such spindly legs bear the weight of that massive torso? He is burdened by a huge chest and broad back; the epaulets square on his shoulders like the silver corner guards of an old-fashioned prayer book;...It is Sheridan, and now Sherman, who helped Grant corner the exhausted Confederate forces near Richmond!...A hundred more, the toast of Congress, the Church, Finance, the Army and the Republic, who have gathered, braving the biting cold, to accompany to the pier where the launch of a warship bound for Venezuela awaits them, the remains...of José Antonio Páez, who with no school but his savannahs, no discipline but his will, no strategy but his genius, and no army but his hordes, freed Venezuela from Spanish rule in a horse race that lasted sixteen years....

The sidewalks are crowded with the curious. This heroic music, this clank of gun-carriages, this clatter of cavalry, these gal500ned uniforms, these public figures in carriages, are a fitting tribute to one who with the water to his chest and the lance between his teeth came out of the wilderness to gain the ranks and riches in the defense of liberty that others gain oppressing it....

Now the procession has reached the pier, through streets where curtains were drawn aside to see the passing stranger. In the poorer sections, the Poles, the Italians, and the Negroes crowded to the curb...to see what was happening....A Colombian Negro, who made his way through the crowd, stood on the sidewalk with tears streaming down his face. The infantry, the batteries and the cavalry troop come to attention. Is it the soul's fond desire, or is it that when the coffin is removed from the hearse the air seems somehow more luminous, and the horses cease to paw the ground, and all is silence? Eight sailors lift the coffin to their shoulders. The band plays "Nearer My God to Thee." Sherman lowers his eyes. Sheridan raises his head. Hats off, gentlemen!

JOSÉ MARTÍ

1965

Stopped opium as sleeping too much and no good effects otherwise. Slept all day and night—dreamed of swimming which is always good.

DAWN POWELL

MARCH 25

1790

Went in the forenoon to the Consecration of Trinity Church, when a Pew was constructed, and set apart for the President of the United Sts.

PRESIDENT GEORGE WASHINGTON

1921

Kenneth Durant [American pro-Soviet journalist] fetched me at six-thirty and we took the over-head-railway and went to [the] East Side. Where, making our way through a maze of playing children, we dined at the Roumanian restaurant. It was as though in a few minutes one had suddenly gone abroad to a foreign country....

In the East Side people talked Italian or else that other strange language that newspapers are printed in, and which looks like a mixture of Russian and Arabic! A newspaper boy brought in the evening papers,... and when I asked him if he couldn't bring in something I could read, the other people laughed. We ordered some steak for our dinner, and when the waiter brought enough for a school treat I exclaimed, and he said, "In Broadway they serve the dishes—here we serve the food!" They did indeed; even sharing it with a starving cat I couldn't get through with it. The restaurant was rather a good one and very clean. I reproached Kenneth for not having taken me somewhere with more local color. I hate being treated as a Bourgeoise.

The evening was very warm, and the restaurant door was open.

East Side has its background of sound like any other place. In Pittsburgh it is the sound of the mills, like the roar of the sea. In New York it is the trams and the traffic and the overhead trains. In the East Side (at night) it is the voices of laughing playing children. What heaps of children! The streets were full of them. One tumbled over them, one bumped into them, one dodged them, as in the side streets of Naples. Some of the smaller children, smaller than [son] Dick, sat crumpled up in a doorway or leaning against a lamp-post, weary and sleepy. It was nearly ten o'clock at night, and they were not in bed. The streets were strewn with papers as after picnic. I said to Kenneth, "Why aren't the streets cleaned," and he said because people were so busy cleaning the streets where I live. I said, "Why don't the children go to bed?" and he said because there were twenty people to a room, and it was easier to leave the children out in the street as long as possible.

CLARE SHERIDAN

MARCH 26

1865

[Edwin] Booth has played Hamlet a hundred nights to crowded houses, and they are going to present him with a Hamlet medal which the Judge is asked to present. All the women are crazy about him. He is, as Stewart, the manager of the Winter Garden, said, "so silent and dark and Gawain-looking and so delightfully indifferent and so distressed (I might add, 'so they think') for the loss of his wife that each and every one would like to do something to console him." He would lose half his popularity if they had heard what I heard this evening of his new love. I believe I have too much reason ever to be amiable or interesting. I hate to do interesting and romantic things.

MARIA LYDIG DALY

1911

After breakfast I got at a cartoon idea in re the frightful fire of last evening in the Triangle Shirtwaist Factory. A black triangle each side marked ("Rents," "Interest," "Profit") death on one side, a fat capitalist on the other and the charred body of a girl in the center.

JOHN SLOAN

1921

We have been here nearly two months, and in [that time] we have learnt that American ideas are on the whole good ideas. There is usually reason in most things that Americans do, and good reasons, as for instance, in Prohibition. But there is another prohibition quite different from that one that most people talk about, and it's unexplained. It concerns Dick. When I say that it concerns him I do not mean that it affects him alone. He is merely voicing the great "why?" of a million children, who may not walk on the grass in Central Park. "Keep Off"—"Keep Off" is written everywhere. It takes a great many men in uniform to enforce this prohibition. Strong men, vigilant men, diligent men, too. Just as the policemen seem to be picked for Fifth Avenue traffic, policemen who seem entirely friendly towards children, whose one idea is to help them across the street and to laugh and joke with them as he does so (Dick has several friends on the Avenue) just so the parkmen seem to be picked for their job. They are hard men, cold men, they smile not, neither do they joke. . . .

On St. Patrick's Day, Dick and I came back through the Park from the Metropolitan Museum and the procession was still passing by. People might not even stand on a rocky eminence to look over the wall. A parkman stood there, whistle in mouth, proudly defiantly, . . . Over the wall came the sound of bands, and the marching feet, but only the park-keeper could see the procession. . . . Should I send Dick to a boarding-school in the country, so that he may enjoy the spring? . . . Must I send him away so that he shall not grow into a law-breaker and a "Revolutioner"?

What we really want to know is: Who does the green grass grow for, in Central Park?

CLARE SHERIDAN

MARCH 27

1869

I took again a bath this morning[,] temperature about the same. On account of the thick fog we proceeded on our voyage by 7 o'clock only, having stopt for the night. Got by 8 a pilot, passed Sandy Hook by 9; splendid panorama of the Bay of New York with Long Island on the one and Staten island on the other hand, both, and particularly the latter, covered with magnificent villas, immense number of ships of all dimensions and also a great many tow and other steamers pass us whilst going up the Bay. Landed only 2 p.m. on Canal street wharf... carriage $1.50. Splendid accommodations at Astorhouse. Everywhere new costly carpets; excellent furniture; interior shutters instead of curtains. Prices dear; common Bordeaux $2 the bottle. Every hour new issues of newspapers with later and always later news from all parts of the world; cries of the newspaper boys. One look from the steamer on the houses adjoining the wharf; one ride or walk through a street satisfies a man that he is here in another world, for nothing is made here for outward show but all is only for practical purposes; in every house are wholesale stores, and of the bustle and business in the streets we are unable to make ourselves the slightest idea in the old world. In nearly every street are 2 and in many cases 4 rails for the large city cars, which cross the town in all senses and directions and of which every one can take 50 passengers; fare 6 cents. Though french [*sic*] politesse is missing, there is nevertheless everywhere a [ready enthusiasm] to render service.

HEINRICH SCHLIEMANN

MARCH 28

1880

Some of the girls got into trouble again last week heaven be praised, not I this time! One night there was a very gay party of gentlemen in the right-hand stage box—about six, I think—who had evidently been having a very jolly time before they came to the theatre, for their faces were flushed, they talked and laughed a great deal, and when the midshipmen came on at the end of the first act they almost fell over the railing of their box in their efforts to applaud us and to make us look at them.... The new girls were the worst; they tried to attract attention to themselves, and behaved in a very unladylike manner. Some of us remembered—at least I did—that certain things had mysteriously come to the Governor's ears, and were on our guard against so much as seeming to be aware of the presence of the merrymakers in the box. Lucky for us that we did, for immediately after the act [who] should come up the stairs but the Governor, with pale face, set lips, and steely eyes.... The next night three of the new girls were missing, and have not been seen since.

DORA RANOUS

1907

Worked on the Madison Square picture in the afternoon till very tired. The weather is very enervating, quite the spring sort.... Rained in the late evening and I saw an idea for a picture in the Flower Shop across the way. Stock out in front and open all night on account of Easter.

JOHN SLOAN

2009

No calls, missed or otherwise, tonight. The blistering honesty of technology.

STAYING PINOY IN NEW YORK

MARCH 29

1845

Old men are apt to be careless and slovenly in their dress—this is wrong....Black is safest, it is peculiarly the garb of a gentleman, and never goes out of fashion. But in this matter of dress one of our great men (than whom there is none greater), Mr. [Daniel] Webster, has a strange fancy. He is not slovenly, but on the contrary tawdry, fond of a variety of colors. I do not remember ever to have seen him in the only dress in which he should appear—the respectable and dignified suit of black. I was much amused a day or two since by meeting him in Wall Street, at high noon, in a bright blue satin vest, sprigged with gold flowers, a costume [as] incongruous for Daniel Webster as ostrich feathers for a sister of charity.

PHILIP HONE

1869

N. York 29th March. I got today my paper as citizen of the U.S. Since no divorce can be obtained in the State of New York except on acct. of adultery, whereas in Indiana even no previous residence is required. I have decided on going on 31st inst to Indianapolis. Peter Cook, the lawyer, procures here divorce in a few weeks by false certificates and perjury; I will have nothing to do with such horrors....

Tonight in the street Railway car a boy, 8 years old, stept in holding in his hand some dozens of small books with paintings, of which he laid a copy on the knees of every passenger singing out 2 cents a peace [*sic*].... It is wonderful indeed to witness how here such little boys are already caring for themselves and gaining their bread.

HEINRICH SCHLIEMANN

MARCH 30

1838

Evening. No meeting of the Philolexian, of which I'm not sorry, for the Freshmen were raising a most infernal row on the green. That's the hardest class in college. They are all up before the Board tomorrow for knocking in a panel of the chapel door, spiking the keyhole and throwing the knobs into the Temple of Cloacina.

GEORGE TEMPLETON STRONG

[The Philolexian is the literary and forensic society of Columbia University.]

2001

I've been avoiding an anniversary blog for my gym notebook ... even though I have a great story about a gorgeous french guy named guillaume.... I'd worn my new camo shorts and a shirt with cutoff sleeves when I dumped this boring party and went to one at the cock. It was crowded. He was my size, with brilliant eyes [and] the wonderful look on his face, intelligent and kind, brilliant, with his head inclined toward the window while our warm legs were interwined romantically. The sex was accordingly wonderful ... we went on a few dates after that, laughed and enjoyed each other's company, fell for him, and he lost interest after awhile, although he remained polite and gorgeously kind.

CHAD THE MINX

MARCH 31

1837

Bookseller's Dinner. [—] This was the greatest dinner I was ever at, with the exception perhaps of that given to Washington Irving on his return from Europe. I had the honor of being an invited guest.

The Association of Booksellers in the principal cities of the Union have a great annual or semi-annual feast, at which eminent literary and scientific men are invited to join the trade. This, I believe, was the first in New York. It was given at the City Hotel, and was gotten up, arranged, and conducted in admirable style.

PHILIP HONE

APRIL 1

1908

A beautiful day. Spring seems to be right in place now. Still necessary to have a low fire in the stove in the north studio.... Took a walk to Central Park...it looks fine, the grass is quite green and the sun is warm. Stopped and looked at the people passing St. Patrick's Cathedral, which represents a temporal value of several million dollars. Noticed the poor men who touched their hats with the customary, half ashamed, furtive air in passing the central door. A baby in carriage has a small parasol held over it by its nurse in passing the same spot! Made a Puzzle in afternoon and evening.

JOHN SLOAN

1921

I have had rather a wonderful morning. I was taken to the apartment of a man who collects Italian primitives. He is young, as yet only about twenty-seven, and one of the amazing products of this country. His mother, they say, was a washer-woman (why not?), and he determined to go through college. At Harvard he paid his own way by buying up the trouser press industry and syndicating it, and putting himself at the head. He made a fortune by pressing the undergraduates' trousers. This is the "on-dit," probably it is quite inaccurate, and he would tell a very different story. Anyway, it's a good story, and the fundamental thing is that he arose, from nowhere.... What his work is now I didn't hear, but he is collecting Italian primitives. We saw them all before he came in. There were Botticellis, Fra Angelicos, Filippo Lippi, Bellini, and countless others. Each one was lovely and one felt much loved. The rooms were simply but beautifully furnished with Italian pieces. In the dining-room the table was laid, and next to the owner's place was a book from which he reads out a little prayer, for grace, before each meal. It sounded affected, but I was assured it came from a deeply fervent spirit. I marvelled much over this young man before I saw him. His bedroom was chaste and hung with Madonnas, he had tall candles and things that suggested holiness! There was only one personal note in the whole place, the photograph of a very modern lovely girl.

CLARE SHERIDAN

1923

In all day, cataloguing letters. Read in *World* how Frank Case has barred the Jews from the Algonquin.

CARL VAN VECHTEN

APRIL 2

1878

We had a test today with Edison in New York and [myself] in Philadelphia of the Edison carbon telephone and the Phelps Magneto telephone. The wire used was a no. 6 wire and runs right along the railroad amongst 22 or 23 other wires some of which were working the Washington "Quad." The induction was very heavy; notwithstanding this Orton and Bentley conversed with perfect ease on the Edison instrument whereas with Phelps not a single distinguishable word could be got. The Edison was the most improved pattern transmitter with thick plate and solid connection between the plate and the aluminum so that it works more by pressure than by vibration[.] The Phelps was a new large magnet and double diaphragm placed as in sketch and when put on the line the usual "frying pan" is put into a complete roar.

CHARLES BATCHELOR

1912

Found this day many a gray hair on the left side of my head, and am growing old, as the song hath it, which thinking of, I to my harmon-icka [*sic*] and play, very sweet and sad.

FRANKLIN P. ADAMS

APRIL 3

1921

Dined with the [Herbert Bayard] Swopes, it being Mrs. Swope's birthday party.

I had a long talk with Barney Baruch who came in afterwards. I had not seen him since that bewildering night when I first arrived, and thought he was Mr. Brooke! I've never forgotten him, he has a dominating personality, and a nose and a brow that I keep modeling in my mind while I am talking to him. But he is "the king with two faces," he can look hard and Satanic one minute, kind and gentle the next. He has a great love of Winston and a loyalty to [Wood-row] Wilson. His ideas about life and the world in general are fine. He has the dynamic force of a Revolutionary, but his idealism is to get the world straight sanely, calmly and constructively, not vio-lently, bitterly and destructively. He believes in an ideal League of Nations, and in reasoning rather than arming. The answer to all that is, that nothing gets done at all except by force, bitterness and violence, and so Russia is the only one among us who has got-ten something done! Perhaps if there were more Barney Baruchs in the world something might evolve, who knows. I don't really know enough about him and his life, and to what purpose he puts his activities.

He talked to me a good deal about his father and mother, espe-cially his mother. He has that Jewish love of family. I always like to hear a man eulogise his mother; it makes me realize my own responsibility towards Dick. If a man can remember the things his mother said to him in early life, then my talking to Dick is not as vain as it would seem.

CLARE SHERIDAN

1944

Exhausted by friends—not so much by revelry as by the responsibility of friends who are so happy to gnaw away at the bones of your energy and talent. Peggy is almost as bad as Portia used to be; she doesn't want to work any more than Portia did. Like 90 percent of women and small boys, however, they do like to pester people who *are* working.

DAWN POWELL

APRIL 4

1790

At home all day—unwell.

PRESIDENT GEORGE WASHINGTON

1842

Sally [canary] laid her first egg.

AUGUSTUS VAN HORNE ELLIS

1937

Stayed in the house all day. Cold and grey. Mary [daughter-in-law] and I played cards. In the evening went to dine with Max Perkins and Tom Wolfe at Cherio's—in 53rd St. We had good dinner and good drinks. Wolfe a huge man 6 ft 4—very alive and sensitive—too easily hurt. He is one of the few real ones.

SHERWOOD ANDERSON

APRIL 5

1842

Sally laid another egg.

AUGUSTUS VAN HORNE ELLIS

1911

The Memorial Funeral Procession for the Victims of the Triangle Waist Co. Fire was held today. A steady pour of rain did not prevent a great turnout—all in silence 200,000 in marching line. (*The Eve. Sun* gives as the number.) Dolly was in the Socialist section. She left before noon and didn't return till nearly six o'clock. Started march at one o'clock. She said it was a big thing, it should make for working class solidarity.

JOHN SLOAN

APRIL 6

1790

Sat for Mr. Savage, at the request of the Vice-President, to have my Portrait drawn for him.

The Company at the Levee [an informal weekly reception] to day was thin. The day was bad.

PRESIDENT GEORGE WASHINGTON

1921

I have spent almost every afternoon at Knoedler, but today, I jibbed, it was too good a day to stay in. Besides, I feel as if I can't bear compliments and praise another moment. It was wonderful at first, one felt flattered, pleased, amused. The various remarks were entertaining, but they are almost without variety, and in the end one longs not to have to smile the smile of appreciation that will not come off, there seems so little to say in reply to "How wonderful! How clever you are, how living they are, how brave you were, what brutes they look———" I just stand first on one leg and then on the other and look silly and feel worse. If anyone bought anything, or wanted to be done [sculpted], it would be different, but I feel that Knoedlers have generously taken a great deal of trouble and been awfully kind, and gained nothing. People treat my exhibition as a sort of free "Madame Tussaud's" and there the thing ends.

CLARE SHERIDAN

APRIL 7

1776

To-day and last night the commotions in the city begin to be greater; attacks have been made on the little islands, and at the watering place.

BROTHER EWALD GUSTAV SCHAUKIRK

1954

Alan [Hovhaness] comes to discuss music for *The Spook Sonata*. We talk with [abstract expressionist Harry] Jackson about the power of evil. Alan believes that Maya Deren is trying to harm him and is the source of a present illness. He played at a party given by Joe Campbell and felt Maya's presence hostile. Jackson suggests exorcism but the idea of bringing the weight of the church on that hell-bent young woman's head is appalling. Jackson: "This is the disadvantage of a liberal church."

JUDITH MALINA

APRIL 8

1865

Captures and victories every day! Lee is so surrounded that he must either disband his army or surrender....

A young woman here of eighteen is lecturing before large audiences upon reconstruction—another Joan of Arc inspired by self-conceit versus patriotism! I supposed she... wishes to make a nice little sum by giving advice. Advice worth nothing is generally given gratis. These young Yankee ladies are sharp enough to charge for it. What fools people are to go and listen!

MARIA LYDIG DALY

1917

Meyer came at 10 A.M. and looked perfectly wonderful in a cutaway coat, striped trousers, gray hat and gloves, silver & headed [*sic*] cane. I wore my black velvet georgette dress, yellow hat and mink scarf and violets. People stared after us—we made such a handsome couple.

Went automobiling in afternoon with Hans and Dorothy. Over at Pauline's in evening—had packs of fun[.] Hilda giving a leg show dance[.] Meyer calls me his baby doll, his sugar plum[,] his sweetest, his spoiled kid. After Meyer hugged me his head was all perspired—some lover he is!

SARA HOEXTER BLUMENTHAL

APRIL 9

1859

Greet[s] the doctor (when he arrived towards 5) as if nothing were the matter with him. Had a coughing spell & laboured breathing after he arrived—the doctor commenced to-day with the glass inhaler & olive tar. Put a tea [*sic*] spoonful of olive tar in the inhaler & inhale whenever cough or difficulty of breathing or asthma are troublesome either by day or night.... May not (dislodge) the phlegm quite so soon as the medicated paper—but the effect the doctor says is more permanent.

PIERRE MUNRO IRVING

1896

J [James Abercrombie Burden, Jr.] & I have finally settled on the day for our wedding, the sixth of June. How I hope the date will be kind and bless us with a glorious day.... J is going to have all the [Porcellian] Club men as ushers.... At our cooking lesson today Alice Shepard said she would like to live in a respectable tenement house for the first year of her married life and do everything herself: cook, wash, and keep house without a servant. She could stand it a week, her husband possibly three days, and then I told her there would be the saloon or the grave.

FLORENCE ADELE SLOANE

APRIL 10

1834

In some of the wards of the City, Riots of an alarming character have occurred, several persons have been severely injured; police officers and watchmen were the greatest sufferers. The riots nearly all occurred at the sixth ward poll and in the immediate neighborhood. The cause of these was the interference of hot headed politicians from other wards in the politics of that ward. The friends of the Bank of the United States are justly chargeable with the crimes of these riots; for, had they not gone to that poll and used language which was sufficient to arouse the angry feelings of almost any man, had they not employed bullies to fight the Jackson men, these riots could not have occurred and our city would have been saved from the disgrace which now attaches to it.

JAMES CRUIKSHANK

1837

One of the signs of the times is to be seen in the sales of rich furniture, the property of men who a year ago thought themselves rich, and such expenditures justifiable, but are now bankrupt.

Markets continue extravagantly high. Meat of all kinds and poultry are as dear as ever. The farmers (or rather the market speculators) tell us this is owing to the scarcity of corn, but the shad, the cheapness of which in ordinary seasons makes them as long as they last a great resource for the poor, are not to be bought under 75 cents and a dollar. Is this owing to the scarcity of corn, or are the fish afraid to come into our waters lest they may be caught in the vortex of Wall Street? Brooms, the price of which time out of mind has been 25 cents, are now sold at half a dollar. But corn is scarce; poor New York!

PHILIP HONE

APRIL 11

1907

We slept till very late.... A reporter from the *Times* named Mac-Adam called to talk to me of the recent elections to the National Academy of Design in which many of the names (Davies, Lawson, etc.) were defeated for membership. Thought there was a feeling against the "younger" element. I told him that it was resentment of good work; that a young man with "fossilized" ideas had no trouble getting in.

JOHN SLOAN

2003

There was a moment in the mirror at the restaurant, after a particularly intense [rugby] practice, and I had so many aches already, such as sore backs of hands and ouched wrists and aching shoulder and bruised nose and I looked in the mirror, in the bathroom, and saw a spot on my face, and thought to myself is that blood or barbecue sauce?

CHAD THE MINX

APRIL 12

1850

Four years ago there was a dreadful famine in Ireland, and we gave up our parlor, and library and dining room for two evenings to hold a fair for them, and all my schoolmates and our friends made things and we sent the poor Irish people over three hundred dollars.

One Fourth of July, my father got a carriage from Hathorn's stable and took [us] out to see the High Bridge. It is built with beautiful arches, and brings the Croton water to New York....

My mother said when she was young everybody drank Manhattan water. Everybody has a cistern or rain water for washing in the back-yard.... The servants had to go to the corner of Broadway and get the drinking water from the pump there. It was a great bother, and so when my grandfather built his new house at 19 Maiden Lane, he asked the aldermen if he might run a pipe to the kitchen of his house from the pump at the corner of Broadway, and they said he could...and it was the first house in the city to have drinking water in it....

My grandfather had ships that went to Holland and brought skates home to his children.... They used to skate on the Canal that is now Canal Street and on the pond where the Tombs is now, and my mother says that the poor people used to get a rib of beef and polish it and fasten it on their shoes to skate on.

CATHERINE ELIZABETH HAVENS

1861

The sad reality of war is upon us. Not a foreign war, but one between brothers of the South & North. My sympathy has been with the South, who would have been satisfied with the recognition of the just rights in the territories, but now that Mr. Lincoln is our President and lawfully elected, all good citizens must stand by him to see that the laws are enforced & that the U.S. property is everywhere protected whether North or South—Fort Sumter having been attacked, I trust the supremacy of the federal government may be sustained under the gallant Major Anderson. The Extra Heralds were eagerly sought after this evening containing the first news of the battle now raging in Charleston harbour. It has been raining all day and everyone you meet is full of war news & express the hope that Major Anderson may be victorious together with the ships sent to his assistance—in forcing the blockade.

EDWARD NEUFVILLE TAILER

APRIL 13

1788

Sunday. At St. Paul's. After church a mob collected at the Hospital, & destroyed all the anatomical preparations; amounting to several hundred pounds value. The cause was, the frequent digging up of dead bodies for dissection—the students of physic having been shamefully imprudent in taking up bodies of respectable people & without sufficient secrecy.

NOAH WEBSTER

1851

Yesterday under the guard of a file of soldiers Thomas Symm a negro was carried off to Savannah as a slave upon the claim of a man who alleges that he ran from his plantation several years ago. The press of the country unites very generally in describing this as a triumph of Constitution and rejoice like fiends over those who tried to protect the poor wretch from the life of bondage which was impending.

JOHN BIGELOW

1860

Downtown after a solitary breakfast. Walter Cutting called to inform me that I had been unanimously elected by some convention or synod of men about town as one of a board or committee of 20, which is hereafter to take charge of polite society, regulate its interest, keep it pure, and decide who shall be admitted hereafter to "Bachelors' Ball" and other annual entertainments. [The] com[mittee] is perpetual and fills its own vacancies. It is to pass on the social grade of everybody, by ballot—one blackball excluding. Outsiders have no voice and nothing to do but to be thankful for the privilege of paying an initiation fee and annual subscription, if we concede them that privilege. Very funny work for me to be concerned in; but I'm in good company. My colleagues are Judge Pendleton, Cha[rle]s King, Ham[ilton] Fish, Anson Livingston, John Astor, W[illia]m Schermerhorn, and others of the same sort. Probably the whole project will come to nothing.

GEORGE TEMPLETON STRONG

1947

I went to bed at seven a.m. At nine, N. and I have a date with Richard Wright to attend a religious service in a Harlem church. The one he's chosen today is renowned for its spirituals and frequented by poor blacks. And although the ceremony is conducted with the same rituals as in the big middle-class church I visited two months ago, the atmosphere is much more vibrant.

Fearing that our presence here might seem shocking (although in northern churches blacks are very hospitable to visiting whites), Wright introduces himself and explains that we are French friends of his. We are seated in the second row, next to the choir in their long, gray robes. There are three groups of singers: one dressed in gray, another in brown, and another in black. They wear square caps, and their outfit recalls that of English undergraduates. One choir has only men.... There are mostly women in the pews, but also quite a few men. All are in their Sunday best, dressed with joyful fantasy: light suits, silk shirts, flowered hats, new dresses in soft colors. The attentive faces go from cheerfulness to laughter as moving songs or familiar speeches are offered.... These churches are generally poor, the pastors are badly paid, and one of the chief resources is the Sunday collection, so it's natural that it should be surrounded by great solemnity. Women in white with blue sashes pass through the rows, plates in hand; offerings are put in directly or slipped into a small envelope made for this purpose. During this time the choirs sing a spiritual. Once the task is completed, the collectors file in front of the dais, holding the collection plate in one hand, with the other hand behind their backs, and stepping in rhythm to the music in what is really a dance step—a most astonishing moment.

Once again, the usual conversation resumes. Among others, the pastor indicates the presence of Richard Wright. He goes forward, speaks, and is applauded. He introduces me as the citizen of a country that is unaware of racial segregation, and all the dark faces smile at me; I'm quite embarrassed when I must say a few words. Another spiritual is sung, and a new preacher stands before the audience. He's young, with an ardent face and a burning voice; his tone is entirely different from that of the pastor. Using modern images, he recovers the pathos and grandeur of the biblical style. The theme is mystical: above all, each man must seek out Jesus in order to see him, speak to him, and draw on his infinite riches.... "No excursion is successful, no sight-seeing tour is worthwhile if you forget to see Jesus." He speaks in a very marked, breathless rhythm that gathers speed by the minute, stressing sentences by moving his feet, his hands, and his whole body. Sweat runs down his face as his voice rises, chokes, breaks, dies away, and begins again. It's a "hot" improvisation; it's the most authentic jazz.

SIMONE DE BEAUVOIR

APRIL 14

1980

I missed Cosmology class. I completely forgot. I never thought about it the whole day till I saw Kenny and he said, "God is light."

KEITH HARING

APRIL 15

1861

Events multiply. The President is out with a proclamation calling for 75,000 volunteers and an extra session of Congress July 4. It is said 200,000 more will be called within a few days. Every man of them will be wanted before this game is lost and won. Change in public feeling marked, and a thing to thank God for. We begin to look like a United North.... Mayor [Fernando] Wood out with a "proclamation."... It is brief and commonplace, but winds up with a recommendation to everybody to obey the laws of the land. This is significant. The cunning scoundrel sees which way the cat is jumping and puts himself right on the record in a vague and general way, giving the least possible offence to his allies of the Southern Democracy.

GEORGE TEMPLETON STRONG

1865

Broadway, N.Y.—In the forenoon, the news had not more than been rec'd. All Broadway is black with mourning—the facades of the houses are festooned with black—great flags with wide & heavy fringes of dead black, give a pensive effect—Toward noon the sky darkened & it began to rain. Drip, drip, & heavy moist black weather—the stores are all closed—the rain sent the women from the street & black clothed men only remained—black clouds driving overhead—the horror, fever, uncertainty, alarm in the public—Every hour brings a great history event on the wires— at 11 o'clock the new president is sworn—at 4 the murder[er] is [arrested.]

WALT WHITMAN

1912

Up early, and reading in the journalls [*sic*] of how the great steamship *Titanic* hath sunk. Thence and away to my office but learn there all on board are saved, of which I am very glad.

FRANKLIN P. ADAMS

1953

Rented a small apartment on 95 Orchard Street. Rent: $13.95 per month.... As a prelude to the new Five Year plan I decided to quit Brooklyn. So here I am, in the pickle and bagel district.

He slept that night in a real bed. It was a large and soft bed, and as he was thinking about it, he became very conscious of the bed. Look, he thought, when did I last sleep in a decent soft bed, and with the smell of a woman hovering over the sheets? All these years, in barracks, in camps, in hard Spartan army cots, in the fields, and in the woods, on hard wood, on stone floors, on stinking mattresses, like a bum. Now here I lie and with my whole body can feel the softness of the blankets and the cleanliness, which is so soothing, so relaxing, so quieting.

JONAS MEKAS

APRIL 16

1912

Absolutely appalling disaster of the *Titanic.* Sank after four hours. No one is thinking of anything else. Only a 3rd enough life boats though more than required by law. Most of the women & children supposed to be saved [on] the *Carpathia* & a few … fearing over a thousand [lost].

MARJORIE RICHARDS REYNOLDS

APRIL 17

1776

We set sail, & at 10 arrived in the City of New York, our desired Port, on the 17 of April. For about 10 Miles below New York the Passage between the Maine & Long Island was very Narrow. On both sides many very elegant Country Seats, & at Hell Gate a handsome & well-constructed Fort lately built by our People. At Turtle Bay are 4 large & beautifull Stores made for the Use of the King's Stores & Amunition &c. From this Place the Yorkers took a very large Quantity of Bombs, & Shot; but the Enemy had conveyed the Powder away before. Near this Place are several elegant & beautifull Country Seats, Several evacuated by the Tories. I visited the Garden of one Gentleman in which was a Summer House which the Gardener shewed me in which were many curious Flowers, &c.; but the greatest Rarity was Orange, Lime, Pomgranet, & Citron Trees all Bearing Fruit. The Lemons were the largest & best that ever I saw, as also the Oranges, both sweet and sour. One Lime tree had 5 different Sorts of Fruit growing at once besside [*sic*] Blossoms.

On our arrival we found Houses provided for both Officers & Men. Our Reg.ᵗ was barracked in Water Street near to Pecks Slip, & we had 2 Rooms for the officers of our Company in D. Barkleys on the Same street.

Lt. Isaac Bangs

1907

A high wind this morning and the pranks of the gusts about the Flatiron Building at Fifth Avenue and 23rd St. was interesting to watch. Women's skirts flapped over their heads and ankles were to be seen. And a funny thing, a policeman to keep men from loitering about the corner. His position is much sought, I suppose.

John Sloan

April 18

1931

I wonder what's going to happen to these plans for novels and plays. I fly at things as frantically as a neurotic rich wife sails into each new hobby. This damn twitching going on under my skin all the time; Joe being tight so much; everything being so insecure. Fat as a fool and quite without any vestige of youth or attraction any more beyond my sterling character....

I must put more theatrical effect into this new play. Realism is all very well but only to serve the highlights of art. If the theater doesn't give you a thrill—of fate dealing the cards, of the Mounted Police coming, of suspense and second act catastrophe, of third act final rescue or magnificent defeat—then what is it?

Dawn Powell

APRIL 19

1776

I spent the greatest part of my Time in viewing the City, which I found vastly surpassing my Expectations. The City is nearly as populous as the Town of Boston; the Publick Edifices greater in number, yet not in general so grand & Magnificent.... I found the Town, or City, scituated [*sic*] between two Rivers. The one Runing [*sic*] about North, called the North River, is the same which is navigable up as far as Albany; the other River is that which seperateth Long Island from the Continent, and runs Easterly, one part of which is called *Hell Gate* (very metaphorically so called). In the Town we found every street leading from the Water almost stoped with Breast Works built by Gen¹ Lee on his arrival in this Town.... On the South west part of the Town, which is a Point between the two Rivers, is a very strong & costly Fort built by the Kings Troops & many masons men for the Protection of the City from the Enemy.

On the outside of the Fort at the Edge of the wall was a Battery, erected at a vast Expence to the King, built of hewn stone, the outside about ten feet high, the inside filled up to form a plane that the Wall was not more than a foot and a half high. Over this the Cannon were to play; but as so low a wall would not be a sufficient cover for our Men, our People were busily employed in making a Turf Wall upon the stone Wall, & when we arrived had almost finished as compleat a Battery as ever I saw. Several other Fortifications were erected in this Town, which made it tolerably strong & safe against any attacks of the Enemy. From the above mentioned Fort a spacious street running east notherly [*sic*] in a right line, reached without the Town about 1 Mile. In this, near the Fort, is the Equestrian Statue of King George 3ᵈ, a Present from himself to this City. The design was in imitation of one of the Roman Emperors on Horseback. The Man George is represented about ⅓ larger than a Natural Man; the Horse, in proportion, both neatly constructed of Lead guilt [*sic*] with Gold, raised on a Pedestral of white Marble, about 15 Feet high,... the 2 lower feet Stone, the remainder of open worked Iron; the inclosure was oval, containing about ¼ of an acre of beautifull green [Bowling Green]. This, with several Churches and other Elegant buildings on either side of the spacious street, form a most beautifull prospect from the Fort.

Lt. Isaac Bangs

1912

The rescue ship *Carpathia* in last night. The accounts of the appalling accident are worse, fearful and [more] terrible than anything I've read. The band played on deck to the very end.

Marjorie Richards Reynolds

1924

"Mariner" bill failure financially—will not last beyond regular 3 weeks.

Eugene O'Neill

1954

It's lunch time and I am walking down 23rd Street toward Fifth Avenue, thinking where to eat. It's hot, Spring underway. I stop at Schrafft's, a stop I seldom make, it's always so damn crowded, mostly with young secretary types.

I eat my ham on rye bread, and I drink my Schrafft's coffee. I order a baked apple. There is nothing else to do at Schrafft's so I leave it and I walk to the Madison Park. I haven't been there since September. There is nothing interesting there during the winter. But now, I see people again straddling the fences, walking in pairs, sitting on benches—as usual at lunch hour.

Jonas Mekas

APRIL 20

1831

While I was shaving this morning at 8 o'clock I witnessed from the front window an encounter in the street nearly opposite between W[illia]m C. Bryant, one of the editors of the *Evening Post,* and W[illia]m L. Stone, editor of the *Commercial Advertiser.* The former commenced the attack by striking Stone over the head with a cowskin; after a few blows the party closed and the whip was wrested from Bryant, and carried off by Stone. When I saw them first, two younger persons were engaged but soon discontinued their fight. A crowd soon closed in and separated the combatants.

PHILIP HONE

1954

At the White Horse [Tavern], Mike Harrington and his friends talk; most of it is chatter, but it's never the solemn defeatism of the Remo. At the White Horse people seem to have some life outside the bar.

JUDITH MALINA

2005

Emerging, Reborn. I feel better today. My fever is gone, I have just been through five days of sweats, shivers, and visions. Today, while I still have a sore throat, hacking cough, and a disheveled appearance, I feel significantly better than I have felt since early Friday. I am not all the way to good health, but I'm almost there.

It's been an interesting experience, and not one I'd wish on anyone else, but transformative. I haven't spent so much time in bed sleeping, or trying to sleep, in years. I found a deeper level of consciousness (or unconsciousness) while snoozing by my open second story window. So many different sounds echoed across the courtyards of Leonard Street in Brooklyn.

In the early morning I could hear the sounds of birds chirping, and could actually discern different types of bird calls. I don't know what they're saying but they seem to be happy that the weather is nice. I could hear old ladies talking to each other in Italian as they tidied up their back alley gardens, and as I felt the warm breeze across my face I could easily imagine myself in Italy.

VICTOR OZOLS

APRIL 21

1906

With my portfolio and Mr. Chapin's letter of introduction, I called on Russell Sturgis, art writer. A handsome old house opposite Stuyvesant Square, a large parlor in good taste, not tasteful. Mr. Sturgis is a healthy looking old gentleman and received me most kindly. He looked at the etchings with interest. He has the art critic's annoying breadth; likes things I like and things I don't like in art. I spoke of my De Kock etchings and he said he would much like to see them. Invited me to call and show them Tuesday p.m.

JOHN SLOAN

1954

On the rounds in my bandbox clothes, my sparkling disguise, I have no identity at all. I could be a mechanical doll. In the offices the receptionists say: "Try next month"; and on Broadway simple-hearted, ugly men make idiotic pleas for affection and companionship that sink to a beastly lechery if one so much as answers in a monosyllable.

JUDITH MALINA

APRIL 22

1946

Tired. My flu comes back. And it's on shaky legs that I get the first impact of New York. At first glance, a hideous, inhuman city....A few details strike me: that the garbage men wear gloves, that the traffic moves in an orderly fashion without policemen at the intersections, etc., that no one ever has change in this country, and that everyone looks like they've stepped out of a B-film....I am just coming out of five years of night, and this orgy of violent lights gives me for the first time the impression of a new continent. An enormous, 50-foot-high Camel billboard: a G.I. with his mouth wide open blows enormous puffs of *real* smoke. Everything is yellow and red. I go to bed sick in both body and soul, but knowing perfectly well that I will have changed my mind in two days.

ALBERT CAMUS

[Dating inferred from content.]

1954

Lunch with [editor] Bob Linscott, where—surprise—was Faulkner—minute, silent, grinning shyly and secretly at odd times, wracked by back pains. He said that he did not like to put things down, but that he went to his typewriter when a job had to be done and did it. He had just been working three months in Europe with Howard Hawks on a film [*Land of the Pharaohs*] about the building of the pyramids. "The same story he always does," Faulkner explained. But he never goes to the movies. He did not know who Marilyn Monroe was, but he remembered Garbo as beautiful. Faulkner is one of the most withdrawn of men, coming into our world only when I talked about dogs. He has some twenty. His eyes seem hazel. He ate scrambled eggs, coffee, one martini, and sat silent for endless minutes—this silence making our talk seem utterly superfluous. He doesn't seem to read. He exists—drinks—writes. I could not say that he was happy to see me. Later Bob called and said: "Bill was very pleased to see you again."

Leo Lerman

April 23

1861

Everyone's future has changed in these six months last past. This is a terrible, ruinous war, and a war in which the nation cannot succeed. It can never subjugate these savage millions of the South. It must make peace at last with the barbarous communities off its Southern frontier. I was prosperous and well off last Nov[ember]. I believe my assets to be reduced fifty per cent, at least. But I hope I can still provide wholesome training for my three boys. With that patrimony they can fight out the battle of life for themselves. Their mother is plucky and can stand self-denial. I clearly see that this is a most severe personal calamity to me, but I welcome it cordially, for it has shown that I belong to a community that is brave and generous, and that the City of New York is not sordid and selfish.

George Templeton Strong

1946

Wake up with fever. Incapable of going out before noon. A little better when E. arrives. I have lunch with him and D., a Hungarian journalist, in a French restaurant. I realize that I haven't noticed the skyscrapers; they've seemed so natural to me. It's a question of general proportions. And then also you can't live all the time looking up.... Magnificent food stores. Enough to make all of Europe drool. I admire the women in the street, the color of their dresses, and the colors—reds, yellows, greens—of all the taxis which look like insects in their Sunday best. As for the stores selling ties, ... so much bad taste hardly seems imaginable. D. affirms that Americans don't like ideas. That's what they say. I'm not so sure.

ALBERT CAMUS

[Dating inferred from content.]

APRIL 24

1896

To-day I drove all over the lower part of the city. I had not been down to the Battery in thirty years or more. I found the streets clean and I was surprised at the many fine buildings. I was glad to see that all the ugly telegraph poles were gone. What an improvement that is.

ELIZABETH CADY STANTON

APRIL 25

1865

Today President Lincoln's funeral procession passes through the city. The body lies in state in City Hall and some three hundred thousand people, they say, have visited it. I shall not go out to see the show, as the Judge is not at home. I will let the servants go instead; I am sick of pageants. Both yesterday and today all business has been suspended and I read that the 25th of May is to be another fast day. Poor Mrs. Lincoln! Circumstances, verily, make the man. A house a few doors nearer Fifth Avenue opposite to us, having not been put in mourning, was tarred and for two days men have been at work at it. Tomorrow the theaters reopen and then, I suppose, all will be over.

MARIA LYDIG DALY

1975

At 12:00 we rolled up outside a modestly fashionable "brownstone" with a recently restored front, on one of the streets somewhere in the East 60ths. This is the studio of Richard Avedon—by all accounts One of the World's Leading Photographers and He has chosen to photograph no less than us. Python is to be immortalized in the pages of *Vogue*.

Avedon turns out to be a slight, wiry, dark-skinned, bespectacled man, who could be between 25 and 55. Full of vitality and easy charm.

We are dazed from our efforts in NY and our early appearance on ABC and he must have found us a lifeless lot as he made us coffee. But after ten or fifteen minutes of uninspired ideas, he leapt on the suggestion, made by Graham and Terry, that we should be photographed in the nude. The idea sounded no worse and a lot better than putting on silly costumes or funny faces, so it was resolved. We would keep our shoes and socks on, though, and I would wear my hat....

Soon the Python group were a little naked gaggle and Avedon was busy arranging us in a parody of the sort of beautiful person photo where all is revealed, but nothing is shown. So our little tadgers had to be carefully hidden behind the knee of the man in front, and so on, and every now and then Avedon would look through the viewfinder of his Rolleiflex and shout things like "Balls!... balls, Graham, balls."...

We dressed, muttering jokingly among ourselves about how ashamed, how very ashamed, we were of what we had done....

As we walked out onto the sunlit street, I felt slightly high and rather relieved, as though I'd been for an exotic medical check-up.

MICHAEL PALIN

April 26

1897

C—came down for Grant's procession tomorrow, which is to be the largest ever held here.

Susan Bliss

1924

To luncheon and met Will Benét and Nelly [Elinor] Wylie, and asked them to come riding with me, and they elated over the notion of … a ride through Westchester, past Armonk, very pleasant, and Nell made up a lullaby that ended—

> "Nets of silver and gold have we,"
> Said Veedol,
> Venida,
> And Tiz.

Franklin P. Adams

1954

This weekend unflawed performances: no self-mocking laughter, no loss of concentration. I credit the hypnotist.

Judith Malina

April 27

1839

They are going on gloriously in the upturning of the City Bank, and we shall have a second edition of the Griswold Quagmire as soon as a rainy day comes. The Merchants Exchange makes a bog of the other side of the street, so there's nothing to be gained by crossing. Then the Merchants and Union and Manhattan! Heaven help the Wall Streeters.

GEORGE TEMPLETON STRONG

1897

Beautiful, clear and cold today. Papa and I left Mama on the front steps about 10:15 and reached the Union League Club stand at about 11. Here we sat until 12 and watched the crowd. One man's umbrella blew away (there was a high wind) and almost knocked over two peaceable ladies. Lots of hats blew around, and sandwiches were around loose but were not good as the color had come off the Japanese paper and they tasted of it, but I made away with two and some chocolate and maple sugar. C—— made a newspaper vest, he was so cold. I took pictures with pocket Kodak and hope for luck. First came some policemen, then (not in order) the 69th, 72nd, and 7th besides marines and cadets. We stayed until 1:30 o'clock and then came home in the L. [*sic*] Mama did not go out; too big a crowd. Ambulance corps on bicycles. Altogether first class.

SUSAN BLISS

APRIL 28

1946

A trip to Staten Island.... On the way back, in lower Manhattan, an immense geological dig between skyscrapers which stand very close to one another; we advance, overwhelmed by a feeling of something prehistoric. We eat in Chinatown. And I breathe for the first time in a place where I feel the expansive but orderly life that I truly love.

ALBERT CAMUS

[Dating inferred from content.]

APRIL 29

1680

We should have left to-day, but our skipper said he could not obtain his passport. We called upon several persons, and among others, upon the woman who had brought up Illetie, the Indian woman, and had first taken her from the Indians.... This woman, although not of openly godless life, is more wise than devout, although her knowledge is not very extensive, and does not surpass that of the women of New Netherland. She is a truly worldly woman, proud and conceited, and sharp in trading with *wild* people, as well as *tame* ones.... This trading is not carried on without fraud.... She has a husband, which is her second one, who is a papist, I believe.

JASPER DANCKAERTS

1775

The past week has been one of commotion and confusion. Trade and public business was at a stand; soldiers were enlisted; the inhabitants seized the keys of the Custom House; and the arms and powder were taken from the Corporation. Fear and panic seized many of the people, who prepared to move into the country.

BROTHER EWALD GUSTAV SCHAUKIRK

1980

Bianca wanted to roller skate so we went to the Roxy in Thomas Ammann's limo.

ANDY WARHOL

APRIL 30

1789

This is a great, important day. Goddess of etiquette, assist me while I describe it....

The President [George Washington] advanced between the Senate and Representatives bowing to each.... The Vice-President [John Adams] rose and addressed a short sentence to him. The import of it was that he should now take the oath of office as President. He seemed to have forgot half what he was to say, for he made a dead pause and stood for some time, to appearance, in a vacant mood. He finished with a formal bow, and the President was conducted out of the middle window into the gallery, and the oath was administered by the Chancellor....

As the company returned into the Senate chamber, the President took the chair and the Senators and Representatives their seats. He rose, and all arose also, and addressed them.... This great man was agitated and embarrassed more than ever he was by the leveled cannon or pointed musket. He trembled, and several times could scarce make out to read, though it must be supposed he had often read it before. He put part of the fingers of his left hand into the side of what I think the tailors call the fall of the breeches, changing the paper into his [right] hand. After some time he then did the same with some of the fingers of his right hand. When he came to the words *all the world,* he made a flourish with his right hand, which left rather an ungainly impression. I sincerely, for my part, wished all set ceremony in the hands of the dancing-masters, and that this first of men had read off his address in the plainest manner, without ever taking his eyes from the paper, for I felt hurt that he was not first in everything.

WILLIAM MACLAY

1865

[John Wilkes] Booth was tracked, found in a barn, and on his refusal to surrender and attempting to fire [his gun], the barn was set on fire and Booth, attempting to escape, was shot through the head. His last words were that he had done it for the good of his country. Poor, mistaken young man! He killed the best friend of the benighted Southern people. The plot will soon be discovered. It was to assassinate all the heads of the departments; a fiendish scheme! Poor Edwin Booth is ruined by his brother's act. His engagement of marriage is broken, his future as an actor blasted. Many go so far as to declare he should never again appear, and that he should suffer for his brother's fault. I said that he suffered doubly already, first as much as any of us, as a loyal American citizen, and secondly as a son and brother. I thought nothing should be added. The melancholy Dane: he will look and act more naturally than ever! This blow has fallen upon him in the height of his fame.

MARIA LYDIG DALY

May 1

1834

Mr. Astor commenced this morning the demolition of the valuable building on the block fronting Broadway from Barclay to Vesey Street, on which ground his great hotel is to be erected. The dust and rubbish will be almost intolerable; but the establishment will be a great advantage, and the edifice an ornament to the city, and for centuries to come will serve, as it was probably intended, as a monument of its wealthy proprietor.

PHILIP HONE

1955

Joe and I walked downtown crisscross the Square and MacDougal and West Houston toward Battery, crossing or turning whenever we saw sunlight or a curious building.

DAWN POWELL

May 2

1864

A verry fine day. This being the Birth day of the Rushan Emperor we hoisted the Rushan Flag at our Fore and at noon fired a salute of thirty one (31) Guns in honor of the occasion. All the Rushan Ships were gaily deck'd out with Flags and wasted a great quantity of Powder.

WILLIAM B. GOULD

MAY 3

1847

People are not half aware of the benefits of regular bathing—a practice which should be "got into" by every man, woman, and child of the land. The cold bath is best, (winter and summer), for healthy persons—with this proviso: not to bathe in it when the body is chilled, but when it has a healthy glow of warmth. This is an important item. At first, and for those to whom bathing is new, tepid water will be best—soon and gradually to be superseded by water of the natural temperature. Nor is any thing absolutely necessary to a bath, except a pitcher of water in one's room, a sponge and a towel; by using these daily, one will feel better and live longer.

WALT WHITMAN

1947

As in all big cities, people use a lot of drugs in New York. Cocaine, opium, and heroin have a specialized clientele, but there's a mild stimulant that's commonly used, even though it's illegal—marijuana. Almost everywhere, especially in Harlem (their economic status leads many blacks into illegal drug trafficking), marijuana cigarettes are sold under the counter. Jazz musicians who need to maintain a high level of intensity for nights at a time use it readily. It hasn't been found to cause any physiological problems; the effect is almost like that of Benzedrine, and this substance seems to be less harmful than alcohol.

I am less interested in tasting marijuana itself than in being at one of the gatherings where it's smoked. No sooner have I stated my wish than it is granted; American willingness to oblige is truly inexhaustible. Z. is going to join some friends who are "vipers," that is, habitual smokers; they are giving a party today. When he comes to pick me up this evening, he tells me that the gathering began in the middle of the afternoon: these sessions last a long time because marijuana seems to make time speed up. He himself has already smoked one cigarette, though nothing in his demeanor gives any hint of this. And he advises me to smoke one, too—a prudent step for a beginner, since it's impossible to tell how your stomach might react.

I'm astonished to find that Z. is taking me into one of the largest hotels in New York. There is a characteristically respectable clientele in the lobby: old gentlemen in gold-rimmed spectacles, old ladies in flowered hats, all full of the decency and well-to-do morality of America. The elevator takes us to the fifth floor; we knock on the door. A circumspect voice asks, "Who's there?" We give our names; the door is quickly opened and shut again. In the comfortable, overheated room, it smells like a hair salon, with a scent of violets or carnations, an odor of perfume. It's an odd group: a young man in pajamas with girlish gestures; a blonde girl, her hair cut short, with the manners of a young boy; a magnificent black-haired woman with dark eyes; and a light-skinned black man who is, Z. tells me, the most interesting person in the group. He is the master of the house, a dancer by profession, and he never goes out without a revolver in his pocket. The idea that a white man might insult him is so unbearable that he has decided that if it ever happens, he will kill the offending party and then himself. He seems to be smiling and relaxed.

They've all smoked already and are feeling high. They offer me a first cigarette: the taste is bitter, unpleasant. I don't feel anything. They tell me that I haven't swallowed the smoke; you have to inhale as though you were sucking on a straw. I inhale conscientiously; my throat burns. Everyone is looking at me: "So?" Nothing. The young man in pajamas carefully gathers up my ashes: no traces must be left. The blonde crushes a perfume-smoked paper against a light bulb and· perfumes us one at a time; the smell of marijuana must also be masked. The black dancer gives me another cigarette.

"They cost a dollar apiece," he tells me dryly. All right. And I know you have to engage in a complicated strategy to get them. Even if the seller has lots of them in his pockets, he pretends that he must go to the other end of town to find them, so that he can charge more. I apply myself; I do my best. Nothing. The beautiful brunette is sprawled on the sofa, her head in her hands, with a desperate look on her face. "I feel so happy," she says. "So insanely happy." I'm curious about feeling such happiness. I persist—another cigarette. Always nothing. They tell me, "Get up and walk around." I get up and walk straight ahead. It seems that I ought to feel lifted up by angels: the others are floating, they tell me—they're flying. The dancer mimes this flight marvelously, and then he does a kind of "slow-motion" number from the movies; he know [*sic*] how to dance. He looks beatific. The brunette repeats, "So insanely happy," with her eyes full of tears. I try one more time, a last cigarette. All eyes are on me critical and severe. I feel guilty; my throat is burning. I swallow all the smoke, and no angel bothers to lift me from the earth: I must not be susceptible to marijuana. I turn toward the bottle of bourbon. I think that now, for a long time, I'll dread even the lowliest cigarette.

Simone de Beauvoir

May 4

1789

I went pretty early to the post-office to deliver letters. As I came back, met General St. Clair. He seemed desirous of speaking with me; said he had been at my lodgings, and asked me what I thought of the President's new arrangements. It was the first I had heard of them. The President is neither to entertain nor receive invitations. He is to have levee days on Tuesdays and Fridays, when only he is to be seen. I told the General that General Washington stood on as difficult ground as he ever had done in his life: that to suffer himself to be run down, on the one hand, by a crowd of visitants so as to engross his time, would never do, as it would render the practice of business impracticable; [*sic*] but, on the other hand, for him to be seen only in public on state times, like an Eastern Lama, would be equally offensive.

WILLIAM MACLAY

MAY 5

1754

[For] Daniel Bontekou Dr.... [I made] A Cofin for a poor French woman.

JOSHUA DELAPLAINE

1976

And so I am a Pulitzer Prize winner.

NED ROREM

1980

I have not seen anything of Nixon in recent weeks. He has been away; so have I. Alexandra has witnessed some of his fitful sorties—even collided with him the other day as she was running to a taxi—but the neighborhood has been without drama—until, that is, a few days ago, when the Secret Service installed a set of cameras, including one on the wall between the Schlesinger and Nixon houses. I am presumably half-owner of the wall, though I have not had a chance to check my deed; and no one consulted with me about placing a camera on it—especially a camera that appears to be trained at us.

ARTHUR M. SCHLESINGER, JR.

MAY 6

1839

I went on Saturday evening to a meeting of the Kent Club at Mr. David B. Ogden's.... The club consists of judges and lawyers, who meet and sup at each other's houses on Saturday evenings in succession; distinguished strangers are invited and a few laymen citizens, in which last number it has been my good fortune to be frequently included. I have not always been able to attend when invited, but when I have the conversation of these learned "luminaries of the law" has greatly instructed and delighted me. The evening is usually divided equally between wisdom and joviality. Until ten o'clock they talk law and science and philosophy, and then the scene changes to the supper table, where Blackstone gives place to Heidsick, reports of champagne bottles are preferred to law reports, and the merits of oysters *pâtés* and *Charlottes Russe* are alone summed up.

PHILIP HONE

1952

Alan Hovhaness' music addressed to Khaldis, an Eastern miracle piece with four trumpets and gong and piano. The little Cherry Lane [Theater] shook with the ritual reverberations.

John Cage's sonatas encompass the minute detail of an aesthetically successful civilization. Alan's music is a primitive outburst of fear, passion and arrogance. Lucia plays a loose piece—formless, yet nonetheless carefully drawn.

The audience is small but responsive. The Cherry Lane itself has a meaning. It is a place.

JUDITH MALINA

MAY 7

1780

An account that the Marquis De La Fayette is arrived at Boston from old France.

HUGH GAINE

1849

Rehearsed with much care.... My hairdresser told me there would be a good house, for there was—an unusual sight—a great crowd outside. My call came; I had heard immense applause and three cheers for Mr. Clarke in Macduff. I smiled and said to myself, "They mistake him for me." I went on—the greatest applause, as it seemed, from the whole house. I bowed respectfully, repeatedly. It still kept on. I bowed as it were emphatically (to coin an expression for a bow), rather significantly that I was touched by such a demonstration.... At length I became sensible there was opposition, and that the prolongation of the applause was the struggle against it.... At last there was nothing for it, and I said "Go on," and the play, *Macbeth,* proceeded in dumb show, I hurrying the players on. Copper cents were thrown, some struck me, four or five eggs, a great many apples, nearly—if not quite—a peck of potatoes, lemons, pieces of wood, a bottle of asafœtida which splashed my own dress, smelling, of course, most horribly.

WILLIAM MACREADY

[Asafœtida is the extract of a reeking herb also known as "Devil's Dung."]

1921

I have had a good week, quite one of the best since I arrived here. I had an order from Mr. C. to do a bust of Miss Spence for the school. Mrs. C., when she came to talk to me about it, told me that Miss Spence had to be treated as Royalty. Royalty do not alarm me, and

I expected Miss Spence would! But she was far more interesting than that.

Every morning except one Miss Spence had sat to me from 10:15 until 1 o'clock—and we have hardly stopped talking the entire time....I like her big heart [and] her adoration of immature youth....

We have talked a great deal about America, and I felt myself talking to the Scotchwoman in her, not to the American born....

To-day there is an account in the *New York Herald* of Lady Astor in the House pleading for mothers, that they may have at least an equal right to their children, and as Miss Spence pointed out, how strange that a woman from *this* country should have to do it for English women!

CLARE SHERIDAN

MAY 8

1849

Theatrical Riot. Mr. [William Charles] Macready commenced an engagement last evening at the Opera-House, Astor Place, and was to have performed the part of "Macbeth" whilst his rival, Mr. [Edwin] Forrest, appeared in the same part at the Broadway theater. A violent animosity has existed on the part of the latter theatrical hero against his rival, growing out of some differences in England; but with no cause, that I can discover, except that one is a gentleman, and the other a vulgar, arrogant loafer, with a pack of kindred rowdies at his heels. Of these retainers a regularly organized force was employed to raise a riot at the Opera-House and drive Mr. Macready off the stage.... On the appearance of the "Thane of Cawdor," he was saluted with a shower of missiles and rotten eggs, and other unsavory objects.... This cannot end here; the respectable part of our citizens will never consent to be put down by a mob raised to serve the purpose of such a fellow as Forrest.

PHILIP HONE

1935

We go over the business of the book. I think publishers are like obstetricians. There is the same fuss of making you feel what a wonderful little woman you are, and then getting down to the facts about the head size, pelvic bones, etc. They have a decided bedside manner. After all, though, they are right, you must get over the feeling that you are accomplishing God's mission.... However, I feel embarrassed talking of clothing my book, just as though the doctors were talking about an unborn child. "You don't *really* mean to say it's going to walk around on two feet like other children?"

At night, to the theater with Neilsons. I am so tired and dizzy from excitement I can't talk. I am buried down somewhere in myself, the way you are when you're in love, and can only say over and over to myself the things they had said in the office.

ANNE MORROW LINDBERGH

MAY 9

1790

Indisposed with a bad cold, and at home all day writing letters on private business.

A severe illness with which I was seized the 10th of this month and which left me in a convalescent state for several weeks after the violence of it had passed; & little inclination to do more than what duty to the public required at my hands occasioned the suspension of this Diary.

PRESIDENT GEORGE WASHINGTON

1883

I went to school and spoke my piece.... After drawing went all by myself to the swimming school and there I dived for a piece of white marble and I got it lots of times.... After that I went to Bob's house and played cricket for a while and I made 7 or 8 runs. I then went home and wrote my prize composition on the next to the last chapter of *Westward Ho!*

REGINALD FAIRFAX HARRISON

1971

I rang Marlene [Dietrich]'s bell, and soon she opened her door—cautiously—a small, not awake, very, very old person—so old that the creature was sexless—bleary blue eyes, a straight line for a mouth. "Oh, who? What?..." She had obviously forgotten that she'd asked me to lunch. She was plastered—ancient and plastered and very small. I gathered her in my arms. She, fragile, relaxed gratefully. I saw that her hair was thin to baldness on top. And when I held her at arm's length and saw her legs—they were ugly, veins knotted. But somehow, deep within this wreck where not one glimmer of her beauty was visible, the young girl peeped out.... She finally pulled herself together and swiftly cooked a hamburger, made a salad, peas, mashed potatoes—all with careful attention to what I could and could not eat. Thinking of Marlene exhausts me.... We ate in the kitchen, where a wig block, with Marlene's hair upon it, led an active life of its own. "They go their way," she said, poking at the tight blond curls. I could see the future thousands, viewing this *Blonde Venus* apparition, "Isn't she marvelous!" She is. Her restorative powers are tremendous.

LEO LERMAN

MAY 10

1780

Some Prisoners brought in from the Bridge, as well as a few taken by the Wood Cutters about the English Neighborhood.

HUGH GAINE

1837

Extensive news in this morning's paper. The banks (except three) have concluded to stop specie payment!!! Glory to the Old General! Glory to Little Matty [vice president, Martin Van Buren], second fiddler to the great Magician! Glory—ay, and double patent glory—to the experiment, the specie currency, and the all glorious humbugs who have inflicted them on us.

GEORGE TEMPLETON STRONG

MAY 11

1837

A dead calm has succeeded the stormy weather of Wall Street and the other places of active business. All is still as death. No business is transacted, no bargains made, no negotiations entered into; men's spirits are better because the danger of universal ruin is thought to be less imminent, a slight ray of hope is to be seen in countenances where despair only dwelt for the last fortnight, but all is wrapped up in uncertainty.... The fever is broken, but the patient lies in a sort of syncope, exhausted by the violence of the disease and the severity of the remedies.

PHILIP HONE

1971

Marlene came to the Russian Tea Room. She talked about her forthcoming engagements [in Denmark, then England for the queen]: "What should I wear? Which dress? That is the question.... The gold, the feather coat? That is too much, too theatrical. The pear-shaped diamonds, the coat, and the dress gray-pavé? The Danes love it and call it the Electric Eel...." That one, I advised, will look wonderful against the penguin orchestra. Then she told me about her various encounters with Prince Philip. "She [Queen Elizabeth] doesn't like me. She has a be-oo-tee-fool laugh" (Marlene says "beautiful" like no one else, almost crooning it, making it an adornment, a warm cover for herself. She makes it into a precious, cozy word). "When I was at the Café de Paris, the first time, she wanted to hear me and it couldn't be in a theater, so they showed me all the private houses, and I picked Astor's. They all came, and Philip danced with me, dance after dance, and finally I told him he must stop, and he was like a child. Then one time he made jokes and she told him to behave himself. And years ago, when I made a picture with Gabin, there was a big reception at Joinville, in the pouring rain.... I went into the reception. There was Philip, and I said, 'What are you doing here in all this rain...?' I was be-oo-tee-fool in a gray dress by Grès...all tucks and...you know...be-oo-tee-fool...with a big hat...." She gestured the hat into being—a huge, soft swirl haloing her head. "And Philip said, 'I came to see you....' He was so nice.... But he is naughty, very naughty.... No she doesn't like me.... But she has such a be-oo-tee-ful laugh."

LEO LERMAN

MAY 12

1910

... Miss Coates came and after dinner she took [John Butler] Yeats [father of the poet] and Dolly and I to the Wild West at Madison

Square Garden. It was my first seeing of this greatly famed show. There is too much to see and the thing though probably done as well as can be is not very convincing to "grown ups." I'd like to be a little boy and see it. A huge light rubber ball used for equestrian football between four Indians and four cowboys was the feature that excited me most. I wished the Indians to win—they did not. The rest of the American Audience seemed pleased. Buffalo Bill is a stiff old puppet but as he advertised this as his farewell season he affected me as a pathetic passing figure. He had on the reddest red shirt in the whole aggregation of gaudy togs.

JOHN SLOAN

MAY 13

1831

The greatest equality seems to prevail between those who occupy very different positions in society.

The authorities seem extraordinarily approachable. On the thirteenth of May, Mr. Morse, a judge at Cherry Valley, introduced us to the Governor of New York, who was living in a boarding house and received us in the parlor without any sort of ceremony whatsoever. Mr. Morse assured us that everyone could always do the same as we had done.

ALEXIS DE TOCQUEVILLE

1997

It is the loveliest day of the year, I have been married a month, and everything is birdsong apart from the jackhammers that are ripping through the foundation of a building next door. I fetch a Tab from the refrigerator. People grimace when they hear I drink Tab in the morning, but that first can of the day tastes sharp and fruity and has the added benefit of eating the plaque right off my teeth. The kitchen is in a shambles. In a moment of grandiosity, I volunteered to furnish the cake for the wedding of my wife's best friend, ... and my education in baking has turned our small Manhattan apartment into something out of "Independence Day" after the aliens have moved on. I am on my eighth trial cake ... [and am] closing in on a final recipe—a golden, white-chocolate butter cake with lemon and raspberry mousseline buttercream. The bad news is that I don't know what will happen when I multiply the recipe by a factor of 10. ...

At lunch time, my lovely new wife, Rachel, and I head to look for a bigger apartment away from the jackhammers. We'd like to move to Park Slope, Brooklyn, where people pushing baby carriages make nice-nice with hand-holding lesbian couples. Dreaming of a more civilized place to raise my children, I swerve to avoid a cab that stops short, ... whereupon a bicyclist calls me a cock and accuses me of trying to kill him. Meaning to explain that I had narrowly averted an accident and to inquire after his welfare, I say instead, "Fuck you, asshole, I wish I had killed you." Rachel finds my behavior disturbing and wonders if I see too many violent movies. I am convinced it is the sugar from all those wedding cakes, or possibly the Tab.

DAVID EDELSTEIN

MAY 14

1844

I have been roaming far and wide over this island of Mannahatta. Some portions of its interior have a certain air of rocky sterility which may impress some imaginations as simply *dreary*—but to me it conveys the sublime. Trees are few; but some of the shrubbery is exceedingly picturesque. Not less so are the prevalent shanties of the Irish squatters. I have one of these *tabernacles* (I use the term primitively) at present in the eye of my mind. It is, perhaps, nine feet by six, with a pigsty applied externally, by way both of portico and support. The whole fabric (which is of mud) has been erected in somewhat too obvious an imitation of the Tower of Pisa. A dozen rough planks, "pitched" together, form the roof. The door is a barrel on end. There is a garden, too; and this is encircled by a ditch at one point, a large stone at another, a bramble at a third. A dog and a cat are inevitable in these habitations; and, apparently, there are no dogs and no cats more entirely happy.

EDGAR ALLAN POE

1953

Agee's smile in the hazy dawn on King Street on the stoop of his little red house.

This summery afternoon on the grass I recall it over and over, with the kisses. He is a balm to my cringings; he almost trusts me.

JUDITH MALINA

MAY 15

1776

Continued very Ill with the Boils. The Doctor visited me several Times; sat up about 1/2 my Time.

LT. ISAAC BANGS

1831

Thus far the Americans seem to us to carry national pride altogether too far. I doubt whether is it possible to draw from them the least truth unfavourable to their country. Most of them boast about it without discernment and with an assertiveness that is disagreeable to strangers and that shows but little intelligence. In general it seems to me that there is much of the *small town* in their attitude and that they magnify objects like people who are not accustomed to seeing great things.

What seems clear to me at present is that this country shows the attainment of outward perfection by the middle classes, or rather the whole society seems to have melted into a middle class. No one seems to have the elegant manners and the refined courtesy of the high classes in Europe. On the contrary, one is struck at first by something both vulgar and disagreeably uncultivated. But at the same time no one is what in France one might call *ill bred*. All the Americans whom we have encountered up to now, even the simplest *shop salesman*, seem to have received, or wish to appear to have received, a good education. Their manners are grave, deliberate, reserved, and they all wear the same clothes.

ALEXIS DE TOCQUEVILLE

1842

Sally hatched another bird.

AUGUSTUS VAN HORNE ELLIS

1852

Thursday evening.... Ellie and I went off to 78 26th [Twenty-sixth] St[reet] and had a private interview with Mrs. Fish and her knocking spirits.... The knockers are much talked of now, from Edmonds' extraordinary publications in the *Shekinah*. One of his two articles is a mere rhapsody or parable, very obscure and ill-written, but the other is meant to be a statement of facts, a vision of Heaven and Hell in which Benjamin Franklin and William Penn and Sir Isaac Newton and the late Mrs. Edmonds appear and express their views. Sir Isaac informs the Judge that he made a great mistake about the Law of Gravitation and the Judge adds a note stating that he had been convinced that it was so for a great many years.... I suppose the vision is a tolerably faithful record of a vivid waking dream produced by opium, drink and mental excitement.

GEORGE TEMPLETON STRONG

MAY 16

1851

Heard Jenny Lind Wednesday night with Ellen. As much pleased as I expected to be, and no more. All that I heard her sing was overloaded with *fiorituri* and foolery, marvelously executed, but I always find that sort of thing a bore. The low and middle notes of her voice are superb, and the high notes as good as such notes can be, but she runs too much on music written for the altitudes. No doubt she does it with perfect ease, but that don't make it the pleasanter to hear. A man who could walk on his head as comfortably as on his feet would be a fatiguing person to look at, if he abused his faculty of locomotion and was habitually upside down. The lady's personal appearance took me much by surprise. None of her portraits do her any justice. She is not pretty nor handsome, nor exactly fine-looking, but there's an air about her of dignity, self-possession, modesty, and goodness that is extremely attractive.

GEORGE TEMPLETON STRONG

MAY 17

1907

In the evening, after dinner, Dolly and I walked out to Miner's Eighth Avenue Theatre and found all the reasonable [*sic*] priced seats were sold out. It is "Amateur Night" and we declined to spend more than 50¢ each on places. So we walked out Broadway, calling on [the Albert] Ullmans, ... but they have moved away. On our way back [to] Sixth Avenue, we stopped in the Manhattan Theatre which is soon to be torn down for some of the underground railroad work, and upon the stage where once appeared Mrs. Fiske, we saw a cheap (10 cents) moving picture show.

JOHN SLOAN

MAY 18

1842

Both [Sally's hatchlings] dead. Dick [her mate] killed them.

AUGUSTUS VAN HORNE ELLIS

1893

I am much worked up over the infamous Geary bill against the admission of the Chinese into the United States. How my blood boils over these persecutions of the Africans, the Jews, the Indians, and the Chinese. I suppose the Japanese will come next. I wonder if these fanatical Christians think that Christ died for these peoples, or confined his self-sacrifice to Saxons, French, Germans, Italians, etc.?

ELIZABETH CADY STANTON

MAY 19

1854

Ex President [Millard] Fillmore is at present in town and is receiving the hospitalities of the city. We proposed visiting the Chrystal [*sic*] Palace this evening and if my head had felt strong enough I should have been most happy to have gone … to spend a few hours in the company of the "President who did his Duty." Instead of which I went to the Gymnasium.

EDWARD NEUFVILLE TAILER

1953

King Street is one of those dark, quaint vestiges of old New York and the route to it from the café is dank with garbage pails and "the yellow smoke that curls."

The room on the first floor floods the street white.

It is fearsomely bright.

Inside, Agee sits at his typewriter acting out each sentence before he writes it. His face moving to the rhythm.

I watch for a long time before he sees me through the window and lets me in.

JUDITH MALINA

1958

Oh this doorless flat, everyone's perpetual awareness of everyone else. It is like having no eyelids. At this moment Matilda is vacuuming the sitting-room (why at this hour?). If rays of hatred could strike her body through the archway that opens out from this parody of a library into the sitting-room, then dead at this instant would she fall. But who the hell do I think I am—Proust?—needing a cork-lined room to write a masterpiece when I am only scribbling in this diary. Are my susceptibilities so exquisite? What would I do if my "dream children" were crying and shouting all around me? A crotchety old bore I am becoming. I have been reading *Justine* by Durrell. It depends on the mood—if you are irritated it will irritate you and you will say it is all shreds and patches of mysticism, aestheticism, and mandarinism. But wait—let the ingredients settle and the brew is seductive, disturbing, with strong, rancid flavours. Now as Popski barks I hear Matilda say in her plaintive high voice, "When he and I are alone together he is never like this, never barks. It is funny, very funny," and she gives a wild pipe of mirthless laughter. She is developing a mania for Popski and a sort of jealousy of us in competition for his love.

CHARLES RITCHIE

May 20

1842

Shot a cat dead, dead, dead.

AUGUSTUS VAN HORNE ELLIS

1925

Called up Essie Robeson about Paul's records. Lunch in alone. After lunch I went to the bank & then up Madison Avenue to Bloomingdale's for records.... On 59th St. met [Miguel] Covarrubias. We went together to Marconi's for some Blues & he walked home with me.... At ten Rita Romilly arrived to tell me that she is having trouble with her family because she knows Negroes.

CARL VAN VECHTEN

1948

No word from Scribner's. Their silence and businesslike judicious patience is driving me crazy with tension, worry, expectation, disappointment—everything. And the novel is yet unfinished, really, and the time has come to start typing it and straightening it out. What a job in this weary life of mine, this lazy life. But I'll get down to it. The news that Jesse James is still alive is very thrilling news to me, and my mother too, but we've noticed that it doesn't seem to impress the New York world at all—which does bear out, in its own way, what I say about New York, that it is a haven for European culture and not American culture. I don't get personally mad at these things any more, because that is overdoing things in the name of culture and at the expense of general humanity, but still, I get personally mad at those who scoff at the significance of Jesse James, bandit or no, to the regular American with a sense of his nation's past.

JACK KEROUAC

MAY 21

1910

Dolly donned her best looking clothes and went to join the Socialist women and the Suffrage Party ladies in a parade and protest
meeting at Union Square. I started out soon after but missed seeing
the parade. Dolly told me that it was all fine. Each of the Socialist women wore a red sash and they carried the much feared Red
Banner of the Party. The color of the Suffrage Party, as they called
themselves, is yellow. I stood through showers and listened to the
speeches of the women. Dr. Shaw, Mrs. Blatch, Miss Clark, Mrs.
Carrie W. Allen (Socialist) and others. They spoke well it seemed
to me, though of course I was already of their belief that women
should have the vote. After the regular speeches Mrs. Blatch and
Dr. Shaw answered questions from the crowd. Very clever replies
they gave and I think many a man in the crowd (which grew larger
as the rain had stopped) got a better opinion of them in this rag-
ging ordeal.... I got in a little hot worded row with a man who was
ridiculing the women, no bloodshed.

JOHN SLOAN

MAY 22

1947

Today I arrived by train in New York City, which I'd never seen
before, walked through the grandeur of Grand Central Terminal,
stepped outside, got my first look at the city and instantly fell in
love with it. Silently, inside myself, I yelled: *I should have been born
here!*

EDWARD ROBB ELLIS

MAY 23

1797

Very fine weather. Read *King* with the boy. Read "Fable of the Bees." ... "Passions may do good by chance, but there can be no merit but in the conquest of them."

WILLIAM DUNLAP

1900

I am told that the women in their clubs are wild over progressive euchre parties, where they gamble and drink cocktails. I ask myself if the young mothers who participate in these vices are aware of the fact that they are making gamblers and drunkards of the next generation? During the nine months of prenatal life, they are stamping every thought and feeling of their minds on the plastic beings to whom they are giving life and immortality.

ELIZABETH CADY STANTON

MAY 24

1790

This was mess-day, and I went at half-past three and found the company already seated and the dinner almost eaten up. I could not stay long, as we had an appointment with [Thomas] Jefferson, the Secretary of State, at six o'clock. When I came to the Hall, Jefferson and the rest of the committee were there. Jefferson is a slender man; has rather the air of stiffness in his manner; his clothes seem too small for him; he sits in a lounging manner, on one hip commonly, and with one of his shoulders elevated much above the other; his face has a sunny aspect; his whole figure has a loose, shackling air. He had a rambling, vacant look, and nothing of that firm, collected deportment which I expected would dignify the presence of a secretary or minister. I looked for gravity, but a laxity of manner seemed shed about him. He spoke almost without ceasing. But even his discourse partook of his personal demeanor. It was loose and rambling, and yet he scattered information wherever he went, and some even brilliant sentiments sparkled from him. The information which he gave us respecting foreign ministers, etc., was all high-spiced. He had been long enough abroad to catch the tone of European folly. He gave us a sentiment which seemed rather to savor of quaintness: "It is better to take the highest of the lowest than the lowest of the highest." Translation: "It is better to appoint a *chargé* with a handsome salary than a minister plenipotentiary with a small one."

WILLIAM MACLAY

1883

Today is the celebrated day of the opening of the Brooklyn Bridge.... I got excused [from school] and cut down to the City Hall on the "L" road and then went to the opening of the Brige [*sic*] and showed my ticket ... and got a place to stand in but no seat. After [waiting] about ½ an hour I got a chair and placed it by the reporters' tables. I had a splendid place there.... The president came over with all his cabinet and the governor with all his staff.... [Brooklyn mayor, Seth Low's] speech was by far the most interesting. He was very young and spoke very well. Then Mr. J. Levy played a coronet solo ... and he was applauded so much that he wanted to keep it up, but Mr. Hewitt wanted to make his oration ... At last the coronet stopped and Mr. Hewitt commenced to talk about New York and its beauties [200] years ago and it was so deep that I left. I had an awful struggle to get through the crowd ... got my dinner and Bob came here and we went downtown on the top of a stage. We were a little too late but we saw most of the fire works. They weren't half what I thought they would be but it was fun.

REGINALD FAIRFAX HARRISON

1907

Walked today, and, at a distance, shadowed a poor wretch of a woman on 14th St. Watched her stop to look at billboards, go into Five Cent Stores, take candy, nearly run over at Fifth Avenue, dazed and always trying to arrange hair and hatpins. To the Union Square Lavatory. She then sits down, gets a newspaper, always uneasy, probably no drink as yet this day. My study is interrupted by Davis, who, satchel full of "Gum Lax" and accessory advertising, comes by with one of his stockholders in the Gum Lax Company, a Mr. Kendall. Walked up Broadway home.

JOHN SLOAN

MAY 25

1777

All Prisoners paraded in hall: supposed to look for deserters.

JOHN FELL

1777

Mr. [Joseph] Brewer and I crossed the East River and took a view of the fortifications made by the Rebels upon Long Island. A fort above the Ferry called Fort Sterling, which commands the city of New York, appears to be a place of strength, but we could not get admittance into it. About a quarter of a mile from Fort Sterling is another Fort called Cable Hill or Mutton Pie Battery by the Sailors. It is a small round Fort but very strong.... When the Rebels were defeated on this Island on the 28th of August last, great numbers of them were killed in attempting to cross a tide-mill dam at low water to get to this Fort, but they stuck fast in the mud and were either killed by our people or drowned at High Water, saw the remains of them sticking up their knees and elbows in the mud.

NICHOLAS CRESSWELL

1917

On an omnibus to the city, and near 53rd Street, a gust of wind took my hat off, and it blew into the street, and I got off, and picked it up, but the omnibus had gone, so I walked to my office, as I had no money soever [*sic*].

FRANKLIN P. ADAMS

1958

One importance of living in the Village for a writer is that it keeps him more fluid generally—more *au courant* with the life around him. For a historical novelist it might not be good—constant struggle between contemporary life and a set dead pattern.

DAWN POWELL

MAY 26

1854

The great eclips came off this afternoon shortly after four o'clock according to announcement in the newspapers.... Sun eclipsed [visible]...very warm at about 20 minutes before 3 this morning saw a black streek cross the sky in the shape of a rainbow but black...a great eclips[e] of the moon tonight. Total darkness. She is somewhat obscured from sight by the flying clouds.... There is a comet vesible [*sic*] and bright in the n. west in the evening and early morning.

JAMES FRANCIS BROWN

1934

At the Chinese dentist (Dr. Wing) he keeps the radio going full blast as he drills. Across the street the Brevoort porters in blue overalls sweep the *terrasse* and prepare for the big long Saturday lunch, though it is misting and people will probably rush to the

Lafayette for good food rather than open chill air. The radio announces "Martial law in Bolivia! Strike in Bolivia! Armament discussion in Japan! Labor riots in Toledo; three killed! Labor riots in New Orleans!" Finally it switches into "The Goody Hour." "Let's all pretend"—as good a solution to the situation as any.

DAWN POWELL

1972

Back in the city and struck by the agreeability of being again among possessions. Thirty years a gypsy, I'm thrilled now by ownership. Others, they say, shed facts in favor of ideas as they age, while I grow increasingly superficial—though why superficial?—and life is a list. *Je tiens aux objets,* especially the paintings by Joe Brainard, the Janes Freilicher and Wilson, Léonid [Berman], Cocteau, Alvin Ross, Tom Prentiss, Marie Laure [de Noailles], Rosemarie Beck and Norris Embry. But there's a high value to the letters and manuscripts and books and deep blue kitchenware too.

NED ROREM

MAY 27

1844

When you visit Gotham, you should ride out the Fifth Avenue, as far as the distributing reservoir, near Forty-third Street, I believe. The prospect from the walk around the reservoir is particularly beautiful. You can see, from this elevation, the north reservoir at Yorkville; the whole city to the Battery; with a large portion of the harbor, and long reaches of the Hudson and East rivers. Perhaps even a finer view, however, is to be obtained from the summit of the white, light-house-looking shot-tower which stands on the East river, at Fifty-fifth Street or thereabouts.

A day or two since I procured a light skiff, and with the aid of a pair of *sculls* (as they here term short oars, or paddles) made my way around Blackwell's Island, on a voyage of discovery and exploration. The chief interest of the adventure lay in the scenery of the Manhattan shore, which is here particularly picturesque. The houses are, without exception, *frame*, and antique. Nothing very modern has been attempted—a necessary result of the subdivision of the whole island into streets and town-lots. I could not look on the magnificent cliffs, and stately trees, which at every moment met my view, without a sigh for their inevitable doom—inevitable and swift. In twenty years, or thirty at farthest, we shall see here nothing more romantic than shipping, warehouses, and wharves.

Trinity Church is making rapid strides to completion. When finished, it will be unequalled in America, for richness, elegance, and general beauty. I suppose you know that the property of this Church is some fifteen millions, but that, at present, its income is narrow (about seventy thousand dollars, I believe) on account of the long leases at which most of its estates are held. They are now, however, generally expiring.

EDGAR ALLAN POE

1925

At 4 o'clock Zora Neale Hurston comes in to talk [with] me, a bright, rangy, intelligent Negro personality. She stays till six. I have dinner alone.

CARL VAN VECHTEN

1972

Flying to New York to research my Wilhelm Reich piece for *The New Yorker* I buy and read Cecil Beaton's latest book of diaries. How lucky—in this one sense—he is to be queer and unmarried and thus constrained to use a diary as the receptacle for his outer life and inner thoughts. In marriage the partners share the outer life, which thus goes unrecorded, and leak away their inner thoughts to each other and probably oblivion. Yet (writing this halfway across the Atlantic) I would not swap [wife] Kathleen for the authorship of a masterpiece.

KENNETH TYNAN

MAY 28

1851

Weather pleasant. On duty. Opened office at 7½ O'clock—then went through Grand, Broom, Spring, Elm, Mulberry, Mott & Elizabeth streets = notifying the junk and second hand dealers to get out licenses = I went to the Dentist. he made another attemp [*sic*] to get my tooth out but was unsuccessful = in consequence of my severe sufferings from Neuralgia I went up & saw Doct Harris—he ordered me to take a teaspoon of mixture composed of 1 oz of tinct = Valere [*sic*] & 1 oz of tinct of Genee…3 times a day—until my gums were well enough to have my teeth extracted—as it was impossible to cure me until they were out he advised me to avoid exertion & excitement. He said I had better remain home for a few days. I went home took the medicine = 5 o'clock I came to the office and remained until 7 O'clock = & went home.

INSPECTOR WILLIAM H. BELL

1859

He slept very well last night from ½ past 11 to ½ past 12.…He woke with disturbing shortness of breath and a sort of hallucination about [a Miss Coldford Jones] as if he were by her side & he had some how or other got to take care of her—could not rid himself of the impression (it could not be the effect of his sleeping potions—cannabis or [illeg.] as he had not had recourse to either).…I made light of the strangeness of the circumstances as if I in a sudden starting from sleep or dream had been consumed in a similar peculiarity of which I could not readily divert myself.... This peculiarity [was] no doubt the cause of him of misgiving about his mind—as if his sanity was threatened.

PIERRE MUNRO IRVING

1872

Inflammatory calls having appeared in the German Press, and our Men waylaid by the strikers, a general Commotion takes place among, [*sic*] they send a Committee and also demand to reduce daily labor from ten to eight hours at same wages as heretofore, and 20% advance for piecework. Agreeable to previous understanding with Albert he tells them to assemble at 8 A.M. the next morning. At L.K. in evening. Before that note down 8 points on which to speak to our men.

WILLIAM STEINWAY

1971

I am going to have a press conference next Tuesday at the end of this Memorial Day weekend to set in motion the machinery that can free New York City and establish it as its own state. We're moving immediately because there is no more time. And we're taking this course because we have to organize the city as its own entity so that people can fight together instead of each group fighting for its own little packages, as has long been the case. After all, we're all in this mess together. The legislature oppresses *all* New Yorkers....

The idea to make New York City a state, in case you didn't know, is not original with me. There's been a long struggle for more "home rule," which, although it hasn't focused on statehood, has sought to get us more control over taxes, services and decision-making. Statehood was first proposed by the Mayor of New York in 1861; it was later advocated by such people as William Randolph Hearst and by William F. Buckley in his campaign for Mayor in 1965. Most people, however, will remember the statehood idea as it was first put forth in Norman Mailer's campaign for Mayor in 1969. He gave the idea some pzazz, but not enough people took it seriously.

BELLA ABZUG

1982
I've just had a couple of days with a fellow by the name of Jim Sleeper, who is writing a piece for the *Village Voice*. He was so pleasant that I lapsed into enjoying myself instead of giving "I love Abe Lincoln" type replies. We'll see how it comes out.... I was reminded [of] my "turtle" story.... Earl Andrews, patrician, white-thatched, elegant rich Virginian and a client of our law firm, patronizing me—a young lawyer—at lunch as the son of "immigrants": "Isn't that nice. Even someone like you can make it to this great City, and eat with the most successful people." Then asking for a clam in his clam juice and giving me a lecture on how that ensures "freshness." And a burst of laughter from everybody at the table but Andrews when I ordered "turtle soup—with a turtle in it!" Sometimes I think the best thing about the past is 20 stories like the turtle story.

MARIO CUOMO

MAY 29

1781
This day are in form'd by people from Newyork that there is New Preposals to the United States for peace, what they are [we] can't yet learn, but am quite sure Nothing Short of Independancy.

JEREMIAH GREENMAN

1856
No new vagaries from the wild men of the South since yesterday.... A few fine specimens have given them a prestige the class don't deserve. We at the North are a busy money-making democracy

comparatively law-abiding and peace-loving, with the faults…
appropriate to traders and workers. A rich Southern aristocrat who
happens to be of fine nature, with the self-reliance and high tone
that life among an aristocracy favors, and culture and polish from
books and travel strikes us … as something different from ourselves,
more ornamental and in some respects better.… Thus a notion has
got footing here that "Southern gentlemen" are a high-bred chival-
ric aristocracy, something like Louis XIV's noblesse, … very gallant
and generous, regulating themselves by "codes of honor" (that are
wrong, of course, but very grand); not rich, but surrounded by all
the elements of real refinement. Whereas I believe they are, in fact,
a race of lazy, ignorant, coarse, sensual, swaggering, sordid, beggarly
barbarians, bullying white men and breeding little niggers for sale.

GEORGE TEMPLETON STRONG

MAY 30

1851

The persons residing in the vicinity of 17th St. & Avenue A. complained to me of a large Pond of stagnated water situated on the
north side of 17th Street about 120 feet east of Avenue A containing a number of carcasses of Dogs and other dead animals. This
pond is not only detrimental to the public health but I think its
dangerous to the lives of our citizens, as within the last year five
persons have been drowned in it. The Pond is on the average 9 ½
feet deep, in some 15 feet. The water is on a level with the side walk
and a person going along their [*sic*] of a dark night is liable to walk
in it & drown before assistance could reach him.

INSPECTOR WILLIAM H. BELL

1862

The South seems to be desperate, and horrible atrocities are committed. Stragglers from our army are found tied by their feet to the trees with their throats cut, and it seems that what was said of their barbarities at Manassas after the battle of Bull Run was only too true, that they did boil the flesh and carry away the bones of our poor soldiers as trophies, their boasted chivalry rivaling [*sic*] the Indians, exceeding them even in barbarity.

MARIA LYDIG DALY

1925

Presents from Marinoff arrive, from London, 3 pairs of pajamas, 4 shirts, 15 ties, many of them Liberty.... Then to The Nest... & the gorgeous new girl who is a marvellous dancer, does the Charleston in slow motion.

CARL VAN VECHTEN

[Van Vechten's wife was the actress Fania Marinoff.]

MAY 31

1797

The weather has become fair. I had an oppertunity for the first time this spring to observe the song of the Cat bird, which tho not so sweet or so varied as that of the ground thrush (*turdus rufus*) is yet charmingly melodious. I have seen the Cat bird repeatedly this spring but it has always been mute.

WILLIAM DUNLAP

JUNE 1

1872

Meeting of nearly all the pianomakers.... After some sharp debates we resolve unanimously to hold out for ten hours daily labor, and leave the Question of Wages to each pianomanufacturers [*sic*]. One of the evening papers has the report, and the workmen resolve in the evening to hold out for the eight hour system. At home in evening it rains hard for several hours.

WILLIAM STEINWAY

1939

Donald Ogden Stewart is a really funny man. I warned him that the mint juleps he ordered at Longchamps would be all ice as he applied himself to the straw. "That's all right," he said. "I'm blowing back in a couple of drinks I had last night." We congratulated him on the deft way he wove in and out of parliamentary rules....

Stewart said he had never been anything but dazed by Roberts' Rules of Order. In fact, Roberts must have been a nasty little man. He thought Mrs. Roberts must have had a terrible life with him. He thought he would write Mrs. Roberts' Rules of Order. He surmised that Mrs. Roberts had spent all her life waiting for a second.

DAWN POWELL

JUNE 2

1975

Erica Jong to lunch in the Rose Room [of the Algonquin]—in coloring, deeply blond, like certain *mittl*-European peasant girls. She seems plump and open-faced and should have sported an enormous length of hair twisted neatly into a huge braid and wrapped around her circular head.... I liked her and we fell into ... a kind of "mutuality:" Henry Miller ("He's one of my 3 literary godfathers." I am also one now.) Colette (One of her gods. She is about to write an introduction to her short pieces.) So, we bated—always in the middle of any topic—with a seemingly complete understanding, but a kind of wariness—at least I felt that.

Stockard Channing arrived (she was coming to lunch at 2:30). They overlapped for a time, talking movie-making and Colette.... She is highly literate, educated, well-dressed, rapidly alert and funny—a dark-eyed, shrewd, life-loving girl. . . . She seems dizzy, but she is not. She [is] dish-faced, but a tight animation, a constant play of intelligence brightens the ovoid of her face. I liked her. She tells stories better than Erica. Erica is a good listener—sort of cannibalistic—and she has a touch of somnambulism, but this is only a screen. So, ... I had a splendid, long, very New York time.

Leo Lerman

June 3

1873

Visited this aft[ernoon] the "Metropolitan Museum of Art" in the late Mrs. Douglas Cruger's palazzo [on] West 14th St[reet]. The Cesnola collection of antiquities from Cyprus is interesting and large. Some of the glass vessels are exquisitely colored with iridescence from partial decomposition or disintegration of the surface.... Some of these things are costly and curious. The specimens of early printing are good (there is a Caxton among them!)...Art treasures (so called) are evidently accumulating in New York, being picked up in Europe by our millionaires and brought home. This collection promises very well indeed. Twenty years hence it will probably have grown into a really instructive museum.

GEORGE TEMPLETON STRONG

1948

Woke feeling nerve-shattered and hating everything to do with New York. Tea-cum-champagne with Gertie [Lawrence], Ray Massey, Beattie [Lillie], Mike Redgrave, etc. plus *Life* photographer.

NOËL COWARD

JUNE 4

1779

I was so indisposed by a Cold, small Fever, and an aching blind Pile as to be obliged to excuse myself from a public Dinner at the Governor's. He would not take the first Excuse and wrote a Letter insisting upon my Appearance, if but Half an Hour, to defeat the Malice of my Enemies. I was obliged to tell him in the 2d letter that I could not set up in Company with Decency under a Disease which permitted me only to walk or lay down.

WILLIAM SMITH

1844

One of the truest curiosities of Gotham is the great raree-show of Messieurs Tiffany, Young, and Ellis, Broadway, at the corner of Warren. They are very tasteful and industrious importers of the various fancy manufactures of France, England, Germany, and China. Their warehouses are, beyond doubt, the most richly filled of any in America; forming one immense *knicknackatory* of *virtu*. The perfumery department is especially rare. I notice, also, particularly, a beautiful assortment of Swiss osier-work; chess-men—some sets costing five hundred dollars; paintings on rice-paper, in books and sheets; tile for fencing ornamental grounds; fine old bronzes and curiosities from the ancient temples; fillogram [*sic*] articles, in great variety; a vast display of bizarre fans; ranging, in price, from sixpence to seventy-five dollars; solid carved ebony and "landscape-marble" chairs, tables, sofas, &c.; apparatus for stamping initials on paper; Berlin iron and "*artistique*" candle-sticks, taper-stands, perfume-burners, *et cetera, et cetera.*

EDGAR ALLAN POE

JUNE 5

1872

I rise at 6 A.M. dress quickly, proceed to the factory,... find Capt. Gunner with 40 Policemen there and an immense crowd of Men in front on 53^d street who yell at every man who enters the factory. It is raining. At 7½ A.M. I tell Capt. Gunner to drive away the crowd which is done without force. At 10 A.M. I meet Albert at Steinway Hall, tell him, he proceeds uptown, have 300 policemen in factory all day, feed them also the Captains at Alberts house. No further trouble this day.

WILLIAM STEINWAY

1935

On 14th Street and 6th Avenue—Theatre Union, line-forming of the Comrades. They stood, jostling each other, eager to grab each other's seats, to make each other as uncomfortable as possible, blow smoke in each other's faces, step on each other's toes, trip over each other's knees. Let us all work together and let us all make each other as uncomfortable as possible.

DAWN POWELL

JUNE 6

1749

RUM, a brandy prepared from the sugar-canes, and in great use with all the *English North American* colonies, is reckoned much wholesomer than brandy, made from wine or corn. (...chiefly owing to the balsamic quality it gets from the sugar...) In confirmation of this opinion, they say, that if you put a piece of fresh meat into rum, and another into brandy, and leave them there for some months, that in the rum will keep as it was, but that [in] the brandy will be quite eaten, and full of holes.

PETER KALM

1910

Made an anti-Roosevelt cartoon which I will take to the *Call.* This took up the better part of an afternoon. Davis came to dinner by invitation. He tells us that he is doing considerable work for Borden's Milk Co. in the way of writing advertisements. He is prospering. Says that he believes in all the ideas of Socialism but has made up his mind to get money if he can. Deliberately shutting out what he really knows is true. In other words, as the "system" still stands to get what he can of the spoils. This does not seem wrong to me, it merely is the position of one who decides not to take up the cause and fight against the present. After D. went about 11 p.m. I started to work on the plate "Copyist in Metropolitan Museum of Art," which I had laid aside nearly two years ago. Worked till nearly 3 a.m.

JOHN SLOAN

1933

Today I posed eating a pineapple at my typewriter for the J. Walter Thompson Agency—the funniest thing I ever heard of, so funny I couldn't help doing it even though Coby Gilman [magazine edi-

tor and Powell's purported lover] thought it was a hideous lowering of myself. People came and went all day—Edgar [Pocock,
brother-in-law], Adolph Dehn, Al Saxe, the little Agit-Prop boy,
etc.—and I wondered how I ever did any work when my days in
New York are so cluttered with people.

DAWN POWELL

JUNE 7

1910

Made a second anti-Roosevelt drawing and took the two down to
the *Call* office. Editor Simpson is rather stupid as an art critic on
the cartoon subject but after I had explained! Then...he was or
said he was glad to have them. I do not charge for this work—like
to do it, and am sorry that the eds. of the paper are not more interested or intelligent on the subject.... I took a walk through the
East Side, most interesting afternoon. I went through the section
between Brooklyn and Williamsburg Bridges. Life is thick! Color-
ful. I saw more than my brain could comprehend, a maze of living incidents—children by the thousands in the streets and parks.
Jack stone season is on, they are bouncing marbles and clutching
the little iron "jacks" on every piece of smooth paving and steps.
The Jews seem to predominate this section. I saw boys and girls
coming from school with violin cases. The Jews believe in education.

When I came home I found Dolly had put in the whole day
cleaning the front room. She had ripped up the old denim floor
cover and thrown it out. It has served there nearly six years. After
dinner at home, I worked a while on the "Copyist" plate. Mr. Yeats
called while I was out and as usual made a sketch of Dolly.

JOHN SLOAN

JUNE 8

1835

In conversation this day with a young man who arrived a day or two since from a whaleing [*sic*] voyage, I devised some knowledge relating to that bussiness [*sic*] from him that is of some interest. The two last voyages he acted as steersman of a whale boat. In this station he received more pay, but the danger and labors were greater. A steersman has to throw the harpoon, use the lance, and to go upon the body of the whale to fasten the hooks into its flesh to draw about the parts wanted. The only parts of a whale used are the lips, throat, brains, fins, and blubber inside the belly. One whale taken yielded One Hundred and Thirty Six gallons oil. The top of the head of a sperm whale usually yields twenty-five gallons. They live by suction [*sic*] always swimming with their mouths open. Thier [*sic*] throats are so small that a mans [*sic*] leg cannot, from appearances, go down. Only one species of whale have teeth, and these only in the upper jaw.

Immense numbers of sharks of the largest size and most ravenous description, constantly follow the whale ships, seizing and devouring the carcasses of the whale the moment they are cut adrift from the side of the ship. Thirty sharks have been counted swimming around a ship at one time.

Nearly all our whale ships fish on the Coast of Africa and around the western Islands [*sic*]. They usually make a voyage in ten months.

JAMES CRUIKSHANK

1864

I have so much to do and think of that I forget my diary, which, in such momentous times, is a *crime* against myself. Should I live to be an old lady, I shall deeply regret this.

Grant's success has been certain but slow; the enemy has been fighting every inch of the way. I had a letter from Badeau from the front, written in pencil, breathing the utmost confidence in the army, its leader, and the final success which, as he speaks from ac-curate knowledge, cannot but give us the greatest confidence. Both armies fight with the greatest bravery.... We have lost some of our best generals—Wadsworth, Sedgwick [James Clay] Rice, and thousands of heroes whose names are known but to their sorrowing families. Our nationality will be born anew in blood and tears, but we trust it will rise purified and ennobled.

MARIA LYDIG DALY

1973

Josephine Baker opened at Carnegie Hall. I have never seen as many black women in white-blond curly wigs—really platinum blond. Josephine Baker, at around sixty-eight, looks forty. Her figure, completely revealed in a body stocking (flowers here and there in sequins, the color of her skin), is slender to emaciation. "I'm so hungry," she murmured, patting her razor-thin thigh, as she moved into the footlights, four feet and more of orange-red ostrich blooms on her head, like an imperial Russian escaping across the wintered steppes—fleeing from the last imperial ball before the Bolshevik hordes! Singers in the aisles like from *My Fair Lady*. The last of Carlo [Van Vechten]'s *Nigger Heaven* was in Carnegie Hall that night. Diana Vreeland about Josephine Baker: "She was my you-th...." How wrong Andy Warhol is when he thinks Josephine Baker and Marlene are the same thing.

LEO LERMAN

JUNE 9

1777

Prepared Lrs [*sic*] for England to go by the Packet. The General [Howe], and other principal officers, departed for the Jersies, and joined the Army.

AMBROSE SERLE

1919

At my office all day, and H[eywood] Broun had us to dinner.... H[arold] Ross and A[lexander] Woollcott...come to call, and we played at dice, and I gained a few dollars, and then took all for drinks, I having a beaker of buttermilk.

FRANKLIN P. ADAMS

JUNE 10

1749

At noon we left *New York,* and sailed up the river *Hudson,* in a yacht bound for *Albany.* All this afternoon we saw a whole fleet of little boats returning from *New York,* whither they had brought provisions and other goods for sale, which on account of the extensive commerce of this town, and the great number of its inhabitants, go off very well.... Some porpesses played and tumbled in the river.

PETER KALM

1851

I...got my dinner and went in search of Junk shops & second Hand Dealers.... At 3 O'clock I called in at the Shop (Licensed) Of Wm Mullen No 302 Front St. [I] saw a man in his employ named Michael Harry buying a small quantity of old rope, rags, etc from a small boy = There were also in there at the time three small girls the oldest upon my questioning her said she lived in Willet St. & that her name was Morris & was 15 years old. I asked her if she would like to get a good situation to work in a respectable family = where she would be well-provided for = She replied that her mother would not let her go = I was informed by an old negro that was in there at the time that the girl was in the habit of going aboard of the Coal Boats in that vicinity and prostituting herself. I remonstrated with Mullen for harboring these children & threatened to

have his licence revoked = he appears to be a very ignorant man
and promised that for the future he would discontinue buying from
Children and would not allow them to come in his place.

                                        INSPECTOR WILLIAM H. BELL

1906

In the afternoon, walking on Fifth Avenue, we were on the edge
of a beautiful wind storm, the air full of dust and a sort of panicky
terror in all living things in sight. A broad gray curtain of cloud
pushing over the zenith, the streets in wicked dusty murk. About
8:30 in the evening we (Dolly, Nan and I) went down to the Bowery
and walked through Chinatown and Elizabeth Street. It was the first
time I had been down there at night—found it right interesting.
Perhaps Chinatown is a little too picturesque for my purposes.

                                                        JOHN SLOAN

1988

Yesterday, rain, not much but steady, enough to make staying in
seem the wiser part of valor. Later, it cleared off and Mary Abbott
and I strolled over to Chelsea Central and ate plates of Wellfleet
oysters ("Canadian Wellfleets," the waitress firmly said) of so varied
and intense a flavor as to be a kind of food one only knows about
from books. Mary was dressed in a rather startling way: shimmering black over dark paisley, and a hat a friend made for her, of slate
green, its shape an enlarged variation on a cloche, lined with orange, with many orange turn-ups and orange surprises: a hat upon
which the late Queen Mary might have cast an eye both incredu-
lous and covetous,... Mary carried it off with gay aplomb.... Actually, the total effect of [her] costume was of a rare, large probably
benign fungus, found deep in the woods. A fungus with a ready
smile, sparkling eyes and well supplied with Navajo jewelry.

                                                    JAMES SCHUYLER

JUNE 11

1859

Improved the day by leaving Wall Street early and set off with G[eorge] A[nthon] and Johnny to explore the Central Park, which will be a feature of the city within five years and a lovely place in A.D. 1900, when its trees will have acquired dignity and appreciable diameters. Perhaps the city itself will perish before then, by growing too big to live under faulty institutions corruptly administered.... We entered the park at 71st St[reet], on its e[ast] side, and made for "The Ramble," a patch just below the upper reservoir.... it promises very well. So does all the lower park, though now in most ragged condition: long lines of incomplete macadamization, "lakes" without water, mounds of compost, piles of blasted stone, acres of what will be greensward hereafter but is now mere brown earth; groves of slender young transplanted maples and locusts, undecided between life and death, with here and there an aboricultural experiment that has failed utterly and is a mere broomstick with ramifications.... The work seems pushed with vigor and system...Narrowness is its chief drawback. One sees quite across this *Rus in Urbe* at many points...Roads and paths twist and twine about in curves of artistic tortuosity. A broad avenue, exceptionally straight (at the lower end of the park) with a quadruple row of elms will look Versailles-y by A.D. 1950. On the 5th Av[enue] side, the hideous State Arsenal building stares at students of the picturesque, an eyesore that no landscape gardening can alleviate. Let us hope it will soon be destroyed by an accidental fire.

GEORGE TEMPLETON STRONG

1862

Dined yesterday at Dr. Ward's and took a drive in the afternoon in the Central Park. If one lived there, no country would be more desirable—one would have all the luxury of a country seat without the trouble or expense. A niece of Dr. Ward, a Virginia lady, is stay-ing there and is a violent secessionist. It is a pity that the abolition female saints and the Charleston female patriots could not meet in [a] fair fight and mutually annihilate each other.

MARIA LYDIG DALY

1906

Started to paint from memory of the Wind and Dust Storm that we saw and felt Sunday. Across the backyards in a room on the second floor I saw a baby die in its mother's arms. The men of the house powerless, helpless, stupid. She held it in her arms after it had started to pale and stiffen. Hope tried to fight off Fact, then Fact killed hope in her. They took it from her. The men smoked their pipes—sympathetic with her anguish and trying to reason her back to calmness. A bottle of whiskey, and a drink for her. I could hear nothing—but the acting was perfect.

JOHN SLOAN

JUNE 12

1844

Brooklyn has been increasing with great rapidity of late years. This is owing, partly, to the salubrity of its situation; but chiefly to its vicinity to the business portion of the city; the low price of ferriage (two cents); the facility of access, which can be obtained at all hours, except two in the morning; and, especially, to the high rents of New York. Brooklyn, you know, is much admired by the Gothamites; and, in fact, much has been done by Nature for the place. But this much the New Yorkers have contrived very thoroughly to spoil. I know few towns which inspire me with so great disgust and contempt. It puts me often in mind of a city of silvered-gingerbread; no doubt you have seen this article of confectionary in some of the Dutch boroughs of Pennsylvania. Brooklyn, on the immediate shore of the Sound, has, it is true, some tolerable residences; but the majority, throughout, are several steps beyond the preposterous. What can be more sillily and pitiably absurd than palaces of painted white pine, fifteen feet by twenty?—and of such is this boasted "city of villas." You see nowhere a cottage—everywhere a temple which "might have been Grecian had it not been Dutch"—which might have been tasteful had it not been Gothamite—a square box, with Doric or Corinthian pillars, supporting a frieze of unseasoned timber, roughly planed, and daubed with, at best, a couple of coats of whitey-brown paint. This "pavilion" has, usually, a flat roof, covered with red zinc, and surrounded by a balustrade; if not surmounted by something nondescript, intended for a cupola, but wavering in character, between a pigeon-house, a sentry-box, and a pig-sty. The steps, at the front door, are many, and bright yellow, and from their foot a straight alley of tan-bark, arranged between box-hedges, conducts the tenant, in glory, to the front-gate—which, with the wall of the whole, is of tall white pine boards, painted sky-blue. If we add to this a fountain, giving out a pint of real water per hour, through the mouth of a leaden cat-fish standing upon the tip-end of his tail, and surrounded by a circle of admiring "conchs"…, we have a quite perfect picture of a Brooklynite "villa."… I really can see little difference between the putting up such a house as this, and blowing up a House of Parliament, or cutting the throat of one's grandfather.

EDGAR ALLAN POE

1911

Great talk of subway plans, yet do they not come, till that I am like to lose my patience. To the Art museum in the afternoon, which thrilled me not at all, though this Sargent has limned some passable portraits.

FRANKLIN P. ADAMS

1924

Sometimes my love makes me sad, as today, with [new husband] Lorin at his office and a tenderness in my heart that I have no means of expressing. We live in a beautiful little furnished apartment (which we have for the summer) at 237 West 11th Street. Our windows look out on the green backyards, with trees and flowers in them, and the sun pours in out of the wide blue sky that we see over the low roofs that surround us. Here is peace and quiet, in which I can write and think.... We had no place to go but Perry Street that first night. Lorin felt my nervous excitement, the tremors that ran thru me when I looked at my wedding ring or at him. He smiled his old comfortable smile and bade me sleep—which I did, like the dead, lying in his arms safe and warm as a child.

WINIFRED WILLIS

JUNE 13

1776

Here in town very unhappy and shocking scenes were exhibited. On Monday night some men called Tories were carried and hauled about through the streets, with candles forced to be held by them, or pushed in their faces, and their heads burned; but on Wednesday, in the open day, the scene was by far worse; several, and among them gentleman, were carried on rails; some stripped naked and dreadfully abused. Some of the generals, and especially Putnam and their forces, had enough to do to quell the riot, and make the mob disperse.

BROTHER EWALD GUSTAV SCHAUKIRK

1833

The President [Andrew Jackson] is certainly the most popular man we have ever known. Washington was not so much so. His acts were

popular, because all descriptions of men were ready to acknowledge him the "Father of His Country." But he was superior to the
homage of the populace, too dignified, too grave for their liking,
and men could not approach him with familiarity. Here is a man
who suits them exactly. He has a kind expression for each—the
same to all, no doubt, but each thinks it intended for himself. His
manners are certainly good, and he makes the most of them. He
is a gourmand of adulation, and by the assistance of the populace
has persuaded himself that no man ever lived in the country to
whom the country was so much indebted. Talk of him as the second
Washington. It won't do now; Washington was only the first Jackson.

PHILIP HONE

1912

Darling mama took myself and servant to Hudson River. We sat
on the pier at water's edge. Lovely and cool. We saw the "Moltke,"
a very large battleship very clearly with aid of a strong glass. Saw
Bremer "Stetjew" [*sic*] and three American warships. Beauties
with high stacks, masts and guns. The American ships saluted the
Germans with 21 shots. The [Germans] answered with 20 shots.
Watched the ships turn slowly. American ships went down the river
first. I waved to the sailors and yao-hoed [*sic*]. Had lots of fun. Sailors waved to me. German Sailors were frantic and waved hats and
handkerchiefs. I called to them too. Had packs of fun.

SARA HOEXTER BLUMENTHAL

JUNE 14

1937

Dinner last night with George [Platt Lynes] and Monroe [Wheeler]
at Katherine Anne [Porter]'s apartment in Perry Street. Her table
handsomely set; raffia cloth and turkey-red napkins, wooden plates,

and four silver goblets, and her new Russian forks of nugget silver, the handles enameled with dark flowers by some Muscovite William Morris.

After dinner, George drove us to Coney Island. We had been there just a year ago, but with Cecil Beaton, Marcel Khill, and Cocteau, when of course I listened and talked back more than I looked. Portals and towers in a fog are all I remember, and long wet wreaths of light bulbs. We arrived after closing time, therefore could only go up and down the street of games and freaks, where I find nothing surprising. No one ever told me of the elegance and infant splendour inside the enclosures, particularly the one called Luna Park.

Last night we saw this at its best, almost empty; it was about to rain. Clean cement esplanades; *gloriettas* and pagodas and *giraldas:* the electricity thickly dotted on the wood, which resembles paper. A child's idea of palaces, never having seen anything but tenements; or an artist's concept of what he will do, before art has begun to deflate and reform and perpetuate it.

The Chutes: a cascade drawn with a ruler; water thinly and decoratively draped over planks. The flatbottomed boats rush down it, under a bridge, and out on the glassy pool, with stiff rapid ribbons of wash and gashes of shadow. How handsome my friends looked to me, profile against profile in the prow!

The Shooting Gallery with its tightly packed targets: clay pipes, revolving white stars, a large resonant pendulum, burning candles, and ducks incessantly sliding across and ducking and returning. Crude and pretty color schemes: one of those sour blues with purple in it, and sky-blue and blotter-green. A bit of charge from Monroe's rifle, or Katherine Anne's, glances back and strikes my forehead, just hard enough to appeal to my imagination.

GLENWAY WESCOTT

JUNE 15

1831

Nothing could be more beautiful than our passage down the Hudson. . . .

As we approached New York the burning heat of the day relaxed and long shadows of evening fell coolly on the beautiful villas we passed. I really can conceive nothing more exquisitely lovely than this approach to the city. The magnificent boldness of the Jersey shore on the one side, and the luxurious softness of the shady lawns on the other, with the vast silvery stream that flows between them, altogether form a picture which may well excuse a traveller for saying, once and again, that the Hudson river can be surpassed in beauty by none on the outside of Paradise.

FRANCES "FANNY" TROLLOPE

[Dating inferred from content.]

JUNE 16

1697

The fort points upon the Entrance from Sea to command ships in theyr [sic] approach to town. . . . The walls of ye Fort are about 20 feet high from without & pallisaded besides. His Exc. Is also maeking a Low Battery of 8 or 10 guns towards the harbour, others toward the land at ye passadge [sic] to the town gate. . . . His Exc. Was farther pleased to walk the town with me and shew me the multitudes of greate & Costly buildings erected since his arrival about 4 years since to be theyr Gouuernour [sic]. Amongst [which] none appeared more Considerable than that of Coll. Abr. Depeisters a noble building of the newest English fashion, and richly furnished with hangings and pictures. The staire case Large, & nobel, ye whole built out of the Sea or Sound within this 2 years past, as are abundance of Lofty brick & stone buildings on the same range, theyr back doores & wharves, warehouses & gardens Lookeing into the Sound & Harbour. parting from Coll. Depeister whose entertainment is generous & like a Nobleman though a merchant by his professions, his Exc. Was pleased to enjoyne me to dine with him at the fort, where was in ye ... hall furnished with armes, where we had a plentifull & well ordered table both of flesh & fish, with plenty of wine, & other good Liquors.

DR. BENJAMIN BULLIVANT

JUNE 17

1697

Having been now 4 dayes at N.Y. I have Learned to say something of its Constitutions, & fashions. . . . The Mayors court is kept every Tuesday, he hath no ensigns of honour but the bearing a white staffe in his hand, Like ye Sherifs of London. . . . The city is well seated for A trade, the ships bound out being quickly at Sea, hath a good and safe harbour. . . . Most of theyr new buildings are magnificent enough, ye fronts of red and yellow or flanders brick Lookeing very prettily, some of them are 6 stories high & built with a Gable end to ye front, & so by Consequence make Very narrow garratts. The 3d story is usually a warehouse, and over it a Crane for hawleing up goods. . . . Very good buildings, & tradesmen of note, it being not regarded where a man lives in N.Y. as to his trade, for all are known. . . . The children of rich parents are usually without shooes or stockens, and young mayds [*sic*] (especially Dutch) weare morneing [*sic*] gowns allday Long and bare footed, indeed I cannot say I saw any of ye Dutch that were tolerably well dresst, though rich enough to wear what they pleased.

DR. BENJAMIN BULLIVANT

JUNE 18

1854

The conjunction of Barnum and [Antoine] Jullien at the so-called Crystal Palace Thursday evening in a so-called "Musical Congress with 1,500 performers" naturally produced one of the grandest humbugs on record.... The crowd was enormous. It is estimated at fifteen thousand by some and forty thousand by others. I've no opinion at all as to the accuracy of either estimate. But for some time after taking our seats I was seriously exercised about the possibilities of falling galleries and panic-stricken multitudes and was tempted to evacuate the building at once.

GEORGE TEMPLETON STRONG

[The "Congress" was held in the flimsy Crystal Palace, which burned in 1858.]

1923

To G[eorge.] S. Kaufman's for dinner, and we talked of this and that, and he told me of the drolleries of George Jessel, and how they were in Fairmont, West Virginia, last week on a hot day, and how it is a coal centre, and very sooty, and next to the tracks were two men sitting on a porch and they were reading newspapers, amid the noise and hot grime, and Mr. Jessel said, If I had a lot of money, that's just what I'd do: come to a place like this and get away from things.

FRANKLIN P. ADAMS

JUNE 19

1777

Received six bottles claret and sundry small articles, but the note not allowed to come up.

JOHN FELL

1859

Gentle & playful this morning sometimes almost childlike in his manner... very playful & pleasant at dinner. Walk round the brook lot in the afternoon—In the evening smoked... in the library & then took his seat at the [hearth?] in parlor and opened a book to read—had been sometime at a loss for a pleasant book.

"I'm reduced to my favorite author"—said he... "The fifth volume of Washington. I think I'll read it now." Had not looked at it since it was put to prep—

PIERRE MUNRO IRVING

1872

The number of piano makers on strike is growing constantly less... all their energy is now directed toward abusing the police and the Indignation meeting at Cooper Institute next friday [*sic*] evening.

WILLIAM STEINWAY

JUNE 20

1854

After the everlasting rain of the spring, we are entering on a period of drowth. The sun sets, a well-defined coppery disk like a red-hot penny in a dark room, and all the western sky is curtained with dull, coppery haze. Cholera is in town and pretty active—fifty-odd deaths this week.

GEORGE TEMPLETON STRONG

1917

Sailed June 20, 1917   Band playing hula hula on the wharf people dancing in and out among the luggage—

Man who wanted paper as a souvenir—"cause you see sir I'm seein' off my son. I don't reckon they'll mind, do you, sir?"

"I don't reckon they'd mind" goes off mumbling. La traversée—
uniforms—smoking room crap games. Singing. Champagne—
   "For we're bound for the Hamburg show to see the elephant and
the wild kangeroo"
   "God help Kaiser Bill
   God help Kaiser Bill
   Oh old Uncle Sam,
   He's got the infantry
   He's got the cavalry
   He's got the artillery...
   Then by God we'll all go to Germany
   And God help Kaiser Bill"
   General... expectation of raising hell in Paris.

                                          JOHN DOS PASSOS

JUNE 21

1776

Agreeable to this day's orders Col Cary and myself, removed to
Head Quarters as Aid de Camps to His Excellency General Washington.
   Some days past, the General received Information that a most
horrid plot was on foot by the vile Torys of this place and the Adjacent Towns and Villages. Having taken the necessary precautions,
at two o'Clock in the morning a number of Officers & Guards went
to different places & took up many of their principals; among which
was David Matthews, Esq., Mayor of the City: and to our great astonishment, we found five or more of the General's life Guard to
be accomplices in this wicked plan—which was, at a proper time,
to Assassinate the person of his Excell[ency] & the other Genl. Officers, blow up the Magazine, spike the Cannon, &c. It was to be put
in Execution as soon as the Enemy's fleet appeared, if no proper

time offered before—but thank God, they are discovered and many
of them in close Custody; where, I hope, they will receive the punishment due such Infamous wretches.

SAMUEL BLACHLEY WEBB

c. 1856

It seems to be quite clear and determined that I should concentrate my powers [on] "Leaves of Grass"—not diverting any of my
means, strength, interest to the construction of anything else—of
any other book.

WALT WHITMAN

1906

Working again in J.M.'s cellar, finished large panel—J.M. leading
a soul to the Burning River's Brink. Jim in the character of the
"angel of the darker drink" a mirror in the face of the misguided
soul—devils rejoicing.... In the evening, Dolly and I went down
again and I painted a smaller panel. Girl combing hair at a window,
a cat on the leads outside.

JOHN SLOAN

1922

To R. Lingley's for dinner, and I had a box of segars [*sic*] with me,
and the old man at the gate was for not permitting me to enter, but I
told him the next time I would have my dinner invitation witnessed
by a notary publick, and he said, Don't you insult me, and I told him
I did not know how, else I should.

FRANKLIN P. ADAMS

1953

Rosenbergs in their coffins. Their faces pale, like the divine masks
of the Noh....
    The bridal white in which they are shrouded adds to the unex-

pected look of composure that seems to belie the turmoil and anger and agony which surrounds their deaths. I think my impression of them hallucinatory, because the newspaper photographs have been so pitifully crass, but I am told that all corpses have this peculiar glow.

Expecting to be horrified, I am instead so awed that my indignation vanishes....

Many people mill about at three o'clock on a Saturday morning on an obscure corner of Brooklyn, reluctant to abandon the dead.

Inside the funeral parlor a rabbi's prayers sanctify the night while a guard (one does not know whether it was of honor or dishonor) stands among the American flags that mock the murdered.

After all the macabre fuss about not executing them on *Shabbos*, the exposure of the bodies is a contradiction. It is alien to Jewish custom to uncover the dead; that's why I've never seen a corpse in a coffin before. But this is well done in the spirit of Mark Antony's, "If I were to show you Caesar's body."

JUDITH MALINA

JUNE 22

1778

The Army was under arms at 4:o'clock in the morning and marched soon after through Slab Town to the *Black Horse*. General Leslie with the 5th Brigade took an intermediate road between that of the Column and Burlington, where it was supposed there might be some Rebel Troops; by that means flanking the baggage. The 5th Brigade afterwards fell into the Black Horse Road and brought up the rear.... A deserter was executed on the march.

MAJOR JOHN ANDRÉ

[Recounting the British retreat from Philadelphia to New York.]

1843

THURSDAY. Fried to death, nearly, and quite broiled besides. It's as hot as an oven tonight, and I'm constantly looking at myself involuntarily, to see whether I've begun to turn brown. But this weather is no joking matter.

And here I'm sitting—positively steaming and stewing—and afraid to open the window and let in what little cool air there may be stirring, for this murderous influenza is going about like a raging hyena, seeking whom it may—not devour exactly—but give a vicious clawing that leaves its victims in a sufficiently pitiable case a week or so. Never knew such an epidemic.

GEORGE TEMPLETON STRONG

JUNE 23

1836

Excursion in the "Novelty." A party of gentlemen consisting of the managers of the Delaware & Hudson Company . . . and others, went on board the Novelty this morning at six o'clock, at the foot of Chambers Street in New York, and came to Albany in 12 hours and 8 minutes.

This was the first voyage ever made from New York to Albany by a steamboat propelled by anthracite coal. Dr. Nott has been engaged for several years in contriving machinery to accomplish this important object, and has now succeeded completely. The great desideratum was to contrive the means of igniting the coal, and producing a flame sufficient to create the steam. This has been effected by condensing hot air, which by injection into the bottom of the furnaces accomplishes this object, and forces the flame into a chamber in which are a great number of iron tubes of the size of gun-barrels, placed vertically. There are four of these furnaces.

The quantity of coal consumed on this trip was about twenty tons (something less), which at $5 per ton amounts to $100.

PHILIP HONE

1948

Julian and I read *Iphigenia in Taurus.* I feel the urge to act again.

Mother and I go to Butler Davenport's Free Theater, where she often took me as a child.

Davenport has grown old. He was to have played Molière's *Affected Young Ladies,* but his cast was decimated by summer stock and he carried on alone with monologues: Chekhov's "Swan Song" and "An Interview with Mark Twain." ...

I never noticed how drab the stage was because I believed in that darkness then, nor did I notice Davenport's failings as Shylock, Hamlet or Cardinal Richelieu because I believed in him.

Now the old actor was apologetic because he had to alter the ending of his plays to get offstage to pull the curtain; there was no one else to pull it.

At the act break, he made his long speech to the audience about social betterment and birth control. It has a quaint, oratorical quality.

A solitary actor in his fortress.

He passed the basket for support.

JUDITH MALINA

JUNE 24

1847

Visited Poe at Fordham whom the wondrous Mrs. Clem has domiciliated [*sic*] in a neat cottage near a rock overlooking the pretty valley with its St. John's College of Jesuits, contiguous hill and forest, the Sound and the blue distance of Long Island. The purity of the air, delicious. At night the whole agreeable impression of the

afternoon reversed by dreams, into which it might have been supposed Poe had put an infusion of his Mons Valdemar with the green
tea, the probable cause of them. All the evil I had ever heard of him
took bodily shape in a series of most malignant scenes.

EVERT DUYCKINCK

[The Mons Valdemar is a hallucinogen, possibly one relating to Poe's "The
Strange Case of Mr. (Monsieur) Valdemar."]

1872

Learn that pianomakers strike ended yesterday, and that all the men
went to work this morning.... At 2 P.M. am at Police Head Quarters,
trial of Capt. Gunner takes place and of Police men who clubbed
the strikers on 42ᵈ street, Officers conduct commended and Complaint dismissed, go to Nanuet by N.R.R. at 5 P.M. Spend evening
there. It rains heavily all night

WILLIAM STEINWAY

1926

Home at 4. I became abusive & Marinoff went out.

CARL VAN VECHTEN

JUNE 25

1834

President Jackson has issued an order to the different command-
ers of the fortified places throughout the United States, direct-
ing them to cause a salute to be fired at sun rise and a gun every
half hour during the day, as a mark of respect to the memory of
General La Fayette.... In this order the President remarks that
Genl. La Fayette was the last Major [*sic*] General of the United
States who fought in the Revolution. He also remarks that the
order as respects the firing of the guns, is the same as that issued

at the death of Genl. Washington whose companion in arms gen'
La Fayette was.

JAMES CRUIKSHANK

1847

President [James K.] Polk's visit to the city and the thermometer at 90°. Missed his part of the procession and the shabby ba-
rouches [carriages with collapsible tops] but came upon a handful
of Continentalers so dressed in the style of the Revolution, with a
characteristic hawk-faced captain, suggestive of oddity, humor and
antiquity. A placard of [P. T.] Barnum's accompanied the procession on the side walk announcing that Santa Anna's Wooden Leg
taken at Cerro Gordo to be seen at the Museum!

EVERT DUYCKINCK

1926

Up at 10. Hot, clear day. Marinoff does not return. Neither does she
call up. I nearly go out of my mind. About 4 Donald [Angus] comes
up. He telephones the Algonquin & finds she is there & I talk to her.
She says she is through forever. If she is, what is there in life for me?
I take a taxi down to the Algonquin but she has left. Then back to the
house. Then to Reg Wallace's. The word is that she is not in. I wait
there for an hour & then I keep my engagement with Bud [i.e., Ru-
dolph] Fisher for dinner at his house. His wife, sister, & mother there.
I am afraid I was a rather glum guest. At 9:30 I come home & find that
Marinoff has been here, packed her bag & left. I walk the floor till
12:30 & finally manage a little sleep with hot milk & whiskey together.

CARL VAN VECHTEN

1927

Margaret & Alice went out to the country. Gene and I took Charlie
to the theatre where he is playing on the east side and went to see the
show ... *Seventh Heaven*—Charlie very good in lead. Left car in garage

during theatre. Went afterwards to [a] restaurant. Came home to 11th Street at about one o'clock   pouring rain, torrents of rain, street deserted. Gene came into the hall with me to let me in & stepped inside to fetch his overcoat, then went out to take car to garage. Returned in a moment to say that the car was gone, stolen. I called up the police at once. A detective came over presently to get the description of the car to all the police [in] Manhattan. I am confident it will be found.

EDNA ST. VINCENT MILLAY

1952

After midnight, after rehearsals, to the San Remo. In spite of the ruthless violence of the current juke box favorites, one can sit still here.

With Weegee, the photographer of the Naked City, I go to his shabby, one-room home behind the Tombs and then to eat at Thau's. Joined by Norman and Nina and Julian, we prowl the dawn streets, and visit the catacombs below MacDougal Street and the Minetta Spring captured in the art nouveau fountain of a fashionable Washington Square hotel.

Last night in the Remo with John Cage and Lou Harrison. Lou, looking splendid in a white suit and a small Edwardian beard, boasts of his exploits like a child recounting his defiances.

Seven of the cast have left us. The recasting is arduous and boring.

JUDITH MALINA

JUNE 26

1859

It is now time to stir first for Money enough to live and provide for M— To Stir—first write stories and get out of this Slough.

WALT WHITMAN

1926

Up at 7. Still no word. I shall go mad.... at 11 I telephoned Reg & found that Marinoff had gone to the country. So I telephone Esther [Marinoff] & find she is there.... I am off for Bergenfield, [New Jersey] arriving slightly after 2. I go directly to the Marinoffs' house where I find Marinoff eating lunch with Esther.... We make up and after lunch take a long walk & pick daisies.

CARL VAN VECHTEN

1927

Telephone call in morning—car found, car & three prisoners held at 68th Precinct Police Station. [illeg.] Staten Island—Had been found at five o'clock this morning. Gene & I took reporter from the *World* & went to Staten Island. Car badly damaged: must be repaired. Meanwhile without a car—unpleasant.

Interviewed by Harry Salpeter for the *World*.

Ugin took me in a taxi to the Mount Sinai Hospital.

EDNA ST. VINCENT MILLAY

1954

Joe Campbell, who has used *The Spook Sonata* as a text for his classes, came to the theater last night and pronounced the production's iconography accurate.

He congratulated Julian on an explication of Strindberg's choice of the hyacinth: the banks of the River Styx were clotted with them.

At the second intermission Joe and I stood together on the fire escape. The night was very warm. I confessed that it was I who had sent him the Japanese love poem.

He is going to India and Japan next month for a year. He promises me a pine cone from Kyoto.

JUDITH MALINA

JUNE 27

1844

Marriage in [the] High Life. No sooner was the session of Congress ended and a few supplementary victims offered up to the Moloch of party, and a few more ruthless assaults been made upon the sanctuary of the Constitution, than the perpetrators of these enormities, shaking off the cares of public life and bidding adieu for a brief period to the palace of which he accidentally became an unworthy occupant, flew on the wings of love (the old fool) to the arms of his expectant bride in New York, where the hymeneal altar was prepared for the happy couple. His arrival here on Tuesday evening was sudden, unexpected and unheralded (the impudent *Herald* was not apprized of the august arrival) and this morning the joyful intelligence which makes a nation happy . . . is thus announced in the papers:

> MARRIED in this city at the Church of the Ascension, on Wednesday the 26th inst., by the Right Reverend Bishop Onderdonk, John Tyler, acting President of the United States, to Julia, daughter of the Hon. David Gardiner, deceased, late of this city.

The illustrious bridegroom is said to be 55 years of age and looks ten years older, and the bride is a dashing girl of 22, the daughter of David Gardiner of Long Island, one of the victims of the dreadful explosion a few months since on board the steamship *Princeton*. She has been an inmate in the President's family since the calamity which made her fatherless, and it is said the engagement was formed before it occurred.

PHILIP HONE

1916

To the playhouse in the evening, and saw "The Follies of 1916," a harlequinade of great beauty, but no wit nor humour save a little of Miss Fannie Brice's. And the shimmering charm of Miss Ina Claire did cheer me, too.

FRANKLIN P. ADAMS

1927

Operated on—operation they call a "D. and c." [*sic*]—not a very big one. Very sick in stomach. Can't keep even water down....

They are lovely here and give me all the morphine I want—ply me with morphine.

EDNA ST. VINCENT MILLAY

JUNE 28

1878

Today at school the boys all put in money and we had Ice Cream, Lemonade, Bananas and cake. Today has been a very hot day. Today I received Jeff Davis' autograph.

ADDISON ALLEN

JUNE 29

1776

This morning at 9 o'Clock, we discovered our Signals hoisted on Staten Island, signifying the appearance of a fleet. At 2 o'Clock P.M. an express arrived, informing a fleet of more than one Hundred Square rig'd vessels, had arrived and anchored in The Hook—This is the fleet which we forced to evacuate Boston; & went to Halifax last March—where they have been waiting for reinforcements, and have now arrived here with a view of puting [*sic*] their Cursed plans into Execution. But Heaven *we hope and trust* will frustrate their cruel designs—a warm and Bloody Campaign is the least we may expect; may God grant us victory and success over them, is our most fervent prayer. Expresses are this day gone to Connecticut, to the Jerseys, &c, to hurry on the Militia.

SAMUEL BLACHLEY WEBB

1798

Attend to business. Read Reviews. Walk out of town with the Boy & Girl to see our militia parade. Evening Theatre, Mrs. Tyler's night "She Stoops to Conquer" in which the fat old woman advertised her last appearance & *did* Miss Neville: to this was added Mr. Williams alias Anthony Pasquin's afterpiece "the federal Oath or [*Columbians*] Americans strike home": this piece is certainly without rival in the Drama, unless it may be Milns's "Flash in the pan": this last by the by is a misnomer, for the *piece* undoubtedly *went off*—and never will be heard of again. The benevolent intention of the benevolent Mr. Williams in his piece—of patch'd work—is to inculcate some grand and novel political truths, Such as, that, we ought to damn all Frenchmen, and that, "two yankee boys can beat four mounseers."

WILLIAM DUNLAP

1926

Dinner in with Marinoff & then to see Mae West in *Sex* at 63rd Street Theatre. After we came home we made 8 quarts of raspberry brandy. In bed about one.

CARL VAN VECHTEN

1930

Those blocks of New York neutral yellow, if even that, traveling above the neutral water of the river, neither gray nor blue, slowly on the summer afternoon, when most people must have

208 · *New York Diaries*

left town—contrasting, through the window of the boat, a plain enough but flesh-bodied girl, fixes her hair by the reflection in the window, with her tanned and reddish-glowing arms contrasting with those neutral walls, plain but still flesh and blood, black curly Jewish-looking hair—.

EDMUND WILSON

JUNE 30

1836

I went out this evening with Margaret to a strawberry party at Mr. Anthon's, Bloomingdale. It was quite a *fête champêtre*. We had our refreshment on the green, between the house and the river, and the young folks, of whom there was a large and agreeable party, enjoyed themselves very much....

Death of Mr. [James] Madison. This enlightened statesman and illustrious citizen, James Madison, former President of the United States, died on Tuesday 28th Instant [last]. He had been gradually sinking for some time past. It is a pity that he had not lingered six days longer, that his death might have occurred, like those of Jefferson and the elder Adams, on the anniversary of the political birthday of the country over which they had severally ruled.

PHILIP HONE

July 1

1950

A séance. Unlikely as I consider the existence of disembodied beings, much more do I doubt their susceptibility to manifestation by ritual rigamarole....

The table moved. The first moment I was startled, but neither before nor after that did I believe anything supernatural occurred....

I believe that Julian controlled the tapping, but I'm sure that he did so unconsciously....

I leave a margin not for the spirits of the dead, but for the unconscious mind trying to speak.

At dawn, New York is at its most spectacular. We stopped to see [surrealist] Adolph Giehoff's display paintings in the windows of Bergdorf Goodman's: landscapes with unicorns and satyrs. They were like the city: an atmosphere of dream into which real objects thrust pale shadows.

JUDITH MALINA

1986

Arnold Schwarzenegger was having a party for the Statue of Liberty at Café Seiyoken and I wasn't even invited. And I wasn't invited to Caroline Kennedy's wedding, either.

ANDY WARHOL

July 2

1776

Part of the [British] Fleet came up to the Watering Place on Staten Island in plain sight of the City; this caused the signals for an

Alarm. The Inhabitants are in great Confusion, removing from the City, &c. Orders were issued that no Man, either Officer or Soldier, should be absent from Camp without leave in Wrighting [*sic*] from the Commander of the Regiment.

Lt. Isaac Bangs

1958

I am alone in the flat. [Wife] Sylvia has stayed on in Ottawa. Matilda and Popski are away on a holiday. I sleep in one bed and then in another and I never make up the one I slept in last. I leave my dirty clothes in piles on the floor. If the light doesn't work, I'm too lazy to change the bulb, so just move to another room....

Had dinner last night with an old friend from Nova Scotia, now a very successful New York career woman. It was interesting to see how the acquired layers of New York "graciousness and culture" came peeling off after the third drink. Thank God they did.

Charles Ritchie

July 3

1830

Took breakfast at the cabin table, for the first time since coming on board, the smell (stench) of the *bilge water,* now beginning to subside, having hitherto induced me greatly to prefer the deck. Fare excellent. Tea, coffee, boiled ham and eggs, anchovies, pickled shad, cold tongue and other meat, bread, of the finest American flour, baked fresh every day. Biscuits, etc, etc.... We have a cow on board which furnishes an abundant supply of milk; four or five fine sheep; half a dozen small pigs; some geese, and ducks and fowls unnumbered. Poultry, however, soon become very poor stuff at sea. I know of no animals which do not suffer by sailing excepting pigs; they appear to thrive at sea quite as well as on land. Our wines and spirits are first rate, champaign [*sic*] especially; ale and London porter equally good, and all supplied unsparingly. In short, whoever could find in his heart to desire more after this fashion, than is funished in the New York packets, deserves to be treated to a bread and water diet for the remainder of his days.

JOHN FOWLER

1838

Giraffes. Two of these beautiful animals are being exhibited in a lot on Broadway below Prince Street; the place is handsomely fitted up, and great numbers of persons pay their respects to the distinguished strangers. The giraffes or cameleopards, as they are called (I like the first name best), were taken by one of our Yankee brethren in the interior of Southern Africa. They are the only survivors of eleven who were taken, and have been brought to this country at a very great expense.

PHILIP HONE

JULY 4

1776

The Militia from all Parts are daily coming in; many have arrived. This Morning our Brigade had liberty to fire each Man two Rounds of Cartridge at a mark; we accordingly turned out and marched to a suitable Place. The first Fire was made singly, in which one—of Capt Hamblens [*sic*] Company in our Reg. accidentally lost his Life. He, thinking that his Piece had snaped [*sic*], was taking it from his Face to cock it again when the Piece went off, kicked him in the Breast, which instantly killed him.

LT. ISAAC BANGS

1781

'Tis said that Washington and the French are at the Bridge in force.

HUGH GAINE

1832

It is a lovely day, but very different from all the previous anniver-saries of independence. The alarm about the cholera has prevented all the usual jollification under the public authority. There are no booths in Broadway, the parade which was ordered has been coun-termanded, no corporation dinner, and no ringing of bells.... Most of the stores are closed, and there is a pretty smart cannonade of crackers by the boys, but it is not a regular Fourth of July.

PHILIP HONE

1837

The 4th of July, the sixty-first anniversary of American indepen-dence!

Pop—pop—bang—pop—pop—bang—bang—bang! Mercy on us!... Well, the Americans may have great reason to be proud of this day, and of the deeds of their forefathers, but why do they get so confoundedly drunk? Why on this day of independence, should they become so *dependent* upon posts and rails for support?...

When the troops marched up Broadway, louder even than the music were to be heard the screams of delight from the children at the crowded windows on each side. "Ma! Ma! There's Pa!" "Oh, there's John." "Look at Uncle on his big horse."

The troops did not march in very good order, because, indepen-dently of their not knowing how, there was a great deal of indepen-dence to contend with. At one time an omnibus and four would drive in and cut off the general and his staff from his division; at another, a cart would roll in and insist upon following close upon the band of music; so that it was a mixed procession—Generals, ... music, cart-loads of bricks, troops, omnibus and a pair, artillery, hackney-coach, etc. etc. Notwithstanding all this, they at last arrived at the City Hall, when those who were old enough heard the Declaration of Independence read for the sixty-first time; and then it was— "Begone, brave army, and don't kick up a row."

CAPT. FREDERICK MARRYAT

[Dating inferred from content.]

1857

The customary din is raging without. The Chinese War has raised the price and diminished the supply of firecrackers, but our peace is not thereby promoted. The ingenious youth of the city adopt horse pistols in their place.

GEORGE TEMPLETON STRONG

1978

The Fourth of July. Raining out, watched *The Brady Bunch* then went to the office (cab $3.50). Victor was calling, wanting me to see his dog-to-be. I tried to talk him out of getting it. I told him he was a dog himself.

At 4:00 Victor and Rupert picked me up and we walked over to McDonald's to have lunch and hand out *Interviews* (lunch $9.50).

Talked about silkscreening while we cruised. The people in the Village were so unattractive, God. They were all the leftovers who didn't get taken away to Fire Island for the holiday. Dropped Victor at the Morton Street pier ($4.50).

ANDY WARHOL

JULY 5

1857

There was a riot yesterday afternoon in the Sixth Ward, and several persons killed.... The Seventh and other regiments are out with ball cartridge. Some of the downtown streets are made impassable by cordons of police, others, (I am told) by barricades.... We're in a "state of siege," and if half the stories one hears be true, in something like a state of anarchy.... I've just returned from prowling (cautiously and at a very respectful distance) round the seat of war; but I don't know what the disturbance is or has been about. It seems to have been a battle between Irish Blackguardism and Native Bowery Blackguardism, the belligerents afterwards making common cause against the police and uniting to resist their common enemy.

GEORGE TEMPLETON STRONG

JULY 6

1776

Have the News of the United Colonies being Declared free & independent States by the Congress....

The whole Choir of our Officers... went to a Publick House to testify our Joy at the happy news of Independence.

LT. ISAAC BANGS

1953

There is really one city for everyone just as there is one major love. New York is my city because I have an investment I can always draw on—a bottomless investment of 21 years (I count the day I was born) of building up an *idea* of New York—so no matter what happens here I have the rock of my dreams of it that nothing can destroy.

DAWN POWELL

JULY 7

1810

We relished our breakfast but very indifferently. The swarms of flies which assailed the food, were very disgusting; and custards which were brought on the table, *mal apropos* exhibited the marks of that insect as a substitute for the grating of nutmeg.

DEWITT CLINTON

1851

No one can walk the length of Broadway without meeting some hideous troop of ragged girls, from 12 years old down, brutalized already beyond redemption by premature vice, clad in the filthy refuse of the rag-picker's collections, obscene of speech, the stamp of childhood gone from their faces, hurrying along with harsh laughter and foulness on their lips that some of them have learned by rote, yet too young to understand it.... On a rainy day such crews may be seen by dozens. They haunt every other crossing and skulk away together, when the sun comes out and the mud is dry again. And such a group, I think the most revolting object that the social diseases of a great city can produce. A gang of blackguard boys is lovely by the side of it.... And what am I doing, I wonder? I'm neither scholar nor philanthropist nor clergyman.... There is that shadow of an apology for my sitting still. But if Heaven will permit and enable me, I'll do something before I die—to have helped one dirty vagabond child out of such a pestilential stink would be a thing one would not regret when one came to march out of this world...and would be rather more of an achievement than the writing [of] another *Iliad*.

GEORGE TEMPLETON STRONG

1911

A relief from the past five days' terrible heat came this morning after a dreadfully hot night. Dolly has started to make me a lot of China silk shirts which will be a great comfort. I was going to say luxury, but, I think, the things usually called luxuries are necessities forbidden to the "lower classes." There are really two sorts of things—necessities and absurdities. A horse dropped on our street today. They worked over him for two hours. A veterinary doctor attended with hypodermic needle, many with kind hearts helped but finally the patient gave six or seven leaps (lying on his side) and hurdled into paradise.

JOHN SLOAN

1952

Tolstoi's journal. He warns of the weakening of the self by "even such innocent means" as cigarettes and wine. I read this as I waken from my darling hashish sleep. The hashish makes me ravenously hungry. The hunger is impractical as there is no money.

JUDITH MALINA

JULY 8

1931

An evening up on the Empire State roof—the strangest experience. The huge tomb in steel and glass, the ride to the 84th floor and there, under the clouds, a Hawaiian string quartet, lounge, concessions and, a thousand feet below, New York—a garden of golden lights winking on and off, automobiles, trucks winding in and out, and not a sound. All as silent as a dead city—and it looks *adagio* down there.

DAWN POWELL

JULY 9

1770

This morning the Committee began to solicit subscriptions & at night it was said the lists had those for nonimp[ortation at] 799.... DeLancey & Walton headed up importers.

ALEXANDER McDOUGALL

1790

Exercised on Horseback between 5 & 7 in the morning.

A letter from Genl. Harmer, enclosing copies of former letters... put into my hands by the Secretary of War. By these it appears that the frequent hostilities of some Vagabond Indians, who it was supposed had a mind to establish themselves on the Scioto for the purpose of Robbing the Boats, and murdering the Passengers in their dissent or assent [*sic*] of the Ohio, had induced an Expedition composed of 120 effective men of the Regular Troops.... This force rendezvoused at the Mouth of Lime-stone on the 20 of April.... In this expedition little was done; a small party of 4 Indians was discovered—killed & Scalped—and at another place some Bever [*sic*] traps & Skins were taken at an Indian Camp....

Many Visitors (male & female) this Afternoon to Mrs. Washington.

PRESIDENT GEORGE WASHINGTON

1878

Five months ago [was death of Theodore Roosevelt, Sr.]. It seems to me that I have aged very much since that bitter day; now I must rely upon myself in difficulties, while before I had always carried everything to him. The vividness with which I can recall his words and actions is sometimes really startling.

THEODORE ROOSEVELT

JULY 10

1776

Last Night the Statue on the Bowling Green representing George Ghwelph alias George Rex... was pulled down by the Populace. In it were 4,000 Pounds of Lead, & a Man undertook to take... 10 oz of Gold from the Superficies, as both Man & Horse were covered with Gold Leaf. The Lead, we hear, is to be run up into Musquet Balls for the use of the Yankies, when it is hoped that the Emanations of the leaden George will make as deep impressions in the Bodies of some of his red Coated & Torie Subjects.

LT. ISAAC BANGS

1834

There has been of late great excitement in consequence of the proceedings of a set of fanatics who are determined to emancipate all the slaves by a *coup de main,* and have held meetings in which black men and women have been introduced. These meetings have been attended with tumult and violence, especially one which was held on Friday evening at the Chatham Street Chapel. Arthur Tappan and his brother Lewis have been conspicuous in these proceedings, and the mob last night ... went down in a body to the house of the latter gentlemen in Rose Street, broke into the house, destroyed the windows and made a bonfire of the furniture in the street. The police at length interfered, rather tardily, I should think; but the diabolical spirit which prompted this outrage is not quenched, and I apprehend we shall see more of it.

PHILIP HONE

JULY 11

1778

The French Fleet, of twelve Sail of the line and four or five ships of inferior force, came to an anchor off Sandy Hook.

MAJOR JOHN ANDRÉ

[France's support of the Continentals helped turn the tide against the British.]

1804

General Hamilton was killed in a duel this morning by Colonel Burr.

GOUVERNEUR MORRIS

JULY 12

1776

Several Deserters from the Enemy informed that it was the Intention of the Enemy to have sent 5 ships up the N. River to stop the Water Communication between Albany & N. York....

Before any of our Reg^t ... arrived to our Alarm Post, the Ships had past it; ... many Balls very near them, & one killed a Cow at a very small distance from them....

It is said that several of the Company out of which they were killed were drunk, & neglected to Spunge, Worm, & stop the Vent, and the Cartridges took fire while they were raming [*sic*] them down.

LT. ISAAC BANGS

1804

I go to town but meet (opposite to the hospital) Martin Wilkins, who tells me General Hamilton is yet alive at Greenwich.... When I arrive he is speechless. The scene is too powerful for me, so that I am obliged to walk in the garden to take breath. After having composed myself, I return and sit by his side till he expires. He is opened, and we find that the ball has broken one of his ribs, passed through the lower part of the liver, and lodged in the vertebrae of his back: a most melancholy scene—his wife almost frantic with grief, his children in tears, every person present deeply afflicted, the whole city agitated, every countenance dejected. This evening I am asked to pronounce a funeral oration. I promise to do so if I can possibly command myself enough, but express my belief that it will be utterly impossible. I am wholly unmanned by this day's spectacle.

GOUVERNEUR MORRIS

1810

To the west the eye was lost in the expanse of [Oneida Lake], there being no limits to the horizon. A western wind gently agitated the surface of the waters. A number of canoes darting through the lake after fish in a dark night, with lighted flambeaux of pine knots fixed on elevated iron frames, made a very picturesque and pleasing exhibition. We walked on the beach, composed of the finest sand, like the shores of the ocean, and covered a few straggling trees. Here we met with an Indian canoe, filled with eels, salmon, and monstrous cat-fish. In another place we saw the native of the woods cooking his fish and eating his meal on the beach. We could not resist the temptation of the cold bath.

DEWITT CLINTON

1885

Awakened at 5:15 A.M.—My eyes were embarrassed by the sunbeams—turned my back to them and tried to take another dip into oblivion—succeeded—awakened at 7 A.M. Thought of Mina, Daisy, and Mamma G—. Put all 3 in my mental kaleidoscope to obtain a new combination à la Galton. Took Mina as a basis, tried to improve her beauty by discarding and adding certain features borrowed from Daisy and Mamma G. A sort of Raphaelized beauty, got into it too deep, mind flew away and I went to sleep again.

Awakened at 8:15 A.M. .... Smoking too much makes me nervous—must lasso my natural tendency to acquire such habits—holding heavy cigar constantly in my mouth has deformed my upper lip, it has a sort of Havana curl.

Arose at 9 o'clock; came downstairs expecting 'twas too late for breakfast—'twasn't. Couldn't eat much, nerves of stomach too nicotinny. The root of tobacco plants must go clear through to hell. ... It has just occurred to me that the brain may digest certain portions of food, say the etherial [*sic*] part, as well as the stomach—perhaps dandruff is the excreta of the mind—the quantity of this material being directly proportional to the amount of reading one indulges in.

A book on German metaphysics would thus easily ruin a dress suit. ...

This by far the nicest day of this season, neither too hot nor too cold—it blooms on the apex of perfection—an Edenday. ...

Dot just read to me outlines of her proposed novel. The basis seems to be a marriage under duress. I told her that in case of a marriage to put in bucketfuls of misery. This would make it realistic. ...

Dot pitched a ball to me several dozen times—first I ever tried to catch. It was as hard as Nero's heart—nearly broke my baby-finger. Gave it up. Taught Dot and Maggie how to play "Duck on the rock." They both thought it great fun. And this is Sunday. My conscience seems to be oblivious of Sunday. It must be incrusted [*sic*] with a sort of irreligious tartr [*sic*]. If I was not so deaf I might go to church and get it taken off or at least loosened. *Eccavi!* I will read the new version of the bible.

Holzer is going to use the old laboratory for the purpose of hatching chickens artificially by an electric incubator. He is very enthusiastic. Gave me full details. He is a very patient and careful experimenter [sic]. Think he will succeed. Everything succeeded in that old laboratory. Just think electricity employed to cheat a poor hen out of the pleasures of maternity. Machine-born chickens! What is home without a mother?

I suggested to H that he vaccinate his hens with chicken-pox virus. Then the eggs would have their embryo hereditarily inoculated and none of the chickens would have the disease. For economy's sake he could start with one hen and rooster. He being a scientific man with no farm experience, I explained the necessity of having a rooster. He saw the force of this suggestion at once.

The sun has left us on time. Am going to read from the Encyclopedia Britannica to steady my nerves, and go to bed early. I will shut my eyes and imagine a terraced abyss, each terrace occupied by a beautiful maiden. To the first I will deliver my mind and they will pass it down to the uttermost depths of silence and oblivion. Went to bed. Worked my imagination for a supply of maidens. Only saw Mina, Daisy and Mamma. Scheme busted—sleep.

THOMAS EDISON

JULY 13

1804

Take Mr. Harrison out to dine with me. Discuss the points which it may be safe to touch to-morrow, and those which it will be proper to avoid.... The first point of his biography is that he was a stranger of illegitimate birth; some mode must be contrived to pass over this handsomely. He was indiscreet, vain, and opinionated; these things must be told or the character will be incomplete, and yet they must be told in such manner as not to destroy the interest. He was in principle opposed to republican and attached to monarchical government.... His share in forming our Constitution must be mentioned, and his unfavorable opinion cannot therefore be concealed. The most important part of his life was his administration of the finances. The system he proposed was in one respect radically wrong; moreover, it has been the subject of some just and much unjust criticism.... All this must, somehow or another, be reconciled. He was in principle opposed to duelling, but he has fallen in a duel. I cannot thoroughly excuse him without criminating Colonel Burr, which would be wrong.... In addition to all the difficulties of this subject is the impossibility of writing and committing anything to memory in the short time allowed. The corpse is already putrid, and the funeral procession must take place to-morrow morning.

GOUVERNEUR MORRIS

1885

[I] tried to shave with a razor so dull that every time I scraped my face it looked as if I was in the throes of *cholera morbus.* If I could get my mind down to details perhaps [I] could learn to sharpen it, but on the other hand I might cut myself.

As I had to catch the 7:30 a.m. train for New York, I hurried breakfast, crowded meat, potatoes, eggs, coffee, tandem down into the chemical room of my body.... Rushed and caught train. Bought *New York World* at Elizabeth for my mental breakfast....

Went to New York via Desbrosses Street ferry. Took cars across town. Saw a woman get into car that was so tall and frightfully thin as well as dried up that my mechanical mind at once conceived the idea that it would be the proper thing to run a lancet into her arm and knee joints and insert automatic self-feeding oil cups to diminish the creaking when she walked.

Got off at Broadway. Tried experiment of walking two miles to our office—65 Fifth Avenue—with idea it would alleviate my dyspeptic pains. It didn't.

Went to Scribner & Sons on way up, and saw about a thousand books I wanted.... Mind No. 1 said, why not buy a box full and send to Boston now. Mind No. 2 (acquired and worldly mind) gave a most withering mental glance at Mind No. 1 and said, You fool, buy only two books. These you can carry without trouble and will last you until you get to Boston. Buying books in New York to send to Boston is like "carrying coals to Newcastle." Of course I took the advice of this earthly adviser. Bought Aldrich's story of a bad boy, which is a spongecake kind of literature, very witty and charming, and a work on Goethe and Schiller by Boynsen, which is soggy literature. A little wit and anecdote in this style of literature would have the same effect as baking soda on bread—give pleasing results.

Waited one hour for appearance of a lawyer who is to cross-examine me on events that occurred eleven years ago. Went on stand at 11:30. He handed me a piece of paper with some figures on it, not another mark. Asked in a childlike voice if these were my figures, what they were about and what day eleven years ago I made them. This implied compliment to the splendor of my memory was at first so pleasing to my vanity that I tried every means to trap my memory into stating just what he wanted—but then I thought what good is a compliment from a ten cent lawyer, and I waived back my recollection. A lawsuit is the suicide of time.

THOMAS EDISON

JULY 14

1776

It was a wettish day, and it looked as if all was dead in the town. The English [Church of England] churches were shut up, and there was services in none, or few of the others; we had not many hearer either.

BROTHER EWALD GUSTAV SCHAUKIRK

1776

A Flag of Truce from the fleet appeared, on which Col°. Reed and myself, went down to meet it, about half way between Governors and Staten Islands. Lieutenant Brown, of the [HMS] *Eagle*, offered a Letter from Lord Howe, directed [to] George Washington, Esqr., which on acc^t. of its direction [lack of deference], we refused to Receive, and parted with the usual Compliments.

SAMUEL BLACHLEY WEBB

[The British refused to address Washington as "his excellency" as the Continentals demanded.]

1908

Working on the last of the drawings for "The Moonstone." A terrific rainstorm came up in the afternoon, the clouds black and gray and wicked green were fine. I went on the roof to look at them.... first rain of any account for a whole month. Dolly and I, after dinner at home, went out for a walk, stopped in Mouquin's.... We had too many Gin Rickeys, too many for us... Came home and to bed in bad condition. We must quit this.

JOHN SLOAN

JULY 15

1850

I have not written in my diary for ever so long, but now school has just closed for the summer, and I have time.

We had a new study last winter, something to strengthen our memories....

We had charts to paint on,... and one-half of the page was a country and the other half was for the people who lived in that country.... Mesopotamia was yellow, and Abraham, who lived there, was royal purple, and so I shall never forget that he lived in Mesopotamia, but I may not remember after all which was yellow, the man or the country, but I don't suppose that is really any matter as long as I don't forget where he lived.

CATHERINE ELIZABETH HAVENS

1997

When you become a Nielsen Family you encounter others similarly anointed, like VW drivers honking at each other on the highway. We have this in common: none of us is honest.... I've completed my first three days of Nielsen viewing, and I lie too, feeling no obligation to serve the commercial interests of the Nielsens. They virtually demand deception, instructing us diarists: "Please remember... This may be your only opportunity to tell the TV industry the programs watched in your home.... This will help to bring you more of the programs you watch." I can imagine few things more hellish than receiving more of the programs I watch. And so, I reward the virtuous (*Dr. Katz, Professional Therapist*), punish the wicked (*Rosie O'Donnell*), and log any show where a friend works (*Politically Incorrect*). It helps the people I care about and, I think, serves the larger society by reminding the Nielsens, the networks, and me to remain skeptical of the phrase "studies have shown."

A "Nielsen Family"

JULY 16

1847

The Chinese junk [is] moored off the Battery. Entrance to it on the payment of Twenty Five Cents. What was added on actual observation to the information that would be conveyed by a print or model was the development of intense curiosity on the part of the visitors—ladies staring with eagerness at the trumpery China plates the companions to which they have been familiar with all their days. For this they knocked their heads against beams, ascended upright ladders, stumbled over bamboo cordage and did impossibilities with the thermometer at 90°. The red and raucous natives have monopolized the fair sex at the ice cream tables in the garden. Bigelow got the ear of H . . . (distinguished as Captain by a worsted top knot) and the latter asked where the women were to be had that night.... Fronting the forecasle a very respectable monkey tenanted the ledge, splendidly bearded and splendidly tailed. Pigeons from the Celestial Empire hovered over the huge stern and New York gentlemen groped in their holes as if there were eggs there of pearl or of gold. It is a money making enterprise worthy of Barnum.

EVERT DUYCKINCK

1985

Cabbed to meet Ric Ocasek of the Cars who's doing a solo album, and we were filming him for our MTV pilot show, *Andy Warhol's Fifteen Minutes* (cab $6).

And there was a big rainstorm with big hailstones and that was exciting. We ran around with buckets, putting them under all the holes in the roof.

ANDY WARHOL

2001

Is it a crime to want to muzzle a mockingbird?

VICTORIA BALFOUR

JULY 17

1956

At the Warwick Hotel in a room full of crones for a movie. A collection of age and failure. I among them, prematurely uglied, am cast as an extra in a film I don't even know the name of.

Before we got into this Greyhound bus that takes us to location on the Lower East Side, I learned what Lester meant when he describes the "shape up" at the docks where some are chosen to work and some are sent away. We were lined up in our costumes while three men with clipboards came in and pointed: "This one. That one. Her. Her."

At Orchard and Rivington, we are surrounded by those whom we are trying to imitate. We stood under a huge banner that said Jimmy Walker for Mayor. The director stood on a ladder and shouted; we cheered as directed.

JUDITH MALINA

1997

A man from Nielsen called this afternoon. I was scared. Had he torn away my veil of anonymity? Mercifully, it was only a follow-up call. Just routine. Once again I was asked if I'd received my diary, was I filling it in, did I have any questions, was I eating well balanced meals and getting plenty of sleep? So far the Nielsens have sent me three postcards and phoned three times. Which reminds me: I should call my mother.

A "NIELSEN FAMILY"

JULY 18

1776

Thursday 18th, was the day appointed when Independence was to be declared in the City Hall here; which was done about noon; and the Coat of Arms of the King was burnt. An unpleasant and heavy feeling prevailed.

BROTHER EWALD GUSTAV SCHAUKIRK

1997

"Now that you have completed your diary, just moisten the gummed edge below, fold it over your address on the cover and seal it. Please drop your diary into the mail right away. We will pay the postage."

It ended so quickly, my week of watching TV as if it mattered. I miss it already. I'm tempted to continue on my own, keeping a pad of graph paper by the TV.... Some highlights from my week:

Fran's latest beau turns out to be her cousin...the kids try to play Cupid to a couple of aging rhinos...a priest's vestment catches fire during a wedding (comedy)...While chatting with a tyrant, Diane Sawyer twinkles seductively...

Just as historians of today delve into 16th-century church records or ancient Roman account books, archaeologists of tomorrow will someday discover a warehouse piled with Nielsen diaries. I already feel anticipatory embarrassment, maybe a thousand years in advance. I knew I should have listed more stuff on PBS.

A "Nielsen Family"

July 19

1776

...Met with Lieu^r. Hayward, & with him took an opportunity to survey the Fire Ships,—the Chiver du frieze [*chevaux de frise*, or sunken barbed barricades] & Ships preparing to sink in the River. The Fire Ships are well constructed, and may do execution; but the Chiver du frieze can be of little service, as it is too weakly constructed to do damage to a Vessell of any Strength.

Lt. Isaac Bangs

1776

A flag appeared this morning when Col^o. Reed & myself went down. Aid de camp to General Howe met us—and said, as there appeared an insurmountable obstacle between the two Generals, by way of

Corresponding, General Howe desired his Adjutant General might be admitted to an Interview with his Excellency General Washington—On which Col°. Reed, in the name of General Washington, consented; and pledg'd his honor for his being safe returned.

SAMUEL BLACHLEY WEBB

JULY 20

1643

A chief of the savages came to me, and told me that he was very sad. I asked him wherefor. He said that there were many of the Indian youths, who were constantly wishing for a war against us, as one had lost his father, another his mother, a third his uncle, and also their friends, and that the presents or recompense were not worth taking up; and that he would much rather have made presents out of his own purse to quiet them; but he could no longer keep still, and that I must be careful in going alone in the woods; that those who knew me would do me no harm, but I might meet Indians who did not know me, who would shoot me. I told him that he ought to go to Commander Kieft at the fort, and tell the same things to him. We went to the fort.... Commander Kieft told this savage he was a chief of the Indians and must kill these young madcaps who wished to engage in a war with the Swannekens [Dutch], and he would give him two hundred fathoms of *zeewan*. I then laughed within myself, that the Indian should kill his friends for two hundred fathoms of *zeewan*—that is eight hundred guilders—to gratify us. It is true that they do so towards each other, when they are at enmity with each other, but not at the will of foreigners.

DAVID PIETERSZ. DE VRIES

1776

About noon, a General Adjutant from Lord Howe came, and had a short conversation with General Washington, in Kennedy's house.

When he went away he said, it is reported, to Washington and the others with him: "Sir and gentlemen, let it be remembered that the King has made the first overture for peace; if it be rejected, you must stand by the consequences"; and thus—which seems to have been the main errand—he departed. Much politeness passed on both sides.

BROTHER EWALD GUSTAV SCHAUKIRK

1925

Wrote first draft of "What's Wrong with the Negro Theatre." ... Paul & Essie Robeson at Rita Romilly's studio. They have a remarkable conversation in which Essie reiterates her desire to completely possess Paul & Paul expresses his resentment of this. They left about 1, and I stayed till 1:30. Home & to bed.

CARL VAN VECHTEN

JULY 21

1779

Lord Cornwallis and his company arrived from England in the *Greyhound.*

BROTHER EWALD GUSTAV SCHAUKIRK

1978

So here is Little T [Truman Capote] in the newspaper again: drunk, pills, not able to finish a television appearance, saying he "would probably end up killing himself accidentally." Adding, "nothing has ever jelled" in his life. What does he really mean? What is this about? The result of having tried for something he could not achieve? His gift was anecdotal, atmospheres, nuances of terror and mystification. He was a remarkable storyteller with a sensitive heart. He was (is, I believe still) an intuitive. The extent was journalism, which made him believe (*In Cold Blood*) that he was a "great" writer, one of the greatest. In his genre (and it was always genre fiction or reporting), he was very good, sometimes first-rate ("Children on Their Birthdays," "Christmas Memory"), but to become this American Proust—I think impossible for him. He has broken himself upon this wheel. He has come undone.... T believed the legend that he made, which the American way of publicity aggrandized. Publicity—media—identical. In a sense, he is Marilyn Monroe. The Strasbergs [Actors Studio] tried to educate her into something she could not be. T could be the Marilyn Monroe of literature.

LEO LERMAN

JULY 22

1776

A poor Black deserted to us this Morning, and came down paddling in a Canoe from the Town. Three or four Whites had agreed to come off with him; but, staying beyond the Time agreed on, the poor Fellow ventured down alone. By him we learnt, that the [Continental] Rebels were much disconcerted on the Passage of the Ships, and that they had six Men killed.

AMBROSE SERLE

1861

This morning we felt flushed with victory, and I began dictating terms to the [Confederate] rebels, lamenting only to Harriet Whetten, who is staying a day or two with me, that Jefferson Davis would not be punished in a general amnesty.

This afternoon came distressing accounts of the sequel of the capture of the batteries at Bull Run; namely, that a panic had seized our troops, General Johnston had joined General Beauregard and had the Federal Army men in full retreat upon Washington with the loss of all of their artillery and 3,000 killed; that it was a complete rout, General Blenker's brigade alone making a stand and retreating in good order. God help us if this is so. I trust we may receive better accounts tomorrow. Charles has gone to the club to hear the last telegrams.

MARIA LYDIG DALY

1863

This afternoon, July 22ᵈ, I have spent a long time with Oscar F. Wilber, company G, 154th New York, low with chronic diarrhoea, and a bad wound also. He asked me to read him a chapter in the New Testament.... He said, "Make your own choice." I open'd at the close of one of the first books of the evangelists, and read the chapters describing the latter hours of Christ, and the scenes at the crucifixion. The poor, wasted young man ask'd me to read the following chapter also, how Christ rose again. I read very slowly, for Oscar was feeble. It pleased him very much, yet the tears were in his eyes. He ask'd me if I enjoy'd religion. I said, "Perhaps not, my dear, in the way you mean, and yet, may-be, it is the same thing." He said "It is my chief reliance." He talk'd of death, and said he did not fear it. I said, "Why, Oscar, don't you think you will get well?" He said, "I may, but it is not probable." He spoke calmly of his condition. The wound was very bad, it discharg'd much. Then the diarrhoea had prostrated him, and I felt that he was even then the same as dying. He behaved very manly and affectionate. The kiss I gave him as I was about leaving he return'd fourfold. He gave me his mother's address.... He died a few days after the one just described.

WALT WHITMAN

1873

Great wealth, unless inherited, or acquired by professional energy and industry, is now, as a general rule, presumptive evidence

234 · *New York Diaries*

against the character of its owner.... Most of the dodges, devices, and complots which Wall Street considers legitimate and in which millions are lost and won (on paper) every day, are, of course, plainly guileful, dishonest, and wicked. But how many of our nice, fresh, ingenuous boys are plunged into this filthy pool every year at eighteen or even younger... though their parents could well afford them a liberal education. Each hopes to win some great prize in that great gambling house, an establishment far less honest than were those of Baden-Baden and Homburg. And so they grow up to be mere illiterate sharpers, with possible fine houses and fine horses and fine Newport cottages and without capacity to appreciate anything higher—men without culture and with damaged and dwarfed moral sense.

GEORGE TEMPLETON STRONG

1909

Worked on the Pirate story during the day and finished in the evening late, after we returned from the "Casalinga" Club. Our first dinner there. The dining room is in the garden of a house on 38th St. We met besides the Henris and the Roberts, Mr. Yeats, the father of W. B. Yeats, Irish poet. Mr. Yeats was a very interesting old gentleman with white beard. Kindly and well-informed, he is a painter, I believe, also a writer.... He represented the *Literary Digest*.... [He] made the statement that liberty-loving nations were peaceful, that it had a soporific effect. The principle being— don't interfere with your neighbor. On the other hand, a nation or people who love "Justice" are turbulent, restless—the French, for instance.

JOHN SLOAN

1986

I've been watching this stuff on Fergie and I wonder why doesn't the Queen Mother get married again.

ANDY WARHOL

JULY 23

1863

At last the [draft] riot is quelled, but we had four days of great anxiety. Fighting went on constantly in the streets between the military and police and the mob, which was partially armed. The greatest atrocities have been perpetrated. Colonel O'Brian was murdered by the mob in such a brutal manner that nothing in the French Revolution exceeded it. Three or four Negroes were hung and burned; the women assisted and acted like furies by stimulating the men to greater ferocity. Father came into the city on Friday, being warned about his house, and found fifteen Negroes secreted in it by Rachel. They came from York Street, which the mob had attacked, with all their goods and chattels. Father had to order them out. We feared for our own block on account of the Negro tenements below Mac-Dougal Street, where the Negroes were on the roof singing psalms and having firearms....

I saw Susanna Brady, who talked in the most violent manner against the Irish and in favor of the blacks. I feel quite differently, although very sorry and much outraged at the cruelties inflicted. I hope it will give the Negroes a lesson, for since the war commenced, they have been so insolent as to be unbearable. I cannot endure free blacks. They are immoral, with all their piety.

MARIA LYDIG DALY

JULY 24

1810

At eleven o'clock... [we] walked to the head of the rapid where we again embarked. From this place to the Seneca Lake the river is one and a-half chains wide, and from eight to ten feet deep. The color is a cerulean or a beautiful sea-green.

DeWitt Clinton

1910

Walked out for the Press and stopped a while in Madison Square where I surreptitiously left three copies of "The Appeal to Reason" *Socialist Weekly* (very rabid) on the benches in the fond hope of spoiling someone's peace of mind.

John Sloan

JULY 25

1778

At 8 A.M. I marched... to what was called the Morris House where his Ex'c'y. General [Wilhelm] von Knypphaussen [*sic*] lived and where the Chasseur [Hunter] Company was to rendezvous. The Company was formed out of the 11 regiments on *York* island,... and consisted in all of 4 officers, 12 subofficers, 3 drummers and 100 privates. General Knypphaussen instructed the Hessian officers and then we marched to a hill *Spakent Hiell*...near *Courthland's* House, 9½ English miles from Donop's camp, where the Yagers [*Jäger,* elite riflemen and stalkers] were stationed. I was obliged to be commanding sergeant and Lieut. Col. von *Wurmb,* who commanded the whole Yager Corps, promised me his aid. We had to build huts here and at first I had a great deal to do, with little rest day or night and not being able to undress.... We had a hard time with our provisions too, getting neither beer nor vinegar.... I was with the Chasseur Company of Capt. Von Hanger's, in camp *Spaken Hüll* [Spuyten Duyvil Hill].

LT. JOHN CHARLES PHILIP VON KRAFFT

1958

Lee [Krasner] has been "dismissed" (her word) by her therapist. In this case dismissal means that he has gotten as much help from her as he can.

B. H. FRIEDMAN

JULY 26

1810

We departed at five o'clock for the Sulphur Springs, in Farmington, six miles distant....

As you approach the Springs, the smell of sulphur reminds you of the Stygian lake, of heathen mythology.... There is a bathing-house adjacent to the spring, for the accommodation of invalids. It is supposed that there is some arsenic in the waters. Having before seen a sulphur spring at Cherry Valley, my curiosity was not much excited.

DEWITT CLINTON

1950

Went to Central Park.

Walked to where they rent out the boats. All boats were out. The pond thick with people.

For while I stood watching a Scotchman playing bagpipes. I thought he was playing just for himself, but on coming closer I saw a crowd of people standing and watching, and his friend was collecting money in a cup. The Scotchman was playing with his back to the people, facing the bush.... Maybe the melody made him remember something sad?

JONAS MEKAS

JULY 27

1786

This morning we have been taking a ride about the City. The objects therein begin to become familiar.... You see a white house, a red house, a yellow house, a green house, a blue house, a high house, a low house, a square house. A zig-zag house,...a clean house (but rarely) or a dirty house in a town.... Yet I confess I like the hurly burly and bustle of a large town.... You may stand in one place...and see a great variety of faces, figures, and Characters as Hogarth...ever drew—"Come Gentlemen, walk into Mr. Rivington's shop for half an hour, and let us take a peep at the Characters and figures that are passing the Door."...Who is that plodding fellow who is passing at this moment. See what a low Bow he made to the Gentleman in a pea Green silk. The Gentleman in Green is a member of Congress and has been a very distinguished partisan officer. He who made him so low a Bow is Mr. Spee [a hypothetical war profiteer]. When the British Army took possession of this place Mr. Spee remained here. To shew his Loyalty to his sovereign and at the same time gratify his own private propensities, Mr. Spee became one of the Contractors for the Army. Thus he served his King and his God Mamon at once. When Continental Currency was first emitted Mr. Spee was one of the first to advise the counterfieting [*sic*] and dispersing it through the rebel colonies.... The royal cause began to decline. Mr. Spee was still ambidexter...N. York is evacuated.... [Spee] determines to brave danger and stay in N. York while his Brother Tories were embarking for Nova Scotia.

Here was a new field for making money—Houses, Lands, Goods, etc., belonging to those timid Souls, went abegging for purchasers.... Spee is sure to be the first to gain advantage by it. He now cringes and bows to every man in power...and anticipates the joy of pillaging both countries.

ST. GEORGE TUCKER

JULY 28

1852

It appears that the Steamboats *America* & *Henry Clay* were racing down the North river, both having left Albany at AM & when the *Henry Clay* was about Yonkers, she was discovered to be on fire, she was burnt to the waters edge—

WILLIAM RANDELL

1861

The more we hear from those who were in the battle of Bull Run, the more exasperating does it seem. Had the officers behaved themselves well, had they been fitted to command, the victory would have been ours....

My flag, which I gave to the 69th, was lost. The ensign dropped it in his retreat, and as he escaped unhurt, has not dared to show his face. The Regiment declared that he shall be shot if he does. He is skulking somewhere about in Washington, and sent on to his wife for nine dollars to enable him to come home. But if he does, the Regiment vows vengeance for the disgrace. If anyone asks me about it, I shall say that one of the ensigns was killed and nothing more. The brave fellows shall not suffer for the fault of *one*. Besides, it was the first battle, and I would forgive the poor fellow and give him another chance.

MARIA LYDIG DALY

1912

My first Callers.

Morton Solomon and George [H] called to visit me. We chatted for a while and ate candy then we sang both ragtime and classical songs. Mr. Solomon has a beautiful voice. It sounded lovely when we two sang together. Then they both sat one on each side of me on our long piano chair and we sang love songs with our own remarks between. It was simply great!! They complimented me very much. Darling Ma served raspberry drinks and…ginger cake…they made me sing "A Perfect Day!" Morton gave a solo also. We sang, all three together—"Silver Threads Amongst the Gold." It was after 10 when they were sent home. Had a great time!!

SARA HOEXTER BLUMENTHAL

JULY 29

1810

Six miles from Abbey's we put up for the night at Matteson's tavern, an open log house, in the town of Murray, where we suffered the want of sleep, and encountered every other privation. Two slept in the garret, three on the floor on mattrasses [*sic*], and I thought myself happy in putting mine on a wooden chest, where I avoided the attacks of kittens. The night was very damp and rainy—the musquitoes abundant; and we were serenaded by the jingling of cow-bells, and the screaming of drunken clowns.

DEWITT CLINTON

1852

Morning Clear & Very Warm…. The finding [of] bodies lost by the *Henry Clay* still continues, and the coroner of Westchester County holding inquest on the same.

WILLIAM RANDELL

JULY 30

1786

Col. Carrington and myself visited Fort Washington which is situated on a considerable eminence on the New York side of the north river.... This place is remarkable for the capture of 2700 Americans, who were mostly starved to death by the British General Howe.... there was some very fine Corn growing. There were also some tatters of American regimental uniforms still to be found on the rocks which are bare in several places.

ST. GEORGE TUCKER

1810

We left this disagreeable place at half-past five, and after a ride of four hours through a wilderness, we arrived at one Downer's, a private house...[where] we partook of a comfortable breakfast on our own provisions....

The rain discontinuing, we proceeded to Sibley's tavern... [where] we halted awhile. The land along this route has been sold by the Holland Land Company for from eighteen to twenty shillings per acre. The Ridge Road was laid out by their agents about two years since, and may be considered as a great natural turnpike. In imagination, one might suppose that this ridge was a great road, created some thousand years ago, by the powerful emperor of a populous State, to connect the lakes with the interior country; ... against incursions from the lakes. Such as it is, the lashing of the waves...has spread this ridge with gravel; and if the stumps of the trees are eradicated, and the cavities filled up, it may be made the best road in the United States.

DEWITT CLINTON

1958

Tomato appeared on roof vine! Potted in shallow pan at that. Also, in the evening an enormous butterfly flew in the window, which I caught. Most beautiful creature, six inch wings almost of delicate pink verging on beige with a sky blue stripe. Cocktails with Malcolm Cowley re: novel at Harvard Club and Algonquin yesterday.

DAWN POWELL

JULY 31

1830

A brilliant morning, but no wind. [We are] beginning to feel it very warm. The pilot reports it the hottest summer they have had since the year 1822, for some days the thermometer in the shade having stood at 93°;—appalling intelligence after the temperature we have been exposed to for the last five weeks, muffled up in top-coats and cloaks, and shivering even then, and now finding our lightest summer attire almost oppressive.—Scarcely a breath of air until four o'clock, when we had just enough to put us in motion for the city, the approach to which is very fine, heightened by the beauty of the day and the extreme clearness of the atmosphere. The shores on each side, though a good deal wooded, have, nevertheless, a rich and cultivated appearance, often ornamented with a handsome villa, and everywhere well guarded with fortifications. Governor's Island, nearer the city, also a military station, is a beautiful object, and soon the Battery, Castle Gardens, many of the churches and public buildings, and Brooklyn on the heights, with crouds [*sic*] of shipping in the Bay, arrest the attention, and cannot fail to excite deep interest in the mind of a stranger.

JOHN FOWLER

1847

Dined with Herman Melville at the Astor House. He is to be married next Wednesday. He is cheerful company without being very [illeg.] or original and models his work on Washington Irving.

EVERT DUYCKINCK

1851

On duty—This morning about 10 o'clock I arrested an Italian woman whom I found begging about the Park—she had a printed petition which she used for the purpose of Begging = the following is a copy

TO THE BENEVOLENT

The bearer Mrs. Mary [Botto?] arrived in this city from Genoa about 9 months since in comparatively good circumstances with her husband and four children. Shortly after their arrival the Husband contracted with that scourge of the human family = the Comsumption: which in the course of a few months caused his death.

The wife spared no expence in procuring such medical aid as was likely to effect a cure or arrest the progress of the disease. In doing so she expended all her means and after the expense of his internment was left almost penniless. We have remitted a portion of our fees & recommend her to the favorable consideration of the public.

Signed

G. S. Watson MD

Dr. S…Valentino Mott. MD

P. S. The bearer is ignorant of the English language—any donations in clothing, groceries, etc shall be thankfully & gratefully received by your humble petitioners.

I took her before Justice Lathrop who committed her to the Penitentiary as a vagrant for 3 months. The woman was unable to speak English and from her actions I understood she had children. Fearing that they would suffer I obtained permission from Mr. Edmonds to allow one of the prisoners in the Tombs who could speak Italian to interpret—upon questioning her I learned she had come to this country with 4 children. She said she lived in Washington St. I went in and requested Justice Lathrop not to send her up until I could find her children & have them provided for by permission of the Magistrate. I took the woman out of Prison and brought her down to this office = Mr. Bang's assisted me in finding an interpreter—we got Mr. Dominico Medina an Italian to translate to us in English. During his examintion [*sic*] learned that she had sold two of her children to a woman for the purpose of Begging. Upon asking her as to when and where she had obtained the Petition she replied she would not tell and said that she had sworn not to tell. I learned that there is a large and well organized gang...of these imposters & that they are sent out here at a [premium?] for the express purpose of begging. She would not tell the number of the house she lived so I told her to go home. I followed her up to No. 479 Washington Street in the rear. When she entered she went up to the top story where there [were] 5 men organ grinders with their monkeys & 6 or 8 small children, one of these was sick. As I should suppose, the small pox. The men were eating their macaroni soup. I told the woman to take her child and go back to prison with me—one of the men said she could not go. I took hold of the woman when three of these men attempted to interfere when I slaped [*sic*] him alongside of the head which set the men women & children a jabbering & crying. The monkeys squealed and was almost frightened to death. After considerable trouble I got the woman & children to the Tombs where she was locked up to be sent to [the] Island.

INSPECTOR WILLIAM H. BELL

AUGUST 1

[BRITISH FLEET SIGHTED OFF SANDY HOOK.]

1776

Lieut. General Clinton, having with him Lieut. General Earl *Cornwallis,* arrived with a large Fleet of transports from South-Carolina.... The 33d Regiment joined the Flying Army. The 50th Regiment came in also, and were soon after drafted into the weakest Regiments; being they were returned unfit for service, and the Corp was sent home to England.

The Landgrave of Hesse Cassel gave his Majesty 12,000 Men, to serve in America. They arrived in Staten Island in this Month under the command of Lieut General De Hester.

The 42nd Regiment, or Royal Highlanders, came also, being 1000 strong: But three Companies of them were taken Prisoners by the Enemy on the Passage.

THOMAS SULLIVAN

1974

Mikhail Baryshnikov yesterday morning. He came to be photographed by Avedon, who came from Fire Island and his illness to do this. He could be any boy on a street corner—pale, stockyish, blond, retiring, but friendly, slight. If he were in a room with other people, he would not be noticed save for his deep-set, heavily shadowed, sad, somewhat doomed blue eyes—eyes curiously related to Marlene's now that she is old and lost, her world gone quite awry. His dancing strength comes from his feet—beautifully shaped feet of enormous strength and flexibility. You feel that he could write with his feet. (Rudi [Nureyev]'s dancing strength comes from his buttocks, Eddie Villella's from his thighs.) When this boy stands on the floor, peering into a long glass, warming up, he becomes noble romantic—a tremendous presence, not flashy but magical. Then suddenly he is airborne: There is no visible preparation. He is so masculine that there is a sort of feminine quality that flavors his dancing. He could be a marvelous Spectre de la Rose or Harlequin or Petrouchka—all of the Ninjinsky roles—but with a different sensibility. Baryshnikov has humor, a sense of fun. Also, he has a sense of atmosphere in stage works.

LEO LERMAN

1991

I've pretty much isolated myself from almost all the people I know, especially since the last two months when I was so fucking ill—constant nausea, head pains,... feeling that my system is poisoning me and having bone biopsy, intestinal biopsy, and blood work.... For a while I was injecting myself with interferon, now I'm on steroids. They made me feel a boost for a week or so but now I have trouble shitting again, fevers 101–102°, nausea all day, on some days head pains again. I'm sick of being sick and it aggravates me to speak to people who have a degree of normalcy in their lives.... Humans obviously can never fathom what suffering feels like; there's a block in the brain that prevents it....

This psychiatrist called me at the bidding of a friend. We talked for about forty minutes. He asked me about my sexual activities, my depression.... He wanted to know if I had been into S/M. I was surprised at the question. I told him of my few experiences and how I realized with low tolerance to pain I wasn't into it....

Anyway, I'll see this psychic next week. Who knows, maybe I can release some of my state of mind and get some relief.... I'll give this guy a handful of sessions and see where it goes. I feel interested to try but also somewhere in my head I wonder at whether another human can actually touch me deeply as I seem to need at this point in my life.

DAVID WOJNAROWICZ

AUGUST 2

1754

[For] Cornelius Rosevelt [*sic*] Dr. . . . [Ordered] a 501b Chocolate box.

JOSHUA DELAPLAINE

1842

A coloured man lectured this evening at Five Corners about slavery.

JAMES FRANCIS BROWN

1948

And now, despite all, or perhaps because of all, of course, to finish the work of the novel once and for all. Got a letter from Neal, had an urge to answer right away, but would end up losing a day's work on a fresh-beginning Monday, so will wait. Worked, slept, walked, worked grudgingly—then, in the middle of the night, a wonderful interlude for myself:—spaghetti with the blood-red sauce and meatballs, Parmesan, grated cheddar, chicken cuts, with red Italian wine and chocolate ice cream, black demitasse coffee; and a 28 cent Corona cigar; and the life of Goethe (and loves),—all in the kitchen. And I never planned this, I just did it. Then I went back to work at 2:00 A.M. Spent night correcting 50 pages of ancient manuscript and rewriting parts, now a 30-page chapter, to be typed. Went to bed at 7 A.M.

JACK KEROUAC

1978

Reentry. Back in the city again. Today I visited my grandparents to prove to myself that not everything here is gray and harsh and mean. On the subway coming home, I was doodling in my note-

books, and as the train began to pull out of the Brighton Beach
station, I glanced up and saw a young black man standing on the
opposite platform. He waved and leered at me and licked his lips.
I frowned pointedly, as always when this happens, and lowered
my head and lifted my pen from my notebook so he could see it
(a weapon?).... I've been thinking about my reaction to him. The
frowning is a carefully acquired habit, something I've trained myself to do when men say anything to me on the street. I suppose that
every woman has to decide sooner or later, if she lives in New York,
how she's going to deal with rude gestures and verbal assaults. You
pick a response, stick to it, refine it, and eventually you respond
that way without having to think about it.

MICHELLE HERMAN

AUGUST 3

1776

The Rebels we could perceive very busy all Day long, and, as our
People suppose, in constructing Fire Stages to consume [our] Ships.

AMBROSE SERLE

1777

A Whisper that Gen. Burgoyne has met with some Check by the
Rebels, but we hope 'tis without Foundation.

HUGH GAINE

1830

Rose this morning vastly refreshed, and feeling myself again. In
the course of the day made a pretty extensive perambulation of
the city.... I was highly pleased with it. The City-hall and the Exchange are indeed noble edifices. Many of the banks, hotels, and
other public places, are very spacious and elegant;... but, as a strik-

ing defect, I noticed a great want of uniformity in the building of the houses, and, in the business streets particularly, of a total inattention to neatness.... Revisited Brooklyn in the evening, of which, the more I see, the more I admire it.... Much of the land in the neighborhood of Brooklyn appears to be devoted to the raising of fruits and vegetables for its own and the New York markets; prodigious quantities of which are taken across the water daily.... I have counted eleven waggons driven off one steam-boat at a time; and a friend...told me there were frequently more. It is besides a place of considerable trade; contains tanneries, distilleries, cotton and linen cloth manufactories, rope-works, market-houses, and a great number of stores, warehouses, &c. There are several places of worship, a Lancasterian school, and other very respectable seminaries.—Thermometer at noon to day 81°.

JOHN FOWLER

1984
Went to Bernsohn, the crystal doctor, and he worked on my pancreas.

ANDY WARHOL

AUGUST 4

1776
A Rifleman (a Native of Ireland) came over the Narrows this evening. He says, that many more would desert the Rebels, if they could escape out of their Hands; but the Coast is strictly guarded to prevent any Step of that Kind. One would think, however, that it would be Wisdom to let such People depart, and have only those in their army whom they may depend upon, as the Desertion of Numbers in the Day of Battle may throw their whole Force into Confusion.

AMBROSE SERLE

AUGUST 5

1778

Some deserters came in from the Rebels. They were Brunswick-ers who had been taken prisoner with General *Burgonne* [*sic*]. They told us much news, for instance, that the Rebels received much and frequent help from the French. The French fleet which did not yet act in open hostility against us was eagerly expected. We passed many nights in this neighborhood without getting the slightest rest (owing to the great number of mosquitoes) and we suffered by day from the swarms of flies.

LT. JOHN CHARLES PHILIP VON KRAFFT

1847

Dull weather and cards. A dull set of vulgarians, jesting and slang-whanging with no wit to redeem the coarseness or an idea, by way of a background to any part of their conversation. There was some... readiness and pleasantry in a lawyer from the city named Barrett. Shall certainly get dyspeptic on these clams. The very name of the place, Quogue, is indigestible. Shall return to morrow morning.

EVERT DUYCKINCK

1909

Roof re-coated with tar-slate composition so that we feel safe from the elements again. This is a great relief.

Today is our eighth anniversary. Married eight years and neither Dolly nor I would have it otherwise. We have had our rubs but we have been very happy together.... Balfour Ker called in the evening. He was much interested in looking at some of my Daumier lithographs and at my etchings.

JOHN SLOAN

AUGUST 6

1849

I am ten years old to-day, and I am going to begin to keep a diary. My sister says it is a good plan....

I can remember as far back as when I was only four years old, but I was too young then to keep a diary, but I will begin mine by telling what I can recall of that far-away time....

Back of our house was an alley that ran through to the Bowery, and there was a livery stable,... and one time my brother, who was full of fun and mischief, got a pony from the stable and rode it right down into our kitchen and galloped it around the table and frightened our cook almost to death....

We moved from Lafayette Place to Brooklyn,...but only lived there one year. My brother liked Brooklyn because he could go crabbing on the river, but I was afraid of the goats.... So we came back to New York, and my father bought a house in Ninth Street. He bought it of a gentleman who lived next door to us, and who had but one lung, and he lived on raw turnips and sugar. Perhaps that is why he had only one lung. I don't know.

CATHERINE ELIZABETH HAVENS

1866

Cholera multiplies. Cases are confined as yet to our disgraceful tenement houses and foul side streets—filthy as pigsties and even less wholesome. The epidemic is God's judgment on the poor for neglecting His sanitary laws. It will soon appear as his judgment on the rich for tolerating that neglect—on landlords for poisoning the tenants of their unventilated, undrained, sunless rookeries, poisoning them as directly as if the landlord had put a little ratsbane into the daily bread of each of the hundred families crowded within the four walls of his pest-house.

GEORGE TEMPLETON STRONG

1950

Took a boat up the Hudson.

On the upper deck a group of teenagers sat and sang, accompanied by two guitars. Somebody beat a bongo drum. On the lower level, downstairs, a piano played and was very crowded. People danced, drank beer and whiskey, and the piano player, and everybody was very exuberant, in shirtsleeves, the girls in swimsuits. I stood leaning against the rail, on the steps leading down, and watched them. They danced, and the dances were unfamiliar to me, American and Latin dances.

Yes, this was life. They lived—I thought.... A few pairs sat under the stairs. I don't know whether they were lovers or had met here just a few minutes before, but they were very close, the girl didn't pay any attention to the people around and was in a trance of kissing and I was the invisible observer of all this. What could I be but a voyeur. A Displaced Person as Voyeur. Immigrant as Voyeur. A good title for my life, right now. That's all I could be, with my shy old world upbringing, in this open scene. But this was life, the real life of people with real roots.

JONAS MEKAS

AUGUST 7

1776

It was pleasing to hear the Hessians singing Psalms in the Evening, with great Solemnity; while, to our Shame, the British Navy & Army in general are wasting their Time in Imprecations or Idleness.

AMBROSE SERLE

1974

It's 6:45 a.m. below. My friends—anxiously watching through shared binoculars, awaiting my first step on the wire—are oblivious to the jostling of early commuters coming out of the subway....

I sit down on the wire, balancing pole on my lap.

Leaning against the steel corner, I offer to myself, for a throne, the highest tower ever built by man; for a ceremonial carpet, the most savagely gigantic city of the Americas; for my dominion, a tray of seas wetting my forehead; while the folds of my wind-sculpted cape surround me with majestically mortal whirls. . . .

I rise, standing up on the wire. . . .

Wire and I together, we voluptuously penetrate the cloudy layer that melts as we approach, as we pass between the twin towers. . . . I walk on air that softens under each step. I glide each foot. I cut through the whitish lump of breeze with the knife of my balancing pole. . . .

But for the crowd, what I just did will remain invisible. . . .

Barely will it distinguish a human being up there, strolling upon a thread. . . .

Already, a news bulletin is reporting the event on all the radio stations. Television networks are sending their crews downtown.

Ambulances, rescue vehicles, fire trucks, and police cars—with furious alarms—are forcing their way through the clogged traffic.

PHILIPPE PETIT

AUGUST 8

1927

Aaron Douglas comes to paint the bathroom & brings a marvellous design. . . . At 5:15 Robert Chisholm, the Australian baritone who is to sing in Arthur Hammerstein's opera, *Golden Dawn,* came in to meet Edna Thomas who is to teach him a Negro dialect.

CARL VAN VECHTEN

1990

Before five, the sky black as the [Chelsea Cinemas] metroplex (favorite new word) lets it get. Somewhat cooler and with a breeze out of the west, which makes the stink of the lobster shells more subtle.

The relief night clerk says, "The President is going to speak in the morning—about this Iraq business." He is laughing and full of gay expectation and hope. From what? The boob on the tube? They, it is said, come armed with chemical weapons: "mustard gas, nerve gas…" We are ready for that: we have gas masks, and more, we have the Stealth Bomber.

Is it a bird? Is it a plane? Is it a bathtub toy? Wait, alas, and see.

JAMES SCHUYLER

AUGUST 9

1776

Nothing material occurred this Day, wch [*sic*] was extremely warm. In constant Expectation of the [British] Fleet, & still disappointed.

AMBROSE SERLE

1854

Walked uptown this afternoon and inspected a quite splendid little conflagration in Elizabeth Street near Spring; two or three wooden shanties blazing and disgorging an incredible number of cubic feet of Irish humanity and filthy feather beds. While I was there, another alarm and red glare to the south sent us on a trot down to Broome Street, west of Centre, where a certain old meeting-house was in vigorous combustion. Saw it burned out and walked home.

GEORGE TEMPLETON STRONG

AUGUST 10

1924

The *Times* just printed "The Death of Thais" which had been returned to me by *The New Pearsons* when they went out of business. I have been at my novel again. I would [have] finished before doing anything else [if] I didn't want some real money quick. Novels are slow and short stories are a gold mine.

WINIFRED WILLIS

AUGUST 11

1778

Ensign *Kleinschmitt* of our Company and of Regiment *Woellwarth* deserted on account of his debts, while under leave of absence from N. York.

LT. JOHN CHARLES PHILIP VON KRAFFT

1864

Mother was telling me at dinner today, how glad she was when peace was declared, after the war of 1812 &c. She said her father told them he hoped they never would be compelled to see the horrors of war, as he had seen them in the Revolution. Mother's brothers were in the army at Brooklyn in 1812. She told me that her father came down to visit the [*sic*] & bring them some things, & she came with him. The camp must have been somewhere in the neighborhood of what is now Washington Park.

WALT WHITMAN

1906

Made a try with my sketch box and find it quite a new thing to paint outdoors. My work of this sort has usually been of city subjects from memory. Can't say that my attempt at the chicken yard back of the house was successful.

JOHN SLOAN

1913

We were all dressed and on deck. It was 2 o'clock and one could vaguely see a city, but very far away. The sea was gray and heavy. How different from the beautiful sea of Spain!...

It was 4 o'clock when the ship began to move again, slowly, as though she approached the great city with fear. Now, leaning on the railing, I couldn't hear anything. My eyes were fixed on the lights that grew closer, I saw the tall buildings, I heard the whistling of the engine, I saw a great deal of movement. Huge buildings went by in front of me. I hated those buildings in advance because they hid what I love most—flowers, birds, fields, liberty....

Although I admire New York for its progress, I hate it, I find it superficial. I saw it as an ugly prison.

ANAÏS NIN

AUGUST 12

1915

To the city in my oil-waggon, without aught untoward till I am come to 22nd Street, when a policeman cometh after me, saying, Why did you not stop? And I telling him I did not see his signal nor hear him call me, he believing me not at all, asked me whether I was blind and deaf, and I, fearing to make him a witty rejoinder, did say, No, sir. Which so enraged him that he bade me to come to the Police Court tomorrow morning at nine, albeit I had liefer [*sic*] go to a tennis court. But I feared to tell him that too, forasmuch as he did speak to me in so loud a voice it terrified me utterly. At my scrivening in the afternoon, but distrait over the imminence of a prison sentence for my so great crime.

FRANKLIN P. ADAMS

1961

Schrafft's at Eighty-eighth and Madison. All of the women have creaking voices like ancient rocking chairs.... Each of the creakers orders a Manhattan and the Diet Lunch. Crockity-crickity they go. One bravely summons the male manager and suggests that more fish be added to the menu. The headwaitresses are close kin to women who supervise "rest homes." "Not in the dining room," says the most rigidly haired one, the one with glittering spectacles in place of eyes and old 5-cent pieces in her throat. "We had that one out before, Mrs. Pomerantz." Mrs. Pomerantz is large and could blubber. Her three companions diminish in size, each a replica of Mrs. Pomerantz: whitened, carefully set hair, and pale, carefully set smiles; wide, wondering, have-lived-for-years eyes huge and aquatic behind glass; mouths satisfied by things, not love, by respect from servants, not admiration. The supervisors have utterly dissatisfied mouths. They hate the "ladies." "Do you have that lovely," one of the ladies' voices suddenly cascades, young and girlish, "black raspberry ice cream I had the other night?"

LEO LERMAN

AUGUST 13

1776

A great many Deserters, chiefly Irishmen, came off to the Ships this Day. It appears very evidently, that the Rebels are surprized with the appearance of so formidable a Fleet and Army. They have been in motion from one Part of their Works to another all the Day long.

AMBROSE SERLE

1915

It is one year, one year I have been in New York, a year full of work, of walks, and of endless dreams.... A year that we are here, that I breathe the air full of ambition that fills New York, and heaven help me not to fall victim to it because ambition counts many victims.

ANAÏS NIN

AUGUST 14

1776

Our Army now consists of about 24,000 men, in a most remarkable State of good Health & in high Spirits. On the other Hand, the Rebels are sickly & die very fast.

AMBROSE SERLE

1916

All day at my labours, and in the evening for a ride in my petrol-waggon to Yonkers. On the journey home I did notice a bicycle policeman toiling up the long Broadway hill from 200th Street to 181st Street, and my heart did sorry for him, as one cyclist's for another, and I bade him take hold of my petrol-waggon and helped him up the hill, for which he was grateful. But going down the hill at 130th Street I did ride rapidly and another policeman, Mr. Winfield Merritt I think was his name, and a fair spoken gentleman he was, too, did bid me halt; and told me to be in court at nine Wednesday morning. Home then, but could not sleep for being irritated at myself in being so foolhardy as to drive fast.

FRANKLIN P. ADAMS

1945

PEACE. At last—everyone going mad with joy.

7 P.M. Truman had surrender of Japs announced & the din was terrific—horns, bells, whistles, etc. Sailors kissing girls & almost broke their backs!

Drove down B'way honking horn—fun—confetti-paper all over.

Mr. Gans had whiskey party in lobby & then for hamburgers!

SARA HOEXTER BLUMENTHAL

AUGUST 15

1849

I know a little girl who has a stepmother, and she has [her] own child, and this step-child, and she dresses her own child very prettily but she makes the step-child wear nankeen pantalettes, and when she plays in the Parade Ground, the boys tease her and call her ginger legs, and she is very unhappy, it is a very sad case.

CATHERINE ELIZABETH HAVENS

AUGUST 16

1881

Everything propitious from the start. An hour's fresh stimulation, coming down ten miles of Manhattan island by railroad and 8 o'clock stage. Then an excellent breakfast at Pfaff's restaurant, 24th Street. Our host himself, an old friend of mine, quickly appear'd on the scene to welcome me and bring up the news, and, first opening a big fat bottle of the best wine in the cellar, talk about ante-bellum times, '59 and '60, and the jovial suppers at his then Broadway place, near Bleecker street. Ah, the friends and names and frequenters, those times, that place. Most are dead.... And there Pfaff and I, sitting opposite each other at the little table, gave a remembrance to them in a style they would have themselves fully confirm'd, namely, big, brimming, fill'd-up champagne-glasses, drain'd in abstracted silence, very leisurely, to the last drop. (Pfaff is a generous German *restaurateur*, silent, stout, jolly, and I should say the best selecter of champagne in America.)

WALT WHITMAN

1916

Up very betimes, and to the police court, where Mr. F. B. House heard my case and fined me a scant thirty dollars, which I might have only spent for something more foolish.

FRANKLIN P. ADAMS

1980

Convention vignettes: in the midst of the hurly burly of the week I glanced one morning out of our bedroom window. Below, sprawled on a deck chair, wearing jacket and tie, was Richard Nixon. Seated near him, wearing an afternoon dress and high-heeled shoes, was one of his daughters. A grandchild was playing. The two Nixons looked as if they were dressed for a garden party: even in his own house, his own garden.

ARTHUR M. SCHLESINGER, JR.

AUGUST 17

1879

Every Sunday we have morning and evening prayers: I wish we could have them every day.

Motherling is just too sweet and pretty for anything; and I doubt if there ever were too [*sic*] more lovely and unselfish girls than dear, noble Bysie [sister Anna], and darling little Pussie [sister Corinne]. These three, and my best friend, old brother Nell, give me as happy a home as a man could possibly have.

THEODORE ROOSEVELT

AUGUST 18

1776

Early in the morning the two men-of-war and their tender, that had been up the North River, came back; which caused again a sharp cannonading till they were passed. Yesterday, a fortnight ago, they had been attacked by the Row-gallies and a Privateer, which were obliged to desist from their attempt; having been greatly worsted by the men-of-war.... Last week they attacked them with fire-ships, but could not obtain their end, and lost one of their captains.

BROTHER EWALD GUSTAV SCHAUKIRK

1865

Definite news from the [Trans Atlantic] cable. It parted on the 2nd and went overboard in 1900 fathoms. The Great Eastern began forthwith dredging for the lost thread and Cyrus W. Field says it was grappled and raised three several times. But the rope always broke. So they anchored a buoy and steamed home to get some rope and try again.

GEORGE TEMPLETON STRONG

[Cyrus Field, an American entrepreneur who conceived of a "transAtlantic cable" for the purpose of telegraphy with Europe and supervised the fitful laying thereof.]

AUGUST 19

1810

The Mohawk country is greatly deficient in fruit trees. We saw no peach trees, but wild plums in great abundance.

DEWITT CLINTON

AUGUST 20

1927

All Harlem is gay with flags for the Elks convention next week.

CARL VAN VECHTEN

1955

To buy books.... I passed a food store. I saw apples, and plums, ripe, in the window. I have been dreaming since my childhood of eating a lot of fruits, someday.... I'll eat and eat and eat until I will not want anymore.... It's still only a dream.

JONAS MEKAS

AUGUST 21

1777

Nothing Worth Notice.

HUGH GAINE

AUGUST 22

[BRITISH INVASION OF LONG ISLAND]

1776

We had last Night a most terrible Storm of Wind, Thunder, & Lightening! So violent as I have not seen since about this time in August 1773.... Several Hundred Men are making a Breastwork still along the River only as a Defence from Musquetry.... Crack: Crack! An Alarm from Red-Hook. Crack! Crack! Crack! The Alarm repeated from Cobble-Hill. Orders are given for the Drums to beat

To Arms. The Enemy have been landing for some time down at the Narrows, &, it is said, have now ashore several thousand.

PHILIP VICKERS FITHIAN

1776

We weighed anchor and lay close over against Long Island. The ships of war came within range of the shore and pointed their cannon at the beach. At eight in the morning the whole coast swarmed with boats. At half-past eight the admiral hoisted the red flag, and in a moment all the boats reached shore. The English and Scotch, with the artillery, were first disembarked, and then the brigade of Colonel von Donop (the only Hessians there). Not a soul opposed our landing. This was the second blunder of the rebels since I have been in America. Their first mistake was when we disembarked on Staten Island, for they might then have destroyed a good many of our people with two six-pounders, and now they might have made it very nasty for us. We marched on, equally undisturbed, through Gravesend, and reached Flatbush towards evening. Three hundred riflemen had been there a little while before us. We sent a few cannon shots after them, set out our pickets, and slept quietly all night. I got two horses as booty, one of which I sent to the colonel and gave the other to my St. Martin for a pack-horse.

HESSIAN [ANONYMOUS]

1778

The Yagers almost mutinied on account of being kept three days without provisions. There was a constant calling for them. We Chasseurs [rapid infantry] got our rations separately and usually on time.

LT. JOHN CHARLES PHILIP VON KRAFFT

1822

Being acquainted with Mr. g. Mansfield Thomson, a clerk with Mr. wiley bookseller corner of Wall and new Street & hearing that he was sick of a disease supposed to be yellow fever went at noon this day to see him. Found not more than fifty persons walking in Broadway between St. Paul and Trinity Churches.... The Docks at the foot of those streets... were completely abandoned.... Found Mr. Wiley's store open.... All of the family of Mr. Wiley had left town from fear.... Thomson was on his back healthy constitution sanguine [temperament]... complained of [headache?] & fever yesterday morning Mr. Wiley gave him a dose of calomel... fever was very high all yesterday—At 8 o'clock last evening a Dr. Bliss threw over him 2 or 3 pails of cold water & at 8 this morning repeated it. When I saw him, pulse was depressed and feeble about 95 a minute—this a little more than natural beat—no difficulty [with] respiration but sighing—some pain in head... anxious look but the intellect of the patient perfectly rational—loquacious but it fatigues... him—I recommended large draughts of hot lemonade—I saw it was a decided case of yellow fever. I told Mr. Wiley confidentially when I came down he having then come in. He & his father both very confused.... He told me Dr. Bliss had called in this morn- ing... but could not determine what it was!... Soon after my leav- ing the patient... found by the bulletin in the evening papers that Dr. Bliss and Stevens had written to the Board that this case had not yet developed any unequivocal symptoms of Yellow Fever!! Being the first case however on the East side of Wall Street a part of the town considered even fit up to that time, it occasioned great alarm & the Eastern House & Banks began immediately to agitate the question of removing—[patient] died Saturday morning following at 8 o'clock at Greenwich whither he had been removed.

PHYSICIAN [ANONYMOUS]

1960

"When will this weather change?" the doorman asked as I stepped out from under the apartment-house awning into the heat of 62nd Street. These hot, sticky days seem to have been with us for so long that we have lost track of dates and can hardly remember when they began or what went before them. The cool sparkle of early autumn seems a distant mirage. Central Park is not really any cooler than the streets but I go there every morning to walk over the burnt grass and under the dusty trees before we have breakfast in the apartment. I get my first cup of coffee in the Zoo cafeteria and take it out on to the terrace. The coffee tastes of dishwater, the terrace tables have not yet been cleaned, and when I put my elbow on the green-painted table surface, grains of sugar stick to the sleeve of my coat....

Every day and every night this week has been occupied by the Security Council meetings on the Congo. Ever since the Belgians granted [it] independence...that country has been in turmoil.... That bloody Kuznetsov attacked me personally in the most insolent terms tonight for the support that Canada is giving to Ireland for the presidency of the Assembly. He said this was a Cold War move on our part. I said that he knew perfectly well that our Minister was, as he had so often proved, totally opposed to the Cold War. He replied that in any case Canada had no independence of its own and this was proved by the fact that we were members of NATO. I lost my temper at this, but my temper has got very frail anyway from sitting it out in this vast hot-box of New York, and I also lost my temper with the waiter at the Côte Basque restaurant.

CHARLES RITCHIE

AUGUST 23

1641

The wind variable. Our sailors again hauled water. A dead horse overboard.

ANTONY DE HOOGES

1776

This morning early we were attacked on the right wing of the advanced guard. We brought up a cannon and drove them back. It rained bullets. Captain Congreve and one Constable were wounded by my side, and an Englishman was shot through. In the afternoon they attacked on the left side of the village and set fire to several houses, and we drew back into the village. Lieutenant von Donop, who stood on the left wing, was wounded in the breast; the ball glanced from his rib. I advanced on the right wing, where I occupied a big garden, with one hundred and fifty men, chasseurs and light infantry. As the enemy had fallen back from here, I relieved Lieutenant von Donop. The rebels were placing cannon on the highway, and our Scotch Highlanders had to make a battery across the road, with embrasures for two cannon. I had to cover the work, and so came to the advanced posts, where, however, I was little disturbed.

HESSIAN [ANONYMOUS]

1788

The Grand Procession in New York to celebrate the Adoption of the Constitution by 10 States. Very brilliant, but fatiguing. I formed a part of the Philological Society, whose flag & uniform black dress made a very respectable figure.

NOAH WEBSTER

AUGUST 24

1776

A hot day. The rebels approached twice, fired howitzers and used grape and ball, so that all our artillery had to come up. At noon I slept a little while, and was waked by two cannon-balls which covered me with earth. The rebels have some very good marksmen, but some of them have wretched guns, and most of them shoot crooked. But they are clever at hunters' wiles. They climb trees, they crawl forward on their bellies for one hundred and fifty paces, shoot, and go as quickly back again. They make themselves shelters of boughs, etc. But to-day they are much put out by our green coats [chasseurs], for we don't let our fellows fire unless they can get good aim at a man, so that they dare not undertake anything more against us.

HESSIAN [ANONYMOUS]

1851

Last night we were at C[astle] G[arden] again. Sat on the terrace and inhaled the sea-breeze, listening only at distant intervals to the not heavy music of *Ernani* [opera by Guiseppe Verdi], and looked out on the bay and the stars above and the stars below—for the night was dark and nothing was to be seen an hundred yards off except the multitudinous lights great and small, near and distant, scattered over the surface of the bay, like another series of constellations below us. Now and then the white sail of a sloop drifting along glimmered faintly through the night and then dissolved out of sight again, in a ghostly manner; but at other times one seemed to be at the edge of the world—the jumping off place—looking up and down at the stars of both hemispheres.

GEORGE TEMPLETON STRONG

AUGUST 25

1776

We barricaded ourselves in the village; and to-night our chasseurs were to take a good rest. About two o'clock the rebels roused us from our slumbers; we quickly quieted them, however, with two cannon and a few rifle-shots. To-day we were attacked again, but after several of them had bitten the dust they drew off. Long Island is a beautiful island, an Arcadia; a most delightful region, full of meadows, corn-fields, all kinds of fruit-trees and pleasantly built houses. There were still a great many cattle there, although the rebels had taken many away with them. Most of the inhabitants had fled from the houses. The rebels advanced in force. General Cornwallis wanted Colonel Donop to retire, but the colonel stayed where he was and intrenched himself.

HESSIAN [ANONYMOUS]

AUGUST 26

1776

During this day we had much trouble, and at night were continually awakened by alarms from the outposts. This was not caused by attacks of the rebels, but mostly by deserters who wanted to come to us; and when the English and the [Hessian] grenadiers heard them approach they at once fired by platoons.... To-day General Von Heister came over to us with six battalions.

HESSIAN [ANONYMOUS]

1839

We are vagrants now on Sundays, poor old Trinity being nearly razed to the ground, and a new church to be erected on the same spot, which will require two or three years to complete. We shall be compelled during that time to hire a pew in one of the uptown churches or quarter upon our friends....

May I not also see in this dilapidation a type of my own decay and speedily approaching removal? When I first went to Trinity Church I was young, ardent, and full of hopes, capable and industrious, and I should now be ungrateful not to acknowledge that in most cases my hopes were realized and my industry rewarded; but the storms within the last three years have beaten upon me, the timbers are decayed, the spire no longer "like a tall bully lifts its head," and the vestry has no funds to rebuild me.

PHILIP HONE

1847

Catarrh and Ennui.

EVERT DUYCKINCK

1926

A flock of reviews, some good, some bad, all stupid.... I am fairly discouraged about *Nigger Heaven*.

CARL VAN VECHTEN

AUGUST 27

[BATTLE OF LONG ISLAND.]

1776

Blood! Carnage! Fire! Our People drove this Morning within their Lines. The Alarm Guns were fired a little before Day. Many Battalions, of excellent Men, went out into the Woods on the right & left Wing of the Enemy;—Alas! Numbers went never to return. The Enemy surrounded them. Those who could, retreated within the Lines.... But many, many we fear are lost.... And the distressed wounded, came crying into the Lines!

PHILIP VICKERS FITHIAN

1776

Having surrendered myself to the 57th: Regt: I was kept under the care of a Guard for some Time, while some others Likewise came in & Surrendered; & at about 5 oClock, I was guarded by sd: Regt:

over on to the Edge of Flat Bush Plain, where I see a Large Body of Hessian Troops (6) on a Hill at our Left; We then took a Turn to the Right, & was March'd by the Front of several Batallions of the Hessians, where I Recd: many Insults from those Formidable Europeans.

JABEZ FITCH

1861

It is about time for another great disaster. It will occur in Western Virginia, probably. Can any disaster and disgrace arouse us fully? Perhaps we are destined to defeat and fit only for subjugation. Perhaps the oligarchs of the South are our born rulers. Northern communities may be too weak, corrupt, gelatinous and unwarlike to resist Jeff[erson] Davis and his confederates. It is possible that New York and New England and the Free West may be unable to cope with the South. If so, let the fact be ascertained and established as soon as possible, and let us begin to recognize our masters. But I should like a chance to peril my own life in battle before that question is decided.

GEORGE TEMPLETON STRONG

AUGUST 28

1776

—Moving out of the city continues and some of the Streets look plague-stricken, so many houses are closed. The dividing of all men bewteen 16 and 50 years into Ward companies, increases the movement.

BROTHER EWALD GUSTAV SCHAUKIRK

AUGUST 29

1869

I entered upon the editorship of the *Times* on Monday the 2d of Aug. I wrote the leading editorial for Tuesday morning on the uses and abuses of journalism which was very widely copied. I made no announcement of my installation in the *Times*. One of the first things I did was to abolish "Minor Topics" as a heading 1st because it was a discrimination against the character of those articles which were not of minor importance but more briefly treated. In the second place I was sick of the twaddle which found shelter under that roof. The press gave me generally a very cordial welcome. The only unfriendly tones or echoes have had their origin in the disappointment of Mr. Conant who aspired himself, to the succession. He has inspired two or three journals of the baser sort to attack me but that will soon cease for I gave him his walking papers on Monday last, and appointed Mr. Bacon the night editor in his place. Mr. B. is worth a dozen of Conant and is besides loyal and zealous.

JOHN BIGELOW

1889

At the Leiter Ball this evening I danced with Mrs. Osgood and Mrs. Anne Wilson. The floor was too slippery for me to feel at ease.

EDWARD NEUFVILLE TAILER

AUGUST 30

1776

Verry rany—Last Night about 10 o'clock our men had orders to retreet [off] Long Island—thay Likwise Did and got [off] all our feild peaces and amunition and the men all got [off] By Sunrise

272 · *New York Diaries*

this morning. The enemy fired som at Last Boats that Left the Island. Our men Left governors Island. The Enemy fired at our Boats
when [we] left govnrs Island and Cilled and wounded 3 or 4.

SOLOMON NASH

1776

In the morning, unexpectedly and to the surprise of the city, it was
found that all [they] that could come back was come back; and that
they had abandoned Long Island; when many had thought to surround the king's troops, and make them prisoners with little trouble.
The language was now otherwise; it was a surprising change, the
merry tones on drums and fifes had ceased, and they were hardly
heard for a couple of days. It seemed a general damp had spread;
and the sight of the scattered people up and down the streets was
indeed moving. Many looked sickly, emaciated, cast down, &c.;
the wet clothes, tents—as many as they had brought away—and
other things, were lying about before the houses and in the streets
to dry.... Many ... went away to their respective homes. The loss in
killed, wounded, and taken has certainly been great, and more so
than it ever will be known.... The Philadelphia, Pennsylvania, and
Maryland people lost the most; the New England people, &c., it
seems, are but poor soldiers, they soon took to their heels.

BROTHER EWALD GUSTAV SCHAUKIRK

1953

The heat is unbearable. We keep gulping down coca-cola, sparkling water, soda, even milk, and water (with some honey, for taste)
and nothing helps. Whatever you drink it immediately comes out
in sweat. I went to the Orchard Beach.... I took a crowded, sweat-
ing, stinking Lexington line, with one million Puerto Ricans, entire
families, including children, carriages, bags of food, blankets. Like
war refugees. In any case, half of their belongings go with them.
    I was sitting in the sand, in this terrible heat, on Pier 17,

with my back leaning flat on a cool concrete wall, looking at the beach.... Suddenly I found myself in the very middle of a crowd.... My neighbors luckily (this time) were pretty girls. They even offered me one corner of their blanket, for which, in turn, I had to help them look through the *New York Times* ads, Sunday edition, jobs for girls—"a good job," they said. Dottie, that's how one of them, the very nice one, but with a nose out of all proportion, was calling herself—Dottie just finished college and wants a "good job" as a typist, or something like that. She knows how to type, that's all she knows, she told me, and I had little doubt that that was the only thing she knew. So I made red pencil marks next to ads that sounded more interesting. Then the girl with the long nose started polishing, filing her nails, and the other one, Flo was her name, wanted to file hers too, but the girl with the nose said, "But mine must be polished, because my fingers will do the work for me and my fingers must look nice to earn the bread."... Then two guys came.... They sat there for an hour or so, making stupid jokes, trying to get some closer connection, but the girls were too absorbed in their nails, so the guys went away, kicking sand in people's faces.

JONAS MEKAS

AUGUST 31

1776

Many Opinions there are about the Retreat from Long-Island— some say it was too secret; some that it was a mark of Fear; some that we are sold—I call it a brave & useful Manoeuvre.

PHILIP VICKERS FITHIAN

1822

Saturday—apprentice of Mr. Rich Taylor—age 19 moved from Wall Street a few doors below Wiley (a cook store) on Monday last—Night before had attack with ordinary symptoms of yellow fever—pain in the head—chill—hot often too. Attended by Dr. C. W. Eddy who politely took me to see him today at 2 P.M.—Took a dose of calomel yesterday morning & drank some hot tea... extremities warm—tongue covered with a yellowish & brown dry fur... Pulse frequent soft strokes—60 to 65 in a minute... sighs frequently... a little wincing at pit of stomach on pressing there with some force—bowels opened by the salts he took last night. He has passed little or no urine—still rejects his drinks. Recovered.

PHYSICIAN [ANONYMOUS]

1844

I was terribly shocked this morning at receiving from young Green (Andrew) the announcement that William Cutter was in the tombs for forgery, and had himself confessed the crime. I scarcely know the man throughout the whole range of my acquaintances whom I would not sooner have suspected than him. He has a wife and five children and a larger intimate acquaintance among the oldest wealthy families of the city of any man I know. Yet these friends have left him & family to starve on $800 per annum until he has finally resorted to criminal means to supply his necessities. I went to see him this mg. in his cell[.] He did not remove his handkerchief from his face when I came but continued sobbing while he extended his hand towards me and asked in grieving tones if that was Bigelow's voice. He was attended by one Jones whom he stated to be a friend and whom from his white cravat and the peculiarly characteristic consolation he offered as he was leaving I took to be a priest. Nothing can be more ridiculous than commending a man of Cutters [sic] education [sic] experience and standing in the church in an emergency of this kind to the consolations of religion.

JOHN BIGELOW

September 1

1776

I walked this afternoon with Ld. Dunmore...over the Rebel Fortifications at Red Hook.... From thence we went to a round Fort, wch the Rebels had constructed with vast Labor at Brookland [*sic*]. Standing on an Eminence, it commanded all the Country for a great way round. This, and the Parts adjacent, is the most beautiful and fertile Spot I have yet seen in America. It is impossible to express the Devastations, which the Hessians have made upon the Houses & Country Seats of the Rebels. All their Furniture, Glasses, Windows, and the very Hangings of the Rooms are demolished or defaced. This with the Filth deposited in them, make the Houses so offensive, that it is a Penance to go into them. Add to all this, putrid dead Bodies are lying in the Fields...as the Army has hardly had Time to bury them.

AMBROSE SERLE

1919

Yesterday afternoon I wrote a short story. Suddenly, unexpectedly, a great many ideas have come to me and I receive them with pleasure, as this doesn't often happen.... I have English at my disposition now, and I can write it better than any other language! Furthermore, I am here in the great country of opportunity, so I can try. And what enthusiasm is tied to this dream of hope and ambition!

ANAÏS NIN

SEPTEMBER 2

1609

We saw a great Fire, but could not see the Land, then we came to ten fathoms, whereupon we brought our tackes aboord, and stood to the Eastward East South-east four Glasses. Then the Sunne arose, and we steered away North againe, and saw the Land from the West by North.... The course along the Land we found to be North-east by North. From the Land which we had first sight of, untill we came to a great Lake of water, as wee could judge it to be, being drowned Land, which made it rise like Ilands, which was in length ten leagues. The mouth of that Lake hath many shoalds, and the Sea breaketh on them as it is cast out of the mouth of it. And from that Lake or Bay, the Land lyeth North by East, and wee had a great streame out of the Bay; and from thence our sounding was ten fathoms, two leagues from the Land. At five of the clocke we Anchored, being little winde, and rode in eight fathoms water, the night was faire. This night I found the Land to hall the Compass 8. degrees. For to the Northward of us we saw high Hils. For the day before we found not above 2. degrees of Variation. This is a very good Land to fall with, and a pleasant Land to see.

ROBERT JUET

1776

We yet be quiet in New-York. No Orders for marching. It is said our People got off several Cannon from Governors Island last Night. Whispers are among the men that this Town is to be evacuated & burned—We do not believe it.

PHILIP VICKERS FITHIAN

September 3

1776

At ten we have Orders to march up the River for Mount-Washington. Adieu, New-York; perhaps forever!

PHILIP VICKERS FITHIAN

1832

The houses are almost all painted glaring white or red; the other favourite colours appear to be pale straw colour and grey. They have all green venetian shutters, which give an idea of coolness, and almost every house has a tree or trees in its vicinity, which looks pretty and garden-like. We reached our inn, the gentlemen were waiting for us, and led us to our drawing room. I had been choking for the last three hours, and could endure no more, but sobbed like a wretch aloud.

There was a piano in the room, to which I flew with the appetite of one who has lived on the music of the speaking-trumpet for a month; that, and some iced lemonade and cake, presently restored my spirits.

FANNY KEMBLE

1951

Marlene says Garbo has only two suits of underwear. They are made of men's shirting. She wears one for three days, then washes it, does not iron it. Then she wears the other. Marlene says she doesn't mind the not ironing, but three days! Garbo uses only paper towels in her bathroom, has two pairs of men's trousers, two shirts, and little else in her wardrobe. She is very stingy.

LEO LERMAN

September 4

1609

In the morning as soone as the day was light, wee saw that it was good riding farther up. So we sent our Boate to sound, and found that it was a very good Harbour; and foure and five fathoms, two Cables length from the shoare. Then we weighed and went in with our ship. Then our Boate went on Land [generally considered to be Sandy Hook but also thought by some to be Coney Island] with our Net to Fish and caught ten great Mullets, of a foot and a halfe long a peece, and a Ray as great as foure men could hale into the ship. So wee trimmed our Boate and rode still all day. At night the wind blew hard at the north-west, and our Anchor came home, and wee drove on shoare, but tooke no hurt, thanked bee God, for the ground is soft sand and Oze. This day the people of the Countrey came aboord of us, seeming very glad of our comming, and brought greene Tabacco, and gave us of it for Knives and Beads. They goe in Deere skins loose, well-dressed. They have yellow Copper. They desire Cloathes, and are very civill. They have great store of Maiz or *Indian* Wheate, whereof they make good Bread. The Countrey is full of great and tall Oakes.

Robert Juet

1776

The Rebels fired a good deal at the *Rose,* yesterday and this day, but as she lies under Blackwell's Island, in such a manner that her Hull is not seen by their batteries, they can do her no great damage with Cannon Shot. This day they threw several Shells over the Island at her, but without effect. She lies however in a dangerous situation.

Lt. Frederick Mackenzie

1777

Horrid scenes of whipping.

JOHN FELL

SEPTEMBER 5

1609

When I came on shore, the swarthy natives all stood around and sung in their fashion; their clothing consisted of the skins of foxes and other animals, which they dress and make the skins into garments of various sorts. Their food is Turkish wheat (maize or Indian corn), which they cook by baking, and it is excellent eating. They all came on board, one after another, in their canoes, which are made of a single hollowed tree; their weapons are bows and arrows, pointed with sharp stones, which they fasten with hard resin. They had no houses, but slept under the blue heavens, sometimes on mats of bulrushes interwoven, and sometimes on the leaves of trees. They always carry with them all their goods, such as their food and green tobacco, which is strong and good for use. They appear to be a friendly people, but have a great propensity to steal, and are exceedingly adroit in carrying away whatever they take a fancy to.

HENRY HUDSON

[Dating inferred from context.]

1832

I have been in a sulky fit half the day, because people will keep walking in and out of our room without leave or license.... Came home up Broadway, which is a long street of tolerable width, full of shops, in short the American Oxford road, where all people go to exhibit themselves and examine others. The women that I have seen hitherto have all been very gaily dressed, with a pretension to French style, and a more than English exaggeration of it. They all appear to me to walk with a French shuffle, which, as their pavements are flat, I can only account for by their wearing shoes made in the French fashion, which are enough in themselves to make a waddler of the best walker.

FANNY KEMBLE

1924

Married life is a headlong rush, interpersed with oases of rich peace—wherefore I have had no time for you, Journal. But I think of you, and after my old habit, am forever making mental notes in you.

WINIFRED WILLIS

SEPTEMBER 6

1609

In the morning was faire weather, and our Master sent *John Colman* with foure other men in our Boate over to the North-side to sound the River being foure leagues from us. They found by the way shoald water two fathomes; but at the North of the River eighteen, and twentie fathomes, and very good riding for our Ships; and a narrow River to the Westward betweene two Ilands. The Lands they told us were as pleasant with Grasse and Flowers, and goodly Trees, as ever they had seene, and very sweet smells came from them. So they went in two leagues and saw an open Sea, and returned; and as they came backe, they were set upon by two Canoes, the one having twelve, and the other fourteene men. The night came on, and it began to rayne, so that their Match went out; and they had one man slaine in the fight, which was an *English*-man, named John Colman, with an Arrow shot into his throat, and two more hurt. It grew so darke that they could not find the ship that night, but labored too and fro on their Oares. They had so great a streame, that their grapnell would not hold them.

ROBERT JUET

1776

The Fleet & Army are now exceedingly well supplied with fresh Provisions & Vegetables from Long Island, which is a pleasing Circumstance both for the Health & Spirit of the Troops. The Hessians, in particular, never fared so well before, and seem remarkably happy in their Situation. Add to all this, the Trees are so loaded with apples, that they seem to defy all the Powers of a fair Consumption.

AMBROSE SERLE

. SEPTEMBER 7

1609

By ten of the clocke they returned aboord the ship, and brought our dead man with them, whom we carryed on Land and buryed, and named the point after his name, *Colmans* Point. Then we hoysed in our Boate, and raised her side with waste boords for defence of our men. So we rode still all night, having good regard to our Watch.

ROBERT JUET

1861

A victory at last! Fort Hatteras, which commands the entrance to Albermarle Sound, with 36 cannon, a thousand stand of arms, three vessels laden with cotton and tobacco, seven hundred prisoners, was taken by General Butler's late mysterious expedition from Fort Monroe. This changes the state of things materially. God grant a speedy success and a cessation of bloodshed!

MARIA LYDIG DALY

SEPTEMBER 8

1609

Very faire weather, wee rode still very quietly. The people came
aboord us, and brought Tabacco and *Indian* Wheate, to exchange
for Knives and Beades, and offered us no violence. So we sitting up
our Boate did marke them, to see if they would make any shew of
the Death of our man; which they did not.

ROBERT JUET

1926

I dream I am a Negro & being pursued.

CARL VAN VECHTEN

SEPTEMBER 9

1609

Faire weather. In the morning, two great Canoes came aboord full
of men; the one with their Bowes and Arrowes, and the other in
shew of buying knives to betray us; but we perceived their intent.
Wee tooke two of them to have kept them, and put red Coates on
them, and would not suffer the other to come neere us. So they
went on Land, and two other came aboord in a Canoe: wee tooke
the one and let the other goe; but hee which wee had taken, got
up and leapt over-board. Then we weighed and went off into the
channell of the River, and Anchored there all night.

ROBERT JUET

1861

I find I can with great difficulty sit silent and hear the Country attacked. Mr. [William] Young of the *Albion* has been publishing such

contemptuous editorials about the American squabble that I almost dislike him and hope that he may keep his distance. We don't ask the assistance or advice of Europeans. He gains his bread here, and if he thinks us all so contemptible, pray why does he not return to glorious Old England and his great naval memories, and his sister and brother, sea princes and princesses of English Commodore blood? Russell too, I confess, I never wish to meet at an American's table. We are too desirous of foreign approbation.

MARIA LYDIG DALY

1906
Sat in Madison Square. Watched the Throbbing Fountain. Think I'll soon tackle a plate on this subject. The sensuous attraction of the spurts of water is strong subconsciously on everyone.

JOHN SLOAN

SEPTEMBER 10

1778
I found a Spanish dollar in the camp without hearing who had lost it.

LT. JOHN CHARLES PHILIP VON KRAFFT

1894
Keep yourself under control completely. Never for a moment let your feelings get the best of you. You will be sorry and unhappy as well if you do. Remember, in a very short time a great deal of harm may be done that it will take weeks and months to make right again. Don't let yourself imagine things, above all don't exaggerate. People do little things out of politeness or kindness, not out of any deeper feeling. You are Miss Vanderbilt.

GERTRUDE VANDERBILT

1953

Today is the Jewish New Year, and the downtown streets are empty and even clean. Orchard Street is black, cold and desolated. Only the children are kicking empty paper boxes along the street. All the shops are closed, all those little shops, clogged from door to door from wall to wall with rolls of cloth, drapes, shirts, neckties, caps, pots and pans and thousands of small, unnamable things for women and men—all of them are closed today. They closed their stores and they closed themselves in their dark rooms for Rosh Hashanah. Even the subway this morning was half empty . . . and I missed several faces which I had gotten used to seeing every morning on the uptown Sixth Avenue F train. They are all sitting now in their dimly lit rooms and thinking about money, the new year, their usual family things, women, their closed shops. I never thought that people could still take their holidays so seriously. I keep forgetting that there are people with traditions, homes, that they have their families in this city, and their memories. . . . And I stand here in my tiny 95 Orchard Street room, looking out the window, overlooking the street—the ceiling is peeling off, pieces of paint are falling down on the books—I am standing here, trying to let my roots grow into this city.

JONAS MEKAS

1977

Walked through Soho and over to Christopher Street, went to the big pier past the old truck lines and Silver Dollar Café/Restaurant where I spent many a night on the streets. Funny I see it all differently—no longer a rush of (many) sad weird feelings hanging out in old areas. Feel real good today—kinda sad—good like a backwards glance over everything and seeing it all as okay and good vibes for the future. . . . Walked onto the pier and sat at the very end with my feet dangling like Huck Finn from his eternal raft with waves plash-plashing beneath every once in a while a great

SWASH of water from a passing party boat or tug. Sunlight drift over New Jersey cliffs illuminates sparse architecture and great warehouses and piers and ships all shapeless from the blinding show of sun making it all look like India with orange postal card skies and you expect a huge herd of cows to be flat-walking over the river surface—where's the Taj Mahal!?

DAVID WOJNAROWICZ

SEPTEMBER 11

1609

Faire and very hot weather. At one of the clocke in the after-noone, wee weighed and went into the River, the wind at South South-west, little winde. Our soundings were seven, sixe, five, sixe, seven, eight, nine, ten, twelve, thirteene, and fourteene fath-omes. Then it shoalded againe, and came to five fathomes. Then wee Anchored, and saw that it was a very good Harbour for all windes, and rode all night [in the upper bay]. The people of the Countrey came aboord of us, making shew of love, and gave us Tabacco and *Indian* Wheat, and departed for that night; but we durst not trust them.

ROBERT JUET

1662

Waldron, the [sheriff] came to my house ... with a company of men with swords and guns (where I was tending my wife being sick in bed, and my youngest child, sick in my arms ...) He told me I must go with him to the General [Stuyvesant]. I told him my family were [*sic*] not in a condition [that I could] leave them. He said he could not help that, he must follow his order, but would not show it to me. So it being too late to go that day, he left his men there and went to drinking in the town. ... So the next day, like a wicked hard-hearted man he carried me in boat to Manhattans... and put me in the Court aguard before the Governor's door.

JOHN BOWNE

[Bowne entries are approximate using Old Style Quaker dating.]

1781

Gen. [Benedict] Arnold has returned from his expedition.

BROTHER EWALD GUSTAV SCHAUKIRK

1862

Since I have been in the city, we have been deeply humiliated, Stonewall Jackson having forced our splendid army and our over-prudent civilian generals across the Potomac, threatening Washington and invading Pennsylvania whilst the pothouse administration in Washington seems as sanguine as ever....

Baron Gerolt tells us that fifteen hundred men were laying for five days, still alive, on the battlefield, and that thousands died from mere starvation, no one going to their succour. The wretched heads of departments know nothing of their duties, and the *honest* fool at their head is content playing President.... I am sure I would not willingly sit at the table of Lincoln or his wife, much less receive them at mine.

MARIA LYDIG DALY

1950

We sat today—talked and talked, Adolfas, Leo—and we dramatically concluded we had come to a dead end. We declared our own bankruptcy....

We thought that up to this moment, this Thursday evening, we had lived our lives right and had nothing to regret.... But now, the new environment, the life around us had begun to thicken, to press against us like a wall. To live our lives justly, correctly and intensely, we really couldn't see, suddenly, how we could do it without dramatic corrections in our directions. Out of the woods!

Krach. Finita. Total breakdown. Everything has to be changed. The Big Crash. The Big Knife.... Good-bye Europe ... Now we are entering the unknown, at the open sea called America ... The moment of separation is here.

JONAS MEKAS

2001

2:30 p.m. The first blast jolted me out of bed!!!! My apartment shook and I heard all these people on the street screaming. Dashed outside—Armageddon??? WTC on fire! Both towers! I watched them burning from the Williamsburg Bridge. Unsure why—no one around me spoke English! Run back inside my apartment no phone—all TV stations static—cell doesn't work—modem does—weird—quickly listen to news on my little battery oper-ated transistor alarm clock radio. Terrorists! Hear first tower COL-LAPSED right outside my window—freak! On radio—radio news people are freaking out—run outside with my bike and camera. Everyone I see on the street is saying shit like "Oh, my fucking God!"—everyone is in weird shock....

In chaotic Chinatown. Looking at only ONE WTC tower—on fire—so surreal. Just one—superbizarre! Was on cell phone with Bryan—only person I could get through to—weird. Camera in hand, as 2nd tower COLLAPSED right in front of me!! You could feel the dull roar in the concrete. Will never forget it—EVER. It was like a ... grey daffodil that bloomed big and then dissipated into dust. An unbelievable image I will never forget. People on street—totally edgy. Super razor blade vibe everywhere—no traf-fic. EVERYONE—MOBS walking AWAY from disaster. I can't be-lieve I am looking up and there are no twin towers—like a fever dream.

MARK ALLEN

2OO1

3:19 PM * watching television after walking 75 blocks home, it feels so distant. i turn from the tv to my computer monitor to not look at it.

i'm scolding myself for being desensitized by an hour of television footage, replaying collapse timelessly. it is not like a movie and i scold myself more than that by saying i saw a plane hit the world trade center today and remembering that i was surprised a second plane came out of the bay and that i had instinctively stepped back from the windows, afraid of a shockwave that would break the windows i was looking through. it only happened once, horribly once. it is not surreal my fellow architects and i knew that without fire suppression systems and help, there was no way the structure was going to survive (structural steel melts after being burned for an hour) and knew exactly how it would fail. you saw several hundred people falling a hundred storeys. each of them fell only once.

CHAD THE MINX

2OO1

6:02:32 PM :: This is getting weird... the news and everyone spoken to who may be an authority seems to have gone from complete shock to pushing for retaliation and perhaps war. Oddly enough, the streets just outside my window seem to be among the calmest place in the nation....

1:34 PM: The World Trade Center doesn't exist anymore. This is very weird.

JEREMIAH McVAY

SEPTEMBER 12

1609

It is as pleasant a land as one need tread upon; very abundant in all kinds of timber suitable for shipbuilding, and for making large casks or vats. The people had copper tobacco pipes, from which I inferred that copper might naturally exist there; and iron likewise according to the testimony of the natives, who, however, do not understand preparing it for use.

HENRY HUDSON

[Dating inferred from content.]

1859

Had been awake til 3—then slept till 4—after which he got no sleep—very nervous in the morning—"Good God!" he exclaimed, "If I could only lie down and die at once it would be a relief to me—but then sleepless nights and dismal days."

PIERRE MUNRO IRVING

2001

buildings smeared across the sky.

Sorry I haven't been around. I went home the other night with Sir, and in the morning slept through the alarm. When I did wake up, around 10am, I went out to get him coffee and apple turnovers as ever. I took my phone with me and noticed that I had a message. I tried to check my voicemail repeatedly, but couldn't, and thought perhaps there had been a broadcast message on the system and people were jamming the system that way. As I walked back with the coffee, the pager on my phone started going nuts with people telling me to turn on my television.

In that block walk back to the house, I kept wondering if a nuclear bomb had been dropped somewhere, and I marveled at the clear blueness of the day and the odd storm cloud obscuring lower Manhattan.

I went into the bedroom to wake Sir. "Something's happened," I said and fumbled with the remote. I worried I was overreacting, being the sucker for news drama that I am. We tuned in just as people were figuring out that the two holes in the WTC were from planes. He woke up quickly then, and we watched. We tried to make calls and couldn't get through to anyone. I had S2 call Sir's mom to let her know he was okay.

He went into the kitchen to try to make some calls, and I watched the towers collapse. Watching the replays of it [isn't] the same, you know what has happened. But the first time you see it live, something incomprehensible happens.

I have been in Queens until just now. Sleeping, watching TV, playing and eating Mexican take out. The towers were visible from his house, and from mine.

I got into Manhattan today. I'm at work, alone, now. Power is wonky, and everyone moves silently as if in a dream. Everything smells burnt. One of my friends, who is an EMT, is not accounted for.

Yesterday, I felt like a writer for the first time, because in the face of things like this, I'm supposed to have something eloquent to say, and I didn't, and I still don't.

Fighter jets continue to go overhead.... They are very loud and always sound like they are flying low even when they aren't. We duck, we hold our breath every time.

Sir's job is closed indefinitely, as it is below the 14th Street perimeter. Everywhere you go, people are quiet and wide eyes. Very little sank in for me until I saw the print photos in the *NY Post* of people jumping out of the towers. I have friends who live and work down there, who saw everything. In fact, as much as I hate the *Post*, you should get it today, there's some amazing photo journalism in it.

So yesterday, I was supposed to be a model, have a photo shoot, today I'm supposed to reschedule it, but can't get my head around that, or calling the dentist to reschedule that either. I'm supposed to shoot tomorrow and this weekend for a photographer from out of town who I'm fairly sure can't get into the city from Chicago, but I need to try to get ahold of him and figure out what is what.

I have a series of photos taken of me on the Brooklyn promenade, with the WTC in the background. Michael took them, and were it not for my squinting my eyes at the sun and a bad hair day, they'd be beautiful photos, he knows his way around a camera, and at that time, around my face. They are pictures I keep meaning to get rid of, they really kinda suck that much, but now they are a memory of a New York that doesn't exist.

I have lived here my whole life, except when I lived in DC. So when yesterday happened, it was the whole world, coming apart by planes.

REIVEATLIVEJOURNAL.COM

2001

Mere months ago I used to work on Water Street, not five blocks from the Trade Center buildings. This is the first time I've been really glad they fired me; I can't imagine having been trapped down there, and I wonder about my former co-workers. And I was the one who talked my roommate out of us moving into a building in that area, because I desperately didn't want to live in the financial district.

At a local deli a worker, clearly of draftable age, told me that he "hope we bomb dem. It's about time we bomb dem." And for the first time in my life it was a sentiment I agreed with....

"I hope it's the Palestinians," said an Israeli girl at a local cafe, "I mean, I'm sorry it happened, but I hope it's the Palestinians because then it wouldn't just be the Israelis against them, but the Americans too and that would be great."

ERIC ROSENFIELD

SEPTEMBER 13

1662

The [sheriff] fetched me to the court where...the Governor bade me put off my hat; but before I could make answer, he bade the [sheriff] take it off. Then he asked me about Meetings, and after some words, said, I had broken their law. So he called for it and read it to me, wherein he termed the servants of the lord [Quakers] to be heretics, deceivers, and seducers, or such like, and then asked me if I would deny that I had kept Meetings. I answered that but that I should not deny meetings; but that I had kept such meetings or entertained such persons as he there read of, I did deny.

JOHN BOWNE

[According to Old Style Quaker calendar, sometime between September 13 and 15.]

2OO1

4:17 A.M. I am holding in my hands a piece of paper from the World Trade Center that I found lying on the ground in the financial district. It is an expense report from a company called "Cantor Fitzgerald," written by a man named David R. Meyer. The Cantor Fitzgerald website is down, but according to this cached Google page it is "historically known as one of the largest third market firms," and according to this cached Google page it was located in the World Trade Center. There are names of people on this document and on these web pages who are probably dead now. How this piece of paper, along with the many hundreds I saw with it in the very heart of the disaster area, are in such good condition, I can only speculate.

ERIC ROSENFIELD

2OO1

12:15:46 PM : I just got back from my first venture out of the day. There's a slight haze over the streets, along with a pointedly bad smell. There are actually a number of eateries, delis, and even storefronts open. To my surprise, St. Mark's Comics was open for business and this week's shipments arrived as scheduled today. I ran into Mike Dauphin on the street and he told me that some of the NYU dining halls that were supposed to be open 24 hours with free food for displaced students had run out of food last night.

JEREMIAH MCVAY

SEPTEMBER 14

1662

I was presently carried ... to a dungeon and there put under strictest charge being given to the guard of soldiers which was by both day and [night] to let no body come or speak with me ... and allowed no thing but coarse bread and water.

JOHN BOWNE

1985

One of those abstract days you just want to block out. Worked until 7:00. Called Jean Michel [Basquiat] and said I'd pick him up and did.

Went over to the Tony Shafrazi Gallery (cab $5) and it was wall to wall. They had a Danceteria doorman. ... Gerard Malanga asked me for my autograph. ... The paintings looked really great, everyone seemed to like them. Iman was on the scene, she's broken up with her husband. Tony had people downstairs for champagne, but it was the same old people and the same old talk. ...

I was wearing the Stefano jacket with Jean Michel's picture painted on the back, but I've decided I can't wear odd things. I look like a weirdo. I'm going to stay in basic black.

ANDY WARHOL

2001

12:46 PM We can't get online at home—earthlink has lost power, apparently—so these are all the pictures I have up, still. We walked over to work just now to get our bikes and check our email—the only reliable form of communication, really. We're about the only people who can get here, because the police aren't allowing pedestrians who don't live south of Houston to cross Houston. The streets down here are totally empty, and a little eerie. There are people walking around, and the fishmarkets in Chinatown are open. But we saw a father teaching his son to ride a tricycle in the middle of Grand Street, which is usually bumper-to-bumper traffic, and we could have sat down in the middle of Broadway for an hour and not risked being run over.

It's an awful sight, the skyline without the towers. The smoke from the fires is filtering the sunlight, making everything look a little jaundiced.

GEORGE WELD

SEPTEMBER 15

1609

I sailed to the shore in one of their canoes, with an old man, who was the chief of a tribe, consisting of forty men and seventeen women; these I saw there in a house well constructed of oak bark, and circular in shape, so that it had the appearance of being well built, with an arched roof. It contained a great quantity of maize, or Indian corn, and beans of the last year's growth, and there lay near the house for the purpose of drying, enough to load three ships, besides what was growing in the fields. On our coming into the house, two mats were spread out to sit upon, and immediately some food was served in well made red wooden bowls; two men were also dispatched at once with bows and arrows in quest of game, who soon after brought in a pair of pigeons which they had shot. They likewise killed a fat dog, and skinned it in great haste, with shells which they had got out of the water. They supposed that I would remain with them for the night, but I returned after a short time on board the ship. The land is the finest for cultivation that I ever in my life set foot upon, and it also abounds in trees of every description. The natives are a very good people, for when they saw that I would not remain, they supposed that I was afraid of their bows, and taking the arrows, they broke them in pieces, and threw them into the fire, etc.

HENRY HUDSON

[Dating inferred from content.]

1776

Shame to Connecticut Valour: it is said, I believe is true, that two Brigades of Connecticut Militia have fled from one hundred & fifty Regulars!—Yes, they fled. New York we have lost this day; the Enemy entered about three o Clock; & we have abandoned the Works on this side.... I pray God I may never see another such a Sabbath.

PHILIP VICKERS FITHIAN

1832

Miss [Fanny] Kemble, like all young persons who have become celebrated, has many and strong admirers. But many dislike her on first acquaintance. Her manners are somewhat singular. Allowance should be made for the peculiarity of her situation, just arrived among strangers, with a consciousness that she is viewed as one of the lions of the day, and as such the object more of curiosity than of affection. Her behavior would be attributed naturally to timidity, were it not that at times she appears to be perfectly self-possessed. She talks well, but will only talk when, and to whom she chooses. She sat at my side at dinner, and I certainly had no reason to complain of her, for I lost my dinner in listening to her and endeavoring to make myself agreeable. She has certainly an air of indifference and nonchalance not at all calculated to make her a favorite with the beaux. Indeed, Henry Hone and I think that she prefers married men.

PHILIP HONE

1832

The women here, like those of most warm climates, ripen very early, and decay proportionately soon. They are, generally speaking, pretty with good complexions, and an air of freshness and brilliancy, but this I am told is very evanescent; and whereas, in England, a woman is in the full bloom of health and beauty from twenty to five-and-thirty; here, they scarcely reach the first period without being faded, and looking old. They marry very young, and this is another reason why age comes prematurely upon them. There was a fair young thing at a dinner today who did not look above seventeen, and she was a wife.

FANNY KEMBLE

2001

12:37:39 PM : We went to Union Square again last night. Candles everywhere. Tried to keep them lit when we could. Some have just burned down to the ground and, in some cases, the ground is burning.

JEREMIAH MCVAY

2001

Last night we sat around at Antarctica listening to one of the rescue workers, a "mole" who climbs down into holes in the World Trade Center rubble to find bodies, talk about his job. He said, "There I am, worst disaster in the world, and I have my choice of 7 kinds of potatoes. I can have my potatoes baked, fried, au gratin, roasted; I can have my hot dogs grilled or fried and with or without cheese; I can get rehydrated, dehydrated, have my eyes washed out and get a massage from a nurse all at the same time. I feel almost guilty down there." He also confirmed what everyone has said—that you can't imagine how monumental the debris piles down there are; and that he'd had it with the journalists trying to get in down there: "They ask me if I've found any bodies, and what do they want me to say?

I'm not going to talk about that. I tell them about the potatoes. If you see me on t.v., talking to a reporter, you can be sure I'm making everything up."

But the mole also told us that he'd never seen a better or more inspiring display of work, that you couldn't imagine how efficient and skilled the effort was. It's like an ant colony, people shoulder-to-shoulder working bucket lines, hanging from cranes with blow torches to cut up girders, the mayor—who, he said, had actually been buried in the rubble himself and had to be rescued right after the buildings collapsed—climbing around in the debris, shaking the hand of every worker.

People keep asking me if I want to get out of the city now. I don't want to get out at all: I feel I've been nailed to this city forever, tattooed as its own.

GEORGE WELD

SEPTEMBER 16

1776

The Rebels have abandoned everything they had in New York. The works they have made, in and about the town, are truly astonishing for their numbers and extent. Many of the Rebels who were unable to make their escape yesterday, are now in the town, and as they have changed their dress it is extremely difficult to discover them. Most of the loyal Inhabitants have fled, or been carried away from the town, so that numbers of the houses are empty.

LT. FREDERICK MACKENZIE

1985

Now life moves so rapidly I can barely record its outline. It's the torrent, the tidal wave, the avalanche I'd feared last month....

Last week, Sept. 10, we went to NYC to see a special screening of *Death of a Salesman,* and to the party afterward at lavish Lincoln Center. Spoke with Dustin Hoffman for some time about the film (which was magnificent—*he* was magnificent), and boxing, and Angelo Dundee (he'd like to make a film based on Dundee's life and he'd like me to collaborate in some way—but I doubt that I will). The next day, an intense two-hour lunch with Michael Shapiro, the sportswriter for the *N.Y. Times* and elsewhere, his primary interest (do I mean interest?—obsession!) being boxing.... We were the last ones to leave Prospect's upstairs dining room and even then we had a great deal more to say to one another.... And now I am going to do a book on boxing, I'm fairly sure, with the photographer John Ranard, who has numerous photographs of boxers, their milieu, etc.,... How to put everything in it! How to leave anything out!

Joyce Carol Oates

September 17

1776

Sad complaints are made of the Hessians, who plunder all men, Friends of Government as well as Foes, indiscriminately.

Ambrose Serle

2001

10:37 PM *this morning (undertown): the train's population dwindles at spring street to a handful of people in my car. whole benches empty, me holding a pole at the exact center, the only one standing in an E train car at 8:50 a.m. i felt a chill; how many fewer people would be on this train, last stop Chambers Street/WTC? i stood up a little, out of respect, or to shrug off the mood, as the train was stopping and i turned and stepped firmly to the door.

8:35 PM * this morning (uptown): managed to get myself out the door without heartbreak setting in. instead, that soberness that hits after a long illness is passing, but has not yet completed its run, as i walk toward ninth avenue. then as i walk to the subway, i notice the sun is out, i'm blinded, a gorgeously deep blue sky, something like i imagine to be the color of my imaginary future boyfriend's eyes, gazing at me, softly brushing my face with that gaze, intent, nearly motionless yet full of life. Life for life and sharing that. the white cirrus clouds bright and figurative, moving to the east. is that the smoke cloud, or the actual sky? too high to be smoke, too pure to be anything but delirious nature.

this morning 2 (downtown): those bright cirrus clouds, those deep blue eyes, that gazing movement happens behind the slowly wafting white cloudlike smoke coming out of the ground where several buildings used to be. the sky is on the ground, yet it's still "a movement space."

this evening (downtown): still bright, still barely cloudy, still moving, still whispering my name with a look.

this evening 2 (uptown): long strings of cirrus clouds are sparkling electric fire orange against a still-blue sky, the same calm attention. the clouds are exactly parallel to the avenues, and i smile and tear in relief: the city is in the sky again. dazzled, i'm stunned by natural beauty for the first time all week, the second-nature beauty of my city moving again in time.

CHAD THE MINX

SEPTEMBER 18

1832

Miss Fanny Kemble made her first appearance this evening in the character of Bianca, Milman's tragedy of "Fazio." It is a fine part, well-calculated for a display of strongest passions of the feminine heart—love, hate, and jealousy. I predicted before we went that it would be no half-way affair; she would make the most decided hit we have ever witnessed, or would fail entirely; and so it proved. I have never witnessed an audience so moved, astonished and delighted. Her display of the strong feelings which belong to the part was great beyond description, and the expression of her wonderful face would have been a rich treat if her tongue had uttered no sound. The fifth act was such an exhibition of female powers as we have never before witnessed, and the curtain fell amid the deafening shouts and plaudits of an astonished audience.

Philip Hone

1916

All day at the office, and in the evening to see "Pollyana," the syrupy sweetness of which was cloying, and only the fact that it was raining, and I was forced to ride in a cab, restored my balance. For insistent optimism I find fermenting.

Franklin P. Adams

1927

House is in perfect condition and I haven't even a desk to clean out. I'm afraid I'll have to start writing!

Carl Van Vechten

September 19

1776

After Breakfast, I took a Trip to New York, and walked both in it & its Environs. It is both delightfully and advantageously situated. The Country round it is the most pleasing of any I have seen since I left Europe. But the Fortifications of the Rebels particularly excited my Astonishment. They have formed Breastworks & Embrazures at the End of every Street or Avenue leading to the Town; Redoubts, Forts, and Lines of Communication every where round about it.

The infinite Pains and Labor, which they must have bestowed, one would have thought, from Regret alone, would have inclined them to make some kind of Stand.

AMBROSE SERLE

1940

NEW YORK, THE BEDFORD.

Anxious—no message from E. [sister Erika]. Only the same terrible reports about the bombardments in London.

KLAUS MANN

SEPTEMBER 20

1776

A little after 12 o'Clock last night a most dreadful fire broke out in New York, in three different places in the South, and windward part of the town. The Alarm was soon given, but unfortunately there was a brisk wind at South, which spread the flames with such irresistible rapidity, that…it was impossible to check its Progress 'till about 11 this day.…

It is almost impossible to conceive a Scene of more horror and distress than the above. The Sick, The Aged, Women, and Children, half naked were seen going they knew not where, and taking refuge in houses which were at a distance from the fire, but from whence they were in several instances driven a second and even a third time by the devouring element, and at last in a state of despair laying themselves down on the Common. The terror was encreased [*sic*] by the horrid noise of the burning and falling houses, the pulling down of such wooden buildings as served to conduct the fire,…the rattling of above 100 waggons, sent in from the Army, and which were constantly employed in conveying to the

Common such goods and effects as could be saved;—The confused voices of so many men, the Shrieks and cries of the Women and children, the seeing the fire break out unexpectedly in places at a distance,... made this one of the most tremendous and affecting Scenes I ever beheld.

Lt. Frederick Mackenzie

1863

Saturday last the Judge went to a clambake at Manhattanville, a singular kind of entertainment. The clambake is indigenous, I think, to this country.... A large hole was dug in the ground and it was filled with large stones. A fire was built in it until the stones were heated red hot, and then a large quantity of seaweed was thrown in, upon which was placed clams, lobsters, chickens, sweet potatoes, potatoes, oysters, ducks, geese, etc., with pans in which were butter, salt, peppers, and lemon to be mulled into sauce. This was then covered over with seaweed and a tarpaulin.... These different articles were distributed in tin basins, and the Judge says everything was admirably cooked. It is an Indian practice. The guests were seated at tables under the trees and had champagne, lager beer, etc. in abundance and had a very jolly time.

Maria Lydig Daly

1927

I get dressed and go to see Ethel Waters at the Palace. I find her in a rage ... in her dressing room because she has made such a success that no one will follow her & she has been given last place on the bill. But I stay to see her succeed in this spot.

Carl Van Vechten

2001

10:15 PM * i had to cling to simple pleasures to keep from being overwhelmed today, today a low day, "it comes and goes," the way the noxious fumes coming from the south were coating my throat and lungs with that horrible taste. i was compelled to fiercely, even selfishly, hold these things tight to survive today, to keep going: the discussion with kerry last night about learning that sex and love and parties and creation are all a celebration and part of the vitality of the city (something that i help make), introducing L to my other friends, a seat on the train during morning rush hour, a compliment from my employer, a beautiful color, the temperature outside and a walk in the rain through SoHo, a discussion with a gallery owner about what art experiences are important and which weather both times of crisis and times of material excess, the serendipitous discovery that we both believe exactly the same thing, a page of mundane details that i took small pride in finishing today, a call from a friend to meet after work before we headed uptown to my apartment, the sudden and soft sight of jonno's face in the darkened gallery at a show opening, talking with keith sonnier about his work, introducing jonno to him and to my other best friends, the constellation becoming more complete, the ability to stay home and separate my thoughts, the satisfaction i feel in knowing i can see more clearly than ever my own idea of "liberty," and why i need to hold it close.

CHAD THE MINX

SEPTEMBER 21

1679

The hatches of the hold were all opened yesterday evening.... As soon as the sun rose, every one climbed aloft in order to look for land.... I must say a word here in relation to our cat; how she was always sick and lame for some days before a storm, and could not walk, and when the storm was over, was lively and nimble again. She had now been very playful for several days, running here and there over the ship, but this morning she was unusually gay. She came running with a spring, leaping into the rigging and going far aloft, turning her head about and snuffing the land, as much as to say, there is the land, you should look out for, and causing great laughter among the folks.... It was about one o'clock when we first saw the land.... Long Island is not very high.... Sandy Hook is low, and stretches out about three miles eastwardly from Rensselaer's Hook, and makes the channel.

JASPER DANCKAERTS

1776

We were up by three this morning to view a great Fire down the River toward New-York; the Fire is indeed considerable but looks compact, so that we cannot think it generl—Many suppose it must be New-York set on Fire by some of our zealous Whigs.

PHILIP VICKERS FITHIAN

1776

This morning about 1 o'Clock, we were alarmed with the Appearance of a Fire in the Town; and presently after it burst out, at several Places, into a most tremendous Blaze. The Wind was rather strong, which increased the Rapidity of the Flames; & these extended in a Line for almost the Length of a mile, consuming onward from the East River, for several Hours together, to the North River up to St. Paul's Church, which wonderfully escaped, while Trinity Church... was utterly destroyed.... Some Rebels, who lurked about the Town, set it on Fire; and some of them were caught with Matches, and Fire-balls about them. One Man, detected in the Fact, was knocked down by a Grenadier & thrown into the Flames for his Reward: Another, who was found cutting off the handles of the Water-Buckets to prevent their Use, was first hung up by the Neck till he was dead and afterwards by the Heels upon a Sign-Post by the Sailors... The New

England People are maintained to be at the Bottom of this Plot, which they have long since threatened to put into Execution.

AMBROSE SERLE

SEPTEMBER 22

1776

A spy for the Enemy [Nathan Hale] by his own full confession/ Apprehended last night, was this day Executed at the 11:00 o'clock in front of the Battery Park.

BRITISH FOOT GUARD

1929

Meyer started kicking about my coats in his closet. Well I'll go. I can't stand this loveless life.

SARA HOEXTER BLUMENTHAL

1940

Yesterday, finally a cable from E. and Friedrich from London: "Safe so far—" Only a qualified consolation. Nevertheless. Moreover, through Kesten, a cable that [Uncle] Heinrich and [younger brother] Golo arrived in Lisbon. Now André *Gide* also wants to go there. I am more excited about him than all the German novelists put together.—

Bouts of great sadness. Again and again the oppressive feeling of being completely detached, of isolation in *every* respect.— One rather despairing evening in Times Square (after eating with [Kesten]). Alone in several Bars. Too much whiskey. Steam bath. Nauseated exit after ten minutes. Half drunk—chatted in Parks with unfortunate vagabonds, gave them money, then hurried off.— Finally, the "unknown soldier" that I take here. He goes to bed but then makes the affectations. I find him disagreeable. I give him something. He goes away, I stay alone—crying like a fool.

KLAUS MANN

SEPTEMBER 23

1679

Having then fortunately arrived, by the blessing of the Lord, before the city of New York,... we stepped ashore about four o'clock in the afternoon, in company with Gerrit, our fellow passenger, who would conduct us in this strange place.... We proceeded on to Gerrit's father-in-law's, a very old man,... who regaled us in the evening with milk, which refreshed us much. We had so many peaches set before us that we were timid about eating them, though we experienced no ill effects.... We remained there to sleep, which was the first time in nine or ten weeks that we had lain down upon a bed undressed, and able to yield ourselves to sleep without apprehension of danger.

JASPER DANCKAERTS

1778

At 6 A.M. we started, taking our two *Amazetten* [amusette, a small cannon, throwing one-pound iron bolt] with the woolen coverings, also one shirt and bottles and kettles. As we had wagons I was only allowed to carry my short musket. We had marched hardly an hour when it began to rain very hard, and as it did not stop and we were near what was called *Philipp's House,* we opened the pretty church there and quartered ourselves in it—but only the Chasseurs and Amuzette-Yagers, in all about 30 men. Finally, a search was begun and a large potato-field was cleaned out and many other luxuries brought in. Fowls, pigs and beef were slaughtered, although everything had to be done secretly. As usual when on the march we received nothing but salt pork, crackers and rum for rations. In short we led, as the Hessians termed it, a Hussar life. The rain continued with surprising violence so that we were glad to have got into such nice dry quarters. We gathered hay and straw and made ourselves good beds. For a mattress I had a cushion covered with green cloth, the covering of which I took with me when we marched away, but disposed of it. The Yagers lay in their camp above Philipp's House very wet, because they had only been able to build huts to protect themselves against the rain. Constant complaints were made to the Yagers and to us that cattle had been slaughtered; but the matter was not very closely investigated.

Lt. John Charles Philip von Krafft

1863

Talk with Ben in Ward A about the tyrannous & unnecessary exposure of the soldiers—how many officers there are who dare not go into engagements nor even out on picket with their men for fear of their lives from their own men—the 8th N.Y. Cav Col David, (killed afterward) who (after Aldie) made the poor sick men, (sick with diarrhea) dismount & mount 13 times to make them do it military style—I have never met a single officer that seemed to *know* American men.

Walt Whitman

1923

Newspaper strike still on. Strange odds and ends of paper come out, dramatic supplement of one, library supplement of another. Lunch at home.... Dinner at Luchow's & home to bed.

Carl Van Vechten

September 24

1679

After preaching, the good old people with whom we lodged...
begged we would go with their son Gerrit, to one of their daughters,
who lived in a delightful place, and kept a tavern, where we would
be able to taste the beer of New Netherland, inasmuch as it was
also a brewery.... But when we arrived there, we found ourselves
much deceived. On account of its being, to some extent a pleasant
spot, it was resorted to on Sundays by all sorts of revellers, and was
a low pot-house. Our company immediately found acquaintances
there and joined them, but it being repugnant to our feelings...,
we walked into the orchard to seek pleasure in contemplating the
innocent objects of nature.

JASPER DANCKAERTS

1869

Have become pretty much discouraged or rather disgusted with
newspaper work & seriously meditate withdrawing next week.

Last evening Dr. Stiefendecker commenced treating me hydro-
pathically. He came to my room with a man who rubbed my legs
with water and the flat of his hand about fifteen minutes. In about an
hour he repeated the operation. The arterial reaction was rapid and
highly satisfactory to the Dr. This mg. the man came at 8, covd. my
back with a wet blanket and rubbed it with the flat of the hand from
the outside for five or six minutes then put on a dry one. He afterwards rubbed my legs as last night. A little soreness was developed.

Jones and Jim Taylor came to my room this mg. and Jones complained that I was running up the expenses of the office and the
standard of the paper was too high for New York. He complained
that I had appointed men on the paper without consulting him and
abolished minor topics also without consulting him....

I told them there is a very easy remedy for all this and I would prescribe it. I could retire the moment they would express the desire.... Jones then complained ... that it looked as if I had no interest in the property. When I replied that I had never worked so hard in my life he said yes I worked too hard and conducted the paper upon too high a standard. I told him that the *Times* when I took it was *demoralized;* it had lost its hold upon the country; there were two ways of conducting it to rally its fortunes. One the sensational and impertinent style following the model of the *Sun.* The other after a model higher in every respect than existed in New York. There was no place in New York for another paper like the *Herald* or the *Tribune* but there was room for a better paper than either and that was what I undertook to make.

JOHN BIGELOW

SEPTEMBER 25

1969

Still I get a bit of strange angst each time I have a biggish sitting. Today lowering skies after the sun spell gave me a foreboding feeling as I got up much too early for the thrice-postponed [Katharine] Hepburn sitting. However, all was well on arrival, Eddie and Japanese assistant *in situ,* and Kate in curlers already made up and looking twenty years younger. I thought the house [Hepburn's on East 49th Street] so much more civilised than when I last saw it, with simple taste, good pieces of dark-brown furniture, monochrome Aubusson carpets, books, Americana and all very polished, and cared for by a Chinese woman who obviously enjoyed her job. Rather touching little bunches of mixed flowers obviously from the country and not from a florist.

The sitting went well with a variety of yearning ship's prow heads to early golfing beauties 1914, sea-spray sports girl, mad moonstruck maidens, jolly good sorts. When I got her to wear a hat pulled down on her face instead of a halo, she really looked marvelous, clear-cut, stylish, such a change. She has a remarkable conglomeration of features; the bad things that have happened, with the cruel years, only accentuate the telegram of her face (the mouth more bitter in repose, the eyes haunted) but she is blessed with a structure that is made for camera and this is at least three-quarters the reason why she has $20 million in the bank.

SIR CECIL BEATON

SEPTEMBER 26

1776

I walked again this Morning upon New York Island to a very handsome & pleasant House [Mrs. Mortier's], which was lately Washington's Head Quarters. Afterwards I called upon Govr. Tryon & [Hugh] Gaine the Printer, to settle the Publication of a News paper which is to be accomplished on Monday next.

AMBROSE SERLE

1780

This Day Gen. Arnold came in from West Point, to the great surprise of every Person who was not in [on] the Secret.

HUGH GAINE

1952

In the downtown morning subway, a crying boy and haggard mother with tear-stained faces. The scene suggests a recent death. His sister sits by apparently unmoved by the family tragedy.

Last night I read Garrick a Babar book in which an elephant turns green and dies from eating a poison mushroom. Garrick asked if he might tear out the page with the bad picture. He trembled, his eyes full of tears, not tantrum tears, but tears of grief.

Julian and I are amazed that our child knows the meaning of death, he who has just been born. We don't know where he learned the fatal sorrow before which all of us stand mute.

JUDITH MALINA

SEPTEMBER 27

1777

A report, that there had been an Action between General Burgoyne and Mr. Gates, in which the former was wounded in the Breast, had lost many Men, and that the Rebels had burnt 150 of his Batteaus, and the General and the Army had retreated to Ticonderoga. I believe this to be a damned Rebel Lie! I am sure it will turn out so.

HUGH GAINE

1778

In the morning a patrol went out from our Corps, of about 300 men. They had met with some Rebels who, however, fled rapidly. They brought back as prisoners three officers of the militia, of whom one was called a Captain and who had an astonishing goitre, who, however, declared that he would never cease to fight for his freedom. They were placed in a prison-house in New York. In the afternoon Capt. *Ewaldt* was sent out on patrol, to the right, with 2 Subalterns and 160 Yagers. He came back on the 29th without having effected anything. On his arrival a Yager threw his musket, out of impatience, upon the ground. It went off and the bullet hit another Yager, who was standing with some others to get some brandy, in the back of his neck and came out of his breast, so that he straightway fell dead to the earth. The wrong-doer was put under arrest, but after a few days was let off with a slight castigation.

LT. JOHN CHARLES PHILIP VON KRAFFT

September 28

1776

I took a very pleasant Walk this Morning upon York Island along the Banks of the East River to Turtle Bay, where our Troops debarked, and think it the most agreeable Part of the Country I have yet seen. The Air was cool, and the Woods & Fields cleared of Musquitos. Our Army & the Rebels remain *in statu quo*. The East River for a great Way up is covered with Ships and Transports, many of wch ('tis now supposed) will soon be ordered on their Passage homewards.

AMBROSE SERLE

1942

Moving to duplex at 35 East Ninth Street, which is considerably cheaper but much more deluxe looking in a sort of modern-improvement Central Park West way. Old battered furniture looks very startled and terrible here but I will not give in to this place and pleasure it with that white decoration sort of thing—the bare tasteful simplicity of the places meant for bare, tastefully bleak personalities.

DAWN POWELL

1979

I was rushing back [from Washington trip] to go to the Board of Management meeting at the Century [Club]. The chief subject on the agenda was the admission of women, and the meeting was full. The issue arose when Jack Greenberg nominated Joan Ganz Cooney (of *Sesame Street*). Dick Dana as secretary replied that the Century, by by-laws if not by the constitution, was a "men's social club" and the nomination was therefore rejected. This reply dissatisfied the committee on admissions, several members of which feared that the issue was being buried.... A few years ago, if anyone had proposed this, a number of members would have condemned the idea roundly. This time, though some people were plainly unhappy, no one openly attacked the idea. It reminded me of the first civil rights debate, I think it was in 1960, when southerners stopped giving speeches about white supremacy. Louis Auchincloss spoke spiritedly in favor of admitting women; the day of the "monosex club," he said, was over. Opponents advocated delay and insisted—quite rightly, I think—that this is a matter the entire membership must decide. I have a sense now that it is only a question of time. (And, though I am strongly in favor of the change—because life has changed—I do feel a certain admixture of regret at the alterations it will inevitably bring to the character of the club).

ARTHUR M. SCHLESINGER, JR.

SEPTEMBER 29

1945

My dear cat Perkins died today—very sweetly, very quietly, daintily, a lady wanting to give as little trouble as possible. She took sick Monday with chills and bladder trouble and threw up her fish. She knew and I knew that this was it. I cashed a bad check to take her to Speyer's where the vet gave me pills and medicine to give her which she hated. She could not eat, either. Nor would she try. Finally she lay on the balcony, exhausted, in the sun. I heard her choke, and she was in a convulsion, but I picked her up and put her in a chair where she managed to fix her sweet eyes on me while I held her paw and moistened her lips with water. It was unbearable....

I forgot my debt to her... until the night after she died when I was alone in the house and suddenly every sound once more became sinister—the escaped lunatic slowly turning the doorknob, the big brute creeping up the stairs. My cat analyst was dead and

ssre4444444444444444444444

my phobias came plunging out of the pits and closets where they had been locked. I cannot have another pet—it would be unfaithful to my little dear who liked no one but me, knew no other cats, no mice, no love but mine. She thought she was my mother—was ashamed and outraged if I was noisy or loud-talking, slapping me if I was blah, avoided me scornfully if I was drunk, approved if I typed. She was the first pet in my life.

DAWN POWELL

1968

Today was the start of the new school year, after the thirteen-day United Federation of Teachers' strike. The same CRMD [Children with Retarded Mental Development] class I taught last term was assigned to me again. Nine familiar faces…, plus two new ones.…

The parents of the two new students came in, both smelling of whisky and in a hurry to get out.… Neither of the two children had had a breakfast, or a summer, that was worth remembering.

JIM HASKINS

SEPTEMBER 30

1679

We came to the plantation of the *Najack* Indians, which was planted with maize, or Turkish wheat…and found there an old Indian woman busily employed beating Turkish beans out of the pods by means of a stick, which she did with astonishing force and dexterity.… Their bread is maize, pounded in a block by a stone, but not fine. This is mixed with water, and made into a cake, which they bake under the hot ashes. They gave us a small piece when we entered, and although the grains were not ripe, and it was half baked and coarse…, we nevertheless had to eat it, or, at least, not throw it away before them, which they would have regarded as a great sin, or a great affront.

JASPER DANCKAERTS

1907

Miss Lawrence brought in Miss Barnes and Mr. [Nathan] and we had them to lunch. Dolly made panned oysters—and we had our chance to study rich people of the time. A turmoil, playing on the piano. Miss Barnes posed after lunch and I made a sketch of her, not very successful.... It doesn't seem that these young people with money have any real good times—not such as we do—who can afford to be artists—a luxury. In the evening Dolly and I dined at Mouquin's and enjoyed ourselves greatly.

JOHN SLOAN

OCTOBER 1

1609

Faire weather, the wind variable.... In the morning we weighed at seven of the clocke with the ebbe, and got downe below the Mountaynes, which was seven leagues. Then it fell calme and the floud was come, and wee anchored at twelve of the clocke. The people of the Mountaynes came aboord us, wondring at our ship and weapons. We bought some small skinnes of them for Trifles. This after-noone, one Canoe kept hanging under our stern with one man in it, which we could not keepe from thence, who got up by our Rudder to the Cabin window, and stole out my Pillow, and two Shirts, and two Bandeleers. Our Masters Mate shot at him, and strooke him on the brest, and killed him. Whereupon all the rest fled away, some in their Canoes, and so leapt out of them into the water. We manned our Boat, and got our things againe. Then one of them that swamme got hold of our Boat, thinking to overthrow it. But our Cooke tooke a Sword, and cut off one of his hands, and he was drowned. By this time the ebbe was come, and we weighed and got downe two leagues, by that time it was darke. So we anchored in foure fathomes water and rode well.

ROBERT JUET

1849

I stopped to get rested a fortnight ago and then I forgot about my diary.

I will now tell about the Ravels. They act in... Niblo's Theater and it is corner of Broadway and Prince Street. My biggest own brother goes there with some of his friends..., and he said he would take me to see the Ravels. But when my father found out about it he would not let me go. He said he did not think it was right for Christians to go to the theater. I went out on our front balcony and walked back and forth and cried so much I hurt my eyes.

CATHERINE ELIZABETH HAVENS

1856

Herman Melville passed the Evening with us—fresh from his mountain charged to the muzzle with his sailor metaphysics and jargon of things unknowable. But a good stirring evening ploughing deep and bringing up to the surface some rich fruits of thought and experience—

EVERT DUYCKINCK

OCTOBER 2

1609

At breake of day wee weighed, the wind being at North-west, and got downe seven leagues; the floud was come strong, so we anchored. Then came one of the Savages that swamme away from us at our going up the River with many others, thinking to betray us. But wee perceived their intent, and suffered none of them to enter our ship. Whereupon two Canoes full of men with their Bowes and Arrowes shot at us after our sterne: in recompence whereof we discharged sixe Muskets, and killed two or three of them. Then above an hundred of them came to a point of land to shoot at us. There I shot a Falcon at them, and killed two of them: whereupon the rest fled into the Woods. Yet they manned off another Canoe with nine or ten men, which came to meet us. So I shot at it also a Falcon, and shot it through, and killed one of them. Then our men with their Muskets, killed three or foure more of them. So they went their way, within a while after, wee got down two leagues beyond that place, and anchored in a Bay, cleere from all danger of them on the other side of the River, where we saw a very good piece of ground: and hard by it was a Cliffe, that looked of the colour of a white greene, as though it were either Copper, or Silver Myne: and I thinke it to be one of them, by the Trees that grow upon it. For they be all burned, and the other places are greene as grasse, it is on that side of the River that is *Manna-hata*. There we saw no people to trouble us: and rode quietly all night; but had much wind and raine.

Robert Juet

1780

Major André is no more among the living. I have just witnessed his exit. It was a tragical scene of the deepest interest....

The principal guard officer, who was constantly in the room with the prisoner, relates that when the hour of execution was announced to him in the morning, he retained a firm countenance, with calmness and composure of mind. Observing his servant enter the room in tears, he exclaimed, "Leave me, till you can show yourself more manly!" His breakfast being sent to him from the table of General Washington, which had been done every day of his confinement, he partook of it as usual, and having shaved and dressed himself, he placed his hat on the table, and cheerfully said to the guard officers, "I am ready at any moment, gentlemen, to wait on you." The fatal hour having arrived, a large detachment of troops was paraded, and an immense concourse of people assembled; almost all our general and field officers, excepting his excellency and his staff, were present on horseback; melancholy and gloom pervaded all ranks, and the scene was affectingly awful. I was so near during the solemn march to the fatal spot, as to observe every movement, and to participate in every emotion which the melancholy scene was calculated to produce. Major André walked from the stone house, in which he had been confined, between two of our subaltern officers, arm in arm.... He betrayed no want of fortitude, but retained a complacent smile on his countenance, and politely bowed to several gentlemen whom he knew, which was respectfully returned. It was his earnest desire to be shot, as being the mode of death most conformable to the feelings of a military man, and he had indulged the hope that his request would be granted. At the moment, therefore, when suddenly he came in view of the gallows, he involuntarily started backward and made a pause. "Why this emotion, sir?" said an officer by his side. Instantly recovering his composure, he said, "I am reconciled to my death, but I detest the mode." While waiting and standing near the gallows, I observed some degree of trepidation; placing his foot on a stone, and rolling it over and choking in his throat, as if attempting to swallow. So soon, however, as he perceived that things were in readiness, he stepped quickly into the wagon, and at this moment he appeared to shrink, but instantly elevating his head with firmness, he said, "It will be but a momentary pang," and taking from his pocket two white handkerchiefs, the provost-marshal, with one, loosely pinioned his arms, and with the other, the victim, after taking off his hat and stock, bandaged his own eyes with perfect firmness, which melted the hearts and moistened the cheeks, not only of his servant, but of the throng of spectators. The rope being appended to the gallows, he slipped the noose over his head, and adjusted it to his neck, without the assistance of the awkward executioner. Colonel Scammel now informed him that he had an opportunity to speak, if he desired it; he raised the handkerchief from his eyes, and said, "I pray you to bear me witness that I meet my fate like a brave man." The wagon being now removed from under him, he was suspended, and instantly expired; it proved indeed "but a momentary pang." He was dressed in his royal regimentals and boots, and his remains, in the same dress, were placed in an ordinary coffin, and interred at the foot of the gallows; and the spot was consecrated by the tears of thousands.

Dr. James Thacher

1909

A parade of school children is going on. I caught glimpses of sections of them from the windows. Crowds of children merry-making always make me sad, rather undefined in origin—perhaps it is the thought of this youth and happiness so soon to be worn away by contact with the social conditions, the grind and struggle for existence—that the few rich may live from their efforts. The struggle to be one of the rich which makes the earnest working slave. *Collier's* phoned asking how the Pirate story pictures were coming on.

JOHN SLOAN

1963

W[orld] Series. Maury Wills out. Jimmy G[illiam] went for over a month without striking out. Willie Davis. Sandy Koufax no runs no hits.... Big Frank Howard the Buckeye Beauty on his way to 2nd. First hit a double. Frank Howard [in] for home he scores 3 run homer brought in by Skowron. *Johnny Roseboro* going going gone. Bringing [in] Skowron and [*sic*]. 9 homers all year and hit off left-handed pitchers. 4 runs for the Dodgers.... Mantle (7) struck out. Sandy K. has had four Yankees & [a] walk back to the dugout. Johnny Roseboro one hands it. Willie Davis has blinding speed... *going* to 3rd. *He's there.* Frank Howard who hit that prodigious double scores.... Koufax pitched K 11th strike-outs in 5 innings.... Cletis Boyer at bat.... When Sandy' gets annoyed, he'll look up in the sky but he hasn't been much annoyed today. First Walk, Elston Howard. Clete Boyar hasn't been out. Mickey ball three, ball four. A manager can now go out as many times as he likes without taking the pitcher out. Maris on deck. Mantle high fly out. ... [Umpire] Paparella looks at the ball. OK. D 5-0. Koufax 11 in 5 innings but no strike outs in the 6th. Tommy Davis 1st to win successive batting honors. Has 3 singles and one up the middle. Kinda strange but the official attendance [exactly] 69,000. Strike-out no 12 for Koufax. Good slow curve for Williams. He picked that up [since?] being a Dodger. He struck out in brief appearances 4. Jim runs outa room. Foul over fence. Koufax is one run f[rom] Erskine of 14. World Series Record & gets an ovation.

MARIANNE MOORE

OCTOBER 3

1789

Sat for Mr. Rammage near two hours to-day, who was drawing a miniature Picture of me for Mrs. Washington.

Walked in the afternoon, and sat about two o'clock for Madam de Brehan to complete a miniature profile of me, which she had begun from memory, and which she had made exceedingly like the original.

PRESIDENT GEORGE WASHINGTON

1798

The Fever thank God, seems to abate, the Hearse being hardly to be seen in this Part of the City, and the few Inhabitants that remain appear more tranquil; many that were down are getting better fast; our Markets are pretty well supplyed and the principal Thing we are most in Want of is MEDICINE.

HUGH GAINE

1862

Now for my special present aggravation and irritation. The Triennial Convention of the Prot[estant] Ep[iscopal] Ch[urch] in the U.S.A. is now sitting in St. John's Chapel.... The church in which I was brought up, which I have maintained so long to be the highest and noblest of organizations, refuses to say one word for the country at crisis. Her priests call on Almighty God every day ... to deliver His people from "false doctrine, heresy and schism," from "sedition, privy conspiracy, and rebellion." Now, at last, when they and their people are confronted by the most wicked of rebellions and the most willful of schisms on the vilest of grounds, viz. the constitutional right to breed black babies for sale...—the church is afraid to speak.

GEORGE TEMPLETON STRONG

1963

Sandy Koufax says he's happy but his curve ball lost its hop in the middle.

MARIANNE MOORE

OCTOBER 4

1609

Faire weather, and the wind at North North-west, wee weighed and came out of the River, into which we had runne so farre. Within a while after, we came out also of *The great mouth of the great River,* that runneth up to the North-west, borrowing upon the Norther side of the same, thinking to have deepe water: for wee had sounded a great way with our Boat at our first going in, and found seven, six, and five fathomes. So we came out that way, but we were deceived, for we had but eight foot & an halfe water: and so to three, five, three, and two fathomes and an halfe. And then three, foure, five, sixe, seven, eight nine and ten fathomes. And by twelve of the clocke we were cleere of all the Inlet. Then we tooke in our Boat, and set our mayne-sayle and sprit-sayle, and our top-sayles, and steered away East South-east, and South-east by East off into the mayne sea: and the Land on the Souther-side of the Bay or Inlet, did beare at noone West and South foure leagues from us....

We continued our course toward *England,* without seeing any Land by the way.

ROBERT JUET

1847

More of the sunshine of October. Found our way to the High Bridge in the afternoon, Evert, Matthews & self. The country has almost the freshness of June. Admired the Roman prospect of the arches and wandered over the higher hills, the blue of the Palisades closing up this last great beauty of the Island of Mannahatta.

EVERT DUYCKINCK

1862

Judge [Edwards] Pierrepont dined with us on Tuesday last. He seems quite at sea. No one seems to know what now to expect. He gave us a most discouraging account of the conduct of our men in the field.... It is incredible, he says, how many slink to the rear pretending want of ammunitions, etc. Some pretend to fall and [are] carried off by half a dozen other friends and all kinds of excuses are found. So our material is not quite as good as the papers make out!... We talked despondently enough of the state of the country. Both of the gentlemen seemed to feel that it would be utterly broken up into four parts at least. New York would be a free city, perhaps, like Hamburg.

MARIA LYDIG DALY

OCTOBER 5

1847

The Historical Society to night unearthed a characteristic letter from Gen Washington to a friend, dated Newburgh 5th Nov 1782, commissioning a pair of leather breeches with the particular injunction, "I shall thank you for reiterating my request that they may be made roomy in the seat." As CM says this was in keeping with the American statesman's idea of enlarging the area of freedom.

EVERT DUYCKINCK

1858

There was an alarm of fire as we emerged from the tunnel at Thirty-first Street, and a majestic column of smoke was marching S.E. [southeast]wardly across the blue sky, and men said the "Crystal Palace" was on fire. So when we reached the twenty-seventh Street depot, I put the party in charge of James (the waiter, known as Pam from the likeness he bears the portraits of a British statesman), who met us there, and then "fled fast through sun and shade" up Murray Hill in pursuit of the picturesque *magna comitante caterva* [a great crowd accompanying]. Up every avenue a miscellaneous aggregate of humanity was racing on the same errand.... Over our heads was rising and wreathing and flowing onward this grand and ominous torrent of vapor, glowing with golden and coppery tints imparted by the setting sun. My run was hard. I panted and perspired before reaching the scene of action. It was the "Crystal Palace." But before I got there, the dome, roof, and walls had gone down. Only a few iron turrets were standing and some fragments of wall that looked like the wreck of a Brobdignagian aviary. The debris was still flaming and blazing furiously....

So bursts a bubble rather noteworthy in the annals of N[ew] Y[ork]. To be more accurate, the bubble burst some years ago, and this catastrophe merely annihilates the apparatus that generated it. Don't know how the fire broke out. The building must have burned up like a pile of shavings. They said in the crowd that many lives had been lost, the swiftness of the fire having cut off egress from the building in a few moments. But I don't believe it. Anyone thus headed off could have kicked his way out through the walls anywhere.

GEORGE TEMPLETON STRONG

1906

Started out to meet [Frank] Crane and the others at a café on 6th Avenue.... Bought R.R. tickets from speculator to avoid the crush and gain time. Got the 3:30 A.M. train in Long Island City. Crowded, jammed, all the roads in sight from the train a steady stream of automobiles with their lights glaring. An hour's ride...to Westbury, L.I. Here the roads were crowded in the foggy night with an army all bound one way with autos so thick we had to pick our way through them....Dawn commenced...and unveiled the crowds. We found a place to stand, the start came at 6:15 A.M. Each car came up sputtering flame and firing broadsides—leaping away. After we had seen the start we walked along the course toward Jericho turn. Amusing incidents all along the road. Now and again the shout "Car Coming!!" The foolish people thronged the road ahead of the cars leaping back just in time to save their craning necks. Such speed I never saw to this day. No doubt the future has greater speed in store for those who then will be alive. The French drivers are wonderful though the fastest "lap" was made by Tracy, an American. Wagner won the cup for France. One spectator was killed by Shepard's car, one out of 250,000 is not a great percentage when the foolhardiness of thousands is taken into consideration.

JOHN SLOAN

OCTOBER 6

1880

Entered the Columbia Law School; I shall be there every day about six hours, from nine till half-past three. Am having a lovely time at Aunt Annie's but miss Alice dreadfully. I am going to give her a diamond crescent a ruby bracelet and a sapphire ring—in all about 2500 dollars! I have been spending money like water for these last two years, but shall economise after I am married. Three weeks from today we are married! I hardly dare believe it; it is too good. Oh my darling, my darling!

THEODORE ROOSEVELT

1911

... We had lunch, then Dolly went up to 84th St. Headquarters and worked on [Eugene] Debs Meeting tickets, etc. Dinner when she came home at 8 o'clock. "Steam heat" today in our apartment. The first experience we have had in N.Y. with this mode of heating. In fact, I have never before had in all my years of studio life. I've always run a coal stove with ashes, etc. Its advantages are few but important. We have been chilly for a week and had I had a coal stove that would not have been.

JOHN SLOAN

OCTOBER 7

1776

An officer & 30 Men deserted from the Rebels last Night to our Camp, by whom we learn, that Sickness prevails very much among them, that they are greatly disheartened, and that great numbers steal away from them to get to their Homes....

The Dread, which the Rebels have of these Hessians, is inconceivable: They almost run away at their Name. Indeed, they spare nobody, but glean all away like an Army of Locusts.

AMBROSE SERLE

1780

Great Lamentations for the Loss of Major André: He is no more.

HUGH GAINE

1923

Up by noon, and to breakfast.... I had a game of croquet with Neysa [McMein] and Dot Parker, and trounced them.... Then there was a game of cribbage.... And they taught me to play, and I was partners with Mistress Dorothy Parker, and we beat Janet Flanner and

Neysa, and I got to like the game greatly, which I was sorry for, as I have too many diversions and distractions as it is.... But I do hold out against dancing, forasmuch as if I got to be a dancer, I should never do any work soever.

FRANKLIN P. ADAMS

OCTOBER 8

1641

The galley got separated from us during the night.... We had a stiff breeze.... A dead heifer overboard.

ANTONY DE HOOGES

1643

In taking leave of [Commander] Willem Kieft, I told him that this murder that he had committed on so much innocent blood would yet be avenged upon him, and thus I left him. Sailed past Staten Island through the Narrows to Sandy Hook, where we were detained two days by contrary winds. Picked each day some blue-plums, which are abundant there, and grow there naturally wild.

DAVID PIETERSZ. DE VRIES

1792

After breakfast went with my Mother-in-Law to Capt. Lawrence's (she went with a design of discoursing about her affairs in London). Left her with him, and went to [Dr. Richard] Bayley's about my usual occupations till 11 A.M. when I went to Smith's between his lectures. Twice a week now. From there I went to the hospital. Bayley [started?] to operate on one Baldwin for a fistulous ulcer in the groin. But so great was the instability and anxiety of him that it was impossible [to] undergo throwing him into such an absolute fit... for he had already worked himself into a light degree of it. This complaint for which the poor devil suffers so much [was] originally occasioned by the effect of unlawful venery. Horrid idea, that.

JOTHAM POST

OCTOBER 9

1844

I went out yesterday to dine at Mr. Blatchford's, at Hell Gate.... Mr. [John Jacob] Astor, one of our dinner companions...presented a painful example of the insufficiency of wealth to prolong the life of man. This old gentleman with his fifteen millions of dollars... would pay all my debts if I could ensure him one year of my health and strength, but nothing else would extort so much from him. His life has been spent in amassing money, and he loves it as much as ever. He sat at the dinner table with his head down upon his breast, saying very little, and in a voice almost unintelligible (the saliva dropping from his mouth,) and a servant behind him to guide the victuals which he was eating, and to watch him as an infant is watched. His mind is good, his observation acute, and he seems to know everything that is going on. But the machinery is all broken up, and there are some people, no doubt, who think he has lived long enough.

PHILIP HONE

1847

Yankee Doodle has dissolved into a monthly—at least the publisher promises the latter on the first of November. He says he has expended more than $4000 upon the engravings of the year but having no [caricaturist George] Cruikshank or even the tenth part of one they have gone for nothing. There are besides essential differences between a publication of the class of Punch in England

and this country. In the former there are institutions and classes to satirize, here there are only individuals, and individuals resent what classes must endure. There are subjects enough here for satire but they are not permanent—before you can catch them they have changed. At best the work of the satirist is not the highest. A spice of it does more good than a cartload. The surest way to put down Evil is to build up good.

Evert Duyckinck

1869

Application from three infatuated young women for admission to Law School. No woman shall degrade herself by practicing law, in N[ew] Y[ork] especially, if I can save her. Our committee will probably have to pass on the application, pro forma, but I think the clack of these possible Portias will never be heard at Dwight's moot courts. "Women's-Rights Women" are uncommonly loud and offensive of late. I loathe the lot. The first effect of their success would be the introduction into society of a third sex, without the grace of women or the vigor of man; and then woman, being physically the weaker vessel and having thrown away the protection of her present honors and immunities, would become what the squaw is to the male of her species—a drudge and domestic animal.

George Templeton Strong

2001

Requiem

Four in the morning. I didn't sleep. I haven't slept in a very long time. The dreams are strong, vivid, of frozen people and terror. I've mostly stopped crying, except late at night in the tub with the water running so the neighbors don't hear. The neighbor whose bedroom backs up to mine doesn't meet my eyes anymore.

Grieve not . . .

In the shower, I wondered idly if Tommy would be around when I went home, and then I remembered.

Tommy's dead. We had a funeral. It was wonderful and awful. So many people. His 29-years-old pregnant wife. His two-year-old daughter. She looks just like him, a miniature smiling Tommy in a black velvet party dress.

Nor speak of me with tears . . .

What I remember: Parking in front of the house I grew up in, unable to get anywhere close to the stone church. Walking with a bunch of my guy friends and their wives and looking up to see Greg, silent, tears running down his face. Grabbing his hand and squeezing it tight and stumbling on the rough hewn steps.

Tommy's family. Wide, expansive, Irish, Catholic, strong. Kennedy grins. His brothers. Twice at his memorial I spotted one or the other of Tommy's brothers, and would think "Oh, there's Tommy." And then seize up when I realized.

But laugh and talk of me as though I were beside you.

I approached one of them outside the hotel, where he was surrounded by his friends, smoking a cigarette and nursing a scotch. He looked up, smiled. Said that Tommy was looking down on us, listening to the Allman Brothers on an 8-track and snaking at a tailgate party in heaven.

Tommy. When I think about him now, I think about a freezing cold night in the middle of winter, laying on a deserted football field with a bottle of scotch and all of our problems.

I think about the tie-dyed t-shirts he'd wear under his flannels. About our kindergarten class picture where he had no front teeth and I was pretending to be a rabbit. Tommy.

I loved you so . . .

I saw the notices tacked up at the church for the others. Too many to count. Newsday said that entire blocks of people from my hometown are missing. What happens, in a town like mine, is that maybe you got a job trading bonds where your dad worked. And maybe he got jobs for a few of your friends, too. Cantor Fitzgerald. EuroTraders. Sandler O'Neill. Aon.

And maybe all of you will die together when a madman decides he's had just about enough of America. Enough of Tommy and all of us who died with him, this perfect cross-section of America. The rich, the middle class, the working class, the poor, the undocumented. Everyone from CEOs to the desperately unlucky delivery boy from a neighborhood deli. Cutting a wide swath through our demographics, a perfect slice of my city.

After, I went to the Saint James to drink myself stuporous, Hillary in tow. A bunch of Tommy's college friends had beat us to the bar. Hillary was a magnet for their grief, she having dated Tommy in college. A burly Irishman with bloodshot eyes cornered her in the alcove where Rob used to steal me away for kisses and wept into her hair, his great shoulders heaving.

I hope it was fast. I hope he didn't suffer. His wife called and spoke to him right after the airplane hit the first building. I don't want to think about it too much, don't want to examine the possibilities. Don't want to think about all of the people we lost. All those daddies.

'Twas heaven here with you.

SARA ASTRUC

OCTOBER 10

1789

Pursuant to an engagement formed on Thursday last, I set off about 9 o'clock in my barge to visit Mr. Prince's fruit gardens and shrubberies at Flushing, on Long Island. The Vice-President, Governor of the State, Mr. Izard, Colo. Smith, and Majr. Jackson accompanied me.

These gardens, except in the number of young fruit trees, did not answer my expectations. The shrubs were trifling, and the flowers not numerous.

The inhabitants of this place shewed us what respect they could, by making the best use of one cannon to salute.

On our return we stopped at the seats of General and Mr. Gouvernr. [*sic*] Morris, and viewed a barn, of which I had heard the latter speak much, belonging to his farm—but it was not of a construction to strike my fancy—nor did the conveniences of it at all answer their cost. From hence we proceeded to Harlaem, where we were met by Mrs. Washington, Mrs. Adams and Mrs. Smith. Dined at the tavern kept by a Capt. Mariner, and came home in the evening.

PRESIDENT GEORGE WASHINGTON

1985

All the governments were just lying so much about the *Achille Lauro* thing yesterday. If I were the Klinghoffers I'd just go to the trial and shoot them, the four of them. I wouldn't be able to get off four shots in a courtroom, but then I'd just get one. I wouldn't care which one. *One* would be enough. I know, I know—yesterday I was so worried about killing a cockroach. But this is different—the cockroach didn't do anything to anybody, and I didn't kill it right so it was squirming and it was so big, it'd lived to be so *big*. Oh, listen, there's going to be a war. Let's stockpile things. Silk stockings. Candy bars (cab $4.30, phone $1.50, newspapers $2).

ANDY WARHOL

OCTOBER 11

1789

At home all day—writing private letters.

PRESIDENT GEORGE WASHINGTON

1860

I begin to be weary of this "sweet young Prince." [Edward Albert, Prince of Wales; later King Edward VII.] The Hope of England threatens to become a bore. In fact, he is a bore of the first order. Everybody has talked of nothing but H[is] R[oyal] H[ighness] for the last week. Reaction is inevitable. It has set in, and by Monday next, the remotest allusion to H[is] R[oyal] H[ighness] will act like ipecac.

It has been a mild, bland, half-cloudy day. By ten o'clock a.m. people were stationing themselves along the curbstones of Broadway and securing a good place to see the Prince. What a spectacle-loving people we are! Shops were closed and business paralyzed: Wall Street deserted.... Lots of Fifth Avenueites sent in letters, tendering a private carriage for the conveyance of HRH to church, with a P.S. [postscript] asking for "a few" tickets. Corporators of Tr[inity] Church bluster about their rights and insist on reserved pews. I fear we are a city of snobs.

GEORGE TEMPLETON STRONG

1908

Today I finally got at a drawing for the American Press story. In the evening, I had a desperate attack of nervous "inability" I'll call it for lack of a better word—just seemed incompetent to draw anything. I suppose it's the modern and American trouble, "neurasthenia."

JOHN SLOAN

OCTOBER 12

1939

Cooler—a grey day. Work doesn't go well here. I shall work on speeches. In the p.m. after the effort to work went to see "Pins and

Needles" [a WPA production]. It seemed still very fresh and alive. Kept wondering what would happen to these girls when they must go back to their shops.

Sherwood Anderson

October 13

1789

At two o'clock received the Address from the People called Quakers.

A good many gentleman attended the Levee this day.

President George Washington

1957

Two very busy weeks have passed. Busy and enjoyable. I am delighted with the cast: the new bits sound good and I am fairly sure I am going to be all right. Everyone made a tremendous effort and was word perfect at the first rehearsal. The result of this is that, in spite of several different members of the company being away with Asian flu, we are now nearly ready to open and have a whole week in hand for polishing....

The Russians have produced a satellite called "Sputnik" which circled the globe in an hour and a half and kept on doing it until it wore itself to shreds. This has shaken the Americans to the core and they are, rightly I think, in a high old frizz. The end of the world we know seems to be drawing appreciably nearer.

Noël Coward

1968

Friday is our scheduled assembly day, and, as usual, we had to deal with behavior problems. Many teachers, mostly white, believe that the children should be allowed to run and play in assembly....

Others, mostly black, disagree.... Generally the white teachers tend to be excessively permissive.

JIM HASKINS

OCTOBER 14

1968

In a taxi past the teachers' strike demonstration at City Hall. The little park, venerable in protests, was filled with orderly lines of teachers and their signs, dignified and sometimes witty, but not very; not a fervent gathering like our demonstrations and without dramatic sense.

But I saw the Panthers for the first time, and they were impressive. They patrolled, in groups of four and five, the outside periphery of the area the cops were patrolling. They wore armbands, berets, were dressed in dark shirts with a white strap from shoulder to waist. They walked with a dramatic bold step. When they passed the police they nodded curtly and politely, like cop to cop, but there was a certain disdain in the mock equality. One is struck by their romantic beauty rather than the incipient violence. Their presence is their challenge....

The "liberals" side with the teachers' union, because it's a union and because they are liberal. The liberal side, because of the dominant Jewish leadership and membership of the teachers...has become the "Jewish side." And there's plenty of black-Jewish, Jewish-black hostility. This hostility is not new. It's been there all the time, but the time of the Choosing of Sides is also the time of unmasking. My dentist, who makes fun of my political activism, says to me/confidentially after the chair, as if it were a great secret/:

"You go to jail for them, you fight for their civil rights, but don't you know they don't like us?"

I take it he means because we're white and I answer accordingly, but he contradicts me: "No, no, they're anti-Semitic! They never liked us!"

And I answer accordingly, but he only hears his own fears. His maid, his cleaning woman, is black—and she told him! He looks at me with sad eyes. He tries to signal me, "Believe me! Understand!" I understand that he feels himself the persecuted, he who narrowly escaped Hitler. The Jewish Refugee.

Suffering has only taught him how to suffer.

JUDITH MALINA

OCTOBER 15

1821

CLIME

Though the warm season in Northeastern America should be considered as nearly spent, yet I feel no small fatigues in perambulations thru city from the heat. What they call the Indian Summer has commenced.... The complexion of the people is very white but appear[s] to vary with the weather. At one time they are more florid than at another. The effects of the sun [seem] to whiten the complexion[;] few are swarthy or sunburnt. Both males and females shade themselves... with Leghorns, straw and other coverings.

BROADWAY

The general plan of the city was made after part of it was built so that irregularity in its structure could not be avoided. Broadway is the Street of fashionable retail business.... With Ladies it is always crowded and it is no easy matter often to get elbowed along through their ranks. The merchants have their goods flying around; their stone doors like jubilee flags. But the finest display of them is on the beautiful figures of the females where the cambrics and silks, velvets, marinos, Leghorns trimmed and decked out make them worthy of recompense from the shopmen for the superior exhibition of their commodities. . . .

The main street does not run up the centre of the city but rather on one side on a ridge with an easy slope on each side down to the Hudson and East rivers. Streets run parallel with Broadway and betwixt it and the rivers and others running across these, river to river, [are] intersected at right angles. No water lies on it; the declivities carry it off. And the air rushing up these Streets from the water render its atmosphere pure and salubrious.

WALL STREET

Walking down Wall Street which cuts Broadway at right angles, [one] is ushered in amidst Money brokers, Stockbrokers, Land-brokers, banks and insurance offices. . . . One does not see here, as on the Exchange of London, the different costumes of so many nations yet . . . perhaps as many different sorts of speculations. . . .

As one goes farther down toward the shore in Pearl Street, Water Street and Front Street, either a new scene presents itself or the same one is brought into more action. Here, the actual exposing of commodities and the accomplishing of sales. The crowding of merchants becomes greater and the noise more diversified. . . . One person stands on a cart calling off by auction hogheads of [illeg.]; another from the Tontine stairs is selling some thousand acres of land to the highest bidder, a third at the corner of a street is knocking off a ship or bales of cotton with the hammer while in the stores around, imported goods are going off in immense quantities by the same process. One hear[s] the salesmen bawling out in every quarter, many of them he can not see and if he pushes his body in a store to learn what is going on, gets wedged fast into a corner overshadowed by leghorn hats which corner him like so many umbrellas. . . . The scene is completely different from that of Broadway, no ladies or sauntering idlers. [Here] sharp faced merchants, clerks, porters, and cartmen are all that are seen. There is room for none else.

SCOT [ANONYMOUS]

1849

My eyes are so bad that I could not write in my diary, and Maggy takes me to Dr. Samuel Elliott's, corner of Amity Street and Broadway, and he puts something in that smarts awfully. He has two rooms, and all the people sit in the front room, waiting, and his office is in the back room; and they have black patches over their eyes—some of them—and sit very quiet and solemn. On each side of the folding doors are glass cases filled with stuffed birds and I know them all by heart now and wish he would get some new ones.

CATHERINE ELIZABETH HAVENS

1892

The Columbus celebration has been a great event this week in New York. The city has been crowded. It is estimated that a million strangers were here the day of the military parade and the unveiling of the monument, which is quite near us. The procession was from ten in the morning until six in the evening passing a given point. In this pageant were soldiers and civilians, governors, senators, and legislators on horseback or in carriages; but not a single woman to represent one-half of the people of the United States was invited to take part. And yet how much Columbus owed to a woman for success in his great enterprise.

ELIZABETH CADY STANTON

OCTOBER 16

1789

About 7 o'clock we left the Widow Haviland's, and after passing Horse Neck, six miles distant from Rye, the Road through which is hilly and immensely stoney, and trying to Wheels and Carriages, we breakfasted at Stamford....

From hence to Fairfield, where we dined and lodged.... The Destructive evidences of British cruelty are yet visible both in Norwalk and Fairfield; as there are the chimneys of many burnt houses standing in them yet.

PRESIDENT GEORGE WASHINGTON

OCTOBER 17

1850

Mr. R.J.L. Austin of No. 693 Greenwich St.

complains that Mr. E. H. Wilcox of No. 393 Broadway who advertises to supply schools with teachers and teachers with schools received from him last November one dollar to get him a situation, he having failed to do so now refuses to return the money. I called upon Mr. Wilcox who informed me that the [City of New York] Corporation sued him for carrying on his business. without a license and got judgement against him for $50 which he settled by paying John Austin, Constable, $5 for his costs—Austin was hired as a witness, and (Wilcox) now refuses to give him back his dollar saying he never agreed to do so.

INSPECTOR WILLIAM H. BELL

1878

Tonight I was looking over some old papers in the barrel in the attic when I found Abraham Lincolns [*sic*] autograph. I ... went and showed it to mama and papa. It is worth $8.00.

ADDISON ALLEN

1942

Apartment a source of delight to servants—incinerator, porters to do heavy work, parquet floors, white kitchen—and as dreary a dump to live in as I've ever seen. Quite charmless, with pitch darkness day and night and no privacy because the delighted servants prance in and out of places with things to put in special Shoe Closets, Hat Closets, etc., and my bedroom-study window looks out over blind brick walls. Too noisy to sleep after 3 a.m. when trucks and street noises begin, and too dreary a sight to open the eyes to in the morning.

Louise's room on roof is very beautiful—probably will start going up there.

DAWN POWELL

OCTOBER 18

1858

People begin to forget the Atlantic Cable, now generally conceded a failure. This is Cyrus's Katabasis. The frantic orgasm of only fifty days ago seems a strange, remote, historical fact. *Punch* is very funny over our extravagances to date. Other English periodicals rebuke them more gravely. We made fools of ourselves beyond all question, but these Anglican criticisms are ungracious. What we exulted over so absurdly was the prospect of closer communication and hourly intercourse with England. The general rejoicing of that time (Charles King says every half-fledged village on the upper Missisippi had its bonfire and its speechifications) is among the healthiest and most hopeful symptoms of this people in my day.

GEORGE TEMPLETON STRONG

[Entry is a play upon the name "Cyrus": From antiquity, a military figure in defeat. Cyrus Field's cable did eventually succeed, in 1866.]

1950

I stood in front of the Latin Quarter [night club], and crowds were pushing around the entrance. Broadway was one big river of humanity. Men, women, sad teenagers, long lonely eyes following the passing girls. Pale neurotic types with their eyes locked on the five-cent nudie movies in the pokerinos.

2 AM it was the hour for "taking you home," "going home," and the teenagers and sailors walked arm in arm with their "women," and the women giggled. At 2 AM in the morning, it seemed, to me, one of the lonely souls, that everybody was walking in pairs, and every smart woman had found her man, and any man worth his pants had managed to hook up with a woman.... Only the poets are free.

JONAS MEKAS

OCTOBER 19

1776

We was Allarmed. It was sd the Lite horse was on thar way to white planes in sight. The Rigement was collected together and under arms some time.

CAPT. PETER KIMBALL

1846

I heard to-day for the first time of a compliment which has been made to me, which touched my feelings very sensibly, and for which I cannot be sufficiently grateful. Twenty gentlemen of New York sent out $500 to Italy to procure my bust, which was begun by Clevenger, and finished, I believe, by Powers. It has arrived, and has been presented to the Clinton Hall Association, where it is intended to be placed in the lecture room. This most acceptable manifestation of the regard of my fellow-citizens is rendered more grateful to my feelings by its location in the hall of an institution with which it has been my pride to have been identified with since its creation, and of which I have been for so many years the presiding officer.

PHILIP HONE

1945

This is really Saturday morning—about 3:06 a.m. I am starting this in an effort to return into myself. It is as though a glass bell has dropped between me and myself. Extrinsically, it looks the same as it has before—the picture seems unchanged—but this is untrue. I am in danger of becoming one of the amputated ones—with all my days and nights given up to the pursuit of wages—not creation. I mean no writing that illuminates—and no true writing at all—not even book reviews. Into those I can work something seedlike. For *Bazaar,* I can give, thus far, only sterility. The surface coruscates, but it is sterile. How to live? I am so luxury-loving. Anaïs [Nin] said today that she could only write a little book behind the door: She gave later; I give here and now. But this is no consolation. She said that she couldn't see how I would have anything left for a book because I was so flamboyant and prodigal. I said that is what's wrong.

LEO LERMAN

1971

American talent does not survive sophistication. It needs to preserve a certain naïveté, a hayseed element, even a touch of the
child, and the primitive, if it is to retain its juice and energy. This is
true of *Huckleberry Finn,* of Scott Fitzgerald (always an outsider in
Paris and the Côte d'Azur), of Hemingway (with the boyish brag-
garty of his virility cult), of the *out-of-towners* who founded and
wrote for *The New Yorker,* of Ring Lardner's ingrained and obsessive
provincialisms, of Whitman, Sherwood Anderson, Runyon, John
Ford.... When urban sophistication lays its hands on the American artist, it is like frost on a bud—witness the aridity of Edward
Albee's recent work and the nonexistence of Truman Capote's.
Tennessee Williams and Arthur Miller, so different in almost every
respect, have more in common with each other than either has
with—say—Nabokov. When US talent goes elegant, New York
really becomes what Spectorsky calls it—"a road-company Europe." Exception: Cole Porter is about the only one I can think of.

KENNETH TYNAN

OCTOBER 20

1844

I moved into Mrs. Elwells [*sic*] rooms with Hurlbut on Wednsday
[*sic*] last, front rooms are appropriated to me[,] the back ones to
him. I pay $5 per week for which I am to have breakfast and tea
added to my room. The misfortune I find is that Mrs. Elwell knows
nothing of cooking, cant [*sic*] make a warm biscuit, nor boil an egg.
I shall take my meals I think at Cowings after tomorrow.

JOHN BIGELOW

1851

Half-past twelve P.M. Thank God, we are happily at the end of the day—the first great peril is over. Ellie was very bright through the morning; played a game of chequers with me, read aloud...her pains occurring every ten minutes or thereabouts. She dined here in the library, and by six o'clock the pains were much more frequent and began to be severe. At about 7:30, she went to bed in a good deal of suffering, and from that time till the finale, suffered terribly, though I suppose no more than is the common lot of women. She bore up bravely, only begging sometimes for chloroform, which Johnston most stoically and imperturbably declined giving. My nerves tingle yet with the remembrance of her cries and struggles of pain. But at ten minutes after ten her baby was born, a boy, and they say a very fine one; certainly vociferous—his ululations first informed me that he had come into the world.

GEORGE TEMPLETON STRONG

1958

It is still before breakfast and the red sun has just risen over the river. I have been standing on the balcony looking down to where it broadens toward Brooklyn Bridge and beyond to the sea. I love that widening of the river. I don't know how I shall live without it when we change apartments.

CHARLES RITCHIE

OCTOBER 21

1776

I was called for teague [fatigue]. Jackman went in my room & I helpt pitch the tent over & afternoon thare was a detatchment of about 600 men sent to ingage the enemy at marnick [Mamaroneck]. 8 out of our company. The next morning all returned but Sim Jackman.

They atackted the enemy about 10 O clock at Night. Took about 36 pisoners.

CAPT. PETER KIMBALL

1798

Very pleasant Weather indeed for the Season; Little said about the Fever, tho' it still rages.

HUGH GAINE

1980

I ran into a boy whose job is to go shopping for John and Yoko, to buy them clothes and things. I asked him if they'd ever made him bring anything back and he said just once. I asked him if they ever *wore* any of the clothes … since they don't go out, and he said, "They're going to make a comeback. They've been wearing them to the studio." Oh, and the best thing he said was that when he started to work for them he had to sign a paper that said, "I will not write a book about John Lennon and/or Yoko Ono." Isn't that great? He said he loves his job. I should find somebody to help me shop.

ANDY WARHOL

OCTOBER 22

1941

Never believing in regrets I have regrets lately. I wish I had finished my novel (which I would have by this time) or else done a play of my own.... I still have a secret passion to live alone and work. I could do as Esther does—live in a $12 a week furnished apartment, live on $25 a week altogether instead of this massive overhead that Joe and I run up.

DAWN POWELL

1963

Began music for *Milk Train*.

Cocktail this evening at James Lord's. Dined later at Glenway Wescott's with Truman Capote in whose mouth reality becomes the verity of Scheherazade as we listen rapt to his tales of research on two assassins, now awaiting capital punishment in Kansas.

NED ROREM

OCTOBER 23

1798

Praise to God for all his Mercies; This FortNight [*sic*] I was taken with the Fever, and am now hearty and well.

HUGH GAINE

1963

Fortieth birthday. I can no longer die young.

NED ROREM

1968

Only one child out of fifteen knows how to spell his father's name. The mother's name presents no difficulties. This holds true even though most pupils live with both parents....

Most of our students spend their time with their mothers and learn from them most of what they know before entering school. Generally, the father works while the child is asleep. The general impression is that most fathers are absent from their homes entirely, but they aren't.

JIM HASKINS

OCTOBER 24

1776

Dined at Governor Tryon's.... The Discourse turned principally
on American Affairs, and the comparative Opulence and Strength
between the two Countries of Britain & America.... We all concluded that, as far as man can foresee, it is impossible that America
shd. carry on the War for any Time in her present Situation.

AMBROSE SERLE

1949

Today I decided to deny the barrier between me and my proper
home—the novel—by giving up this formless second Marcia book
as so much petit point to be done another day. It is not necessary to
do the nostalgic child book. Max was bad for me in that way. I cannot feel at home there. I *am* New York—this minute—now. I know
more about it than anyone—not historically but momentarily. I
must do a New York novel to be happy—one in the *Magic Wheel*
series. Suddenly I remembered meeting Glenway Wescott in the
Lafayette and he said how much he liked *The Locusts*. "No one but
you," he said, "is doing for New York what Balzac did for Paris." It
illumined my whole disorder.

DAWN POWELL

OCTOBER 25

1854

Cholera seems suddenly to have taken a fresh start.... Oysters are
charged with several cases.

GEORGE TEMPLETON STRONG

1911

Read in Mr. Theodore Dreiser's new book "Jennie Gerhardt," which beginneth as it were a great tayle, yet wrote without grace nor humor.

FRANKLIN P. ADAMS

1923

Vogue reviews. All eight mine. Sis has a baby girl. "A little girl, one of us, to grow up in the same sort of eager, bitter childhood that Sis and I lived together."

WINIFRED WILLIS

OCTOBER 26

1777

What shall I say? Poor Burgoyne is at last a Prisoner! He and his whole Army taken by Capitulation about the 15th by the Troops under the Command of Gen. Gates. The Troops that went up the North River returned this Evening having been as high as Esopus.

HUGH GAINE

1837

Red Brethren. Broadway in the neighborhood of the City Hotel has been crowded for the two last days by curious spectators, watching to obtain an occasional glimpse of a large party of Indians who, after having made a treaty at Washington by which their "broad lands" are diminished in quantity the trifling amount of a million and a quarter of acres, are now making a tour of the principal cities, receiving presents and being stared at for the benefit of theaters, fairs, and lectures. There are two tribes, amounting in all to seventy individuals. The Sauks and Foxes, who constitute the most important part of the deputation, are at the City Hotel, and the Sioux at the National, opposite; for these two tribes are not on a friendly footing, and their white keepers do not think it expedient to get up a real war fight for the edification of the spectators.

PHILIP HONE

1939

I went to New York Tuesday noon. Mayor [Fiorello] La Guardia had a car waiting for me at the station and it was at my disposal during my stay. In the afternoon I went down to see Judge [John] Mack, whom I had not seen for over two years before he became ill....

Then Raymond picked me up at the Roosevelt and we went with Paul Moss to La Guardia's apartment at 107th Street and Park Avenue or thereabout. This is one of the humble sections of New York. The building in which the Mayor lives is really a tenement, although not of a bad type.... Other tenants in the building are pushcart peddlers, etc., but it is in a decent, respectable, even if humble, neighborhood.

Fiorello was lots of fun. I kidded him about Nathan Straus and told him that I was certain that he (Fiorello) was a candidate for something; otherwise he would not have supported Straus at the expense of Rheinstein. But Fiorello is good at sparring and he can't be made to talk except when he wants to and then he can be very frank. He was lovely with his two young adopted children. We had several rounds of cocktails and then went to Henri's in Fifty-second Street where we had a good dinner. Fiorello can always be depended upon to serve good food. Afterward we went to the theater to see *Too Many Girls,* a musician show which was light and amusing. Then I went to the hotel and to bed.

HAROLD L. ICKES

1980

The neighbors' house is dark, sealed, a new white window standing out from the others on the right. In it, a piece of paper.... I wonder what it says, what they look at before gazing out their window? But they are concerned with the interior and with replacing defective glass. The rain poured into their two downstairs loft windows yesterday as I looked out. Tonight, one solitary light is on down there. A mystery, a new one. Meanwhile, the old neighbors assert themselves and the loft building that rises tall behind those two buildings shines with a multitude of cheery windows that give me a sense of neighborhood. There are many of us down here, many wake in the night to a loud sound thinking, *is this it, is this the end of everything?*

CAROLE AKA "IONE" BOVOSO

OCTOBER 27

1777

Is a very rainey morning, & the latter part of the past night hath been considerably stormy; The weather being uncomfortable abroad, I keep house cloes this day, & apply'd myself chiefly to reading. In the Afternoon Lt. Brewster made me a Visit; Old neighbour Stilwell was also in here & set with us some time. I have been this day fourteen months in Captivity.

JABEZ FITCH

1781

The report of Lord Cornwallis' surrender was confirmed. This unfortunate event was caused through wilful neglect.

BROTHER EWALD GUSTAV SCHAUKIRK

1846

I witnessed this morning, from the steps of Clinton Hall, a scene which is calculated to cause alarm as to future collisions between the citizens of this country.... A negro boy, named George Kirk, a slave from Georgia, secreted himself in a vessel commanded by Captain Buckley, and was brought to New York. Here he was arrested and confined, at the instance of the captain, who is subjected to severe penalties for the abduction of the slave. The claim of the master to have the fugitive sent back to Georgia was tried before Judge Edwards.... The judge's decision set the boy free, for want of evidence to prove his identity; and such a mob, of all colours, from dirty white to shining black, came rushing down Nassau and into Beekman Street as made peaceable people shrink into places of security. Such shouting and jostling, such peals of negro triumph, such uncovering of woolly heads in raising the greasy hats to give effect to the loud huzzas of the sons of Africa, seemed almost to "fright the neighborhood from its propriety." A carriage was brought to convey the hero of the day from his place of concealment, but it went away without him. This is all very pretty; but how will it end? How long will the North and the South remain a united people?

PHILIP HONE

1931

Trilogy splendidly received. Carlotta & I overjoyed!

EUGENE O'NEILL

OCTOBER 28

1776

We Lay on our arms. The enemy appeard all Round on every hill the Riflemen Afiring on there gards. One of the Riflemen kild this day & at night our gard was Alarmed. Another fired and kild Capt Buntin [the Battle of White Plains].

CAPT. PETER KIMBALL

1777

The Rain continues, and extreme bad Markets indeed.

HUGH GAINE

1972

Except for their apparently bottomless store of sinusitis-producing substances, these long fall weeks have brought sheer light. From day to day, almost from hour to hour, Central Park—the world's eighth wonder—merges from mercury to magenta to slate with no less flamboyance than the Iroquois foliage of Pennsylvania. Whatever the weather I walk there each afternoon now that we live so close. No Paris garden surpasses Central Park in surreal luxury. We used to say that the spired skyscrapers on Fifth Avenue were male, those split ones on the west side were female, and that when no one was looking they flew into the sky and clashed by night.

NED ROREM

1988

The sun coming up turns the fragmentary cloud cover the colors lingerie—ladies' delicate unmentionables—used to be: peach, Nile green. But when the sun goes down, it sets New Jersey on fire and lights up the western flanks of Manhattan's ugliest buildings in beauty.

JAMES SCHUYLER

OCTOBER 29

1844

I told Mrs. Elwell this evg. that I should leave her board and if she pleased would retain my room. There was a terrible time, but my mind was so fully made up that I was not to be shaken by all the tears and sighs in woman.

JOHN BIGELOW

1884

Went to school and after my French I went out to the gymnasium and there fooled around awhile and then went in and made stump speeches and danced a Virginia Reel.... Then walked down in the dripping rain and saw business mens [*sic*] Republican parade. Blaine was there and in the drenching rain waved a thoroughly wet handkerchief to the countless thousands that passed.

REGINALD FAIRFAX HARRISON

1949

Yesterday, about 10 PM the *General Howze* pulled into the Hudson River. We stood on the deck and we stared. 1352 Displaced Persons stared at America. I am still staring at it, in my retinal memory. Neither the feeling nor the image can be described to one who hasn't gone through this. All the wartime, postwar D.P. miseries, desperations and hopelessness, and then suddenly you are faced with a dream.

You have to see New York at night, from the Hudson, like this, to see its incredible beauty. And when I turned to the Palisades— I saw the Ferris wheel all ablaze, and the powerful searchlights were throwing beams into the clouds.

Yes, this is America, and this is the twentieth century. Harbor and piers ablaze with lights and colors. The city lights merged with a sky that looked man-made.

In the North there was a massive cloud, then it thundered, and lightning cut through the cloud lighting it up briefly, and then falling on the city to be incorporated into New York's lighting system. This gigantic manifestation of nature became just another neon sign.

Early this morning there was a heavy fog over the harbor. The city appeared and disappeared. The Statue of Liberty appeared for a moment—to greet us!—and disappeared in the mist again.... Slowly, the ship moved into the very heart of New York.

The ocean was still in our ears, in our flesh. We were both dizzy and ecstatic, as we touched the ground.

According to the immigration papers, we had to board a train for Chicago, ... [but] we stood on the elevated platform at Pier 60 looking at the New York skyline. And we both said it, at the same time, Adolfas and myself: "We are staying right here. This is it. This New York. This is the center of the world. It would be crazy to go to Chicago when you are in New York!"

JONAS MEKAS

1985

I broke something and realized I should break something once a week to remind me how fragile life is. It was a good plastic ring from the twenties.

ANDY WARHOL

OCTOBER 30

1748

About eight o'clock in the morning we arrived at the place where we were to take the ferry for New York.... We saw a kind of wild duck in immense numbers upon the water: the people called them "blue bills" and they seemed to be the same as our pintail ducks, or Linné's *Anas acuta,* but they were very shy. On the shore of the continent we saw some very fine sloping cultivated fields, which at present looked quite green, the grain having already come up.

PETER KALM

1866

First rehearsal in our new Hall.

WILLIAM STEINWAY

1926

Langston [Hughes] appears at 7 o'clock, & after dinner begins work immediately on the songs for *Nigger Heaven*. He has completed rough drafts of all ... before we go to bed. He stays with us.

CARL VAN VECHTEN

1969

First thing this morning I went down to the guidance counselor to discuss the two children the principal assigned to my class on Friday.

Also, I wanted to discuss an after-school clinic at North Side, which one student in my class but not on my register attends. He is on sedatives, which affect his performance in class. The guidance counselor told me to discuss it with his mother.... I wrote to the mother.... She can't read, but perhaps a neighbor will read the note for her. I can't call her because there's no phone in the house. The boy is brighter than most of my pupils, and if he can ever get off the sedatives that keep him glassy-eyed all day he can really make progress. He is not retarded, but he is disruptive when he is not drugged.

JIM HASKINS

OCTOBER 31

1748

The sea near New York yields annually a great quantity of oysters. They are found chiefly in a muddy ground, where they lie in the slime and are not so frequent in a sandy bottom: a rocky and stony bottom is seldom found here. The oyster shells are gathered in great heaps and burnt into a lime which by some people is used in building houses, but it is not reckoned so good as that made of limestone. On our journey to New York we saw high heaps of oyster shells near the farmhouses upon the seashore, and about New York we observed that people had scattered them upon the fields which were sown with wheat. However, they were whole and not crushed.

Peter Kalm

1765

Several people in mourning for the near Issue of the stamps and the Interment of their liberty. Descended even to the Bag-gammon Boxes at the merchant's Coffee House, being covered with Black and the Dice in Crape. This night a mob in 3 squads went through the Streets crying "Liberty" at the same time breaking the Lamps & threatening particulars that they would the next night pull down their Houses. Some thousands of windows Broke. Major James of the Royal Artillery—threatened to be buried alive by the Populace as Commanding the Troops in the Fort for the protection of the Stamps. Merchants of this place met to Know whether they shall carry on trade or not. Agreed in the negative till the 1st of May.

Capt. John Montrésor

1776

Many idle Reports are daily propagated concerning the Army and its Successes, which, like the Eastern Insect, live only for a few Hours. There are many pretended Friends in N. York, who are ready enough to do any Mischief, if they dared: Some of them have secretly injured or stolen the English Horses brought over for the Use of the Army, and do communicate all they can to the Enemy.

Ambrose Serle

1860

Republicans refuse to believe secession possible (in which I think they are wrong), and maintain that were it accomplished it would do no lasting mischief. I am sure it would do fatal mischief to one section or another and great mischief to both. Amputation weakens the body, and the amputated limb decomposes and perishes. Is our vital center North or South? Which is Body and which is Member? We may have to settle that question by experiment.... Bisection is disaster and degradation, but if the only alternative is everlasting submission to the South, it must come soon, and why should it not come now? What is gained by postponing it four years longer?

GEORGE TEMPLETON STRONG

1866

Inauguration Concert by the Bateman Concert troupe. Everybody is delighted with the acoustic qualities. House filled to overflowing. Great Success. Supper afterwards, jolly time til 3 AM.

WILLIAM STEINWAY

1985

I walk in the Village Halloween parade with [folksinger] Ted Hoagland. He's dressed like a fox and we stop midavenue and howl. The streets are packed, blocked completely from traffic and everywhere I look I see smiling faces—a glorious moment for New York. The parade is made up of undulating dragons, twenty-foot-high puppets, dancing skeletons, African drummers, a single Puerto Rican dandy, coyote-women and wolf-men, all of us carrying tall corn stalks, our flags, our pledge of allegiance to maize. After the parade breaks up at Washington Square, we drift west, through carless streets. One 6′8″ transvestite dressed in a girl's cheerleading suit twirls a baton and, holding a ghetto blaster under the other arm, strides to a Sousa march. On Bleecker Street, a man with a raincoat leans back against stairs. As we pass, he flashes: a huge fabric penis springs out toward us—ten feet long, to much laughter.

GRETEL EHRLICH

November 1

1748

Clams. Among the numerous shell-fish which are found on the sea-shore, there are some which by the English are called clams and which bear some resemblance to the human ear. They have considerable thickness, and are chiefly white, excepting the pointed end, which both without and within is of a bluish color, between purple and violet. They are found in vast numbers on the seashore of New York, Long Island and other places. The shells contain a large amount of meat which is eaten both by the Indians and Europeans settled here....

The shells of these clams are used by the Indians as money and make what they call their wampum; they likewise serve their women as ornaments, when they intend to appear in full dress. This wampum is properly made of the purple part of the shells, which the Indians value more than the white part. A traveller who goes to trade with the Indians and is well stocked with it, may become a considerable gainer, but if he takes gold coin, or bullion, he will undoubtedly be a loser, for the Indians who live farther back in the country put little or no value upon these metals which we reckon so precious.... The Indians formerly made their own wampum, though not without great difficulties, but at present it is made mostly by the Europeans, especially by the inhabitants of Albany, who make a considerable profit by it.

PETER KALM

1776

Gaine, the Printer of the *New York Gazette*, escaped from Newark this Morning, and arrived in Town. From him I derived the following Information; That the Army of the Rebels, opposed to Genl.

Howe, consisted of about 30,000 Men, who had been drained from every Part to compose such a Force, that Dr. [Benjamin] Franklin sailed on Sunday last from Philadelphia for France.

AMBROSE SERLE

1880

We are all alone in the comfortable country house, with its roaring wood fires and warm rooms, and it is beautiful autumn weather. Mary Ann & Kate are model servants; and the old negro Davis (who always alludes to Alice as "the good lady") takes excellent care of the horse. The horse, by the way, and a dear, clumsy, handsome colly dog, Dare by name, are really friends, as much as if they were human, and besides them we have an idiotic small calf and a melancholy cat, both of which Baby can never resist teasing. It is impossible to describe the lovely, little teasing ways of my bright, bewitching darling; I can imagine no picture so pretty as her sweet self seated behind the tea things in the daintiest little pink and gray morning dress, while, in my silk jacket and slippers, I sit at the other end of the table. She seems in beautiful health; and she looks even prettier than she ever has before, the little laughing, blushing darling, with her sweet, winsome ways; and oh, she is such a tender and devoted little wife. We have the loveliest drives and walks together; we play a great deal of tennis, being about equally matched; and wander about the woods and shores. In the evenings I read aloud while she sews; or she plays on the piano; or we play cards together.

On Tuesday I drove over to Norwich to deposit my first vote for president—for Garfield.

THEODORE ROOSEVELT

1982

An astrologist sent me a horoscope that said I was going to die on election day. I don't know if she meant literally or figuratively. Just in case she means it literally, I think I'll vote early.

MARIO CUOMO

November 2

1748

[In New York] the streets do not run so straight as those of Phila-delphia, and sometimes are quite crooked; however, they are very spacious and well built, and most of them are paved, except in high places, where it has been found useless. In the chief streets there are trees planted, which in summer give them a fine appearance, and during the excessive heat at that time afford a cooling shade. I found it extremely pleasant.

PETER KALM

1863

Came through to-day from Washington to Brooklyn. Got home in the evening—very pleasant trip, weather fine country looks good, the great cities & towns through which I passed look wonderfully prosperous—it looks anything else, but war—every body well drest, plenty of money, markets boundless & of the best, factories all busy—I write this in Brooklyn.

WALT WHITMAN

1915

To the booth to vote for woman suffrage, and it did not take me over one minute, all going smoothly. How now, Mr. Pepys, said a registration clerk, shall you make game of us again in your jour-nall? And I told him, No, only when you deserve it, as was so at the registration-time.... All the things I did vote for were defeated, as usually they are.

FRANKLIN P. ADAMS

NOVEMBER 3

1908

Outside on 23rd St. the din of the thoughtless celebrating "Election Night" filled the air and penetrated our walls. Henri and I walked out a few minutes to buy cigarettes for Mrs. H. . . . Bryan is defeated for the third time in his attempt to be President. . . . I voted for him for I feel that some stop must be put to the rottenness in the Republican administration. But, as usual, I'm on the losing side. "Bill" Taft, a jolly looking fat man designated by Roosevelt as his successor, gets the office—and the cancerous growth is to have four more years. I'm not a Democrat, I am of no party. I'm for change—for the operating knife when a party rots in power. I am certainly ashamed of the cowardice of the American voters.

JOHN SLOAN

1969

The scenery [for the musical *Coco*] was coming by very slow degrees into the theater, so no rehearsals and the chorus were being sent in droves for fittings on the clothes recently arrived from London. Mercifully, only minor alterations were necessary and many of the costumes delighted me, and sent the workroom and their wearers into ecstasy. . . .

Dinner was a delight, with Ruth and Gar[son Kanin] at the re-flowered Grenouille. I was afraid they would pump me about their great friend Kate, but mercifully they only asked "between the family" what I thought of the show, which Garson had once turned down as director. We talked about dope-taking, methods of work and, interspersed with the usual name-dropping, Ruth was extremely funny and powerful on a variety of subjects. It amazes me that Garson, who is so bright, no longer seems to write or produce in films anything of the slightest merit. The two seem to live in the greatest luxury and Ruth had what she called a huge "limo" to take her a few blocks home. They are two of my old friends that never play the same record too often and I laugh a great deal in their company. They terrified me with an account of how at the end of a picture, *Suddenly, Last Summer,* K.H. asked Mankiewicz if all shooting, dubbing, play bashing etc. etc. was over, and when told yes she spat in his face. She then repeated the performance to Sam Spiegel.

SIR CECIL BEATON

NOVEMBER 4

1765

The Stamps refused to be taken on board of the men of war by order of Captain Kenneday, as per papers of the Corporation refusing both them & the L^r Governor.... Advertisements throughout the Town threatening the lives of particulars. Many stragglers thronging in with arms from several parts even Connecticut, for plunder &^{c}. The Fort pretty well under cover this night. The Governor's Family obliged to seek protection on board His Majesty's Ship the *Coventry*.

CAPT. JOHN MONTRÉSOR

1971

Party for Virgil's seventy-fifth birthday.... Black tie. As in high school, I'm required to "escort" Rita Gam, and so I do, though we have nothing to talk about, but being older than in high school, know how to fake it. Among the guests: Anne Baxter, Carol Channing, Alexis Smith, Ethel Merman, the Bernsteins, Alexei Haieff and Sheila Bridport (who didn't like anyone, but I was dazzled), and Maureen Stapleton whom I offered to bring home, and did, since she was high and lives across the street. No one, not Einstein, nor

Cleopatra nor Margaret Mead nor Mae West, not even Maureen Stapleton, nor Ned Rorem, is clever when drunk.

NED ROREM

1978

No one gives me a seat on the subway unless I take my catalogue of maternity fashions out of my briefcase and read it while I cling to a strap or a pole. Then little old ladies vie with one another to see who can give me her seat first. Men never get up.

MARGARET RYAN

NOVEMBER 5

1907

Election Day. Took a walk in the afternoon and saw boys in droves, foraging for fuel for their election fires this evening...an old lady—a bull dog had a hand bag tearing it up—apparently hers. She wrested it from him, and then discovers to the uproarious amusement of the crowd that hers is safely on her arm. After dinner...out again and saw the noisy trumpet blowers, confetti throwers and the "ticklers" in use—a small feather duster on a stick which is pushed in the face of each girl by the men, and in the face of men by the girls. A good humorous crowd, so dense in places that it was impossible to control one's movement. A big election bonfire on Seventh Avenue with a policeman trying to keep its creators from adding fuel. They would creep through the dense crowd, and when he was busy, over the heads a barrel or box would sail, into the flames. And a shout of ridicule would meet the policeman's angry efforts to get the culprit stoker.

JOHN SLOAN

1942

Had luncheon coffee with Pauline Hemingway. Pauline seemed sharp-edged, too eager, brown and desperate. Her confessionals, her rosaries, that kept her head up during the bad years (so that she amazed everyone with her poise) do not after all fill the major gap in her life and give it a frittering quality that does not flatter. She should have a cause, beyond Saks-Fifth Avenue, and a philosophy, instead of a religion.

DAWN POWELL

NOVEMBER 6

1978

The cleaning woman is thrilled that I am pregnant. She tells me stories: about her daughter's breech birth, and how she was in labor for three days before finally having a Caesarean. About the birth of her own fourth child, who was coming before the doctor got there, and how the nurse tried to hold the child in with a towel, pressing against its head, and about the child's neck breaking.

MARGARET RYAN

NOVEMBER 7

1884

Cleveland is now certainly elected. The official count of New York state gives 1,000 and more Democratic plurality. At school the Republicans were still defiant—hoping against hope. At recess I read a dispatch sent by Jay Gould to governor [*sic*] Cleveland congratulating him on his victory. This *must* be final.

REGINALD FAIRFAX HARRISON

[Gould. A grand financier of scandalous repute, he leaned whichever way the political wind was blowing.]

NOVEMBER 8

1849

My diary has stopped on account of my eyes, and I have not studied much.

Ellen is here, and we have had fun. We have been down to Staten Island to one of my sisters. She has ice cream on Thursdays.... One day I ate it so fast it gave me a pain in my forehead, and my brother-in-law said I must warm it over the register, and I did, and it all melted, and then they all laughed and said he was joking, but they gave me some more.

CATHERINE ELIZABETH HAVENS

1881

Was elected to the [New York] Legislature from the 21st Assembly District by a majority of *1501* over William Strew, the Democratic candidate.

THEODORE ROOSEVELT

NOVEMBER 9

1965

Early this morning Roger LaPorte burned himself to death at [the] U.N. Tonight a black-out. Failure of electricity from Ontario to N.J. All New York in the dark.

A strange and terrible day.

DOROTHY DAY

[LaPorte was a member of the Catholic Worker movement and a staunch opponent of the Vietnam War.]

1987

Walking at 6:30 in the barely morning, I watched a moon with a torn edge hanging in a discolored sky above the Carteret (once a hotel now an apartment house next to the Chelsea [Hotel]) when it was rubbed out, as though on a gray blackboard.

Yesterday, coming back from Saks Fifth Avenue with a red sweater in a black box, I stopped at my bank and when I came out, there in the mist (which was also smoke blown from West Virginia) was the Empire State Building, silvery and half erased and more beautiful than I've ever seen it. Not everything gets worse: that, and round-the-clock banking. Imagine, withdrawing big bucks on Sunday!

JAMES SCHUYLER

NOVEMBER 10

1776

Our brigade went down to King's Bridge under Col. Rall, since Col. Bose, in whose command we had first been, was ill; we were to reinforce Lt.-Gen. von Knyphausen's brigade. The enemy had erected a fort on a high rocky elevation, which seemed fortified by nature itself, which they called Fort Washington. Human skill had also been employed to make it very strong. Without possession of this fort we could not keep up communication with New York, nor could we think of advancing any farther, much less get quiet winter-quarters.

CAPT. ANDREAS WIEDERHOLD

1776

By the intercepted Letters, it appears that Washington is much dissatisfied with his officers, and informs the Congress, that the Northern & Southern People do not agree in the Army, and that there will be a Necessity to form two Armies in order to divide them. It is easy to see, whither all this tends, and what will be the probable Consequence of such a Division. If they cannot find Spirit to act under the Encouragement of their present Numbers, there is little Reason to believe, that their Courage will increase upon a Reduction of their Strength.

AMBROSE SERLE

1949

Now I ask myself, is this October or November? And what day is it? The days got lost. The end of my second week in America is coming to an end.... In the Employment agencies there are hundreds of little desks, and hundreds of people looking for work, with their eyes on the bulletin boards, reading the tiny labels with job descriptions. For two weeks we sat on those sad benches, and moved from table to table, from one board to another, and kept hearing "Nothing. Come tomorrow." The eyes get blank, the face becomes long, apathy sinks in. Work, work, work. Sometimes you come very close, you almost have it—and then it crumbles again.

Now I have a job. I am an "assembly worker" at B.M.Co. Manufacturing, 13-08 43rd Avenue, Long Island City. My check number is 431. For two days I have been assembling miniature toys. I am going out of my mind from the monotony. My fingers have holes from screwing tiny screws. Today, I could barely grasp them....

Saw Van Gogh show at the Museum of Modern Art, I revived.

JONAS MEKAS

NOVEMBER 11

1869

The grand *Vanderbilt* Bronze on the Hudson River Railroad Depot "unveiled" yesterday with much solemnity. There was a prayer and there were speeches. Vanderbilt began life penniless. He acquired a competence—honestly, I assume—by energy, economy, and business tact, and then increased his store to a colossal fortune of sixty millions (as they say) by questionable operations in railroad stocks. Anyhow, he is a millionaire of millionaires. And, therefore, we bow down before him, and worship him, with a hideous group of molten images, with himself for a central figure, at a cost of $800,000.

GEORGE TEMPLETON STRONG

1953

Put my right hand through a pane of glass in a fit of fury and emerge bloody but only scratched. I take satisfaction in such violence and no little pride in the ability to be so reckless and unthinking, though I think of myself as a cautious person.

JUDITH MALINA

NOVEMBER 12

1935

Pear & pastry in room—more conversation with young Cuban. Dolph phoned—I lunched in dining room—he came in just as I was finishing. We walked—sat in Square—to Whitney Museum—Shaker Exhibition—beer in Bar on 8th St. To Russian Inn—2nd Avenue. Assorty [*sic*] Russe-Bortsch-Shashlik Caucasian, Apple cake, . . . Muscatel, Crème de Menthe. Made date with Russian guitarist—he's short, solidly built, short dark hair, a crooked smile, a dimple, wears glasses—has a nice smile—a look in his eyes that promises a good bedfellow.

EUGENIA HUGHES

NOVEMBER 13

1953

Dylan Thomas' funeral

In St. Luke's Chapel, a block from the Cherry Lane, where I went to sit quietly on the days when the theater's worries pressed too hard.

Though the full roster of writers and artists is here, there is neither ostentation nor the unease evoked by coffin and flowers. It might be a mass in any church where all the parishioners know one another, nod, and afterward stop in the winter sunlight to exchange a few benign words.

JUDITH MALINA

1987

DREAM. I unlock a door of an apartment, it's a small studio with one partial wall separating the windowed room from the front door hallway. I'm inside without locking the door.... I hear a sound of some person as I come in.... I turn, it's night. I look toward a wall shielding the front door, no one there. I feel a slight shiver of fear. A bed nearby. This isn't my apartment. I've come through the night streets of a foreign city someplace and someone is allowing me to stay in this room/studio.... Suddenly this guy comes around the wall and pushes me backwards onto the bed. I am pushing him with my arms but he's too strong and heavy. His silhouette is muscular, but he's entirely covered in small spots of Kaposi's cancer. He's wearing no shirt, he has an almost shaved head. He lowers himself onto me and opens his mouth in some sort of grin, his teeth are rotted and wet, saliva spilling from behind them. He leans close to my face to kiss me, first saying, You would have thought I was sexy and cute if you had seen me before I got ill. I'm upset but I give him a quick kiss so he won't think I'm rejecting him completely because he has AIDS. I feel sorry for him just briefly, but I push him off me and rush out the door into the hall and staircase.

DAVID WOJNAROWICZ

NOVEMBER 14

1935

Bad cold—can't breathe properly-pain-pulse rapid—could hardly eat breakfast—felt nauseated. Julius phoned. Arranged to meet at 1.30. Did so—he was very well-dressed—skin sallow but clear—took him to Roma—I ate lunch. minestrone & spumoni. To "Berkeley Square" on 8th Street. Darkest theatre I've ever been in—he sat with his arm around me—his hand through the neck of my dress on my breast—very comforting—bit my ear lobe—we had a marvelous time. hope the patrons weren't disturbed by our breathing—he'll be gentle I think. Won't have him if he isn't.

EUGENIA HUGHES

1979

Pieces of the same thing at different times. I'm talking into these boxes these boxes keep time these boxes can take this time and make it a different time. Pieces of time in boxes. Putting things in boxes. Putting pieces of the same thing in different boxes. Pieces of the same thing at different times. It's the same thing.

KEITH HARING

NOVEMBER 15

1931

Took [son] Jojo to Empire State Tower. A storm up in the clouds. The most magical spot in the world. Bizarre, theatrical—it is impossible to believe in it and people jumping off are (I'm sure) caught on rubber mattresses a few feet below their jumping off place.

DAWN POWELL

NOVEMBER 16

[THE CAPTURE OF FORT WASHINGTON.]

1776

16 November.—was fixed for the attack.... At 11 o'clock the boats with two brigades of English came down Harlem creek in order to make a landing near the woods on the left to make a feigned attack. At this moment the real attack was begun near us, and we stood facing their crack troops and their riflemen all on this almost inaccessible rock which lay before us, surrounded by swamps and three earthworks, one above the other. In spite of this every obstacle was swept aside, the earthworks broken through, the swamps waded, the precipitous rocks scaled and the riflemen were driven out of their breastworks, from where they had been seconded by their artillery—and we gained this terrible height, pursued the enemy who were retreating behind the lines and batteries;... one of which lay on the very top of the rock, and we followed the fleeing enemy to the fort proper.

CAPT. ANDREAS WIEDERHOLD

1776

Fort Washington... This day I, William Slade was taken with 2,800 more. We was allowed honours of War. We then marched to Harlem under guard, where we were turned into a barn. We got little rest that night being verry much crowded.

WILLIAM SLADE

1840

My dear, beloved Mary left this world of trouble and affliction, and as I firmly and confidently believe, joined her sister angels in Heaven, on Friday morning at half past six o'clock. Long and severe as her illness has been, and great as her sufferings, at times she has appeared to be so much better that the blessed rays of hope have shone round her, and we have indulged the delusive expectation that the cherished flower would be reanimated and bloom once more in its former loveliness.... The body was deposited in its coffin, and placed in the back parlor. After the family had all gone to bed, I obtained the key of the room and taking a lamp went into the chamber of death, seated myself at the side of the cold remains of my darling child, and for half an hour held in imagination delightful converse with the spirit which had of late animated it. The countenance was unchanged, the expression intelligent and lovely as it was wont to be, and that smile, sweet as the smile of a seraph, still hung upon her half-closed lips, and I gazed with fixed eyes upon it, until I almost fancied it moved and spoke to me again. It is strange that I could derive consolation from looking upon the wreck of that which my heart held so dear, and yet it was a half hour of delightful employment. Never shall I desire to have it effaced from my remembrance.

PHILIP HONE

1909

Isadora Duncan! Mrs. Roberts (dear kind woman) sent us tickets, box seats, and we saw Isadora dance. It's positively splendid! I feel that she dances a symbol of human animal happiness as it should be, free from the unnatural trammels. Not angelic, materialistic—not superhuman but the greatest human love of life. Her great big thighs, her small head, her full solid loins, belly—clean, all clean—she dances away civilization's tainted brain vapors, wholly human and holy—part of God. I'm in a way regretting that I did not know all her art stood for when I met her at Roberts' on Sunday.

John Sloan

1949

Another week is over. I am still working at G.M.Co. For two days I screwed little screws. For another two I drilled little holes. For yet another two days I drilled big holes. During the last hours of the day my hands can no longer pull the drill handle. The only way I can still continue is by pressing the handle down with my whole body. Chest and stomach muscles are all on fire.... Thoughts are jumping around, like dead sparks, with no center—one thought here, one thought there....

There is a gang of fatso girls working here also, they do the packing.... But most of the time they giggle, with their teeth showing. Or they sing under their noses, in high voices, and they have been going after me like fat flies....

The smell of steel and iron pervades the place. I carry this smell out into the street, and sometimes I think that maybe the whole of New York smells like steel.... Steel is not eternal, no. Steel also dies, like wood, like grass. Steel and Iron turn to dust.

Jonas Mekas

November 17

1778

At daybreak this morning I went on furlough to New York to buy some necessary shirts. I stopped at a German's house, who was a lamp-cleaner in Robinson street near the Colleges which were now used as an English hospital.

Lt. John Charles Philip von Krafft

1780

A report that Ethan Allen has joined the King's Troops at Ticonderoga; 'Tis believed.

HUGH GAINE

1944

Not drinking for a week gives the world a strange opium dream quality. I realize that I drink to make the fantasy rattle down to reality.

DAWN POWELL

NOVEMBER 18

1776

We were called out while it was still dark, but was soon marchd to New York, four deep, verry much frownd upon by all we saw. We was called Yankey Rebbels a going to the gallows.

WILLIAM SLADE

1778

In the morning I saw for the first time two sailors, on an English man-of-war, hoisting up a yellow flag between the masts until it had reached the very tip top—the common sign that a person has to lose his life on account of some crime. At 3 P.M. I left New York and reached our camp, which was 11 miles distant, at sun-down. Our camp there was very poor, because many of the huts which lay around the foot of the hill, among them mine, got full of water whenever it rained. The drinking water was also very bad, and in every respect matters were in such a state, that if no change is made, diseases must unavoidably arise.

LT. JOHN CHARLES PHILIP VON KRAFFT

1909

I worked on hands of second Yolande B. with purple shawl and it seems to be a good thing still.... I finished Puzzle in the evening. Oh these (I've got to hope) everlasting!! Puzzles. "The Pen is mightier than the Pig"—original adage to be used to express how a man is held in by circumstances.

JOHN SLOAN

[Yolande Bugbee was sixteen when Sloan first hired her as a model. She would become the subject of eight of his portraits.]

NOVEMBER 19

1947

Dark Eyes came to my house tonight and we danced all night long, and into the morning. We sat on the floor, on the beautiful rug my mother made for me, and listened to the royal wedding at six in the morning. My mother was charming when she got up and saw us there. I made Dark Eyes some *crêpes suzette*. We danced again, & sang.

JACK KEROUAC

1971

Tonight I was the guest speaker at my own synagogue, the Town and Village.... When I arrived, I discovered I had forgotten my glasses, so the first thing I had to do was go around the synagogue to find somebody of about my age with my degree of farsightedness so I could read my notes.

Once I found a similar prescription to mine, I gave my speech, which was a report of my meeting with Sisco. Afterwards, Martin and I went downstairs for what they call the *Oneg Shabbat*, where they serve cake, coffee and wine. As usual, one guy cornered me and started badgering me about my views on Israel.

BELLA ABZUG

November 20

1780

Pretty Pleasant. Some Prizes brought in, said to be Rebel Privateers.

HUGH GAINE

1848

Conflagrations. The bells were ringing nearly the whole of Saturday night, and the heavens were illuminated in four different quarters.... The greatest destruction was in the burning of Murphy's omnibus stables, corner of the Third Avenue and Twenty-seventh Street. I went up this afternoon to see the ruins, and a "sad sight" it was. The whole of this extensive establishment is destroyed, with twenty-six omnibuses and sixteen of those man-of-war sleighs which convey in winter the population of the city from up to down town.... But the saddest and most disgusting sight of all is the blackened and bloody carcasses of one hundred and fifty horses, some of whom were valuable; all of them burned at their stalls, unapproachable and inextricable. Carts were employed in conveying away the mangled remains of these noble animals. The burning of omnibus stables has become frequent of late, and is without doubt the work of incendiaries.

PHILIP HONE

1953

Several nights with Jim. One ice-cold night at Cornelia Street with only the fireplace red with old *New York Post*s for both light and heat; once in King Street where we made love fearful of every sound.

Jim is much troubled by Dylan's death. He makes efforts to cut down on his drinking, boasts about it less, attends meetings of Alcoholics Anonymous, rations himself to five drinks a day.

JUDITH MALINA

1966

I will be going [with Diana Vreeland] to Truman's £10,000 party. About this I have mixed feelings. I would feel that I had missed quite an event if I didn't go, but I know I will be angry. It seems to me such a terrible waste of money to spend so much in one evening. After six hours he will have nothing to see for his cheque except a lot of press clippings. The foolishness of spending so much time organizing the party is something for a younger man, or a worthless woman to indulge in, if they have social ambitions.

What is Truman trying to prove? At any rate it is a masterstroke of publicity though of the wrong sort. Cocteau fought to keep himself away from the costume balls of de Beaumont. As much as he would have liked it, he knew that his image was being made too frivolous if he was photographed in *Vogue*. So he kept away. Now things are different. Truman had delivered himself of a very good book. Nothing can take away the fact that as a popular writer, of the greatest sales, he has "arrived." That this is a book of importance is also undeniable. The party will be a very brilliant occasion with all café society present, but while the two bands are blaring and the champagne drunk, who will remember the two murderers but for whose garrulous co-operation, as Jonathan Miller remarked, the book could not have been written. It is going to be very hard for me to hide my feelings.

SIR CECIL BEATON

1979

Last night Kenny and I went to Times Square to do Polaroid photographs after seeing Barbara Buckner's video tape—*Pictures of the Lost*—at the Donnell Library. We watched this incredible black

woman in a fluorescent orange poncho playing an electric organ.
She was the best organ player I've heard in a long time. She would
go through these incredible abstract chord changes. She was totally unaware of the preconceived structures of songs and the only
way you could tell what she was playing was by listening to the
words. She did the most far-out version of "Blue Suede Shoes"
I ever heard. We were the only people watching except for two
other men.

KEITH HARING

NOVEMBER 21

1780

Little worth Notice; some firing at Newark, where the Refugees
went for some Cattle; but they were beat away, by a Part of General
Washington's Army.

HUGH GAINE

1980

I just finished *Goldberg Variations*—it was horrible. I felt each entrance that I could not do it. The moment I set foot on stage, it
wasn't me. I charge to the dressing room, look at my face in the
mirror under a cloud of cigarette smoke. My makeup is beautiful;
my hair is divine; I look great, even magnificent. But out there I was
numb. Looking in the mirror re-establishes me; then the thoughts
flow into a barrage of hatred for mirrors, our obsession. I dance far
better for myself in front of a mirror. At least then I know I have a
receptive audience. Oh dear, this is not good dancing. I'm definitely
missing the point. I have prepared myself to be beautiful and to be
chosen for that beauty. But I feel unchosen.

TONI BENTLEY

November 22

1780

The Anspachers entered the North Church for Winter Quarters, and their Major, de Seitz, was billeted on us.

Ewald Gustav Schaukirk

1873

Boss Tweed the *Meister-Dieb* sentenced to 12 years and a moderate fine. Good as far as it goes.

George Templeton Strong

1935

In *Turn, Magic Wheel*, I believe firmly that I have the perfect New York story, one woman's tragedy viewed through the chinks of a writer's book about her, newspaper clippings, cafe conversations, restaurant brawls, New York night life, so that the story is tangled in the fritter of New York—it could not happen anyplace else. The front she keeps up is the front peculiar to the New York broken heart; peoples' deeds and reactions are peculiarly New York. "What? Our friend committed suicide—that's terrible … that's the kind of suit I'm going to get, there in Altman's…. She jumped out of the window? No!—are you getting out here, why don't you get a gold belt?…"

The truth is that in New York, a city of perpetual distraction—where superficial senses are perpetually forced to react to superficial impressions—the inner tragedies, no matter how intense, are viewed through the tawdry lace of New York life.

Dawn Powell

1980

Still dark out the window of the 10th floor of the Wellington, muffled sounds of auto engines revving up in the background. A car going by occasionally. Andrew's parrot—or whatever—silent, standing perched on a lamp in the second bedroom. Andrew asleep. A good time to think.

MARIO CUOMO

NOVEMBER 23

1859

Uncle finishes the *Deerslayer*—Character of Natty Rumps [Bumppo] rather overwritten—some interest in the story, but an immense deal of twaddle in the conversations.

PIERRE MUNRO IRVING

1934

On Wednesday we had a staff meeting of PWA [Public Works Administration], followed by a meeting of the board at two o'clock. On the list of projects to be submitted for approval were several for New York City, aggregating a considerable sum. All of these I struck off the list before the meeting. I have been insisting for some time that Mayor La Guardia get rid of Robert Moses as a member of his Triborough Bridge Commission. This has been at the instance of the President. It seems that Moses is a bitterly persistent enemy of the President's, and the President has a feeling of dislike of him that I haven't seen him express with respect to any other person. La Guardia has been putting me off for months. Then came the campaign in New York with Moses as the Republican candidate for Governor. Naturally I had to declare a truce during that period in order to avoid a charge that I was playing politics. Since the election I have called La Guardia twice. The last time he told me he could not get rid of Moses, unless he was willing to resign, without preferring charges. I told him that that was his funeral and not mine and that I did not see any reason why we should be expected to go in on a Federal project with a man who criticized the Federal Administration as bitterly as Moses has. Accordingly, I have decided not to make allocations for any more projects in New York City until this matter has been adjusted, and I am considering refusing to honor requisitions for funds on pending projects.

HAROLD L. ICKES

1981

We just had a hilarious time in *Rubies* as a new girl happily jogged all around the stage sixteen counts early while the rest of us stood stationary. She looked like an escaped jumping bean.

We are discussing our new contract, and, typically, very few of us are interested in such things as raises and union rules, but tomorrow there is a promise of fudge and brownies at the meeting, so I predict a large turnout.

TONI BENTLEY

NOVEMBER 24

1863

I am happy to begin another book with the account of Grant's victory over Bragg at Chattanooga, and the release of Tennessee.... Phil [her brother] is at Knoxville with the Ninth Army Corps. He gives a sad picture of his accommodations (five in a tent), and when he is thus uncomfortable, what must be the condition of the private soldiers?... The news came on Thanksgiving Day. It is quite remarkable how often good news has arrived on festival days.

MARIA LYDIG DALY

1937

I had my first day in the room I've got, at the old Broadway Central Hotel, in Lower Broadway. It should be a grand place to work.

Spent most of the day at letters. Sneaked off to the Old Glory horse sale at 94 and Madison. Very sad that I could not bid for some of the beautiful yearlings. In the evening Mary, E and I to eat lobster at the Grotto.

SHERWOOD ANDERSON

NOVEMBER 25

1783

Today all the British left New York, and Gen. Washington with his troops marched in and took possession of the city.

BROTHER EWALD GUSTAV SCHAUKIRK

1864

Attempt by southerners to burn the City.

WILLIAM STEINWAY

NOVEMBER 26

1776

We spent in cooking for wood was scarce and the church was verry well broke when done, but verry little to eat.

WILLIAM SLADE

1777

We were informed this morning, That the House of General De Lancey at Bloomingdale was burnt to the Ground by the Rebels last Night, his Lady and Children abused, and Cash to the Amount of £500 Ster. taken away.

HUGH GAINE

1941

KEROUAC/STUPID JOURNAL

Up till September 1941 I had been regarded (and was regarding myself) as a college man, a "star" athlete, an unusual hunk of youthdom, a "writer," a loyal son and an industrious young man—headed *somewhere*, as it were.

Actually, I was this:

I was an unjustified egoist: I was child-minded; I was an athlete, and still am, but I used to walk around with the athlete complex, thinking that being so I might be looked upon as superior, in some haphazard way or other. I was headed nowhere, really.

I returned to college in the Fall, but my mind wasn't at rest. My family was not any too well fixed; I felt out of place, the coaches were insulting, I was lonely; I left and went down to the South to think things over. Since then, on my own, I have been learning fast, writing a lot, reading good men, and have been slowly making up my mind, seriously & quietly. Either I am loathsome to others, I have decided, or else I shall be a beacon of rich warm light, spreading good and plenty, making things prosper, being a cosmic architect, conquering the world and being respected, myself grinning surreptitiously. Either that, Sirs, or I shall be the most loathsome, useless, and parasitical (on myself) creature in the world. I shall be a denizen of the Underground, or a successful man of the world. There shall be no compromise!!! I mean it.

JACK KEROUAC

NOVEMBER 27

1765

Reported that the Mob are for having their assembly first to have the stamp act repealed.... Mr Peter Delancey obliged to resign his office as Inspector and Stamp distributor for the Provinces of Canada, Nova Scotia and New Hampshire. The Governor sent for Sears, a ringleader, to preserve the peace of the city.

CAPT. JOHN MONTRÉSOR

1931

Last night the [Alfred] Knopfs gave a box party at Carnegie Hall to hear to Boston Symphony Orchestra, and a supper later at their city apartment, 400 East 57th Street, in honor of the conductor, Koussevitzky.... Willa Cather surprised me by saying that [Mahler's Ninth Symphony] was too much for her, but that she liked the Ravel. The latter was a very cheap piece of trash....

After the concert... we went to [the] Knopf apartment.... A lot of miscellaneous introducing. I got but one drink—a small straight Scotch. Dashiell Hammett, the writer of detective stories, came in drunk, and became something of a nuisance. After we left, so Blanche told me today, she had to get rid of him. William Faulkner, the Mississippian, who came in late also got drunk. At 4 A.M. Blanche and Eddie Wasserman decided to take him to a speakeasy to dispose of him. Unfortunately, all the speakeasies in the neighborhood were closed, so they had to haul him to his hotel. He still talked rationally, but his legs had given out, and he couldn't stand up.

H. L. MENCKEN

1940

Visiting the Greenwich Prison—Women's new House of Detention. Top floor for rehabilitation work where in one room a little colored girl was drumming at a piano, trying to learn; another room had a history class (all prostitutes); here was a group rehearsing the Xmas play; here was the ward for social diseases; here was the kitchen where the girls did the cooking, sewing, etc.; here was the library; here was where they talked (through closed windows and amplifiers so no tools could be exchanged); here were the locked doors everywhere; here were the little bunks, stockings being dried, *Screen Guide* on a bed, but barred doors and windows; here was a cop bringing in two new streetwalkers, one colored, one drab white, and here, coming from one assembly hall, was a chorus of incorrigibles lifting happy voices in "Hark, the Herald Angels Sing." We heard them as we went down the hall, the matron unlocking one heavy door after another on our way to tea at her private suite.

DAWN POWELL

1980

There are some basic rules for rehearsal clothes. Everything must be soft, old, borrowed, pinned, cut up and oversized. And worn only once—variety is essential. Only new company members wear anything that actually fits, a sure giveaway of their youth. We go through fads: big sweat shirts, Capezio's latest leg warmers, or triple layers of leg warmers. New articles are very suspicious; they contain no personal identity, so the scissors are instantly applied to the neckline (as low as possible, please!). The basic premise is to cover up and keep warm. Layer upon layer is essential so that we can peel off at appropriate intervals when sufficient warmth and confidence for self-exposure is reached. When we are onstage in tutus and leotards, it is the most naked we've been all day. Layers also give a wonderful feeling of possibility; after all, one can always take them off. Adding layers also happens but less frequently; it's a sign that things aren't going so well in the security area.

The one and only time we all strip is for Mr. Balanchine. He demands to see exactly what he is getting. He does not take kindly to paraphernalia. After all, we are hired to show our bodies, so those layers are rather defeating the purpose.

TONI BENTLEY

NOVEMBER 28

1859

On retiring for the night... Sarah, who always took charge of his medicines, went into his room to arrange them as usual. He said to her, "I must arrange my pillows for another weary night. I feel no dread. Fully [downhearted]" and then exclaimed—"if this could only end."... [A]lmost at the same moment he gave a slight exclamation, as if of pain—placing his hands on his left side—repeated the exclamation & the pressure of the hand. Caught at the foot boards of His bed, and fell backwards.... I was in the parlour—heard the sound & the cries of Sarah which immediately followed brought me in an instant to his side. I raised his head in my arms—he was to all appearances unconscious & he gave but a few [final?] gasps (or breaths) and expired. Though [continued] to administer brandy... [told] Helen to bathe his arms & feet... but it was evident to her it was in vain.... We went at once on the alarm for Dr. Caruthers—and when he came—more than an hour—he pronounced Life extinct.

PIERRE MUNRO IRVING

NOVEMBER 29

1641

At daybreak we ran to the *Sandpunt* [Sandy Hook] and as we rounded it too close we got aground on a reef which had formed there within a year. After two hours we got afloat again. God be praised, we suffered no damage and with good speed passed between the [headlands] and in the afternoon came to anchor at the *Manhatans* in front of the *Smits Valeij* [on the East River] in four fathoms. At anchor there we found a flute [transport vessel], called *de witte Valck* [*The White Falcon*] laden with salt and sugar. Thus the

Lord delivered us at last after much adversity, for which be He praised forever. Amen. The next day a dead horse overboard.

ANTONY DE HOOGES

1783
In the evening about 8 o'clock, we felt a slight shock of an earthquake; and about eleven, there was a more violent one, which shook all the city in a surprising manner. We felt it in bed—enough to arouse us from our first sleep.

BROTHER EWALD GUSTAV SCHAUKIRK

NOVEMBER 30

1954
Last night's rally for Joe McCarthy in Madison Square Garden was a cocked gun that failed to fire because the triggerman was in Washington with a bum elbow. The explosive charge was packed tight and dry: the "martyrdom" of McCarthy, the jiggled and juggled signatures of the boobocracy on the anti-censure petition, the 13 Americans jailed by the Chinese Reds, the vest-pocket war off the China coast, the issue of co-existence, the GOP defeat in the election and Joe's subsequent loss of his chairmanship, the renewed public snufflings of the Christian Fronters and America Firsters.

All the necessary ingredients, primed for a big BANG! Instead, the rally went pfff—f-f-f—ttt.

Hitler would have sneered, Huey Long would have guffawed. The three witches in *Macbeth* would have slunk away, disconsolate at the plot that misfired. . . .

Last night the tin-headed admirals and generals and majors turned truth inside out. Unwittingly revealing their own lust for power, they wailed that they had been brainwashed, that we are advancing toward a totalitarian state, that there is danger of a man on horseback—in those very words. *Their* man on horseback, of course. St. McCarthy.

To the frenetically shrieking people they declared that everything they said was cold rationalism. We believe in law and order, they shouted, even as they ejected a girl photographer who had broken no law, committed no disorder. This is a government of laws and not of men, they shrilled, ignoring the fact that McCarthy had appealed on television for all federal employees to break the law and give secret information to him, a single man, not the whole government. They said more, much more, but they failed to spew the words that could have unleashed the beasts. The mob wanted to hear about mob-given laws. It wanted to be told that it had ascended the throne....

For a few suspenseful minutes it seemed that Roy Cohn might help the mob make love to itself. "Discovered" in a box seat on the south side of the arena, a would-be Caligula with a thumb ready to point down, a flayer of all enemies of McCarthy, Roy was photographed repeatedly by newspaper and television cameramen whose lights enabled the mob to realize that their champion was in their midst, and so there arose a throaty chant: "We want Roy, we want Roy!..."

And Cohn, the violet who shrinks toward the sun, the bear-trap mind beneath gleaming patent-leather hair, humbly bowed to fate and arose and began striding along a balcony toward the speakers' platform. Two Garden guards, sudden bearers of a sacred treasure, marched self-importantly ahead of him to clear his path to the platform. Like a low-lying cloud bristling with electricity on a sullen summer night, the audience rumbled expectantly. *Roy* would tell everyone! *Roy* had all the answers! He stepped in front of the snake-slim microphones and pursed his fat red lips and then began to speak. *This* was the moment! But—he fizzled out.

A lawyer by trade, he unreeled long and involved sentences, spun out clauses and phrases, served pap when the mob wanted red meat. However, into the mob he did shoot one dose of hyperbole: "If the Senate," said Roy sonorously, "votes to censure, it will be committing the blackest act in our whole history!"

From near and far there came applause, but it merely pattered like an April rain, rather than booming like a cannonade. Had he machine-gunned bursts of short emotional words into that audience, he would have carried the night—and maybe the entire history of the nation. Greased with the poison of lies, they would have found their mark and killed the soul of an entire people. Instead, he shot over their heads. He should have aimed at their bellies. Surprise! Surprise! The golden moment gone.

EDWARD ROBB ELLIS

1980

It is Sunday night, a special night to us because tomorrow is our free day—the one day of the week when we try to make up for all lost living time: laundry, bills, friends, meals, sleep. We just closed with a magnificent *Stars and Stripes*. Since it is the last ballet of the week we are all tired, very tired, yet we muster up more energy than ever from the inspiration that afterwards we will be free. Heather Watts and Peter Martins pulled out all the stops tonight. The wings were filled with cheering, smiling faces, applauding and yelling with delight. I hope the audience was as thrilled as we were. Peter's eyes constantly glanced into the wings as if for more food. It worked somehow; we loved them, and they rose to the occasion. There was a wonderful, warm family feeling—it happens more often than you might imagine. No more complaints or axes or anxieties, but all pure goodwill flowing out for the success of *Stars and Stripes*, of the evening, and of NYCB. We were magnificent tonight.

TONI BENTLEY

1985

I'm starting to think that crystals don't work. Because look what's happened lately when they're supposed to be *protecting* me—my rug has cancer from the moths, I stepped on a beautiful old plastic ring and crushed it, and I was assaulted at the book signing. But I've got to believe in *something,* so I'll continue with the crystals. Because things could always be worse.

ANDY WARHOL

December 1

1765

It being Sunday—no work to-day. A son of liberty stabbed with a Bayonet by one of the Royal Artillery.

Capt. John Montrésor

1832

Persuaded my father to come down and take a breathing on the Battery with me. And a breathing it was with a vengeance. The wind blew tempestuously, the waters, all troubled and rough, were of a yellow green colour, breaking into short, strong, angry waves, whose glittering white crests the wind carried away, as they sank to the level surface again. The shores were all cold, distinct, sharp-cut, and wintry-looking, the sky was black and gloomy, with now and then a watery wan sunlight running through it. The wind was so powerful, we could scarcely keep our legs. My sleeves and skirts fluttered in the blast, my bonnet was turned front part behind, my nose was blue, my cheeks were crimson, my hair was all tangled, my breath was gone, my blood was in a glow: what a walk!... The keen cutting wind whizzed along the streets; huge masses of dark clouds, with soft brown edges, lay on the pale delicate blue of the evening sky. The moon was up, clear, cold, and radiant; the crowd had ebbed away from the busy thoroughfare, and only a few men in great coats buttoned up to their chins, and women wrapped in cloaks, were scudding along in the dim twilight and the bitter wind towards their several destinations, with a frozen shuddering look that made me laugh. I had got perished [*sic*] in the coach, and see-ing that the darkness covered me, determined to walk home, and bade the coach follow me. How pleasant it was: I walked tremen-dously fast, enjoying the fresh breath of the north, and looking at the glittering moon, as she strode high in the evening sky. How I do like walking alone—being alone; for this alone I wish I were a man.

FANNY KEMBLE

DECEMBER 2

1776

Early in the morning we was calld out and stood in the cold, about one hour and then marchd to the North River and went on board the *Grovnor* transport ship. Their was now 500 men on board, this made much confusion. We had to go to bed without supper. This night was verry long, hunger prevaild much. Sorrow more.

WILLIAM SLADE

1935

Lunch with John Farrar. He told me how fine my book was; it probably wouldn't sell, etc. Lunch with him is taxing for he is such a complete self-dramatizer.

DAWN POWELL

DECEMBER 3

1920

I find the town grown callously indifferent. It may be that the warr [*sic*] hath soaked to saturation our capacity for indignation. A building fell Wednesday and yesterday five persons were burned to death in a fire in a small house, yet the town is not aroused to any great wrath. Until it is, such things will continue... For the only advance ever made was pushed by the wrath of somebody.

FRANKLIN P. ADAMS

1978

Halston and Stevie Rubell gave Bianca a beautiful fur coat. Dr. Giller paid for the collar, and Halston and Steve paid for the rest of the coat. It cost $30,000 or $40,000. I'm surpised they didn't ask me to give her an arm. (*laughs*) And Halston said, "I think everyone should have furs, jewels, and Andy Warhol paintings."

ANDY WARHOL

DECEMBER 4

1839

The Daguerrotype. I went this morning by invitation of M. Francois Gouraud to see a collection of the views made by the wonderful process lately discovered in France by M. Daguerre.... The reflection of surrounding images created by a camera obscura upon a plate of copper, plated with silver and prepared with some chemical substance, is not only distinctly delineated, but left upon the plate so prepared and there remains forever. Every object, however minute, is a perfect transcript of the thing itself; the hair of the human head, the gravel on the roadside, the texture of a silk curtain, or the shadow of the smallest leaf reflected upon the wall, are all imprinted as carefully as nature or art has created them in the objects transferred; and those things which are invisible to the naked eye are rendered apparent by the help of a magnifying glass.... How greatly ashamed of their ignorance the by-gone generations of mankind ought to be.

PHILIP HONE

1852

Two more lectures by [William Makepeace] Thackeray, spirited and original, though not so striking as the first two. They are still crowded.... Lamentable commentary on the Vanity of Human

Greatness in Thackeray's inquiry ... —"Who is a Mr. Astor who has left a card for me?"

GEORGE TEMPLETON STRONG

1907

Miss Niles wrote Dolly and sent her a nice pair of shoes and two pairs of gloves, little worn and useful. While poor, we are thus proved not proud.

JOHN SLOAN

1923

Early up and to the office, where till four, and so up town, and met Mistress Neysa McMein and Dottie Parker, and they asked me to walk with them and look in windows, which I promised to do if they would not beg me to buy them this or that, and they said they would not, but they teased me for everything they saw, from emerald necklaces to handkerchiefs. But I was firm and bought them never a thing.

FRANKLIN P. ADAMS

1923

Mrs. [Elinor] Wylie—I saw her a few nights ago. Her face looked softer, and she had some color. Whether suffused by nature or by art, it was very becoming—She looked less like one of those birds wh. remind you of their reptilian origin.

MARIANNE MOORE

1969

Last year when I began work on my Pollock biography, I asked Lee what color Jackson's eyes were. I couldn't remember if they were light hazel or gray. To my surprise, Lee couldn't either—Lee, who gave fifteen years of her life to Jackson while he was alive and who has already given almost as many since his death. I called some friends and determined that his eyes were hazel.

B. H. FRIEDMAN

DECEMBER 5

1949

Yesterday I took [daughter] Susie to a party on Fifth Avenue given for their daughter by a French-Swiss couple. The pretty parlor-maid, the melodious French voices, the pink rooms, the smell of candy and perfume like an expensive confectioner's on a late-winter afternoon; and my own awkward shyness. I asked the elevator man to wait for me and left her at the door, although I can at least do this much better. Then walking down Fifth Avenue; the crowds pouring out of the Metropolitan, the people walking north from the Frick gallery, where the Stradivarius had been playing a Beethoven quartet. The light in the sky is sombre, there is a brume in the air. The dead city trees of Central Park are massed like a thicket in the somber light. In the brume the long double track of street lamps seems yellow. This appears to be a city of the Enlightenment—like Paris or London at the turn of the century; the irreducible evidence of man's inventiveness; progress.

JOHN CHEEVER

1949

Still with G.M.Co. Putting together scissors, pliers, screwdrivers, but most of the time I don't even know what. When we get an order of drills, the palms get covered with blisters. I can't even touch anything, even with gloves. They keep rotating the workers from one table to another, but it's of little help.

The fingers are working automatically. They lead their own automatic lives. I may as well let them. Who cares about the fingers. I leave them alone. They keep moving.... Suddenly I catch myself dreaming, making plans, completely unconscious of the activities of my fingers. I have no idea what they did in the meanwhile. Maybe they strangled somebody. I wouldn't know. I am not responsible for my fingers at all. I am a space traveller.

I am taking off again! Next to my knees the radiator is boiling. I am standing at a long table, with my back to other workers. The radiator sizzles. Behind my back a monotonous noise. In another corner some women are singing, their voices are very high. It's their own form of space travelling. They must be off to somewhere.

Went to see *Firebird* (Balanchine).

JONAS MEKAS

DECEMBER 6

1864

Sunday evening last, the 3rd, Mrs. [Jessie Benton] Frémont came just as dinner was put upon the table. She stayed until nine o'clock. She is very brilliant and original, has somewhat the manner of one accustomed to rule and direct others, fond of gentlemen's society, as most clever women are, has some affectations of *thought* and idiosyncracies of taste and feeling, but no affectation of manner and no hypocrisy. I'm afraid she is too positive and truthful to be popular in New York. Nobody likes so much fresh breeze and so much sunlight; it disturbs the lazy and frightens the hypocritical.

MARIA LYDIG DALY

1892

Jay Gould was buried yesterday. He was but 57 years old and died of consumption. He had about as little of the respect of the country as any man it ever produced and seemed as perfectly indifferent about [it] as a skunk or a rattlesnake. He was a phenomenon. With many domestic virtues, he seemed wholly lacking in philanthropy.... He was a most [left blank] husband and father, ascetically temperate—due perhaps as much or more to his health than anything else—and was even religious in his way, [though] no cutpurse or highwayman seemed to have less scruples about the way he took to get into other peoples safes.

JOHN BIGELOW

DECEMBER 7

1847

St. Nicholas [Society] dinner last night. Instead of sitting down at five, it was half-past six before feeding commenced, and as I'd been ass enough to omit my usual dinner, my gastric juice was by that time eating up the coats of my stomach and I was in that disgusting state of faint, weak, headachy misery to which a postponement of pabulum always reduces me, for dinner deferred maketh the stomach sick. And then sitting down with an omnivorous appetite and filling myself up with 1. Oysters, 2. Soup, 3. Fish, 4. Turkey, 5. Venison, 6. Canvasback duck, 7. Miscellaneous trifles, the enumeration of which under 17 several subdivisions I omit for the present, this promiscuous kind of abundant pasture, moistened by a little hock and a little champagne and a tolerable sufficiency of sherry and a few sips of vitriolic Schiedam—all this swinery or hoggishness, or whatever it may be called, gave me a shocking sick headache, which I deserved.

GEORGE TEMPLETON STRONG

1935

Julius phoned today—he introduced me to the dancer whose room we made such good use of Wednesday night. The dancer is very

Russian—has a charming voice—wanted me to have dinner with him at the Russian Bear & stay for the floor show, in which he dances at one A.M. I had to say no. Felt too rheumatic—he'll phone Monday at 3—his first name is George—wonder if Julius thinks two lovers are better than one—I'm really quite content with J.

EUGENIA HUGHES

1983

A choice on Tuesday between dining with the Donald Newhouses or the king and queen of Spain. Having promised the Newhouses months ago, I regretted the royals. A vengeance on the Inquisition.

LEO LERMAN

DECEMBER 8

1704

I Riss, ... about three in the morning, Setting up by the Fire till Light, ... wee took our leave of Monsier and about seven in the morn come to New Rochell, a french town, where we had a good Breakfast. And in the strength of that about an how'r before sunsett got to [New] York. Here I applyed myself to Mr. Burroughs, a merchant to whom I was recommended by my Kinsman.... Mr. Burroughs went with me to [the] Vendue where I bought about 100 Rheem of paper wch was retaken in a flyboat from Holland and sold very Reasonably here.... And at the Vendue I made a great many acquaintances amongst the good women of the town, who curteosly invited me to their houses and generously entertained me.

The Cittie of New York is a pleasant, well compacted place.... The Buildings Brick Generally, very stately and high, though not altogether like ours in Boston.... The inside of them are neat to admiration, the wooden work for only the walls are plastered.... The House where the Vendue was, had Chimney Corners like ours, and they and the hearths were laid wth the finest tile that I ever see, and the stair cases laid all with white tile which is ever clean, and so are the walls of the Kitchen wch had a Brick floor. They were making Great preparations to Receive their Govenor Lord Cornbury from the Jerseys, and for that End raised the militia to Gard him on shore to the fort. . . .

The English go very fasheonable in their dress. But the Dutch, especially the middling sort, differ from our women, in their habitt go loose, wear French muches wch are like a Capp and a head band in one, leaving their ears bare, which are sett out wth Jewells of a large size and many in number. And their fingers hoop't with Rings, some with large stones in them of many Coullers as were their pendants in their ears, which You should see very old women wear as well as Young.

SARAH KEMBLE KNIGHT

1838

A Dinner-Party Disturbed by an Unexpected Visitor. We had to dine with us to-day Mr. Christopher Hughes, American chargé at Stockholm, Col. Webb, Mr. William B. Astor and Dr. Francis. Whilst we were at dinner there was a ring at the street doorbell. The boy Daniel went out and found nobody there; but there was a basket on the sill of the door, which he brought into the dining room, and it was found to contain a lovely infant, apparently about a week old, stowed away nicely in soft cotton. It had on a clean worked muslin frock, lace cap, its underclothes new and perfectly clean, a locket on the neck which opened with a spring and contained a lock of dark hair; the whole covered nicely with a piece of new flannel, and a label pinned on the breast on which was written, in a female hand, Alfred G. Douglas. It was one of the sweetest babies I ever saw; apparently healthy. It did not cry during the time we had it, but lay in a placid, dozing state, and occasionally, on the approach of the light, opened its little, sparkling eyes, and seemed satisfied with the company into which it had been so strangely introduced. Poor little innocent—abandoned by its natural protector, and thrown at its entrance into life upon the sympathy of a selfish world, to be exposed, if it should live, to the jeers and taunts of uncharitable legitimacy!... My feelings were strongly interested, and I felt inclined at first to take in and cherish the little stranger; but this was strongly opposed by the company, who urged, very properly, that in that case I would have twenty more such outlets to my benevolence. I reflected, moreover, that if the little urchin should turn out bad, he would prove a troublesome inmate; and if intelligent and good, by the time he became an object of my affection the rightful owners might come and take him away. So John Stotes was summoned, and sent off with the little wanderer to the almshouse.

PHILIP HONE

1867

Meet Chas. Dickens at our Hall.

WILLIAM STEINWAY

1979

The "Fashions of the Hapsburgs" [Costume Institute] gala, on Monday last at the Metropolitan Museum—A perfect moment came when the whole lavish crowd was traipsing the long, narrow, grenadier-scarlet carpet away from the wretched dinner, a quarter-mile path between black-tied musicians, who stood on either side effusing waltzes. So potent was this magic, that the diners swirled from the carpet, waltzing among the Greek, Roman, and Etruscan sarcophagi, broken-nosed statues, and dead dancers now immobilized in marble, in terra-cotta—a dazzling, unexpected moment. The most beautiful party of the year, with memories of long-ago parties. The reopening of the museum after the war, with ranks of royals standing beneath their remote ancestors in the medieval and Renaissance halls, when suddenly the lights blew—blackout—and when they suddenly blazed again, a moment of terror clearly frozen in time on every royal face. Then relief composed those history-worn faces into sureness—not yet—not yet. You could smell the terror. You could hear the exhalation of relief.

LEO LERMAN

DECEMBER 9

1909

Yolande Bugbee posed today—the last occasion for the present. I have very much enjoyed the hours passed painting from her. She has a bright, fanciful mind and has been a great incentive to work. I hope to have her again before long. But models are an expensive luxury when no pictures are being sold.... The Ullmans were [to dinner]. Ullman...insisted on giving a demonstration of the wonderful "One Minute Washing Fluid" which he is about to exploit. Very amusing incidents. He messed in the kitchen till it got on Dolly's nerves.

JOHN SLOAN

DECEMBER 10

1849

My eyes are better and I will write a little while I can....

On the corner of Broadway and Ninth Street is a chocolate store kept by Felix Effray, and I love to stand at the window and watch the wheel go round. It has three white stone rollers and they grind the chocolate into paste all day long. Down Broadway, below Eighth Street, is Dean's candy store, and they make molasses candy that is the best in the city. Sometimes we go down to Wild's, that is way down near Spring Street, to get his iceland moss drops, good for colds....

I roll my hoop and jump the rope in the afternoon, sometimes in the Parade Ground on Washington Square, and sometimes in Union Square. Union Square has a high iron railing around it, and a fountain in the middle. My brother says he remembers when it was a pond and the farmers used to water their horses in it. Our Ninth Street stages run down Broadway to the Battery, and when I go down to the ferry to go to Staten Island, they go through Whitehall Street, and just opposite the Bowling Green . . . there is a sign over the store, "Lay and Hatch," but they don't sell eggs.

CATHERINE ELIZABETH HAVENS

1958

Cocktails with Bryan R[obertson] here. Dinner at Cedar [Tavern]. Decided Village is my creative oxygen. Buy house down there—let out basement to super and janitor and other floors to others to have income on honorable property.

In apartment hotel life—the lightness of no impedimenta has effect of making one more inward-turning. Ailments are more urgent and alarming because of absence of the million background ailments—a cough is TB; a nosebleed or headache submerged in the bills, cooking, cleaning and clatter of apartment house life becomes a major matter.

DAWN POWELL

DECEMBER 11

1863

This forenoon Mr. [John T.] Trowbridge has been with me—he had a talk yesterday with the Sec of the Treasury S[almon] P Chase about me, presented [Ralph Waldo] Emerson's letter to Mr. C—he said some commonplaces about writing to oblige R W E, & Mr. Trowbridge—then said he considered Leaves of Grass a very bad book, & he did not know how he could possibly bring its author into the government service, especially if he put him in contact with gentlemen employed in the beaureaus—did not think he would be warranted in doing so—he considered the author of Leaves of Grass in the light of a decidedly disreputable person—Mr. T. mentioned to him my employment for a year past... the wounded & sick soldiers—it did not seem to make a difference.

Walt Whitman

1864

A very stormy day. Stayed at home, wrote to Phil, said my prayers, read a little, pondered much upon the present condition of society. It is a bad sign when women become lax, and what I see and hear of *le beau monde* suggests this to be the case, at least in that circle.

Ellen Strong [wife of George Templeton Strong] came in painted like a wanton at Mrs. Bancroft's with a huge bouquet sent by one of her little *beaux,* without her husband. What must he think? What can he mean by thus leaving her so much to herself? Mrs. Dr. [John Charles] Peters was in church last Sunday afternoon with one of her little lovers.... Could he not sigh just as well and more comfortably at home? Or would the Doctor have been in the way? I was malicious enough to think of going up and congratulating her upon having her son at home, but the idea pleased me so much that it relaxed all my muscles and I felt I could not keep my countenance.

Maria Lydig Daly

1880

There was a grand reception at our house; I enjoyed it very much, as I could move around and talk to whomever I wanted to. I like some of the New York girls (more especially the married women, as Mrs. Astor, Mrs. Cutting & Mrs. Newbold) very much, but I am not very fond of going out. However, Alice is universally and greatly admired; and she seems to grow more beautiful day by day.

She *couldn't* grow any sweeter, or lovlier [*sic*]. She seems very happy; and oh, how happy she has made me!

THEODORE ROOSEVELT

DECEMBER 12

1967

When it rains our school is a miserable place—as are most schools, I suppose. The children cannot go outside to play, and they are all over the halls, the auditorium, and the gym. Most teachers on duty do nothing about it; they are afraid to discipline the children because of the parents.

Many children stay home on rainy days because of bad shoes or insufficient clothing.

JIM HASKINS

1971

All morning the telephone in my New York apartment has been ringing off the wall. Seems like I finally arrived at that special plateau in American culture—I made it into *The New York Times* Sunday crossword puzzle. Sixty-six across. Hint: Bella Abzug is one. Answer: Woman of the House.

BELLA ABZUG

DECEMBER 13

1916

Walked nearly a mile this morning, and then rode to the office, where all the day, striving to write a poem, but throwing away all my sad attempts as unworthy of print. I despair of ever being able to write a poem, forasmuch as when I was twenty, I would say, Wait until I am come to twenty-five; and then thirty; and then thirty-five. And now I have grown to believe that it is not years alone that make a poet.

Franklin P. Adams

1968

Can a composer imagine a more satisfying experience than mine last night in Town Hall? A capacity crowd listened carefully as I accompanied three friends in a whole program of my songs. Paul Gramm in white tie sang a group of Theodore Roethke and Paul Goodman poems, Beverly Wolff in green satin sang *Poems of Love and the Rain* and Phyllis Curtin in black velvet sang a miscellany. Then together we performed the premiere of *Some Trees* (John Ashbery) for three voices and piano, and everyone clapped long and loud, after which we all went to Virgil's at the Chelsea for cold salmon, cheese, white wine and chocolate cakes (paid for by Boosey & Hawkes). This morning *The Times* is approving, while Beverly [Sills] on the phone apologizes for not having come to the party because she had performed with a temperature of 103°.

Ned Rorem

1986

Benjamin picked me up and we went down to Arman's on Washington Street. It was supposed to be for lunch but since I told them I don't eat lunch, there (*laughs*) wasn't any and I was starved. And I got so jealous, he showed me the jewelry he's doing, he gets little hearts and redoes them in gold and glues them down. I asked him to be on our TV show. And then I got even more jealous when he told me about the dresses he's making—a "sleeve dress" made all of sleeves, a "pocket dress" all made of pockets. *I* mean, why couldn't *I* have thought of those?

Andy Warhol

December 14

1634

Jeronimus wrote a letter to our *commis* (factor), Marten Gerritsen
and asked for paper, salt, and *atsochwat*—that means tobacco for the
savages. We went out to shoot turkeys with the chief, but could not
get any. In the evening I bought a very fat one for two hands of see-
wan [wampum]. The chief cooked it for us, and the grease he mixed
with our beans and maize. This chief showed me his idol; it was a
male cat's head, with the teeth sticking out; it was dressed in duffel
cloth. Others have a snake, a turtle, a swan, a crane, a pigeon, or the
like for their idols, to tell the fortune; they think they will always
have good luck in doing so.

HARMEN MEYNDERTSZ VAN DEN BOGAERT

1776

Busied in preparing the Pardons for Rebels, who have surrendered.

AMBROSE SERLE

1793

Purchase a share in N York Library.

NOAH WEBSTER

1949

Saw a great show at Bop City. Lionel Hampton's wild "going" band;
and George Shearing's piano. Was with Neal, who has one-arm
room in E. 76th St. slums, and is writing his novel on the Harcourt
typewriter I got. Told Neal how I had changed in past month. Was
surprised that when you change, others seem to change too(!). We
discussed this by the stove in the parking lot shack....

Meanwhile, *On the Road* is on the road, that is, moving.

JACK KEROUAC

December 15

1880

The horse is in superb spirits, and the weather is beautiful; I enjoy my drives with Alice most intensely; especially when we go up the Riverside Park by the beautiful Hudson. When my sweetest little wife can't go I always take the dear little mother. It is lovely to live as we are now; it would be hard to imagine a pleasanter home. The little wife is just the brightest, prettiest little queen imaginable; and I perfectly worship her. How I marvel at my good luck!

THEODORE ROOSEVELT

1925

Up at 8 am, with a kind of hangover.... To Rivoli Theatre where my name is on the front in electric lights [for film version of *Tattooed Countess*].... At 5 I had my first Charleston lesson.

CARL VAN VECHTEN

December 16

1776

Employed myself after the Morning in writing. In one respect, this Town is like Athens: Though it has little or none of its Refinement or its Literature, "it is always seeking to hear or see some new thing."

Walked awhile with Col. Dalrymple, who with me is of Opinion, that Power is never more to be trusted, with any Degree of Safety, in the Hands of this People.

AMBROSE SERLE

1852

The sale of pictures of the American Art Union going on today at the Gallery 497 Broadway. They bring good prices in the present prosperity of this golden age. The builders of fine houses begin to look for something to cover their walls. The first taste was for European copies of the old Masters—now, within a very few years, a desire to possess the original works of moderns, and latterly—great through the art Union—of American works has sprung up.

EVERT DUYCKINCK

1935

Victor phoned—wanted to take me to a movie—I declined the offer—he has a heavier accent than either Serge or Walter—I have enough Russians—two lovers are more than I can please.

EUGENIA HUGHES

DECEMBER 17

1835

Unparalelled Calamity by Fire. How shall I record the events of last night, or how attempt to describe the most awful calamity which has ever visited these United States! The greatest loss by fire that has ever been known with the exception perhaps of the conflagration of Moscow, and that was an incidental concomitant of war. I am fatigued in body, disturbed in mind, and my fancy filled with images of horror which my pen is inadequate to describe. Nearly one half of the first ward is in ashes: 500 to 700 stores, which with their contents are valued at 20 to 40 millions of dollars, are now lying in an indistinguishable mass of ruins. There is not perhaps in the world the same space of ground covered by so great an amount of real and personal property as the scene of this dreadful conflagration.... The night was intensely cold, which was one cause of the unprecedented progress of the flames, for the water froze in the hydrants, and the engines and their hose could not be worked without great difficulty. The firemen, too, had been on duty all last night, and were almost incapable of performing their usual services.

PHILIP HONE

1947

What a depressed, beleaguered, lonely night last night! (Just like the old days.) No work today, went peddling my screen story (in vain, I'm afraid)—but I did get that marvellous film "A Tree Grows in Brooklyn." A great story, by a greater director, Elia Kazan. And I went to see people and none of them were in: it was as though all my friends had suddenly vanished like ghosts in N.Y. This often happens in N.Y., by the way, and it is eerie, and enough to drive one insane when it happens. What is even more eerie is that I ran into two of them on Time Square and they never saw me, and I followed them awhile, and they too eventually vanished (so perhaps it was just an illusion of mine).

JACK KEROUAC

DECEMBER 18

1789

Read over and digested my thoughts upon the subject of a National Militia, from the plans of the militia of Europe, those of the Secretary at War, and the Baron de Steuben.

PRESIDENT GEORGE WASHINGTON

1969
"D-DAY"

This date has loomed large the past six months. At last it was terrifyingly upon us. . . .

I waited at the corner of 55th Street in awful draughts for the Wrightsman car in which Lee [Radziwill] was my special escort (in absence of Diana V[reeland] ill with flu). Lee looked very beautiful with Japanese landlady hairdo. At the theatre the usual mêlée of excited onlookers, a vast crowd of not very impressive first-nighters, expectation, cool excitement backstage, packages, flowers, K.H.'s door tight shut.

Our seats were in the second row, nearer than I've ever been even at rehearsal and they gave one [no] feeling of the bulk of the ship at back of one. It was like being in the prow, and perilously near K.H.'s mottled face and legs. I enjoyed the evening, for the show has improved enormously and goes with a zing....

I...was thrilled to have the cheers for the little black dresses, and there seemed to be applause for many of the sets and costumes. But in the interval people said there was no show but for me. That did not forebode well. However, I was buoyed and excited. The audience enthusiastic about everything they could enjoy, but quite silent when not amused.

For me K.H. was without any magic, her timing as erratic as ever, her overemphasis quite horrible. She was in no way resembling Coco, in no way doing an impersonation of anyone but herself. Lee cooed that the improvement in the show was immense.... Then the finale cheers, the red dresses having created their usual effect, and a standing ovation for K.H., who suddenly shed 30 years and looked far too young for the part.

SIR CECIL BEATON

DECEMBER 19

1634

We received a letter from Marten Gerritsen dated December 18, and with it we received paper, salt, tobacco for the savages, and a bottle of brandy, and secured an Indian that was willing to be our guide to the Sinnekens We gave him half a yard of cloth, two axes, two knives, and two awls. If it had been summer, many Indians would have gone with us, but as it was winter they would not leave their land, because it snowed very often up to the height of a man. To-day we had a great rainfall, and I gave the guide a pair of shoes.

Harmen Meyndertsz van den Bogaert

1935

Johnny Mosher was over at Dos [Passos]'s. He talks and feels about himself as a very dear eccentric aunt and wherever he goes watches his own amusing reactions as if he were his own pet, too precious to be left in the baggage car but rather to be tenderly borne on the lap....

As for his friend, Miss Newell, he sighed, "Yes, we get along much better now. I'm too old for her at last, thank God." He is a faintly funereal wag, smelling of old ladies and mothballs, and Victorian parlors, expecting cancer with a smile, welcoming decent calamity with great good nature so long as it's something slow and fatal and respectable rather than garish and dramatic. He, like so many other gifted young men about town, slipped somehow into one of Henry James' lesser mantles, assuming with authority the role of Dean of Letters, without going to the bother of writing. This slight lapse in preparation passes unnoticed now, when others of his own generation have stopped writing anyway, so no one can be sure which witty critic once wrote a fine novel, a successful play or poem, and which never did anything but show promise.

Dawn Powell

2008

Down at Swifty's the lunchtime conversation was about...one guess...Bernie Madoff and his Made Off with Billions. The discovery is still-ongoing for as widely revered as he was in his world, he was unknown, or almost, to many others … and, it turns out, even to those who knew him. Or thought they knew him.

There is a large contingent of people who are gleeful about the losses of others. There is another contingent who would like to see the worst happen to the man. Then there is an even larger contingent still confounded *that he would do such a thing*. To the friends, to the people who loved and respected him. Somehow there's the life lesson for all of us in the last one. How could he?

The image you see in the papers is that of one who looks sanguine. Self-assured and self-possessed. Of course we can't read minds. But after making off with tens of billions of Other People's Money, he ironically appears to be most concerned about his privacy.

He asked someone in the William Wayne shop in the ground floor of his building if he could use their access to the … elevators so that he could avoid the press and paparazzi waiting to ambush him. His request was refused. …

What must he be thinking? He must be dying inside. Somewhere, sociopath or no, he must be dying a thousand deaths. Or ten thousand. And it will never be okay.

DAVID PATRICK COLUMBIA

DECEMBER 20

1862

I have had no heart to write. Since I opened my diary last, the battle of Fredericksburg has occurred and our repulse with the loss of 14,000 killed, wounded, and missing. … It is surprising how people spend despite the present distress. The artists say they have never been so busy. Bierstadt is even offered more than he has asked for his pictures, and every place of amusement is crowded.

MARIA LYDIG DALY

1944

I discussed at length [with Lenny] the question of F.D.R. I told him: The Pres. has high blood pressure, feels that his muscles are gradually weakening, has had a lump in his left side which is supposed to be weak muscles which cannot keep the organs in, at that point, but there is no pain or even discomfort.

Lenny said he had watched F.D.R.'s pictures on the screen and has diagnosed his case thus, plus what I have told him: the spleen is the organ that is making most of the trouble....

Lenny added that of course he may find an entirely different condition when he sees the Pres. I told him of my plan: When the Pres. can fix an afternoon, I will telephone Lenny & he will take the 2 P.M. from Grand Central. He will be smuggled into the library & the President will come up "for tea" with the family [at Wilderstein, the Suckley family estate on the Hudson]. Just as soon as the S.S. have gone out of the front door, the family will leave the library and Lenny will start working on F.'s feet—I am almost afraid of this meeting, for *so much* depends on it—

MARGARET "DAISY" SUCKLEY

["Lenny" was Harry Setaro, a former boxer and trainer and later masseur, whom Suckley believed to be a healer.]

DECEMBER 21

1860

That termagant little South Carolina has declared herself out of the Union and resolved to run away and go to sea. How many of the Southern sisterhood will join the secession jig...remains to be seen.... It's a grave affair for any family if one of its members goes mad. But as an offset, we have the influx of gold from England and the growing hopes that Northern cities will get through the winter without the panic and crisis and uprising of hungry mobs that our Southern friends complacently predict.

GEORGE TEMPLETON STRONG

1956

Strange faces in the subway—the minute I sat down I realized I had power to see them straight in the eye and dig the eternal moment's mask—as they ride by dreaming rocked in the dark with neon on their faces.

The 59th St. stop—recollecting Burroughs and Lucien, Columbus Circle, IRT Station, the dark pavement and endless outpouring of students and ballet dancers and musicians and fairies on this platform, waiting in their youth for life to begin—while I come back here dead (for the fourth time), disconnected.

ALLEN GINSBERG

DECEMBER 22

1779

As I foresaw, this garrison is distressed for fuel. [Governor] Tryon tells me they consume 600 cords of wood per week. Yesterday they seized the private supplies of sugar and still houses and breweries and got but seventy cords. Carts are pressed to [go] out tomorrow and cut in this island and orders issued... at Brooklyn to deploy 300 axes in the woods nearest to the landings. These attacks upon private property great[ly] offend. Some excoriate the General, others the police and the barrackmaster. The Commandant talks of taking from the private stock of the citizens.

WILLIAM SMITH

DECEMBER 23

1634

A man came calling and shouting through some of the houses, but we did not know what it meant, and after awhile Jeronimus de la Croix came and told us what this was—that the savages are preparing and arming. I asked them what all this was about, and they said to me: "Nothing, we shall play with one another," and there were four men with clubs and a party with axes and sticks. There were twenty people armed, nine on one side and eleven on the other; and they went off against each other, and they fought and threw each other. Some of them wore armor and helmets that they themselves make of thin reeds and strings braided upon each other so that no arrow or axe can pass through to wound them severely; and after they had been playing thus a good while the parties closed and dragged each other by the hair, just as they would have done to their enemies after defeating them and before cutting off their scalps. They wanted us to fire our pistols, but we went off and left them alone. This day we were invited to buy bear meat, and we also got half a bushel of beans and a quantity of dried strawberries, and we bought some bread, that we wanted to take on our march. Some of the loaves were baked with nuts and cherries and dry blueberries and the grains of the sunflower.

HARMEN MEYNDERTSZ VAN DEN BOGAERT

1845

Well, last night I spent... at Mrs. Mary Jones's great ball. Very splendid affair—"The ball of the season," I heard divers bipeds more or less asinine observe in regard to it. Two houses open—standing supper table—"dazzling array of beauty and fashions." Polka for the first time brought under my inspection. It's a kind of insane Tartar jig performed to a disagreeable music of an uncivilized character. Everybody was there and I loafed about in a most independent manner and found it less of a bore than I had expected. Mrs. Jones, the hostess, is fat but comely; indeed, there's enough of her to supply a small settlement with wives. Came home with Charley at about half-past one, but didn't get asleep all the rest of the night—an abominable wooden kind of cadence upside down in one of those polka tunes haunted me like an evil spirit.

GEORGE TEMPLETON STRONG

1922

To [Harold] Ross's and found nine at cards, and I played too, with great good luck,... and so home, at near five in the morning, and found on my bed a fine Christmas gift from my wife, three night-gownes of linen with my initials worked on them, which I shall try to remember to tell her is a great convenience,... when there are dozens of us in a bed it will be easy to distinguish me by the embroidered initials.

FRANKLIN P. ADAMS

DECEMBER 24

1852

A green Christmas. The fog at Barnum's Circus [to the South] gave an English atmosphere and distances to the street view. Christmas Trees offered for sale on the sidewalk in front of the Hospital, the [tops] of evergreens set in a square of wood and the branches hung with a few showy ornaments. This German Christmas tree within the last ten years has become quite an inhabitant of our parlors.

EVERT DUYCKINCK

December 25

1840

Hurrah for Christmas!... Alas for our schismatic city, but few among its churches were open today.... One would think that even if the matter-of-fact dissenters did consider it not quite demonstrably certain that this is the anniversary it professes to be, and if the Papaphobic dissenters did esteem its celebration a relic of popery, they wouldn't be quite blind to all its glorious associations, quite oblivious that from all corners of Christendom, save those they occupy, the anthem of thanksgiving rises this day unanimously, and all mankind are happier under the influence, I believe, of better and kinder feelings from its recurrence. One would think that they couldn't find any great evil in setting apart one day even if not the right one for such an object.

GEORGE TEMPLETON STRONG

1865

Had a most satisfactory and delightful morning. Went to eight o'clock mass, saw the sun just rising above the buildings and park as I crossed Waverly Place, the sky as bright and clear as spring. I thought of the words of the old carol, "Royal day that chaseth gloom." And I went to St. Joseph's where the congregation was mostly poor people; I like to go to church with the poor, particularly on Christmas.

MARIA LYDIG DALY

1878

This morning I got up very early and got my Christmas things... lots of candy, an orange, and some figs, a nice large Magic Lantern, a book, a steam Engine. Mamie got a [scarf], candy, an organ, a book, a chain and locket and other things. Grace got a necktie, a bottle of cologne and other things. Walk got two books, a pin and other things. Mama got a gold thimble from Auntie and a teapot-stand from Mamie. Papa got some handkerchiefs. Last night Mama and I took Auntie around some presents.... I have had an ear-ache fearful bad all day so I could not enjoy myself.

ADDISON ALLEN

1909

Christmas Day. Dolly had made Bess and Nan [his sisters] nice presents of stockings etc. I gave checks. Simple but useful cash. Nan gave me a set of gold buttons, very nice indeed—but Christmas is a rather dreadful institution.... Now that Mother is gone it would seem to me to be wasted hypocrisy to go to services which are full of ideas and formulas of life which I think positively against the intentions of that great Socialist Jesus Christ. He was a Revolutionist. The Church backs the Exploiters by preaching content to the victim. I know that my state grieves my hyper religious sisters—they probably pray for me, with tears.

JOHN SLOAN

1986

I got up early and walked to Paige's and she and Stephen Sprouse and I went to the Church of the Heavenly Rest to pass out *Interviews* and feed the poor. It wasn't as crowded as it was at Thanksgiving. Afterwards Stephen and I walked down the street, and I had told John Reinhold we'd come by and he could take us to tea and he did, at the Carlyle, and that was sort of, I don't know, young guys waiting for their grandmothers to die. Stephen dropped me. Got a lot of calls to go to Christmas parties but I just decided to stay in and I loved it.

ANDY WARHOL

DECEMBER 26

1864

I am writing this in the front basement in Portland Avenue, Brooklyn, at home. It is after 9 o'clock at night. We have had a wet day with fog, mud, slush, and the yet unmelted hard-polished ice liberally left in the streets. All sluggish and damp, with a prevailing leaden vapor. Yesterday, Christmas, about the same.

[Brother] George's trunk came by express early in the forenoon today, from City Point, Virginia. Lieutenant Babcock, of the 51st [New York Regiment], was kind enough to search it out and send it home. It stood some hours before we felt inclined to open it. Towards evening Mother and Eddy looked over the things. One could not help feeling depressed. There were his uniform coat, pants, sash, etc. There were many things reminded us of him. Papers, memoranda, books, knick-knacks, a revolver, a small diary, roll of his company, a case of photographs of his comrades (several of them I knew as killed in battle), with other stuff such as a soldier accumulates.

Mother looked everything over, laid out the shirts to be washed, the coats and pants to hang up, and all the rest were carefully put back. It made me feel pretty solemn. We have not heard from him since October 3rd; either living or dead, we know not.

I am aware of the condition of the Union prisoners...from lately talking with a friend just returned from...the exchange at Savannah and Charleston of which we have received twelve thousand of our sick. Their situation, as of all our men in prison, is indescribably horrible. Hard, ghastly starvation is the rule. Rags, filth, despair, in large, open stockades, no shelter, no cooking, no clothes.... The guards are insufficient in numbers, and they make it up by treble severity, shooting the prisoners literally just to keep them under terrorism....

I cannot get any reliable trace of the 51st officers at all. I supposed they were at Columbia, South Carolina, but my friend has brought a list purporting to be a complete record of all in confinement there, and I cannot find any of the 51st among them.

WALT WHITMAN

[George later found alive, a prisoner at Danville, Va.]

1869

The Low-Pierrepont wedding came off Thursday...& was supremely gorgeous.... Noone [*sic*] but invited guests were admitted, & the seats were filled with what the "papers" would have called the "elite" òf Brooklyn & New York. Every one was very "swell," & the scene was quite animated.... Finally at one o'clock (the organ) swelled into a wedding march, & the bridal procession entered. First came two "ushers," Gussie Jay & Mr. Brevoort, followed by six groom's men two-by-two, & then [the groom, Henry Pierrepont] Harry with his Father. Then the six bride's maids in pairs, dressed in alternate pink & white dresses, with over skirts of "crêpe de chine," looped up "en panier" & trimmed with morning glories. Then Mrs. Low in yellow satin & white lace, leaning on her son Seth's arm, who...looked as handsome as a picture; & then came the bride [Ellen Low] with her Father. The great Paris "Worth" made her dress...white satin with a long train, & sprays of white orange blossoms falling all over it, & to crown all a beautiful lace veil, made expressly for her.... Jay & Seth were as devoted as they could be, for acting as ushers they had to attend to every one, fat ladies, old gentleman & so forth.

JULIA ROSA NEWBERRY

DECEMBER 27

1776

Three men of our battalion died last night. The most malencholyest night I ever saw. Small pox increases fast. This day I was blooded. Drawd bisd and butter. Stomach all gone. At noon burgo [a kind of porridge]. Basset is verry sick. Not like to live I think.

WILLIAM SLADE

1797

Extreme cold indeed! Last Saturday there was a little Confusion on the Dock with the Capt. of the British S. [sloop] of War *Hunter,* about impressing [*sic*] American Seamen.

HUGH GAINE

1833

The holidays are gloomy, the weather is bad, the times are bad, stocks are falling, and a panic prevails which will result in bankruptcies and ruin in many quarters where but a few short weeks since the sun of prosperity shone with unusual brightness. It will be worse before it is better.

PHILIP HONE

DECEMBER 28

1778

No Abatement of the Frost. The Fleet sailed yesterday. Seven Vessels lost in our Harbor in the Storm. Three Sentinels found frozen in their Boxes.

WILLIAM SMITH

1866

I am rather glad I have not money enough to go to Paris this spring.... That city has been a maleficent blowhole of poisonous gas over all Europe and over all the world since the days of Henry IV. Louis IX seems to have been the last Christian ruler of France. He was a soldier and a gentleman.... This Louis Napoleon seems to be neither.

GEORGE TEMPLETON STRONG

1971 ·

A group of young Vietnam war veterans has seized the Statue of Liberty. They're going to stay there, they say, to remind the American people the war is still going on. And to underscore the point that Nixon has ordered massive bombing of North Vietnam, the heaviest since 1968. This is how he's winding down the war! Some American pilots have been downed, and so now there are *more* American prisoners of war, not [fewer]....

In the meantime, I've announced that I'm going to introduce a resolution to censure the President for flouting the will of Congress. Some people want me to introduce an impeachment resolution, but I tell them that the voters will do it their own way.

I live in hope....

BELLA ABZUG

DECEMBER 29

1789

Being very snowing, not a single person appeared at the Levee.

PRESIDENT GEORGE WASHINGTON

1958

Having watched the indefatigable industry with which the New York Life skyscraper has been painting angels, Christmas trees on its windows ever since Thanksgiving, now equally industriously rubbing them out.

DAWN POWELL

DECEMBER 30

1836

I went this evening to a party at Mrs. Charles H. Russell's, given in honor of the bride, Mrs. William H. Russell. The splendid apartments of this fine house are well adapted to an evening party, and everything was very handsome on this occasion. The home is lighted with gas, and the quantity consumed being greater than common, it gave out suddenly and in the midst of a cotillion.... Gas is a handsome light, in a large room like Mr. Russell's, on an occasion of this kind, but liable (I should think) at times to give the company the slip, and illy calculated for the ordinary uses of a family.

PHILIP HONE

1920

Mina Loy.—She's writing a novel—Her husband was drowned & it knocked her up a good deal—She was really in love with him and her novel's all about that and her life with him—I haven't seen her for a good while. I used to take her out to lunch—almost every day for a while—I had the money and she hadn't and I thought maybe she isn't eating regularly.... She hasn't got her wardrobe and spoke of it—She was almost down & out she said she could go into the movies but she hadn't any of her clothes.

MARIANNE MOORE

DECEMBER 31

1662

Came the [constable] in the morning.... He said the governor would set me free if I would promise to remove myself and family out of his jurisdiction in a month's time.... I went to his house and was called into a private room where he [was] with one of his writers.... I told him I had heard that he meant to send me away in a ship and I did desire to know wherefore.... I also asked what the ship's master should do with me and he told me put me ashore either in Holland, or anywhere the ship put in.... My things were put in a boat but by who I know not[.] Then on the 3rd day of the week...the [constable] put me in [a] boat and so I was Carried onboard...and we set sail about the middle of the day and went out to sea.

JOHN BOWNE

[Entry approximate, per Quaker calendar.]

1909

Ullmans came after dinner and took us to see Maude Adams in "What Every Woman Knows" by J. M. Barrie. This I enjoyed quite well. Miss Adams is overly cute and too conscious of the humor of her part in relation to her stupid husband. We did not mix in the crowd of New Year's Eve celebrators but came home and got a pitcher of chop suey from the Chinese restaurant and at 12 o'clock began the New Year on tea and Chinese lunch.

JOHN SLOAN

1921

Up betimes and to my new office, and found there many things to do, such as arranging my books and papers, which tasks I hate; yet are pleasanter than scrivening. Home to supper, of a chine [backbone] of beef from last night....and my wife and in good health and I greatly pleased with her much of the time; the nation in no great prosperity but better off than most; all, meseems [*sic*], in a bad way because of greed and jealous envy that is in the world. So to Heywood Broun's, where a great party and merry as can be, and we acted a play, J. Toohey being the most comickall of all. Saw there Mistress Clare Sheridan, in the prettiest pink dress ever I saw her wear; and she rallied me for not having gone to see her one day, and charged me with having forgotten, which was true. Saw H. G. Wells, too, and he wrote his name on a card for me, to give little Janet Wise, and very gracious too, using my back for a desk. I loved Mistress Dorothy Parker the best of any of them, and loath to leave her, which I did not do till near five in the morning, and so home.

FRANKLIN P. ADAMS

1953

I stayed away entirely from the San Remo except when Agee has called me to come. For all that he gives me, he is too torn for me to lean on.

The Ballet Theater project ended dreadfully.... The ballet was lousy, pantomiming the brash Hemingway sentiments. Our props looked fine. The decadent benefit audience loved everything.... We watched from a box in the Metropolitan's crescent. In Mrs. Vanderbilt's box, next to ours, four young balletomanes sat eating cheese sandwiches.

JUDITH MALINA

1978

Fred's in the Amazon—no, wait. The Andes. I talked to David Bourdon, he was going to go to Rosenquist's New Year's Eve party. Rosenquist was hiring a live band again. It was so successful the year before that he's doing it again.

I worked all afternoon at the office. It was nice working on New

Year's Eve. I painted backgrounds. Walter Steding came over to help me. Ronnie was having an Alcoholics Anonymous New Year's, and Brigid stopped by to pick up some tapes.

I didn't know the evening at Halston's was going to be so chic, my dear. I'd asked if I could bring Jed and Halston said fine so we went over. Catherine brought Tom and Winnie—Halston'd said fine to that, too. Tom told me that he was giving Catherine and me points in the movie, and that they had to reshoot a little more, that somebody had just given $150,000 so they could. Bianca was in a Dior....

Diana Ross looked beautiful. And she had asked Halston over the phone if he was going to serve black-eyed peas at midnight because it was good luck. So Steve went around town getting soul food. And when she got there Halston was cooking ham hocks and ribs. A few people said to her, "Don't you want to check on the black-eyed peas?" They knew the peas were her idea, and they were just trying to be nice. I guess she took it as an insult, though, because she said, "No, thank you, darling. I think I've checked them enough."

And Mohammed the houseboy had a girlfriend there and she was Jake LaMotta's daughter. He's that boxer Bobby De Niro's playing in the new Scorsese movie. She's pretty.

While we were sitting at Halston's we had the radio on and it was "live from Studio 54," and we heard the announcer saying, "Oh yes! Here they come! Halston, Bianca, and Andy Warhol! They're walking in the door right now!"

Then we all did go to Studio 54. They had decorated it great, put silver glitter on the floor, and they had someone on a trapeze, and white balloons. And they were saying that Bobby De Niro had been there since 10:00. They'd been having a press party.

The whole night was spent losing and finding and looking and finding and looking. John Fairchild, Jr. has a crush on Bianca so we were looking for her, and then losing her, and then losing him and finding her, and then losing me, and looking for me, and losing him....

I was sober. I had lots of Perrier. The place was still jumping at 7:00. Went outside, it was warm out, and people were still waiting to get in, as if it were only 1:00. Only the light was different.

ANDY WARHOL

About the Diarists

Dates refer to entries made.

ABZUG, BELLA. [1971] Labor lawyer. Elected congresswoman from New York's 19th District. Kept diary of her first year in Washington and its reverberation back home. Published as *Bella! Mrs. Abzug Goes to Washington.* New York, Saturday Review Press, 1972. Used by permission of Dutton, a division of Penguin Group (USA) Inc.

ADAMS, FRANKLIN P. [1911–1925] Newspaperman who wrote a popular column, "The Conning Tower," in the style of Samuel Pepys. Entries originally published in the *New York Evening Mail,* the *New York Tribune,* and the *New York World.* Later collected, in part, as *The Diary of Our Own Samuel Pepys: 1911–1925.* New York, Simon & Schuster, 1935.

ALLEN, ADDISON. [1878] Adolescent boy whose family moved from East Orange, NJ, to the white middle-class neighborhood of

Harlem in the late 1800s. Enthusiastic collector of stamps and autographs. In manuscript at the New-York Historical Society.

ALLEN, MARK. [2001] A blogger whose 9/11 diary entries were published on the website www.nycbloggers.com. He lives in New York.

ANDERSON, DR. ALEXANDER. [1795] Known as "the father of American wood engraving." Published in *Old New York: A Journal Relating to the History and Antiquities of New York City,* Vol. 1. edited by W. W. Pasko. New York, W. W. Pasko, 1890.

ANDERSON, SHERWOOD. [1937–1940] An Ohioan from humble origins. He became a successful businessman, then gave up everything, including family, to become a writer of short stories. Author of the collection *Winesburg, Ohio.* His peers included E. E. Cummings, John Dos Passos, and Orson Welles. *The Sherwood Anderson Diaries. 1936–1941.* Athens and London, University of Georgia Press, 1987.

ANDRÉ, MAJOR JOHN. [1778] A handsome and charismatic British officer who conspired to turn Benedict Arnold traitor. His tactical account of warfare is considered to be among the most accurate from the British perspective. Even George Washington liked André and was deeply saddened to condemn him to death by hanging. Published as *André's Journal, An authentic record of the movements and engagements of the British Army in America from June 1777 to November 1778 as recorded from day to day by Major John André,* edited by Henry Cabot Lodge. Boston, H. O. Houghton & Co., at the Riverside Press, 1903. Entries here drawn from *Major André's Journal: Operations of The British Army under Lieutenant Generals Sir William Howe and Sir Henry Clinton, June 1777 to November, 1778.* Tarrytown, NY, William Abbatt, 1930. Copyright 1904 by The Bibliographical Society, Boston.

ASTRUC, SARA. [2001] Former online diarist Sara Astruc (www .astruc.com) left New York after September 11. She now lives and writes in the Pacific Northwest.

BALFOUR, VICTORIA. [2001] Freelance writer. Excerpt appeared in *The New York Times*'s "Metropolitan Journal."

BANGS, LT. ISAAC. [1776] New Englander and Harvard graduate who fought as an officer with the patriots during their ill-fated stand against the British in New York. Published as the *Journal of Lieutenant Isaac Bangs.* Cambridge University Press, John Wilson & Son, 1890.

BATCHELOR, CHARLES. [1878] British-born mechanical engineer who assisted Thomas Edison with some of his most important innovations in telegraphy, telephony and electric lighting. He kept a detailed record of their experiments: *Charles Batchelor's Recollections of Edison*, the Edison Papers, Part II: Series Notes. Menlo Park Notebooks, 1878–1882. From *The Papers of Thomas A. Edison: The Wizard of Menlo Park, 1878*, edited by Paul B. Israel, Keith Nier, and Louis Carlat. Baltimore and London, Johns Hopkins University Press, 1999.

BEATON, SIR CECIL. [1966–1969] British photographer of the rich and famous. Diaries reveal hectic experience of costume design for the Broadway musical *Coco*, based on the life of Coco Chanel, starring Katharine Hepburn. Published as *Beaton in the Sixties*, edited by Hugo Vickers, copyright © 2003 by The Literary Executors of the late Sir Cecil Beaton. Used by permission of Alfred A. Knopf, a division of Random House, Inc.

BEAUVOIR, SIMONE DE. [1947] Feminist philosopher who spent two months in New York after World War II. She was taken in tow by Richard Wright, among others, in whose company she explored

Harlem and Greenwich Village. Her descriptions sometimes resemble those of an interplanetary visitor trying to explain such simple phenomena as ear muffs. Published as *America Day by Day*. Berkeley and Los Angeles, University of California Press. University of California Press, Ltd. London. Translated 1999 by the Regents of the University of California. Translated from *Simone de Beauvoir L'Amerique en jour le jour*. Paris, Editions Gallimard, 1954.

BELL, WILLIAM H. [1850–1851] New York City Police detective who inspected junk shops and pursued the criminal activity surrounding them. Participated in the return of a fugitive slave to his owners in Virginia. Diary available in manuscript at the New-York Historical Society.

BENTLEY, TONI. [1980–1981] Australian-born dancer with the New York City Ballet. During a personally difficult year, she kept a journal on a yellow legal pad. Her humorous and poignant entries express the tension between the demands of art and the human desire for love and comfort. Published as *Winter Season: A Dancer's Journal*. New York, Random House, 1982.

BIGELOW, JOHN. [1844–1892] Author, editor, and diplomat. One of the socially prominent Bigelows of Gramercy Park. His journal may be found among the Bigelow family papers at the New York Public Library's Rare Manuscripts collection.

BLISS, SUSAN. [1897] Daughter of a prosperous New York banker. Diaries reside in The New York Public Library's Manuscript and Archives Division.

BLUMENTHAL, SARA HOEXTER. [1912–1945] A young Jewish woman from a well-to-do German family, who documents her coming of age at the turn of the twentieth century, and subsequent disappointments in marriage. Handwritten diaries in manuscript form and an extract in typed notes can be found at the New-York Historical Society. Published by courtesy of Dr. Myron Blumenthal.

BOGAERT, HARMEN MEYNDERTSZ VAN DEN. [1634] Most likely, the surgeon of Fort Orange under the Dutch West India Company. Entries chronicle a journey among native tribes. Published in part as *Narrative of New Netherland (1609–1664), 1634–1635,* edited by J. Franklin Jameson. New York, Charles Scribner's Sons, 1909.

BOVOSO, CAROLE "IONE." [1980] African-American poet, painter, and journalist. Her entries dwell heavily upon content from her dreams and explore an "internal landscape." Published by consent of the author.

BOWNE, JOHN. [1650–1694] Quaker leader arrested by Peter Stuyvesant for his religious beliefs. Bowne returned to Europe to appeal to Stuyvesant's backers, who subsequently granted freedom of religion to the nascent New Amsterdam. That case is held to be the first test of religious freedom in the New World. *Journal of John Bowne 1650–1694,* transcribed and edited by Herbert F. Ricard. New Orleans, Friends of the Queensborough Community College Library and Polyanthos, 1975. Also published in *The American Historical Record and Repertory of Notes and Queries Concerning the History and Antiquities of America and Biography of Americans,* edited by Benson J. Lossing. Vol. 1, No. 1, January 1872.

BRITISH FOOT GUARD. [1776] Anonymous officer who recorded in a daily orderly book the execution of twenty-one-year-old patriot and Continental spy Nathan Hale. The book may be found at the New-York Historical Society.

BROWN, JAMES FRANCIS. [1854] A fugitive slave from Baltimore who escaped north along the Underground Railroad and found refuge in the Hudson River Valley. He was a self-educated horticulturalist whose jottings are chiefly about the weather and other celestial events. The entries published here are from *"On the Morning Tide": African Americans, History and Methodology in the Historical Ebb and Flow of the Hudson River Society.* By A. J. Williams-Myers. Africa World Press, Inc., 2003.

BULLIVANT, DR. BENJAMIN. [1697] New England pharmacist and onetime attorney general of Massachusetts who visited British New York in the late 1600s, leaving a detailed description of the town and its inhabitants. Published as *A Glance at New York in 1697: The Travel Diary of Dr. Benjamin Bullivant,* edited by Wayne Andrews. Revised from *The New-York Historical Society Quarterly,* January 1956.

CAMUS, ALBERT. [1946] French novelist and philosopher. Arrived for a visit just after World War II, suffering from influenza. Journal entries over the following two weeks reflect ambivalence toward America and Americans. He was awed, however, by the size and bizarre ambience of New York. *Albert Camus' American Journals,* first published in Great Britain, Hamish Hamilton, 1989. London, Penguin Group, 1978; Editions Gallimard. Copyright 1988 Paragon House [first English-language edition].

CAYLEY, GEORGE JOHN. [1844] A cultivated young gentleman, thought to have been English, who describes business and social life in Manhattan in the mid-nineteenth century. He lived as a ward of one "Mr. Goodhue" and was employed on Wall Street. He consorted with Van Rensselaers and DePeysters. His diaries are unpublished and may be found at the New-York Historical Society.

CHAD THE MINX. [2001–2003] Screen name of New York blogger Chad Smith, an architect, writer, martial artist, and club team rugby player. His 9/11 diary entries were published on the website www.nycbloggers.com.

CHEEVER, JOHN. D. [1949] Short story writer and novelist. Diary entry records his experiences escorting daughter Susan to a birthday party in Manhattan. Entry here from *The Journals of John Cheever,* by John Cheever. copyright © 1990 by Mary Cheever, Susan Cheever, Benjamin Cheever, and Federico Cheever. Used by permission of Alfred A. Knopf, a division of Random House, Inc.

CLINTON, DEWITT. [1810] Scion of a prominent Revolutionary War family. Served as a U.S. senator from New York, three-time mayor of New York City, and two-time governor of New York State. When he was mayor, in 1810, he and an exploratory party scouted out a path for the prospective Erie Canal. *The Private Canal Journal, 1810,* is taken from a detailed account he kept during that trip. From *The Life and Writings of DeWitt Clinton* by William W. Campbell. New York, Baker and Scribner, 1849.

COHEN, RANDY. [1997] The ethicist behind "The Ethicist," a weekly column in *The New York Times Magazine.* Cohen penned these entries for *Slate* shortly after being fired as head writer of *The Rosie O'Donnell Show.* They were published in *The Slate Diaries,* edited by Jodi Kantor, Cyrus Krohn, and Judith Shulevitz. Introduction by Michael Kinsley. New York, Perseus Book Group, 2000. Copyright © 2000 by Michael Kinsley. Reprinted by permission of Public Affairs, a member of the Perseus Books Group.

COLUMBIA, DAVID PATRICK. [2008] Publisher of the website "New York Social Diary" (www.newyorksocialdiary.com) and a lifelong admirer of George Templeton Strong.

CORNELIUS, DR. ELIAS. [1778] Continental surgeon's mate, taken prisoner by the British in 1777. Excerpts published in *American Pris-*

oners of the Revolution by Danske Dandridge. Charlottesville, VA, the Michie Company, Printers, 1911.

COWARD, NOËL. [1948–1957] British playwright who spent much of his professional life in New York, where he enjoyed a love-hate relationship with the city. Published as *The Noël Coward Diaries.* Boston & Toronto, Little, Brown and Company, 1982.

CRESSWELL, NICHOLAS. [1777] British Loyalist living in New York during the Revolutionary War. Published as *The Journal of Nicholas Cresswell 1774–1777.* New York, The Dial Press, 1924.

CRUIKSHANK, JAMES. [1834–1835] Prominent New York merchant, an intellectually curious man fascinated by the details of such diverse processes as tea-making, banking, and whaling. Manuscript resides at the Rosenbach Musem and Library, Philadelphia.

CUMMINGS, E. E. (EDWARD ESTLIN). [1925] Imagist. One of the premier American poets of the twentieth century. Diary in manuscript at Houghton Library, Harvard University. Excerpt from the unpublished diary entry of January 30, 1925, by E. E. Cummings. Copyright by the Trustees for the E. E. Cummings Trust.

CUOMO, MARIO M. [1980–1982] Former governor of New York. Kept a diary during a gubernatorial campaign and other significant events from 1980 to 1983. Published as *Diaries of Mario M. Cuomo: The Campaign for Governor.* New York, Random House, Inc., 1984.

DALY, MARIA LYDIG. [1861–1865] A patrician who, over her family's strong objections, married the son of Irish immigrants Charles Patrick Daly, a Democratic reformer and one of the most respected jurists in New York. A northern Democrat, Lydig expressed contempt for New England abolitionists whose zeal she blamed for inciting the Civil War. Her published journal reveals her particular antipathy toward Abraham Lincoln. Her entries cover the Civil War and its aftermath. Caustic and amusing observations upon New York society. Published as *Diary of a Union Lady, 1861–1865*. University of Nebraska Press, Lincoln. Copyright 1962 by Funk and Wagnalls Company. Reprinted by permission of HarperCollins Publishers, Inc. Introduction to Bison Books Edition copyright 2000 by the University of Nebraska Press.

DANCKAERTS, JASPER. [1679–1680] One of two explorers from a dissident Catholic sect, the Labinists, who visited North America from 1679 to 1680 to scout out a potential colony. An officer of the Long Island Historical Society found the manuscript in a bookstore in Amsterdam. The manuscript is currently the property of the Long Island Historical Society. Published as *Journal of Jasper Danckaerts, 1679–1680*, edited by Bartlett Burleigh James and J. Franklin Jameson. New York, Charles Scribner's Sons, 1913.

DAY, DOROTHY. [1965] Radical American journalist who converted to Catholicism and cofounded the Catholic Worker, "a faith-based, grassroots movement for peace and social justice through nonviolent direct action." Entry published in *The Duty of Delight: The Diaries of Dorothy Day*, edited by Robert Ellsberg. Marquette University Press, 2008.

THE DEADICATED GROUP. [2009] Entry appeared in www.nyc bloggers.com.

DELAPLAINE, JOSHUA. [1754] Quaker cabinetmaker and merchant of New York City. Excerpts from his account books, spare as they are, offer a revealing glimpse into the commerce of the time. Diary may be found in manuscript at the New-York Historical Society.

DICKENS, CHARLES. [1842] *Charles Dickens: American Notes for General Circulation.* The famed British novelist published an account of his first visit to the U.S. A generally disapproving report—some Americans termed it libel—but he left a vivid portrait of New York. First published in 1842 and reprinted in 1868 by D. Appleton and Company, New York, 1868.

DOS PASSOS, JOHN. [1917] American novelist. Entry made on a troop carrier to Europe during World War I. Published in *The Fourteenth Chronicle: Letters and Diaries of John Dos Passos.* Boston, Gambit, 1973.

DUNLAP, WILLIAM. [1797–1798] Theater manager and dramatist. Journal published as the *Diary of William Dunlap, 1766–1839: The Memoirs of a Dramatist, Theatrical Manager, Painter, Critic, Novelist, and Historian.* Printed for the New-York Historical Society, 1930.

DUYCKINCK, EVERT. [1847–1856] Evert and his brother, George, were editors of *The Literary World* between 1848 and 1853 and editors and publishers of the *Cyclopedia of American Literature.* Duyckinck Family Papers may be found at the Manuscripts and Archives Division of the New York Public Library.

EDELSTEIN, DAVID. [1997] Film critic for *New York* magazine. Entry originally published in *Slate.* Later included among *The Slate Diaries,* edited by Jodi Kantor, Cyrus Krohn, and Judith Shulevitz. Introduction by Michael Kinsley, New York, Perseus Book Group, 2000. Copyright © 2000 by Michael Kinsley. Reprinted by permission of PublicAffairs, a member of the Perseus Book Group.

EDISON, THOMAS. [1885] Celebrated American inventor whose credits include the telephone and the telegraph. A personal diary, kept for only part of one month in 1885, records his attempts to perfect his own education by reading. Permission granted for material from *The Diary and Sundry Observations of Thomas Edison* by the Philosophical Library, New York. Published as *The Diary and Sundry Observations of Thomas Alva Edison,* edited by Dagobert D. Runes. New York, Greenwood Press, 1968.

EHRLICH, GRETEL. [1985] American travel writer and novelist. Her entry was taken from *Antaeus Journals, Notebooks & Diaries.* New York, Ecco Press, 1988.

ELLIS, AUGUSTUS VAN HORNE. [1842] Youthful keeper of canaries. Died at the Battle of Gettysburg. Manuscript resides at the Museum of the City of New York.

ELLIS, EDWARD ROBB. [1947–1954] Longtime journalist with *New York World Telegram.* A midwesterner by birth, he promptly fell in love with New York. Published as *Edward Robb Ellis: A Diary of the Century: Tales by America's Greatest Diarist.* New York, Kodansha America, Inc., 1995.

FELL, JOHN. [1777] *American Prisoners of the Revolution.* Danske Dandridge, Charlottesville, VA, the Michie Company, Printers, 1911.

FITCH, JABEZ. [1776–1777] Continental soldier from the 17th Connecticut Regiment. He was captured by the British in New York and held, with officers, on a prison ship and under house arrest elsewhere. His journal records that time spent in captivity. Published as *The New-York Diary of Lieutenant Jabez Fitch of the 17th (Connecticut) Regiment from August 22, 1776, to December 15, 1777.* Copyright 1954 by W.H.H. Sabine. In manuscript at New York Public Library.

FITHIAN, PHILIP VICKERS. [1776] Presbyterian chaplain to the Continental Army. He witnessed and wrote a vivid account of the rout of Washington's forces from New York. Published as *Philip Vickers Fithian: Journal, 1775–1776, written on the Virginia-Pennsylvania frontier and in the army around New York,* edited by Robert Greenhalgh Albion and Leonidas Dodson. Vol. 2. Princeton, NJ, Princeton University Press, 1934. Original volumes are in the Manuscripts Division, Department of Rare Books and Special Collections, Princeton University Library.

FOWLER, JOHN. [1830] British visitor whose task it was to assess New York State as a prospective settlement for English farmers. Published as *Journal of a Tour in the State of New York in the year 1830 with Remarks on Agriculture in Those Parts Most Eligible for Settlers,* by John Fowler. London: Whittaker, Treacher, and Arnot, 1831.

FRIEDMAN, B. H. (BERNARD HARPER). [1958, 1969] Friend of abstract expressionist painter Lee Krasner and biographer of Jackson Pollock. Friedman supplied an introduction to *Lee Krasner* by Robert Hobbs and published by Harry N. Abrams. Copyright © 1999 by Independent Curators International, New York. Was published in conjunction with the traveling exhibition of Lee Krasner, organized and circulated by Independent Curators International (ICI), New York. Guest curator for the exhibition: Robert Hobbs, the Rhoda Thalheimer Endowed Chair, Virginia Commonwealth University.

GAINE, HUGH. [1777–1798] A colonial printer and journalist sympathetic to the British cause. Allied with the Loyalist James Rivington, who published the *New York Gazette.* Was printer to His Majesty. Published as *The Journals of Hugh Gaine, Printer,* ed. by Paul Leicester Ford. New York, Dodd, Mead & Company, 1902.

GINSBERG, ALLEN. [1956–1957] Poet of the Beat Generation. Lived in San Francisco but spent a great deal of time in New York with Neal Cassady, Jack Kerouac, and others. Published as *Allen*

Ginsberg Journals Mid-Fifties 1954–1958. New York, HarperCollins, 1955.

GOULD, WILLIAM B. [1864] An escaped North Carolinian slave who served as a sailor helping to enforce the Union blockade of the South. His spare but literate entries were published as *Diary of a Contraband: The Civil War Passage of a Black Sailor.* Palo Alto, CA, Stanford University Press, 2002, by the Board of Trustees of the Leland Stanford Junior University. The Diary of William B. Gould and "A portion of the Cruise of the U.S. Steam Frigate 'Niagara' I Foreign Waters Compiled from the Journal of Wm. B. Gould."

GREENMAN, JEREMIAH. [1781] Continental soldier from Rhode Island who rose to the rank of an officer, regimental adjutant, for RI troops. Captured by the British in Westchester, he spent the summer and autumn of 1781 as a British prisoner at Gravesend, Long Island. He was released only a few days before the Continental victory at Yorktown. Published as *Diary of a Common Soldier in the American Revolution, 1775–1783: An Annotated Edition of the Military Journal of Jeremiah Greenman,* edited by Robert C. Bray & Paul E. Bushnell. Dekalb, Northern Illinois University Press, 1978.

HARING, KEITH. [1979–1980] Pop artist of the eighties. Published as *Keith Haring Journals,* with an introduction by Robert Farris Thompson and a preface by David Hockney. New York, Viking, 1996.

HARRISON, REGINALD FAIRFAX. [1883–1884] Fifteen-year-old schoolboy with a keen interest in politics. Unpublished manuscript may be found in the Museum of the City of New York as "Diary of Reginald Fairfax Harrison for the Year 1883–1884."

HASKINS, JAMES. [1969] Harlem teacher who chronicled his experiences for one school year in the late sixties during a strike by a radical wing of the teachers union. Published as *Diary of a Harlem Schoolteacher.* New York, Grove Press, ca. 1969.

HAVENS, CATHERINE ELIZABETH. [1849–1850] Ten-year-old heiress from a wealthy American shipping family who offered frank observations about her rather delightfully pampered life. *Diary of a Little Girl in Old New York* was first published in 1919. Second edition, New York, Henry Collins Brown, 1920.

HERMAN, MICHELLE. [1978] Editor and writer of short fiction. Entry originally published in the anthology *Private Pages: Diaries of American Women, 1830s–1970s,* edited by Penelope Franklin. New York, Ballantine Books, 1986. Republished by permission of the diarist.

HESSIAN [ANONYMOUS]. [1776] From the letter diary of an unidentified Hessian mercenary who participated in the British assault upon Long Island. These entries appeared in the magazine *Die Neuesten Staatsbegebenheiten,* published at Frankfort-on-the-Main in 1777. Found excerpted in *The Hessians and the Other German Auxilliaries of Great Britain in the Revolutionary War.* By Edward J. Lowell, New York, Harper & Bros., 1884. (Lowell posits that the account was written by an officer of the chasseurs, either Major von Prueschenk or Lt. von Grothausen.)

HIRSCHORN, MICHAEL. [1977] Former editor in chief of *Spin* magazine and later contributing editor to *The Atlantic.* Entry originally published in *Slate.* Later included in *The Slate Diaries,* edited by Jodi Kantor, Cyrus Krohn, and Judith Shulevitz. Introduction by Michael Kinsley. New York, Perseus Book Group, 2000. Copyright © 2000 by Michael Kinsley. Reprinted by permission of PublicAffairs, a member of the Perseus Books Group.

HOLT, JIM. [1997] American humorist. Formerly editor of *The New Leader*, a political biweekly and contributor to *New York* magazine, *The New York Times Magazine*, and *The New Yorker*. Entry originally published in *Slate*. Later included among *The Slate Diaries*, edited by Jodi Kantor, Cyrus Krohn, and Judith Shulevitz. Introduction by Michael Kinsley. New York, Perseus Book Group, 2000. Copyright © 2000 by Michael Kinsley. Reprinted by permission of PublicAffairs, a member of the Perseus Book Group.

HONE, PHILIP. [1825–1851] A New Yorker of humble origins, he enjoyed success as partner in an auction house and served as mayor for one year in 1825. Is better known as a prodigious diarist who for twenty-five years chronicled events great and small: the Boz Ball for Charles Dickens, stage appearances of Fanny Kemble, the ravages of cholera, the distant rumblings of the Civil War. Manuscript at the New-York Historical Society. Also published as *Diary of Philip Hone, 1828–1851*, edited with an introduction by Allan Nevins. New York, Dodd, Mead and Company, 1927.

HOOGES, ANTONY DE. [1641] A young Dutchman who became secretary and business manager for the settlement of Rensselaerwyk. His entries recount a stormy voyage from the Netherlands to New Amsterdam (conditions seemed particularly lethal to the livestock on board). Diary may be found in the Van Rensselaer Bowler Manuscripts. Entries here published in *Narratives of New Netherlands: 1609–1664*, edited by J. Franklin Jameson. New York, Charles Scribner's Sons, 1909.

HUDSON, HENRY. [1609] British navigator who, sailing under the flag of the Dutch, ventured into the New World in search of a sea passage to China. This proved nonexistent, but in the process, he explored the length of the river that would later be named in his honor. From *Henry Hudson the Navigator: The Original Documents in Which His Career Is Recorded, Collected, Partly Translated, and Annotated*, with an introduction by Georg Michael Asher. London, Elibron Classic series © 2005. Adamant Media Corporation. This edition is an unabridged facsimile of the edition published in 1860 by the Hakluyt Society, London.

HUGHES, EUGENIA. [1935] Greenwich Village artist and free spirit. Her unpublished diary manuscript may be found in the Manuscripts and Archives Division of the New York Public Library.

ICKES, HAROLD L. [1934–1939] Secretary of the Interior under Franklin Delano Roosevelt who kept detailed journals of his experience with that administration. Reprinted with the permission of Pocket Books, a Division of Simon & Schuster, Inc., from *The Secret Diary of Harold L. Ickes,* Volumes I, II, III by Harold L. Ickes. Copyright © 1953 by Simon & Schuster, Inc. Copyright renewed © 1981 by Harold M. Ickes and Elizabeth Ickes. All rights reserved.

IRVING, PIERRE MUNRO. [1859] The nephew of Washington Irving, to whom he refers as "Uncle" or "W.I." Pierre attended his uncle as the latter struggled with asthma and depression at his Hudson River estate, Sunnydale. These entries are rich in medical detail. Moreover, they recount the elder Irving's heroic work on a biography of George Washington, finishing only hours before his death. These entries are found in manuscript at the Berg Collection of the New York Public Library.

ISHERWOOD, CHRISTOPHER. [1939] British-born poet and novelist best known for his sketches of life in pre–World War II Berlin, later the basis for Bob Fosse's *Cabaret.* He came to the U.S. with the British poet W. H. Auden during the war. Not enjoying success in New York, he moved to California, where he took up the study of Hinduism, later becoming a naturalized citizen. Published as *Christopher Isherwood Diaries, Volume One: 1939–1960,* edited and introduced by Katherine Bucknell. New York, Michael di Capua Books, HarperFlamingo, 1996. First published in Great Britain in 1996 by Methuen London.

JOHNNY/QUIPU BLOGSPOT. [2003] www.nycbloggers.com.

JUET, ROBERT. [1609] Crew member, possibly first mate, on the *Half Moon.* His entry of September 11, 1609, records the first European expedition into New York's Upper Bay. Juet's diary was first published in 1625 in *Hakluytes Postumous, or Purchas His Pilgrimes,* by Samuel Purchas, who acquired it from Richard Hakluyt. The text of this edition, reprinted in 1906 as *Juet's Journal: The Voyage of the Half Moon from 4 April to 7 November 1609,* published by the New Jersey Historical Society, 1959. Found also in Georg Michael Asher's *Hudson The Navigator,* printed in London for the Hakluyt Society, 1860.

KALM, PETER. [1748–1749] A Finnish naturalist who visited North America on behalf of the Swedish Academy of Sciences looking for seeds that could be transported to the harsh climate of Scandinavia. He was the first scientist to record phenomena in the New World methodically and publish widely. His diary appears in several editions. The entries here are taken from *Travels into North America* by Peter Kalm. Vol. II. Printed and sold by T. Lowndes. London, 1771.

KEMBLE, FRANCES "FANNY." [1832] This actress, a niece of John Philip Kemble and Sarah Siddons, was a member of the "first family" of British thespians. In 1832 she accompanied her father, tragedian Charles Kemble, to America. Over the following two years, the pair toured and gave performances from New York to

New Orleans. She made an unhappy marriage to a southern plantation owner, Pierce Butler, and the two were eventually divided by their sentiments on slavery. F. Kemble recorded her often acerbic observations of American institutions and manners. Published as the *Journal [of] Frances Ann Butler*. Philadelphia, Carry, Lea & Blanchard, 1835.

KEROUAC, JACK. [1941–1949] Beat poet whose "mood diaries" tracked his creative process and life in New York. He was living in Ozone Park, Queens, with his mother when most of these entries were written. Some were published in *Windblown World: The Journals of Jack Kerouac 1947–1954*, edited with an introduction by Douglas Brinkley. New York, Viking, 2004. The manuscripts are held in the Berg Collection of the New York Public Library. Reprinted by permission of SLL/Sterling Lord Literistic, Inc. Copyright by John Sampas Literary Rep.

KIMBALL, CAPTAIN PETER. [1776] A New Englander who joined Washington's army after the evacuation of New York in 1776. Excerpts of his camp diary are published as "The Diary of Capt. Peter Kimball." *The Granite Monthly*, Vol. 4, 1881.

KING, NAOMI R. [1899] Wrote *My Visit to New York*, the travel diary of a twelve-year-old girl from Indiana who visited New York City for the first time in January 1899. The entries published here give a detailed rendering of New York as she found it during her stay with relatives on the Upper West Side. Available only in manuscript, which may be found in the Manuscript and Archives Division of the New York Public Library.

KNIGHT, SARAH KEMBLE. [1704] A thirty-eight-year-old Bostonian who made a trip by horseback from Boston to New York in the early 1700s. Her observations include minute aspects of daily life during the British colonial era. She jotted them down before retiring and probably used a form of shorthand. Published as *The Journals of Madam Knight and Rev. Mr. Buckingham. From the Original Manuscripts, written in 1704 and 1710*. New York, Wilder & Campbell, 1825.

KRAFFT, LT. JOHN CHARLES PHILIP VON. [1778] A German mercenary who, after failing to obtain a commission in the Continental army, joined the British and served with two Hessian regiments during the Revolutionary War. From the *Journal of Lt. John Charles Philip von Krafft* [sic] *for the Year 1882*. Collections of the New-York Historical Society, 1882.

LERMAN, LEO. [1945–1983] Condé Nast editor and esthete who kept a copious diary of the doings of café society. Particularly fascinating are his portraits and reminiscences of grandes dames Marlene Dietrich, Lynn Fontanne, and Cathleen Nesbitt, among others. Published as *The Grand Surprise: The Journals of Leo Lerman*, edited by Stephen Pascal, copyright © by Stephen Pascal. Used by permission of Alfred A. Knopf, a division of Random House, Inc. Lerman's papers are on file at Columbia University's Rare Book and Manuscript Library.

LINDBERGH, ANNE MORROW. [1935] Wife of the "world's most famous man," Charles Lindbergh. Diaries reveal her attempts to establish herself as a writer in her own right. Their baby son was kidnapped and murdered in 1932. The entry included here was written three years later. Published in *Locked Rooms and Open Doors: Diaries and Letters of Anne Morrow Lindbergh, 1933–1935*. New York, a Helen and Kurt Wolff Book, Harcourt Brace Jovanovich, 1974.

MACKENZIE, LT. FREDERICK. [1776] Officer of the Welsh Fusiliers in the Revolutionary War. Published as *Diary of Frederick Mackenzie:*

Giving a Daily Narrative of His Military Service as an Officer of the Regiment of Royal Welch [sic] *Fusiliers during the Years 1775–1781 in Massachusetts Rhode Island and New York.* Vol. 1. Cambridge, Harvard University Press, 1930.

MACLAY, WILLIAM. [1789–1790] Pennsylvanian senator to the first U.S. Congress in New York City. A vocal populist agrarian and anti-Federalist. His account is one-sided but offers a valuable and unsentimental view of his colleagues, notably Thomas Jefferson, John Adams—whom he characterized as "Bonny Johnny"—and the president, whom he continued to call "General Washington." Maclay was appalled by Alexander Hamilton's fiscal innovations on grounds that they favored speculators and the urban financier. Published as *The Journal of William Maclay, United States Senator from Pennsylvania, 1789–1791,* edited by Edgar S. Maclay. New York, D. Appleton and Company, 1890.

MACREADY, WILLIAM. [1848–1849] British actor whose performance at the Astor Place Opera House in 1849 provoked a partisan riot that became symbolic of the class struggle between the city's privileged anglophiles and the poor—chiefly Irish—immigrants. Published as *Macready's Reminiscences and Selections from His Diaries and Letters,* edited by Sir Frederick Pollock. New York, Macmillan and Co., 1875.

MAILER, NORMAN. [1955] American novelist. Excerpts taken from entries appearing in *Antaeus, Journals, Notebooks, and Diaries.* New York, Ecco Press, 1988.

MALINA, JUDITH. [1948–1968] Immigrant of a German-Jewish family, she married Julian Beck, a modern expressionist painter; later, they, cofounded the Living Theater. Together they were pioneers of experimental drama. They had an open marriage. She had

affairs with several men, notably James Agee, and a one-sided in-
fatuation with the mythologist Joseph Campbell. Published as *The
Diaries of Judith Malina: 1947–1957,* New York, Grove Press, 1984.
Also *The Enormous Despair: The Diary of Judith Malina, August 1968–
April 1969.* New York and Canada, Random House, 1972. Reprinted
by permission.

MANN, KLAUS. [1940] German essayist and novelist and son of
Thomas, who, along with his sister, Erika, emigrated to the U.S. in
1937. The latter two spent their energies saving writers and members of the intelligentsia caught behind enemy lines. Klaus edited
an expatriate magazine, *Decision,* published as *Tagebücher* by Klaus
Mann. Vol. 5. 1940–1943. München: Spangenberg, 1989.

MARRYAT, CAPTAIN FREDERICK. [1837] British officer and author
of popular naval fiction. His *Diary in America with Remarks on its Institutions,* Volume I, was printed for Longman, Orme, Brown, Green
& Longmans. London, 1839.

MARTÍ, JOSÉ. [1888] Cuban patriot and journalist who lived and
wrote in New York from 1880 to 1895. An art critic for the *New York
Sun.* His entries are drawn from the *Selected Writings of José Martí:
The America of José Martí.* Translated from the Spanish by Juan de
Onís, with an introduction by Federico de Onis. New York, Noon-
day Press, 1953. Excerpts from "New York Under the Snow" and
"José Antonio Páez: An American Hero," from *The America of José
Martí,* translated by Juan de Onís. Translation copyright © 1954,
renewed 1982 by Farrar, Straus and Giroux, LLC. Reprinted by
permission of Farrar, Straus and Giroux, LLC.

MAVERICK, MARIA LOUISA. [1848] Diary and memorandum book
of Maria Louisa Maverick, a single woman living in New York City
during the late nineteenth century. Brief entries regarding "current

events and family news." The unpublished manuscript is owned by the New-York Historical Society.

McDougall, Captain Alexander. [1770] One of the original Sons of Liberty. After being imprisoned by the British for eight days, he wrote a brief political journal in which he expressed the difficulties of organizing a boycott of British goods. Available in manuscript at the New-York Historical Society.

McVay, Jeremiah. [2001] A blogger whose 9/11 diary entries are published on the website www.nycbloggers.com.

Mekas, Jonas. [1949–1955] Lithuanian, a survivor of a German concentration camp. Filmmaker, writer, critic, and president of the Anthology Film Archives. He was relocated to the U.S. by the United Nations after World War II. He wrote film reviews for *The Village Voice*. Diary published as *I Had Nowhere to Go*. New York, Black Thistle Press, 1991.

Mencken, H. L. [1931] Co-editor of the *Smart Set* and co-founder and editor of *The American Mercury* from 1925 to 1933. Mencken was an iconoclast with a wicked—arguably cruel—wit. A prominent detractor of fundamentalist Christianity, he famously named the prosecution of the biology teacher John Scopes the "Scopes Monkey Trial." Entry taken from *The Diary of H. L. Mencken*, edited by Charles A. Fecher. New York, Alfred A. Knopf, 1989. Copyright 1989 by the Enoch Pratt Free Library.

Millay, Edna St. Vincent. [1927] Pulitzer prize–winning poet. Contemporary of Edmund Wilson and Max Eastman. Excerpts of diaries written by Edna St. Vincent Millay, Collection, Library of Congress. Reprinted by permission of Holly Peppe, Literary Executor, The Millay Society.

MITCHELL, JOHN CAMERON. [1998] Writer, actor, and director whose work includes the rock musical *Hedwig and the Angry Inch* and the film *Shortbus.* Diary entries originally published in *Slate.* Later included among *The Slate Diaries,* edited by Jodi Kantor, Cyrus Krohn, and Judith Shulevitz. Introduction by Michael Kinsley. New York, Perseus Book Group, 2000. Copyright © 2000 by Michael Kinsley. Reprinted by permission of PublicAffairs, a member of the Perseus Books Group.

MONTRÉSOR, CAPT. JOHN. [1765] British officer who recorded firsthand the colonial disturbance occasioned by the Stamp Act. *The Montrésor Journals* from the Collections of the New-York Historical Society for the year 1881. Published 1882.

MOORE, MARIANNE. [1920–1963] Modernist poet. Editor of *The Dial* from 1925 to 1929. During the sixties, she acted as "unofficial hostess" for the mayor of New York. She was an avid baseball fan. Manuscripts at the Rosenbach Museum and Library in Philadelphia. Permission granted by David M. Moore, administrator for the Literary Estate of Marianne Moore. All rights reserved.

MORRIS, GOUVERNEUR. [1804] Wealthy young revolutionary and familiar of Alexander Hamilton. Was present beside Hamilton's deathbed and gave the funeral oration. Made fascinating diary entries on those occasions. Published as *The Diary and Letters of Gouverneur Morris, Minister of the United States to France: Member of the Constitutional Convention, etc.* New York, Charles Scribner's Sons, 1888.

NASH, SOLOMON. [1776] Massachusetts soldier who recorded events surrounding the Battle of Long Island and Washington's flight across the East River. Privately printed in 1861 as the *Journal of Solomon Nash: Soldier of the Revolution, 1776–1777* by Charles J. Bushnell.

NEWBERRY, JULIA ROSA. [1869]   Young Chicagoan. Daughter of Walter L. and Julia Butler Newberry of the wealthy and distinguished "Newberry lot." The family traveled to and from Europe, stopping in New York to visit friends and relatives. Julia's description of a society wedding, in which her older sister was a bridesmaid, is so vivid as to leave a reader feeling that he is a member of the bridal party. Published as *Julia Newberry's Diary.* New York, W. W. Norton & Co., Inc., 1933.

A "NIELSEN FAMILY." [1997] A New York humorist is tapped to keep a weekly journal of his television watching on condition of anonymity. He appears elsewhere in these bios under his real name. Hint: an arbiter of New York ethics. Published by permission of the author.

NIN, ANAÏS. [1913–1919] Frenchwoman of letters. At age eleven she emigrated to New York with her mother and two brothers. Finding the city "ugly" and "superficial," she feared falling victim to its pulsing ambition. Over the next six years, however, her sentiments changed as she came to see ambition as a creative force in her work. Her entries are published as *Linotte: The Early Diary of Anaïs Nin 1914–1920.*

OATES, JOYCE CAROL. [1985] Author and poet. Excerpt taken from entries published in *Antaeus, Journals, Notebooks, and Diaries.* New York, Ecco Press, 1988.

O'NEILL, EUGENE. [1924–1931] Twentieth-century American playwright who got his start at the Provincetown Playhouse. His spare entries on a line-a-day diary reflect public reception of his works. The Eugene O'Neill Papers, Yale Collection of American Literature, Beinecke Rare Book and Manuscript Library.

OZOLS, VICTOR. [2005] Brooklyn-based writer, editor, and blogger.

PALIN, MICHAEL. [1975] Member of Monty Python. From *Diaries 1969–1979. The Python Years.* Thomas Dunne Books, 2007.

PETIT, PHILIPPE. [1974] French aerialist who walked a tightwire between the Twin Towers of the World Trade Center, to much acclaim and eventual arrest. Published as *To Reach the Clouds: My High Wire Walk Between the Twin Towers.* New York, North Point Press, 2002.

PHYSICIAN [ANONYMOUS]. [1822] This diarist is most likely James L. Phelps, who kept a journal during the yellow fever epidemic of 1822. He followed forty cases with the name of the patient, age, occupation, address, nationality, symptoms, course of illness, treatment, and other physicians involved, keeping notes on "Pathology & Peculiarities of the Disease." The diary is in manuscript and owned by the New-York Historical Society.

POE, EDGAR ALLAN. [1844] American poet who wrote audaciously caustic dispatches concerning New York to the Columbia [PA] *Spy*. These were later published as *Doings of Gotham*. Old typeset edition by Jacob E. Spannuth, publisher, 1929. Is an "authorized facsimile."

POST, JOTHAM. [1792–1793] Physician and "drug importer." Post kept a journal of his experiences as a student at the College of Physicians and Surgeons, Columbia College. This handwritten diary can be found in manuscript at the New-York Historical Society.

POWELL, DAWN. [1931–1965] Midwestern-born novelist and playwright. Her diary details struggles with a difficult marriage, a handicapped child, and lack of financial security. Though she yearned for broader public recognition, she received it only after her death.

Gore Vidal reportedly called her "America's only satirist." Published as *The Diaries of Dawn Powell, 1931–1965*. South Royalton, VT, Steerforth Press, South Royalton, 1995.

RANDELL, WILLIAM M. [1852] Secretary of the Committee on Fire Patrol of the New York Department of Fire Underwriters. Brings his powers of description to bear upon the wreck of the steamboat *Henry Clay*. His manuscript resides at the Museum of the City of New York.

RANOUS, DORA. [1880] An erudite young actress who spent her early years in Augustin Daley's theatrical company. She later gained fame as a translator of French and Italian literature into English. Ranous's performance in *The Middy* is chronicled in *Diary of a Daly Débutante*. New York, Duffield and Company, 1910.

REIVEATLIVEJOURNAL. [2001] 9/11 blogger. Diary entries published on the website www.nycbloggers.com. Screen name of Racheline Maltese, a working actress and pop-culture commentator in New York City.

REYNOLDS, MARJORIE RICHARDS. [1912] Diarist who described the particulars of everyday life in New York during the early twentieth century. The manuscript resides at the New-York Historical Society.

RITCHIE, CHARLES. [1958–1960] Canadian ambassador to the United Nations. He kept a detailed diary observing not only world events but the social mores of New York, which he adored. Excerpts from *Diplomatic Passport: More Undiplomatic Diaries, 1946–1962*. Copyright © 2001 by Charles Ritchie. Published by McClelland & Stewart. Used with permission of the estate and the publisher.

Roosevelt, Theodore. [1878–1884] Twenty-sixth president of the United States. Scion of a wealthy and socially prominent New York family. The diary entries published here encompass the six years from the early courtship of his first wife, Alice Lee, through the tragic deaths of Alice and his mother on the same day, February 14, 1884. Entries pertain chiefly to his marriage and his intense grief over the loss of his father. Published in *Theodore Roosevelt's Diaries of Boyhood and Youth.* New York, Charles Scribner's Sons, 1928; also found among the *Theodore Roosevelt: Private Diaries 1878–1895* published by the Library of Congress.

Rorem, Ned. [1961–1982] Pulitzer Prize–winning composer and marathon diarist. Published as *The Paris Diary and New York Diaries of Ned Rorem, 1951–1961.* Copyright © 1966 and 1967 by Ned Rorem, and *The Later Diaries of Ned Rorem 1961–1972,* by Ned Rorem. Copyright © 1974 by Ned Rorem. Both reprinted by permission of Georges Borchardt, Inc., on behalf of the author. And one brief, but very lovely entry from *The Nantucket Diary of Ned Rorem, 1973–1985.* San Francisco, North Point Press, 1987. Copyright © 1987 by Ned Rorem.

Rosenfield, Eric. [2001] A writer and web programmer, he has been blogging in New York since the late nineties. His 9/11 diary entries are published on the website www.nycbloggers.com. He lives in Brooklyn.

Ryan, Margaret. [1978] Poet and freelance writer. Kept a pregnancy journal. Excerpted in *Ariadne's Thread: A Collection of Contemporary Women's Journals,* edited by Lyn Lifshin. New York, Harper Row, 1982.

Schaukirk, Brother Ewald Gustav. [1775–1883] Moravian missionary living in New York under British occupation during the

Revolutionary War. His journals, penned as *The Diary of the Moravian Congregation,* appeared in several parts as *The Occupation of New York City by the British* by *The Pennsylvania Magazine of History and Biography,* Vol. 1, No. 2–3, 1877, and Volume X, No. 4, 1886, published by the Historical Society of Pennsylvania.

SCHLESINGER, JR., ARTHUR M. [1979–1980] Historian and author of biographies of the Kennedys and Franklin Delano Roosevelt. During the eighties, he kept a residence in New York from which he and his family had an exceptionally clear view of their incoming neighbors, the Richard Nixons. The excerpts here were taken from *Journals 1952–2000,* Arthur M. Schlesinger, Jr., edited by Andrew and Stephen Schlesinger, copyright © 2007 by the Estate of Arthur M. Schlesinger, Jr. Used by permission of the Penguin Press, a division of Penguin Group (USA) Inc.

SCHLIEMANN, HEINRICH. [1869] German archaeologist famed for his excavation of the ruins of Troy. Visited New York on the way to Indiana to take advantage of that state's liberal divorce laws. Manuscript resides in the Lilly Library, Indiana University, Bloomington.

SCHUYLER, JAMES. [1987–1990] American poet of the New York School; also a novelist and contributor to *The New Yorker.* Published as *The Diary of James Schuyler,* edited by Nathan Kernan. Santa Rosa, CA, Black Sparrow Press, 1997.

SCOT. [1892] An anonymous Scottish visitor with an unusually keen eye for topological and engineering detail (his name cannot be discerned). Manuscript at the New-York Historical Society.

SERLE, AMBROSE. [1776–1777] Secretary to General Sir William Howe. His reports indicate that Loyalists were telling him what he wanted to hear about progress of the Revolution. He seems to have been responsible, in part, for influencing the New York press in the interests of the British, and he also oversaw publication of the *New-York Gazette.* Published as the *American Journal of Ambrose Serle, Secretary to Lord Howe 1776–1778.* Edited and with an introduction by Edward H. Tatum, Jr., San Marino, CA, the Huntington Library, 1940.

SHERIDAN, CLARE. [1921] Celebrated British artist who traveled the world sculpting busts of the famous—Guglielmo Marconi, Nikolai Lenin, Mohandas Gandhi, among them. Her work for Soviet subjects caused her to be labeled a "Bolshevik" during her visit to the U.S. in the early twenties. These excerpts are taken from Sheridan's *My American Diary,* published in New York by Boni and Liveright, 1922.

SLADE, WILLIAM. [1776] A Continental volunteer who was captured by the British shortly after his enlistment and confined, under pitiful conditions, in a notorious prison ship, *The Grosvenor.* Excerpts published in *American Prisoners of the Revolution* by Danske Dandridge. Charlottesville, VA, the Michie Company, 1911.

SLOAN, JOHN. [1906–1911] Cartoonist and illustrator. One of "The Eight," a school of American painters, cartoonists, and illustrators from the so-called Ashcan School of Realism who broke with the academic school of art and ran with the Village Bohemian circle during the early twentieth century. (The others included William Glackens, Robert Henri, George Luks, Everett Shinn, Arthur B. Davies, Ernest Lawson, and Maurice Prendergast.) Published as *John Sloan's New York Scene: from the diaries, notes, and correspondence 1906–1913.* New York, Harper & Row, copyright © 1965 by Helen Farr Sloan, renewed 1993 by Helen Farr Sloan. The Helen Farr Sloan Library & Archives contains the John Sloan manuscript collection at the Delaware Art Museum, Wilmington. Reprinted by permission of HarperCollins Publishers.

SLOANE, FLORENCE ADELE. [1896] A debutante of the Gilded Age. Subject of a biography published as *Maverick in Mauve: The Diary of a Romantic Age* by Louis Auchincloss. Garden City, NY, Doubleday & Company, Inc., 1983.

SMITH, WILLIAM. [1779] A Whig-Loyalist who hoped to find a middle ground in the American Revolution. Smith's diary from 1753 to 1783 and other notes are contained in nine red morocco leather volumes owned by the New York Public Library.

STANTON, ELIZABETH CADY. [1890–1900] Feminist writer and lecturer. Published as *Elizabeth Cady Stanton As Revealed in Her Letters Diary and Reminiscences*. New York and London, Harper & Brothers Publishers, 1922.

STAYING PINOY IN NEW YORK. [2005–2009] Anonymous Filipino ex-patriate whose evocative entries on the website www.nycbloggers .com chronicle both his cultural estrangement and the beauty he finds in urban life.

STEINWAY, WILLIAM. [1864–1872] Scion of the famed German-American family of piano manufacturers. Scrupulous, if terse, Steinway's entries cover thirty-six years. Included here are details of a labor strike and the inauguration of Steinway Hall, one of the city's preeminent cultural and performance venues. Excerpts from Steinway & Sons Records and Family Papers. Archives Center, National Museum of American History, Smithsonian Institution.

STRONG, GEORGE TEMPLETON. [1835–1875] Lawyer from a privileged New York family. A conscientious diarist who chronicled the American Civil War, among other events, for posterity: impressions of the nascent Central Park and Metropolitan Museum of Art. Strong offers opinions on wide-ranging subjects: Jenny Lind; the moral degeneracy of Wall Street; contempt for European royalty; and an abiding hatred of anarchists. Manuscript owned by the New-York Historical Society.

SUCKLEY, MARGARET "DAISY." [1943–1944] A cousin and close confidante of FDR's. Roosevelt's advisers could not understand the nature of her relationship with the president and were annoyed when she tried to put forth a radical, alternative cure for his degenerative illness. Published as *Closest Companion: The Unknown Story of the Intimate Friendship Between Franklin Roosevelt and Margaret Suckley,* edited and annotated by Geoffrey C. Ward. Boston and New York, Houghton Mifflin Company, 1995. Reprinted by permission.

SULLIVAN, THOMAS. [1776] Irishman who served with the British in the American Revolution, notably at the Battle of Brooklyn Heights. He later defected to the Americans. Published as *From Redcoat to Rebel: The Thomas Sullivan Journal.* Westminster, MD, Heritage Books, Inc., 1997, 2004. A handwritten manuscript at the American Philosophical Society in Philadelphia.

TAILER, EDWARD NEUFVILLE. [1854–1891] Prominent New York merchant and banker with proslavery sensibilities. Kept a diary from boyhood to old age, notable for its chronicling of café society. Manuscript at the New-York Historical Society.

THACHER, DR. JAMES. [1780] A surgeon to the Continental Army, he witnessed the hanging of Major John André. His account appeal in *Military Journal of the American Revolution* by James Thacher, M.D. Hartford, CT: Hurlbut, Williams & Company, 1862.

TOCQUEVILLE, ALEXIS DE. [1831] French nobleman who, with companion Gustave de Beaumont, traveled America for nine months to study and evaluate democracy. The sojourn culminated in the publication of *De la Démocratie en Amérique*, which became a sensation on both sides of the Atlantic. The original Tocqueville papers deposited at the Château de Tocqueville in Normandy have been lost. Reproductions can be found at Yale University's Beinecke. The entries reproduced here are taken from *Tocqueville and Beaumont in America*, by George Wilson Pierson. New York, Oxford University Press, 1938. Tocqueville's travel diary published as *Journey to America*, edited by J. P. Mayer, New Haven, 1959.

TROLLOPE, FRANCES "FANNY." [1831] British visitor to U.S. After attempting a grandiose business venture that failed, she wrote a scathing critique of the new democracy. While most of America displeased her, she was fond of New York. Her entries are not dated, but the account of her trip on the Hudson can be dated by external events. Published as *Domestic Manners of the Americans*. London, Penguin Group, Penguin Books Ltd, 1832. Also published in New York by Dodd, Mead, in 1927, and Penguin Classics, 1997. It is also available as a free eBook from Project Gutenberg.

TUCKER, ST. GEORGE. [1786] A Virginian and one of the original signers of the Declaration of Independence. After the Revolution, he visited New York, then the national capital. Detailed observations of the sights and sounds of the city. First published in 1832 as *A Virginian in New York*. Also published in the *Quarterly Journal of the New York State Historical Association*, New York History, April 1986, Vol. 67, No. 2. Originals in the Tucker-Coleman Papers, 1664–1945, Special Collections Research Center, Swem Library, College of William and Mary.

TWAIN, MARK. [1867] Pen name of Samuel Langhorne Clemens, American poet, writer of short fiction, and humorist. During a trip east in 1867, Twain kept travel diaries for the San Francisco *Alta California*, which published them as columns.

TYNAN, KENNETH. [1971–1976] Theater critic for *The New Yorker*. Published as *The Diaries of Kenneth Tynan*, edited by John Lahr. New York and London, Bloomsbury, 2001.

VAN VECHTEN, CARL. [1923–1930] Photographer and prominent figure in the Harlem Renaissance (as a white enthralled by black culture). Friend of Paul Robeson and Ethel Waters as well as the Alfred Knopfs. Married to the actress Fania Marinoff, to whom he refers simply as "Marinoff." He and cohorts apparently passed days and nights in a boozy state of delirium that he recorded in brief journal entries. Published as *The Splendid Drunken Twenties: Selections from the Daybooks, 1922–1930*, edited by Bruce Kellner. Urbana and Chicago, University of Illinois Press, 2003.

VANDERBILT, GERTRUDE. [1894] Daughter of Cornelius Vanderbilt II, she was heiress to one of New York's great shipping and railroad fortunes. She married a wealthy banker, Harry Payne Whitney, and later strayed from her social set into Greenwich Village, where she kept a studio for sculpture. Her works and those of other American artists later found a home when the artist-socialite founded the Whitney Museum of American Art. This entry, in which the young heiress, Gertrude Vanderbilt, describes her own place in the world, is found among the unpublished papers of Gertrude Vanderbilt Whitney at the Archives of American Art.

VRIES, DAVID PIETERSZ DE. [1643] Dutch mariner who, in February 1643, witnessed a brutal attack by the Dutch governor's forces upon an encampment of Indians. Published in *Narratives of New Netherland,* edited by J. Franklin Jameson. New York, C. Scribner's Sons, 1909.

WARHOL, ANDY. [1978–1986] Born Andrew Warhola. A painter and chronicler of pop art, he dictated his journal every morning by phone to an amanuensis. He was wounded in pre-diary days by a would-be assassin. In later years, he reflected upon celebrity, art, and his own mortality. Excerpts from *The Andy Warhol Diaries,* by Andy Warhol. Edited by Pat Hackett. New York, Warner Books, 1989. Copyright © 1989 The Estate of Andy Warhol, reprinted by permission of the Wylie Agency.

WASHINGTON, GEORGE. [1789–1790] Most of Washington's presidential diaries are missing. Those included here reflect the first year of his presidency, spent in New York City. Excerpts here from *The Diary of George Washington from 1789 to 1791,* edited by Benson J. Lossing. New York, Charles B. Richardson & Co., 1860.

WEBB, SAMUEL BLACHLEY. [1776] An aide-de-camp to "His Excellancy, George Washington" on the eve of the British occupation of New York. Excerpts taken from *Correspondence and Journals of Samuel Blachley Webb,* collected and edited by Worthington Chauncy Ford. Vol. 1, 1772–1777. New York, 1893.

WEBSTER, NOAH. [1788–1793] Editor of the *American Magazine* and *The American Minerva* and compiler of the *American Dictionary of the English Language.* Spare entries of his life in New York. Published as *The Autobiographies of Noah Webster: From the Letters and Essays, Memoir, and Diary.* Columbia, University of South Carolina, 1989.

WEILL, KURT. [1950] German-Jewish composer, best known for *The Threepenny Opera* with dramatist Bertolt Brecht. He immigrated with wife, singer-actress Lotte Lenya, to America in 1935 where he became a naturalized citizen and composed such Broadway works as *Lady in the Dark* and *Street Scene*. Diary is at Yale University. Reprinted with permission of the Kurt Weill Foundation for Music, New York. All rights reserved.

WELD, GEORGE. [2001] A writer whose 9/11 diary entries appear on the website www.nycbloggers.com. He is also a cook and restaurateur from Brooklyn.

WESCOTT, GLENWAY. [1937–1939] Novelist and art impresario and friend of Truman Capote and Ned Rorem, among others. Published as *Continual Lessons: The Journals of Glenway Wescott, 1937–1955*, edited by Robert Phelps with Jerry Rosco. New York, Farrar, Straus & Giroux, 1990. From *Continual Lessons*, copyright © 1990 by the Estate of Robert Phelps. Reprinted by permission of Harold Ober Associates Incorporated. Copyright © 1990 by Anatole Pohorilenko. Copyright © 1990 by the Estate of Robert Phelps.

WHITMAN, WALT. [1847–1865] Journalist and poet uniquely identified with New York. Journalist/editor in Brooklyn. Member of the Pfaffians, early bohemians who were forerunners of the Beats. Best known for *Leaves of Grass*. Diaries published as *The Collected Writings of Walt Whitman*. New York University Press, 1963–64 and 1984. Also *Complete Prose Works, Walt Whitman*. Philadelphia, David McKay, 1892; *Notes and Fragments* by Walt Whitman and edited by Richard Maurice Bucke. London, Ontario, printed by A. Talbot & Co., 1899; *Walt Whitman, the Man*. By Thomas C. Donaldson. New York, Francis P. Harper, 1896; and *The Uncollected*

Poetry and Prose of Walt Whitman, collected and edited by Emory Holloway. Vol. 1. Garden City, NY, and Toronto, Doubleday, Page & Company, 1921.

WIEDERHOLD, CAPTAIN ANDREAS. [1776] Hessian officer who served with the Knyphausen Regiment during the capture of Fort Washington. From *The Pennsylvania Magazine of History and Biography,* Vol. XXIII. Philadelphia, The Historical Society of Pennsylvania, 1899.

WILLIAMS, TENNESSEE (THOMAS LANIER). [1943–1955] American playwright, author of *The Glass Menagerie* and *A Streetcar Named Desire,* among others. Published as *Tennessee Williams, Notebooks,* edited by Margaret Bradham Thornton. New Haven, CT, and London, Yale University Press, 2006. Copyright © 2000 by the University of the South. Reprinted by permission of George Borchardt, Inc., for the University of the South.

WILLIS, WINIFRED. [1923–1924] Daughter of a successful journalist, she pursued a career as a writer and playwright. Her attempts were hampered by a bad marriage and mental illness. Though she wrote for *The New Yorker, The Saturday Evening Post, Ladies' Home Journal,* and the *New York Herald Tribune,* her poignant diary remains her most enduring legacy. Some of the selections here can be found in *Private Pages: Diaries of American Women, 1930s–1970s,* edited by Penelope Franklin. New York, Ballantine Books, 1986. Willis's complete diary is available in manuscript at the Schlesinger Library, Radcliffe Institute for Advanced Study.

WILSON, EDMUND. [1927–1955] American poet, editor, and man of letters. He kept a diary from the 1920s through the 1960s. Excerpts here are drawn from the above. Set piece published in *The Fifties: From Notebooks and Diaries of the Period,* edited by Leon Edel. Copyright © 1986 by Helen Miranda Wilson. Reprinted by permission of Farrar, Straus & Giroux, LLC.

WOJNAROWICZ, DAVID. [1977–1991] Painter, photographer, and filmmaker who died of AIDS. Excerpts from *In the Shadow of the American Dream,* copyright © 1999 by the Estate of David Wojnarowicz. Used by permission of Grove Atlantic, Inc.

ACKNOWLEDGMENTS

A special thanks to the following: Dr. Isaac Gewirtz of the Berg Collection, Edward O'Reilly of the New-York Historical Society, Elizabeth Fuller of the Rosenbach Library, and the NYPL's rare manuscripts archivist, Thomas G. Lannon—all of whom steered me toward previously unpublished materials.

I am grateful for the continuing assistance of Dr. Alice Birney, literary and cultural historian in the Manuscript Division of the Library of Congress, and for the contributions large and small of Dr. Louise Bernard, Dr. Don C. Skemer, Maurita Baldock, Dave Stein, Charles P. Griefenstein, Dr. John Fleckner, Carol Rusk, Lindsay Turley, Joy Weiner, Elizabeth Fuller, Karen Schoenewaldt, Dr. George Campbell, Christine Nelson, Vin Barnett, Holly Peppe, Bruce Kellner, David M. Moore, Olga Tsapina, Anna Karvellas, Tom Cary, Dr. Gilbert Schrank, Susan Mulcahy, Brad Burgess, Alexis Gelber, Tammy Kiter, Alison MacKeen, Dr. Richard Cochran, Anne W. Brown, Scott Carpenter, Levi Thomas, Dr. Myron

Blumenthal, Sean Henry, Flip Brophy, Robert Guinsler, Anne-Marie Mente, John Sampas, Jesse Rosenthal, and Iris Fodor.

I was fortunate to enjoy the counsel of Frederick Courtright of the Permissions Company, Inc., and the research back-up of Stephen Pascal, Ian Beilin, Stacy Horn, Mervyn Keizer, and Victoria Wright of Bookmark Services. I'd like to give a warm thanks to the production personnel at Random House. Vincent La Scala, Benjamin Dreyer, Debbie Foley, and M. Beth Thomas, and especially to Christopher Zucker, who created the beautiful design for this book. I owe an accruing debt to my editors, David Ebershoff, Judy Sternlight, John Flicker, and particularly Jonathan Jao, who, with assistant Sam Nicholson, shepherded this detailed project with meticulous care and attention through to completion. And a special thanks to my publisher, Tom Perry, for his thoughtful and patient oversight.

As always, abundant and ongoing gratitude to Esther Newberg and Kari Stuart of ICM. And, of course, to my family: Steven, who provides the loving care and support to keep me at my desk; and Andrew, who was lucky enough to be born a New Yorker.

INDEX

Permissions Acknowledgments

Grateful acknowledgment is made to the following for permission to use both published and unpublished material:

Mark Allen: Diary entry by Mark Allen. Used by permission of the author.

American Philosophical Society: Excerpt from a diary entry of Thomas Sullivan from August 1, 1776. Used by permission of the American Philosophical Society.

Sara Astruc: Diary entry by Sara Astruc. Used by permission of the author.

Beinecke Rare Book and Manuscript Library: Six diary entries by Eugene O'Neill from the Eugene O'Nell Papers, Yale Collection of American Literature, Beinecke Rare Book and Manuscript Library at Yale University. Used by permission.

Toni Bentley: Excerpt from *Winter Season: A Dancer's Journal* by Toni Bentley, copyright © 1982 by Toni Bentley. Used by permission of the author.

Bloomsbury Publishing Plc.: Excerpts from *The Diaries of Kenneth Tynan,* edited by John Lahr (London: Bloomsbury Press, 2001). Used by permission.

Dr. Myron Blumenthal: Diary entries by Sara Hoexter Blumenthal as found in the Sara Hoexter Blumenthal papers, 1910–1951 housed in The New-York Historical Society Archives. Used by permission.

Georges Borchardt, Inc., and Ned Rorem: Excerpts from *The Paris Diary & The New York Diary 1951–1961* by Ned Rorem, copyright © 1966, 1967 by Ned Rorem; excerpts from

ABOUT THE EDITOR

TERESA CARPENTER is the author of four books, including the *New York Times* bestseller *Missing Beauty*. She is a former senior editor of *The Village Voice*, where her feature articles on crime and the law won a Pulitzer Prize in 1981. She lives in New York City's Greenwich Village with her husband, writer Steven Levy, and their son.

www.teresacarpenter.com